The King
of Content

The King
of Content

Sumner Redstone's Battle
for Viacom, CBS, and Everlasting Control
of His Media Empire

KEACH HAGEY

HARPER
BUSINESS

An Imprint of HarperCollins*Publishers*

HarperCollins books may be purchased for educational, business, or sales promotional use. For information, please email the Special Markets Department at SPsales@harpercollins.com.

FIRST EDITION

Library of Congress Cataloging-in-Publication Data

Names: Hagey, Keach, author.
Title: The king of content : Sumner Redstone's battle for Viacom, CBS, and everlasting control of his media empire / Keach Hagey.
Description: First edition. | New York : HarperBusiness, [2018]
Identifiers: LCCN 2018002946 (print) | LCCN 2018009806 (ebook) | ISBN 9780062654113 (ebook) | ISBN 9780062654090 (hardback) | ISBN 9780062848666 (audio)
Subjects: LCSH: Redstone, Sumner. | Mass media—United States—Biography. | Businesspeople—United States—Biography. | Viacom International—History. | Columbia Broadcasting System, Inc.—History. | BISAC: BIOGRAPHY & AUTOBIOGRAPHY / Business. | BUSINESS & ECONOMICS / Corporate & Business History. | BUSINESS & ECONOMICS / Industries / Media & Communications Industries.
Classification: LCC P92.5.R33 (ebook) | LCC P92.5.R33 H34 2018 (print) | DDC 302.23092 [B] —dc23
LC record available at https://lccn.loc.gov/2018002946

18 19 20 21 22   LSC   10 9 8 7 6 5 4 3 2 1

To Wesley, Belle, and June

Contents

The King
of Content

Sumner Redstone with his daughter, Shari, in 2012. By 2018, Shari had ascended to the top of her family's empire, becoming a media mogul in her own right. *(Mark Sullivan/WireImage/Getty Images)*

Prologue:
"I Don't Want to Sell Paramount"

One afternoon in February 2016, Viacom chief executive Philippe Dauman drove through the heavy metal gates of the exclusive Beverly Park neighborhood overlooking Beverly Hills, past the Olympian estates of movie stars like Sylvester Stallone and Eddie Murphy, and up to the sprawling, butter-colored mansion of his longtime boss and mentor, Sumner Redstone. Such visits had long been a monthly routine for the lifelong Manhattanite, who ran the New York–based public company that the ninety-two-year-old Sumner overwhelmingly controlled. Usually the two former lawyers would mix business talk with reminiscences of their past corporate conquests, watch a little baseball or CNBC, and gaze at the giant aquariums of Sumner's beloved saltwater fish.

But on this day, Dauman had come to discuss a particularly delicate matter. Viacom was considering selling nearly half of Paramount Pictures, the glamorous Hollywood studio whose takeover in 1994 had defined both men's careers. They had wrested it from rival media titans Barry Diller and John Malone in an epic bidding war, and owning America's oldest continuously running studio—the home of *The Godfather*, *Chinatown*, and the Indiana Jones series—had cemented Sumner's status as a mogul.

Yet Viacom's stock had been in a tailspin, losing half its value during the previous two years, and investors were clamoring for some kind of dramatic action. Some big Chinese companies had gotten Hollywood's attention in the last few months with their interest in studios, and it seemed like a good moment to capitalize on the century-old Paramount's romantic allure—even if it, too, had been in a years-long slump. After one prospective buyer expressed interest in a deal that valued the beleaguered studio at more than $10 billion—more than twice what most analysts thought it was worth—Dauman wanted to explore a joint venture. Perhaps the right partner could not only provide the cash Paramount desperately needed to restock its nearly bare cupboard of franchises but also help the studio's movies get better access to international markets in an era when 70 percent of Hollywood's movie revenues came from overseas.

He knew it would be a hard pitch. Redstone was an amasser, not a divester, and few things had brought him greater pleasure over the last two decades than his intimate dinners at Dan Tana's or The Ivy with Paramount's management, albeit often at the inelegantly geriatric hour of five p.m. To own a studio in Hollywood was to be a king, a status beyond money. And Paramount was not just any studio. It was the original Hollywood monopoly, the creator of the studio system business model and the first studio to take Sumner seriously when he was nothing more than the executive vice president of his father's drive-in theater chain.

Dauman's task would also be challenging because communication with Sumner these days was nearly impossible. The mogul who had once famously declared that "Viacom is me" had suffered a precipitous decline in his health in eerie parallel with Viacom's stock price, after an episode of inhaling food into his lungs in 2014 that had left him dependent on a feeding tube and barely able to speak. A few months earlier, his former live-in companion had alleged he was completely non compos mentis, unable to follow the thread of a conversation or the plot of a film. And a few months after this visit, Dauman himself would make a similar charge. But for now, he tried to communicate with Sumner the way he had been for months, by doing his best to interpret his grunts.

Often, visitors to the mansion got help deciphering Sumner's speech from his nurse Jeremy Jagiello, dubbed "the Sumner whisperer." But Dauman's task was too sensitive for that. For months, he had assumed that the mansion was either bugged or filled with spies loyal to his longtime rival, Sumner's daughter, Shari Redstone. Shari and Dauman, both sixty-one, had long competed for the role of Sumner's heir apparent, but in recent years, Dauman seemed to have definitively clinched the prize as Shari's relationship with her father deteriorated. That had all changed since the fall, however, when the two live-in companions half Sumner's age to whom the mogul had bequeathed some $150 million (whom Shari referred to as her father's "little sluts") were thrown out of the mansion, paving the way for Shari to reconcile with her father. Dauman had been concerned enough about Shari that he had announced his visit when he was just twenty minutes away, in order to avoid giving his East Coast rival enough time to get on a plane and position herself next to her father through their meeting, just as Sumner's former companions had done with all of Sumner's visitors during the two years before their ejection. Still, he assumed—correctly—that anything Jagiello heard would be relayed back to Shari.

So as he walked in to find Sumner watching television in the "fish room," the sitting room lined with aquarium-scale fish tanks, he asked Jagiello if he could step into the next room so that he and Sumner could discuss some sensitive corporate information. The nurses were not allowed to let Sumner out of their sight, in case they had to jump in and suction from his throat the saliva that was constantly threatening to choke him, but Jagiello moved through the open doorway between the aquariums. Dauman pulled a chair up next to Sumner, so that Jagiello could only see his back, and leaned in close to whisper his news. He asked Sumner if he had understood him, and Sumner nodded.

A few days later, Dauman held a board call to discuss the Paramount stake sale. Worried about leaks, he had not told anyone in advance, not even Paramount chairman Brad Grey, what the call was about. As he had expected, Jagiello had told Shari about the visit, the whispering and the nodding, and she called Dauman repeatedly in the hours leading up to the board call, worried about what machinations her rival was up to. But the call itself proceeded without drama.

Dauman addressed the board members one by one, including Sumner and Shari, and got no objection from any of them.

The next day, Dauman announced that Viacom had received "indications of interest from potential partners seeking a strategic investment" in Paramount and had decided to pursue the discussions. In case any other potential partners were out there, the press release touted the studio's deep library, "robust pipeline with proven franchises," and "high potential" (read: nascent) television production operation. An undeniable For Sale sign had been planted in front of Paramount's iconic Spanish Gate.

Anyone familiar with Sumner's history was stunned. He was famously fickle about his executives, but Paramount was the love of his life. And, indeed, within a few days of the announcement, Sumner began repeating "I don't want to sell Paramount" to anyone who would listen—to household staff, to Dauman over the phone, and finally, on Saturday, February 27, the day before the Oscars, to Grey, who wasn't so thrilled about the idea himself. Still, at the next board meeting, which Sumner dialed into remotely, he voiced no opposition, and management charged ahead with the plan. Sumner's protestations would not become public until April 11, when they were reported in the *Wall Street Journal*.

Just how he came to utter this phrase is a matter of some dispute. Some people close to Viacom believe his household staff or some other ally of Shari's goaded him into saying it by misinforming him that Viacom planned to sell the entire studio. Others think he was coached to repeat the phrase the way he repeated, parrot-like, other phrases like "Manuela is a fucking bitch" or "I kicked Shari out of the house" by people close to him who had an interest in having him say those things. Still others argue this was his own, authentic opinion.

Regardless of how they arrived on Sumner's tongue, the impact of these six words was devastating and would become the fulcrum for one of the greatest corporate power struggles in American business history.

How had it come to this?

Sumner Murray Redstone, once feared as the "mad genius" of media who would dump his chief executive officers for mere wobbles in his companies' stock price, had built one of the world's greatest media empires through a series of audacious takeovers constructed to ensure that he always maintained control. Today, as the majority owner of the family theater chain National Amusements, he controls roughly 80 percent of the voting shares of both Viacom Inc. and CBS Corp., a $36 billion media empire encompassing MTV, Comedy Central, Nickelodeon, BET, VH1, Paramount Pictures, CBS, Showtime, Simon & Schuster, and the Showcase Cinemas and Cinema de Lux movie chains. He spent decades performing meticulous estate planning so that his control would extend beyond the grave (which he loved telling reporters he would never lie in), constructing trusts designed to make it impossible for his heirs to sell his companies after he dies. "Unless they start doing terribly," he told the *Wall Street Journal* in 2012, "which they will not."

Sumner's confidence at the time was not misplaced. His life up to that point had been a story of exceeding expectations—starting as the son of a liquor wholesaler with underworld connections in the immigrant tenements of Boston's West End to Harvard Law School and a federal clerkship, from the president of his father's regional drive-in movie theater chain to the owner of Viacom, from a cerebral lawyer who shopped at Filene's Basement to the owner of a coveted Hollywood studio, and ultimately, after the Viacom-CBS merger (the biggest media deal up to that point in U.S. history) to the controlling shareholder of one of the largest media empires in the world. Most famously, he had survived a hotel fire by hanging out a window while flames singed his wrist to the bone, an experience that left him with a gnarled claw for a hand, burns over 45 percent of his body, and a steely resolve never to be beaten at anything. That resolve made him the most feared negotiator in all of media. The credo that he coined and repeated for decades—"content is king"—turned out to be truer in the digital world than he could have ever guessed.

With the exception of Rupert Murdoch, no other titan of media so personally shaped the companies he controlled, at times swooping in to act as CEO when his frustration with management got too great. Like Murdoch, he had inherited a regional company from his father and turned it into a global behemoth. And like Murdoch, he sought to continue this control by passing it on to his children.

But the very ruthlessness that made Redstone a great businessman made him a terrible father. His relationship with his son, Brent, ended in 2006 when Brent sued him for unfairly shutting him out of the company and using the company as a private piggy bank. His relationship with his daughter, Shari, had run hot and cold for decades, at one point becoming so strained that they communicated only by fax. Other family members fared little better. Sumner had also squared off in court against his brother, Eddie; his nephew, Michael; his wife Phyllis; and his granddaughter Keryn. The theme running through much of the litigation was Sumner's obsession for total control of the family business and his willingness to push aside anyone he had to, including—indeed, especially—his own flesh and blood, to get it.

But again and again, what threatened this control most was not his family but his tumultuous love life. When his philandering made his wife of fifty-two years, Phyllis, finally divorce him, he risked losing control of Viacom. And when he threw ex-companion Manuela Herzer out of his life, she turned around and filed a lawsuit challenging his mental capacity, a legal maneuver that would shake his media empire to its foundations. The case riveted Hollywood, in part because of the salacious details it leaked out about Sumner's fixation on daily sex and steak, but mostly because it spoke to the industry's deepest suspicions about why no one had seen or heard from Sumner in more than a year. When an activist investor started buying up Viacom stock that winter, he released a scathing PowerPoint presentation criticizing Dauman's leadership, illustrated with stills from *Weekend at Bernie's*, the 1989 comedy about two guys who drag their boss's dead body around pretending he's still alive so that they can continue to enjoy his luxurious home.

While CBS—bolstered by its sports rights and the programming prowess of its former actor CEO, Leslie Moonves—had been able to hold its stock price steady in the age of cord-cutting, Viacom's fall had been dizzying. At the time of Dauman's visit, ratings at its biggest cable networks, which include MTV, Comedy Central, Nickelodeon, BET, and VH1, had been falling double-digit percentages for years. A few small cable companies, annoyed at Viacom's demands for price hikes for their entire package of dozens of channels when ratings were so weak, dropped them altogether in 2014—a move widely viewed as a canary in the industry coal mine. Revenues and profits had dropped in the previous twelve months, and hundreds of employees were laid off. One analyst compared Viacom to Eastman Kodak, the ultimate corporate cautionary tale, saying that both were "once dominant companies where the product that provides the majority of their profits (film; TV networks) is made obsolete by a digital world."

Some of Viacom's struggles in 2016 were happening because the television business was in the midst of seismic change. Subscription video services like Netflix, which allow people to avoid both advertising and expensive cable TV bills—the dual lifebloods of the cable television business that makes up the bulk of Viacom's profits—were by this point in nearly half of American homes. The young audiences that had long been Viacom's target viewers now watched video on Snapchat or YouTube instead of traditional TV, and they signed up for cable in ever-smaller numbers. Meanwhile, the industry was still having a hard time measuring the TV viewing that happens on iPhones and Roku boxes, which meant that Viacom had a hard time getting paid for its offerings.

But many media investors, analysts, and executives placed much of the blame for Viacom's woes squarely at the feet of Dauman, a mergers and acquisitions lawyer who grabbed on to Redstone's coattails in 1986 at the age of thirty-two and never let go. Compared to his ayahuasca-sipping predecessor, Tom Freston, who built MTV Networks into a global juggernaut and is beloved in Hollywood, the gold cuff link–sporting Dauman was never embraced by the creative community. Critics loved to point out that not a single one of Viacom's biggest hits—things like *Beavis and Butthead, Dora the Explorer, SpongeBob SquarePants, The Daily Show,* and *South Park*—was developed since Dauman took the reins in 2006. While rival companies were investing in digital properties like Bleacher Report and Maker Studios, Viacom under Dauman actively unwound its joint venture with Vice Media, which went on to become the most valuable digital media company at more than $5 billion. In the months before Dauman's visit, Hollywood's distaste for him had spread to Wall Street, with some of Viacom's largest investors openly saying he lacked programming chops and the company would be better off without him. They were baffled how Sumner, who famously fired a string of CEOs before Freston, including Frank Biondi and Mel Karmazin, was putting up with Dauman's performance.

It turns out that Dauman's performance was not enough to get him fired. But his attempt to sell a piece of Paramount after Sumner asked him not to? That was disloyalty worthy of beheading. As Dauman drove away from the mansion that day, he didn't know it yet, but he was a dead man walking.

CHAPTER 1

Rain at Sunrise

A ugust 10, 1938: Darkness descended on what would prove to be an inauspicious beginning for a media empire.

It was opening night of the first drive-in theater in New York State. Rain drummed the domed metal roofs of the six hundred cars creeping through the mud of the abandoned airport along the Sunrise Highway in Valley Stream, Long Island, threatening to blur the picture and drown out the dialogue of the feature film the intrepid moviegoers had come to see: *Start Cheering*, an antic Columbia Pictures musical comedy starring Walter Connolly and Jimmy Durante about a film star who leaves Hollywood for college. Aside from some jelly-legged tap dancing by Hal Le Roy, a few cameos by the Three Stooges, and the spectacle of vaudevillian Chaz Chase eating a book of lit matches, the film didn't have a lot to recommend it—not to mention that it had already been showing at indoor theaters for six months.

But as would often be the case for the drive-in industry for the next half century, the capacity crowd had come to the Sunrise Drive-In as much for the experience as for the movie itself. Coming in off the lonely stretch of highway along the railroad tracks just beyond the New York City limits, they had driven past the glowing marquee beckoning drivers to "Sit in Your Car" and "See and Hear the Movies" for thirty-five cents, past the scrubby evergreens planted to keep outsiders from stealing a glimpse of the screen, past the five-story steel-and-concrete screen splashed with turquoise and terra-cotta. At the entrance, fresh-faced young men in pale jackets, black bow ties, and soda jerk hats guided the cars to their place in the concentric semicircular ramps tilted to ensure that no one's Chevy, no matter how big or boxy, blocked anyone else's view. These same young attendants went from car to car, delivering refreshments from enormous wooden boxes slung over their shoulders. For weeks leading up to the premiere, the theater's developers, the New York architectural and building firm led by Irwin Chanin, had been in the news, touting their latest creation as if it were the eighth wonder of the world. The Chanin Organization was already well known for building architectural marvels in Midtown Manhattan, such as the sumptuous Roxy Theatre, one of the largest movie houses in the world when it was completed in 1927, and the Art Deco landmark Chanin Building, the tallest building in Manhattan when it was finished in 1928. So when they turned their public relations machine to promoting the twelve-acre drive-in theater they had carved out of their vast Green Acres suburban housing development, it wasn't hard for them to get most of the press to print that their sixty-by-forty-eight-foot screen was "said to be the largest ever made" and "on the basis of ground area it may be considered the 'largest' theater in the New York area." "World's Biggest Movie Screen for Outdoor Theater," blared a headline in *Popular Science*, beneath a photograph of a man standing, for scale, like a tiny speck in front of an Art Deco ziggurat.

But as the premiere approached, the task of drumming up interest in the drive-in fell to a far less known entity: Max Rothstein, a slight, soft-spoken Bostonian with piercing blue eyes, a long face, and a thick sweep of hair that made him look not unlike a movie star himself. Rothstein was the public face of Sunrise Auto Theatre, Inc., a hastily assembled, Boston-based corporation founded earlier that summer, just as the Long Island zoning officials had decided to approve the creation of a drive-in. On July 3, Chanin announced that he had leased the $50,000 theater "for the long term," according to the *New York Times*, to Sunrise, which would operate it. It was quite a coup for a thirty-six-year-old father of two who had neither the money to lease a drive-in nor any experience running one. Nowhere in all the press reports was there any word about how Rothstein came into that money. Not until years later would it emerge that he had a silent partner: Harry "Doc"

Sagansky, a Boston dentist-turned-bookie, who at that point was five years into his career as one of the most famous illegal gambling figures of the twentieth century.

"They were partners together for forty-four years," said Sagansky's son Robert Sage. "My father helped put money into the theaters, starting with the Sunrise."

But for obvious reasons, Sagansky remained in the background, and so it was left to Rothstein to be the barker. While Chanin, a developer to the core, went for superlatives and grandeur, Rothstein emphasized drive-ins' practicality and accessibility. Drive-ins mainly served the "family trade," Rothstein told the *Brooklyn Daily Eagle*, with a high concentration of what the paper called "cripples and aged people who are not able to walk into ordinary theaters but who can be brought to the automobile theaters." The Boston-area theaters were particularly popular, Rothstein noted, because they took cars off the street and reduced traffic congestion—a somewhat peculiar pitch for a drive-in located along one of the earliest tentacles of Long Island's suburban sprawl. Freedom to smoke and talk through the movie without annoying fellow audience members was, he said, another key advantage.

If it seemed like Rothstein was doing everything humanly possible to erase any mental images of necking teens before they even had a chance to form, that's because he was. He was well acquainted with the risks of doing otherwise. He pitched himself to the New York papers as an expert in drive-ins, having "been interested" in the operation of those that had popped up in suburban Boston in the last couple of years. But what he did not mention was that, less than a year before, suburban Boston had also been the site of one of the first and most ferocious community outcries over a proposed drive-in that the fledgling industry had seen. The previous October, 250 people had packed into the town hall building of Dedham, on the southwest edge of Boston, to protest a proposed drive-in at the intersection of the newly constructed Route 1 and Route 128. The chairman of the board of selectmen of Westwood, an adjoining community, said the proposed theater "would be a menace and a moral danger to the community."

The plans were nixed. (More than a decade later, Rothstein and Sagansky would open up a drive-in on the site, which has since become the luxurious Cinema De Lux multiplex at Legacy Place that serves as a centerpiece of Rothstein's descendants' theater chain.)

The ad in the local papers for opening night summed up the pitch: "Sunrise Drive-In Theatre. The *latest* thing on Long Island. New, open-air way of seeing the movies. Sit in *your own car*. No parking problems, no waiting in line, dress as you please, smoke, chat, be comfortable. New show every Sunday, Wednesday & Saturday. 35 cents per person—your auto free. 8:30 and 10:30 nightly."

And then the all-important words: "Rain or shine."

*   *   *

By 1938, drive-ins were not quite as novel as Rothstein's ad copy would suggest. The first one was opened just over the Camden, New Jersey, town line on June 6, 1933, by Richard Milton Hollingshead Jr. shortly after he received a patent for his design of terraced ramps that enabled cars to come and go without distracting their fellow moviegoers.

Hollingshead, the son of an auto products dealer, originally concocted his outdoor movie theater as a mere feature of a more grandiose plan for a Hawaiian fantasy-themed gas station, complete with palm tree–shaped gas pumps, but for perhaps obvious reasons, only the outdoor movie innovation survived. At least a dozen drive-ins popped up over the next five years, but Hollingshead had little luck getting them to pay him license fees for his patent without suing them. Among those tangled up in early litigation were two in the Greater Boston area that had likely inspired Rothstein: the Weymouth Drive-In Theatre in Weymouth, Massachusetts, opened in 1936, and E. M. Loew's Open Air Theatre in Lynn, Massachusetts, opened in 1937. By the spring of 1938, the trade publication *BoxOffice* wrote of the New England drive-in industry: "There are already more law suits on drive-in theatres in this territory than there are drive-in localities."

Many years later, Rothstein's son Sumner would claim that the Sunrise was "maybe" the third drive-in in the country. According to newspapers of the day and subsequent studies, it was probably closer to the fifteenth, with drive-ins in New Jersey, Pennsylvania, Texas, Massachusetts, California, and Ohio predating it.

But what it lacked in novelty, it made up in size and style.

*   *   *

The Sunrise was the first truly grand suburban drive-in in the country, built for five hundred cars but expanded to accommodate two thousand, with a playground for children and even a Ferris wheel.

It was part of an ambitious suburban vision by Irwin Chanin and his brother Henry, who in 1936 purchased a 335-acre tract of empty land just beyond the New York City limits and carved it up into a unique "residential park" community of eighteen hundred Cape Cods, colonials, and English manor houses, mostly on cul-de-sacs connected by footpaths, called Green Acres. Both the development and the drive-in were harbingers of a new mode of American life as the country emerged from the Great Depression, one built around middle-class families with disposable income, roomy cars, and easy access to endless miles of freshly built highways. Drive-in theaters would expand modestly to about one hundred across the country by the start of World War II and then stop dead, halted by tire and gas rationing. But as soon as the war was over, they took off, exploding to more than two thousand by the 1950s. Foreseeing this boom, Rothstein told the papers that his company was named "Sunrise Auto Theatres," suggesting there would soon be more of them, even though it was actually named Sunrise Auto Theatre, Inc., in corporate filings and land records. And though it took a decade for Rothstein and Sagansky to open their second theater, eventually their ambitions were realized. Despite what a *New York Times* reporter described as a "torrential downpour" and a still-primitive sound technology, the Sunrise's opening night had been a success. The bad weather at the opening had proven that, as the *Wave* newspaper put it, "even with the windows of an automobile closed the roof of the car acts as a sounding board to bring inside the sound from the battery of directional amplifiers located atop the 80-foot-high screen. Under all conditions the quality of sight and sound are equal to those in the conventional indoor theatre." The Sunrise Auto Theatre became the cornerstone of a chain of drive-in theaters that would come to dominate the Northeast and, by the end of the 1950s, remake itself with an even more forward-looking name: National Amusements Inc.

Under the leadership of Rothstein's son Sumner, who worked at the Sunrise selling popcorn and soda during his teenage years, National Amusements would go on to take control of Viacom Inc. and CBS Corp. and build one of the world's largest media holdings. Along the way, it has shaped culture in immeasurable ways, defining global pop culture for generations and inventing the reality television format at MTV, giving platform to the leading satirical voices of the last two decades with *South Park* and *The Daily Show*, pioneering the very idea of a dedicated children's channel with Nickelodeon, reviving the once-beleaguered CBS to a prime-time powerhouse with hits like *Survivor* and *The Big Bang Theory*, and showing Hollywood that critical acclaim and commercial success need not be mutually exclusive with hit movies like *Titanic, Forrest Gump*, and *Braveheart*.

It would turn Sumner Redstone into one of the richest men in the world, with a Beverly Hills mansion, girlfriends half his age, and a Rolodex of Hollywood royalty for dining companions. And ultimately, control of it would pass into the hands of Sumner's daughter, Shari, and her children amid one of the greatest boardroom battles that corporate America has ever seen. But before any of that could happen, Max Rothstein would have to become Mickey Redstone.

*   *   *

Max Rohtstein was born on April 11, 1902, in Boston, the fifth of ten children raised by Morris and Rebecca Rohtstein, who were part of the great wave of Jewish immigrants fleeing rising anti-Semitism and desperate poverty in Eastern Europe in the late nineteenth and early twentieth centuries. Morris grew up the eldest son in a family of dark-haired, brown-eyed bakers in Kozova, a shtetl in a section of modern-day Ukraine known then as Galicia, the poorest province of the Austrian empire, just as the formation in the 1880s of Christian economic cooperatives designed to exclude Galician Jews from commercial life was prompting a mass emigration to the United States. In 1892, at the age of eighteen, he boarded the steamship *Friesland* from Antwerp, Belgium, bound for New York. There he joined his father, Isaac, who had arrived the previous year, and they made their way to Boston. Over the next two years, Morris's little brothers, Harry—traveling alone at just eight years old—and Barnett, known as Barney, would join them. In a hint of family strife to come, each would go on to found his own bakery supply company, named after himself, just blocks away from each other in the working-class Boston neighborhoods of Charlestown and the West End: M. Rohtstein Co., H. Rohtstein & Co., and B. Rothstein & Co. (Barney had given in early to American bureaucrats' tendency to flip the "h" and the "t" in public documents, while Morris's family held out longer but eventually followed suit, with Max going by Rothstein by the time he was a teenager). Their descendants would run them for the better part of the next century, though the lack of family solidarity would baffle them a bit. "They were all competitors," said Harry Rohtstein's grandson, Steven Rohtstein, who remains in the flour and sugar distribution business in Massachusetts to this day. Although he was the straggler, only entering the flour supply business after a stint in antique dealing, Harry would end up the most successful of the brothers. By the mid-twentieth century, Harry Rohtstein & Co. would become one of the nation's largest flour distributors.

But it was Morris's branch that was bound for the true heights of American business. On March 14, 1894, Morris married Rebecca Bornstein, an eighteen-year-old "tailoress" from Vilnius, Lithuania, with brown, wavy hair, a wide smile, and an ample figure well-built for the rapid-fire baby production that was to come. Their first child, Sarah, arrived nine months later.

Boston's immigrant population was exploding, particularly from Southern and Eastern Europe. From 1880 to 1920, the city's population swelled from 362,000 to 748,000, nearly three-quarters of which

were first- or second-generation immigrants. Like many of the immigrants flooding into Boston from Eastern Europe at the time, Morris
and Rebecca got their first foothold in the North End, a lobe of land
jutting into Boston's Inner Harbor densely packed with four- and five-
story tenement buildings, where bathrooms were usually shared with
several other apartments and rents were cheap. By the time their son
Max was born, the neighborhood was dominated by Jewish and Italian
immigrants.

After a few years in the North End, Morris did well enough to move
his growing family across the Charles River to Somerville, where Max
attended elementary school and high school, and then to the West
End, a slightly more comfortable immigrant landing place, where
Morris owned bakeries and a baker's supply shop. They bought an
apartment in a redbrick building at 6 Poplar Court, just behind the
famous Charlesbank Homes tenement, a five-story redbrick building
of 305 two-, three-, and four-room apartments built as an early, private form of affordable housing by philanthropist Edwin Ginn. Once a
Yankee bastion, the neighborhood received so many successive waves
of immigrants—beginning with the Irish in the 1840s, followed by
the Eastern European Jews in the 1880s and then the Italians in the
1890s—that by the time the Rohtsteins lived there in 1920 it was the
most densely populated neighborhood in the city and just 10 percent
of its inhabitants were native-born. It was the West End, where Max
lived as a teenager, that would shape the rest of his life.

By age seventeen, Max had dropped out of high school to work as a
chauffeur in his father's company. Although he had savvy and ambition, he was not the heir apparent. That role went to his older brother,
Jacob, who would one day take over the bakery supply business, turn
it into a trucking outfit, and pass it on to his son. Max had to forge his
own path.

*   *   *

One of Max's West End neighbors was Harry Sagansky, a stout, lugu-
briously dark-eyed middle child of Lithuanian immigrants four years

Max's senior. Sagansky was born with a hustle in his blood, a passion for baseball, and a mind for numbers. By the age of twelve, he was selling newspapers on the streets of the West End, and by sixteen, he had begun a gambling career that would last until he died peacefully in a Boston nursing home at the age of ninety-nine.

Sagansky got his first taste of gambling at Boston Red Sox and Boston Braves games, where he discovered that his facility with math gave him an advantage. After briefly flirting with the idea of parlaying his good grades in school into a career as a lawyer, he fulfilled his upwardly mobile parents' dreams by enrolling at Tufts University School of Dental Medicine at eighteen. But he made sure not to let his studies get in the way of his extracurricular activities. "He arranged his laboratory work when he was going to college to do that in the morning," Sage said. "In those days, you played baseball in the afternoon. He would gamble on the games."

In 1919, he set up his practice in Scollay Square, Boston's red-light district, above a pharmacy that functioned as a secret liquor store just as the country was descending into Prohibition. The area had become known as the "Sailor's Haven," according to Boston historian David Kruh, because it was just a quick subway ride from the Charlestown port and offered "many theaters and cheap restaurants and rent-by-the-hour hotels and motels in an area that was, by the '20s and '30s, beginning to run down." Sailors, who had notoriously poor dental care, stopped by a row of dentist shops in the square amid their carousing. But dentistry, which was hard on Sagansky's bad back and provided few accommodations in those days for the left-handed practitioner, turned out not to be the path to economic stability he had hoped. "The next-to-last patient told him he couldn't pay my father for his dental work, so he gave him a live chicken," Sage said. "That was the final straw." By 1931, the year of the birth of his third child, he had left dentistry behind to become a full-time bookmaker. The only legacy of his trade would be his lifelong nickname, "Doc."

Before the arrival of state-sanctioned lotteries, the black-market lottery was big business in the working-class neighborhoods of American cities. It went by a variety of names—numbers game, numbers pool, numbers racket, policy racket—but in 1930s Boston everyone called it "nigger pool," ostensibly because it was popular in black neighborhoods. But bookies hung out in bars, barbershops, and factory floors all over the city's working-class districts, ready with their notebooks and pencils to mark down which three-digit numbers their bettors thought might be the total amount bet at the local racetrack. The winning number was published daily in the *Boston American*, and winners would get their winnings—usually at 600:1 odds—via runners the next day. "Everybody did it," said Joe McDonald, a third-generation West End resident and president of the West End Museum board of directors. "Old ladies, grandmothers, workers. There was a bookie on every corner."

By July 29, 1932, a thirty-four-year-old Sagansky had made it far enough up the hierarchy of the numbers rackets to be invited to a closed-door meeting on the fifteenth floor of the Hotel Manger, a grand Art Deco affair at the northern tip of the West End, to sort out the future of the lottery business in the city. North End gang leader Joseph Lombardi had convened the meet to address the rise of "chiselers," newcomers to the numbers game who didn't pay out when the numbers hit. But police, on the hunt for information about a recent gangland murder, raided the conference room and arrested all twenty-six men inside, charging them with "suspicion of knowledge" about the murder, the *Boston Globe* reported. Sagansky identified himself to the officers as "Harry Jasper," a version of the "Doc Jasper" moniker that many of his clients (as well as the Federal Bureau of Investigation) would know him by for decades to come. It was the first time that Sagansky would find himself in the news for his illegal livelihood, but far from the last. As would often happen in the decades that followed, the charges failed to stick.

When Prohibition ended the next year, the numbers game took on an even bigger role in the underworld economy of the North and West Ends, and so did Sagansky. He became the "bank" for all of the other bookies in the neighborhoods. "Doc Sagansky put together a group of his old friends—Mickey Redstone was one of them—who chipped in to cover the bets," said one longtime North End resident and historian. "They were a group of Jewish guys who grew up together in the West End and the other Jewish sections of Boston." According to Gary Snyder, the grandson of Mickey's youngest sister, Ethel, Sagansky became a key ally of the Irish Mob that controlled Boston for much of the first half of the twentieth century, through figures like four-time mayor James Michael Curley. "Sagansky was, simply put, their Jew," Snyder said. "If Capone's Mafia had Meyer Lansky, Boston's Irish Mob had Harry 'Doc Jasper' Sagansky."

*   *   *

Another of Max Rothstein's West End neighbors was Bella Ostrovsky, the most beautiful of the four girls born to Bension and Esther Ostrovsky and the first to be born on American soil, shortly after they immigrated from Kiev at the turn of the century. In the old country, Bension had been a successful lawyer, but without a solid grasp of English, he took work in a raincoat factory, where the din from the machinery gradually deafened him. For a while, the family lived together in a rented apartment in Cambridge, but eventually Bension and Esther, a noted beauty with a fiery temperament, divorced while their youngest child, Ida, was still quite small—a highly unusual decision for Jewish families at the time. "When this was mentioned to me as a young person, it was regarded as extraordinary, maybe a little scandalous," said Russ Charif, grandson of Rose, the Ostrovskys' eldest child. Rose and Ida went to live with their mother, while the middle daughters, Sarah and Bella, went with their father. By the time Bella was in her late teens, they were living at 112 Poplar Street in the West End, around the corner from Max Rothstein. Blond, blue-eyed, and bright, Bella—who would later change her name to Belle as the whole family further anglicized their names—was from more modest circumstances than the Rothsteins, but she was no less ambitious. "Belle worshipped her father—how many men of that time raised two daughters alone?—and when she met her future husband, she saw a relentlessly ambitious and authoritative figure who would take care of her as well as her father had," wrote Judith Newman, Sarah's granddaughter, in *Vanity Fair* in 1999.

In 1921, when she was eighteen or nineteen, Max and Bella Rothstein were married and began their journey toward becoming Mickey and Belle Redstone. (Max was called "Mickey" from childhood, as his mother's accent made "Maxie" sound like Mickey, family members say.) That journey began humbly enough, with a move a few doors down the street to the Charlesbank Homes.

In his autobiography, Sumner recalls the apartment having no toilet. Richard Hartnett, a West End Museum board member who grew up in the Charlesbank Homes two decades after Sumner lived there, said the larger apartments did have bathrooms inside. "We had steam heat with janitor service. We had five rooms and we were paying $18 a month. It was great." Children played on the rooftop, amid the hanging laundry, or at a nearby playground designed by Frederick Law Olmsted. The Rothsteins didn't stay in the tenement for long. Family members say that during Prohibition, Morris Rohtstein's fleet of flour and sugar company trucks were put to more lucrative use ferrying liquor from Canada to various points throughout the Northeast. And thus Mickey, the bakery "chauffeur," joined a singular fraternity of young men from the immigrant ghettos of America's large cities who came of age just as Prohibition was extending them a truly once-in-a lifetime business opportunity.

Bootlegging in Boston was controlled by Charles "King" Solomon, a portly, thick-lipped crime boss whom the feds called the "Capone of the East." The son of Russian Jews, Solomon had begun with the drug and lottery rackets before creating what customs officials dubbed "the wealthiest liquor syndicate ever built up in New England." He became a member of the "Big Seven" bootlegging syndicate and attended the 1929 Atlantic City conference to divvy up territory alongside Meyer Lansky, Charles "Lucky" Luciano, Frank Costello, Frank Erickson, Bugsy Siegel, Dutch Schultz, Abner "Longy" Zwillman, Al Capone, Waxey Gordon, and Enoch "Nucky" Thompson. By the time he was gunned down in a nightclub men's room in 1933, he was under federal indictment for running a vast rum-running operation that allegedly brought in ships of booze from Canada and Europe and guided them up the East Coast by secret radio frequencies. After his death, the business was taken over by his lieutenants Joseph Linsey, Hyman Abrams, and Louis Fox.

Fox, who was arrested in 1921 for the "illegal transport of liquor," was a longtime business partner of Mickey and Sagansky's. So, too, was Linsey, a convicted bootlegger identified by federal agents as the New England chief of a consortium that bought Canadian liquor from Seagram founder Samuel Bronfman and distributed it in the United States, alongside Lansky and Al Capone associate Joseph Fusco. After repeal, Linsey—like another famous Bostonian with whom he is often associated, Joseph Kennedy—went into the legitimate liquor distribution business, becoming president of Whitehall Company, distributors of Schenley liquors. Linsey's business partnerships with Mickey stretched from the liquor business to drive-ins to dog racing. Linsey would not be bought out of his business interest with Mickey until the early 1980s, when Mickey's son Sumner cleaned house in preparation for a run at the upper reaches of American legitimate business.

Just how deep Mickey got into bootlegging, and whether his partnership with Sagansky led him there, is unknown. But there were some hints that this street-smart kid was willing to break the law—and adept at talking his way out of a jam. At age nineteen, in the same year he would end up marrying Bella, he was arrested and held for questioning over a missing bag owned by Boston's boxing commissioner, Carl Barrett, which contained his wife's $700 fur neckpiece and a 250-year-old empty jewel case from France. A man in the counting room in a local newspaper office had seen a woman walking past with the fur on her shoulder, and when officers asked her about it, she said it was a present to her sister from Max Rothstein. Max told the police that he had bought the fur for $40, and apparently, that was the end of it.

What is clear is how porous the boundaries were between legal and illegal, enterprise and racket, in the interbellum Boston in which

Mickey began his working life. The dominant political figure of the
era, James Michael Curley—four-time mayor, two-time congressman,
and one-disastrous-time governor—served part of his last mayoral
term from prison. His predecessor in the mayor's office, John "Honey
Fitz" Fitzgerald, founder of the Kennedy political dynasty and grandfather of John F. Kennedy, dealt with his own allegations of graft and
corruption during his administration and remained a power broker
for decades. Mickey learned early how to navigate the city's Irish-
dominated power structure. He bought a used truck, opened his own
trucking firm, and, according to Newman, secured a carting contract
from the city of Boston with the help of friends like "Honey Fitz." His
granddaughter Shari's earliest memory of him was driving and singing old Irish songs.

He also began to invest in real estate very early, with help from his
own entrepreneur father. At twenty-three, he got a bank loan to buy
a $2,000 investment property in Brighton, a heavily Irish neighbor-
hood of ample Victorians and lush yards. Years later, his wife, then
called Belle, wrote her younger son, Eddie, amid a family dispute,
holding up the loan for the property as evidence that Morris had been
stingier with his children than Mickey was with his. "I remember
when Sumner was a little boy Dad needed $1500," Belle wrote. "He
asked his father for a loan. His father arranged for a bank to make the
loan and Dad signed a note [which] his father endorsed and he paid it
back 'with interest.' He evidently wanted to be different with his children!!" But the loan was a crucially important mechanism for Mickey
to build credit beyond the underground economy. Just two years later,
he moved his young family to Brighton, to a roomy, four-bedroom
clapboard house with a yard at 5 Bothwell Road.

By this point, in 1930, with Prohibition still going strong, Mickey
was formally listing his occupation as a floor covering proprietor.
This is how his son Sumner first remembers him. "My father peddled linoleum and I have a clear picture of him in my mind toting a
huge roll over his shoulder and carrying it out to the truck," Sumner
wrote in his autobiography. Then, more dubiously: "With the money

he brought in, he supported not only my mother, me and my younger brother, Edward, but his own parents and my mother's family as well."

There's little evidence to suggest this is true. Morris and Rebecca were wealthy enough to have a live-in maid, several property holdings, an eldest son who was in line to take over their business, and, by 1933, a comfortable Victorian in fashionable Brookline. But if Mickey really was supporting his parents in the final years of Prohibition, it is unlikely that he did so from linoleum alone. Family members believe that linoleum was a side business to the bootlegging and other vice rackets. By the end of the decade, Boston had four thousand speakeasies—four times the number of licensed bars in the entire state in 1918—and fifteen thousand people involved in selling illegal booze. When the bonanza suddenly ground to a halt with repeal in 1933, Mickey found a perfect next business: liquor wholesaling. And that business would lead Sagansky and him into a whole other aspect of the entertainment industry.

CHAPTER 2

The Conga Belt

ew Boston businesses flourished more under Prohibition or struggled more with its repeal than Club Mayfair, a fashionable nightclub at the edge of the theater district in Boston's gas-lamp-lit and brick-sidewalked Bay Village neighborhood. The club had an impeccable nightlife pedigree, founded as the Renard Mayfair Club by Jacques Renard, a classically trained violinist–turned–jazz band leader who had previously cofounded the Renard Cocoanut Grove up the street in 1927. The Cocoanut Grove, resplendently kitschy with fake palm trees, rattan-covered walls, and zebra-patterned chairs, would go on to be "Boston's number one glitter spot and the axis around which Boston's night life revolved," the *Record American* put it a few years later.

But during Prohibition, Renard forbade the Cocoanut Grove to serve alcohol, and business suffered—particularly after the stock market crash of 1929. The local underworld was not impressed. Renard's daughter recalled to journalist Stephanie Schorow how some of them expressed their desire to see alcohol introduced. "They took my mother for a proverbial ride. Put her in the backseat of a Roadster and covered her up with a blanket and took her for a ride to Revere beach. She said there were machine guns under the sheet with her."

Renard and his partner, master of ceremonies Mickey Alpert, couldn't take it. They sold the club for a mere $10,000 to Charles "King" Solomon, who in 1931 donned a tuxedo and attempted to remake himself an elegant nightclub impresario. On his last night on earth, he was entertaining two young dancers at the Cocoanut Grove before heading to another nightclub, where he was shot to death, uttering the final words, "Those dirty rats got me."

Renard, meanwhile, went up the street and opened the smaller Mayfair to compete with the Cocoanut Grove. After another change of ownership, the club began to do well selling illegal liquor, according to the
Boston Globe:

> With a membership reported to run in the thousands, lack of in-
> terference, and backed by popular fancy, the club prospered until,
> in the final days of prohibition, Gov. Ely told Police Commissioner
> Hultman to raid all suspected speakeasies. With police officers sta-
> tioned inside and outside, the Mayfair finally posted a sign: "Closed
> for alterations." It has not opened since.

In the wake of repeal, it was sold and reopened as a restaurant,
and later a nightclub struggling with the decline of vaudeville. Then,
suddenly, on January 29, 1940, the *Boston Globe* ran a large photo of a
dashing man in a smart suit accented by a crisp pocket handkerchief,
smiling confidently and shaking hands with a bandleader beneath the
headline "New Owner-Manager of Mayfair." The photo didn't lie: it
was Max Rothstein's face, but the name, for the first time publicly, was
Michael Redstone.

*　　*　　*

The name change was a common maneuver for Jewish immigrant
families, even in the best of times, and these were not the best of
times.

Germany had just invaded Poland the previous September, and the
Nazis were forcing all of Poland's Jews to wear identifying badges. In
the United States, where the increasingly anti-Semitic radio broadcasts
of Charles Coughlin had been drawing tens of millions of listeners
throughout the last decade, a 1939 Roper poll found that just 39 percent of Americans felt Jews should be treated like everyone else, while
51 percent were somewhere on a spectrum of belief ranging from wanting Jews not to mingle socially to wanting them deported. Within this
group, 31 percent agreed that "Jews have somewhat different business

methods and therefore some measures should be taken to prevent Jews from getting too much power in the business world."

"They felt a less conspicuously Jewish name would be helpful from a business perspective," said Russ Charif. One close family associate said Mickey had been in line to buy the Friendly's ice cream chain, "but when they found out he was a Jew, they refused to sell it to him." (A spokeswoman for Friendly's, founded in Massachusetts in 1935 by brothers S. Prestley and Curtis Blake, said, "Since the brothers are now 100 and 103, they don't really recall this.")

Moreover, given the particularly colorful history of Boston's night-life district, known as the Conga Belt, "it was also to avoid confusion with Arnold Rothstein, who was accused of fixing the World Series," Charif said. Rothstein, who was shot over gambling debts in 1928, was the leader of New York's Jewish mob and the first to run his gambling and bootlegging rackets like a corporation. In an ironic twist, the mobster used the pseudonym Redstone Stable for his racehorses—"red stone" is a literal translation of the German name Rothstein—and his character in HBO's *Boardwalk Empire* uses the alias "Redstone" for his banking transactions.

Sumner makes a similar argument in his autobiography, but some who know the family say his real concerns were about Rothsteins closer to home. His cousin Irving Rothstein—the son of Mickey's big brother Jake—was a longtime figure in the gambling rackets in Boston, having married the sister of Burton "Chico" Krantz; Krantz became famous late in life when he became a key witness in the case against Whitey Bulger. Another cousin, Edward Rothstein—the son of Mickey's uncle Barney—was also wrapped up enough in the boot-legging, gambling, and loan-sharking rackets to wind up stuffed in the trunk of a car in 1960 with five bullets in the back of his head.

Sumner, who had been bar mitzvahed and grew up attending temple on holidays, described the name change as an idea of his father's that he accepted only reluctantly. "Redstone sounded so solidly American, so ecumenical, so Christian," Sumner wrote in his autobiography. "I thought my father was trying to walk away from our being

Jewish." But people close to the family say it was more his idea than his father's. "Sumner was going into a clean field and didn't want to be involved with that," said one family associate.

Regardless whose idea it was, the Rothsteins became the Redstones just as both father and son were in the midst of social transformation. Sumner had always been exceptionally clever, and his mother had resorted to any means necessary—including lying down on the floor and faking a guilt-inducing heart attack—to ensure that he devoted his every waking moment to study. A few months after Mickey took over the Mayfair, Mickey and Belle sat in the wood-paneled auditorium of the prestigious Boston Latin School and beamed as they watched their firstborn walk to the podium again and again, scooping up nearly every award that the country's oldest school had to bestow on its graduating seniors. The modern prize. The classics prize. The Benjamin Franklin Award for being first in his class. A scholarship to Harvard University, to which his academic record granted him admission without even having to take the college boards.

Sumner entered Harvard College the next fall as "Sumner Murray Redstone."

*   *   *

Mickey, meanwhile, was also entering a new echelon of society. The Sunrise had been a success, and he and Doc Sagansky were looking to expand their partnership to new ventures. By the late 1930s, Club Mayfair was owned by Benny Gaines, who was booking vaudeville circuit regulars like Belle Baker, the singer famed for "My Yiddishe Mama," and the singing comedy duo Cross and Dunn. But vaudeville was dying, and Gaines was having trouble making a go of it. Mickey told the *Boston Globe*'s nightlife columnist, Joseph Dinneen, a few years later that he took the Mayfair as a "gift" in 1939 and stepped out of the wholesale liquor business to run it. "A discouraged owner handed him the night club lock, stock and barrel and said: 'When, as and if you make any money there you can pay me for it,'" Dinneen wrote. "Mickey has made considerable money there and has paid for the club."

Just how he paid for it was always a matter of some mystery. It would come out in court a few years later that Mickey borrowed $10,000 from Sagansky to buy the club in 1941, and the corporation he set up to own the Mayfair would borrow another $11,000 from Sagansky over the next two years, paying him back with $3,000 interest. "Mickey came along and told my dad about the nightclub, and because they were successful with the drive-in together, they invested in the two nightclubs," Sagansky's son Bob Sage said. "They had been partners ever since."

At that point, the partnership was simple. Redstone would run the club, and Sagansky would put up the money. "It was my father's money," Sage said. "The Redstones didn't put any money in it, I don't think, until 1949 or 1950. My father paid for all the theaters, and he paid for all the nightclubs."

Mickey had a good feel for talent and an even better touch with the press. He took chances on a new generation of up-and-coming comedians, like the rotund Romo Vincent, whom several years later Dinneen declared the "funniest man in America." Mickey had the influential Dinneen wrapped around his little finger. By 1942, with America's involvement in World War II in full swing and Boston's harbor crawling with sailors and other servicemen looking for a good time, the Mayfair was making money hand over fist along with the rest of the Conga Belt. So Mickey and Sagansky decided to double down on their nightlife empire by taking over the much-higher-profile Latin Quarter.

*   *   *

The Latin Quarter was the brainchild of Lou Walters, a slim, elegant talent agent with a British accent, a bookish streak, and a glass eye, whose daughter Barbara would go on to become the pathbreaking broadcasting legend.

In her memoir, Barbara Walters describes her father's innovation when he opened the nightclub in 1937 in a deconsecrated Greek Orthodox Church at 46 Winchester Street, a few blocks away from the Mayfair and Cocoanut Grove:

Boston had its share of nightclubs already. What Boston did not have was an inexpensive nightclub that served a full dinner for under ten dollars and was naughty enough for grownups but tame enough for families. My father toyed at first with using the Congo as a theme, with lions and tigers painted on the walls and a chorus line of pretend native dancing girls. His next idea was to re-create a more bohemian club, like those in New York's artsy Greenwich Village. But after seeing the new movie Gold Diggers in Paris, *starring Rudy Vallee as a nightclub owner with a chorus line of American girls transported to Paris, he decided to do the same thing in reverse: He would bring Paris to Boston.*

No bank would give him a loan for a nightclub, she writes, so he scraped together money from friends and family. He got his liquor license by calling "his old patron and friend" Joe Timilty, Boston's police commissioner, who turned around and called "his close friend" then governor James Michael Curley. He spent the weeks before the opening melting candle wax around the necks of empty wine bottles to create a Parisian ambience.

It was an instant success. There were two shows nightly featuring singers, acrobats, and the occasional comedian, but the main attraction was the chorus line of barely clothed, besequined girls whom Walters had recruited from local dance schools. He called them his "petite mamzelles." "For the finale," his daughter wrote, "they would drop, one by one, into a deep split, raising their skirts over their heads and showing their ruffled panties."

The formula worked so well that Walters took it to Miami and eventually, in April 1942, to New York, where it was such a phenomenon that the corner of Broadway and Forty-Eighth Street, where it was located, is named "Lou Walters Way." In July 1942, Walters sold the Boston Latin Quarter to the L.Q. Corporation, a newly formed company whose three officers included a Boston lawyer named Louis Winer. In typical fashion, the founding documents bore no mention of the name Redstone, but Winer would go on to become one of Mickey's most trusted advisers, serving as general counsel for National Amusements for decades and as a trustee of the trust that Mickey would leave to his grandchildren. Winer would go on to cofound a law firm with a younger lawyer named George Abrams, who began arguing cases for the Redstones around 1960 and would remain one of the family's most trusted advisers for more than half a century.

On September 10, 1942, just as Boston's nightclub scene was enjoying its best business in years, the Latin Quarter opened for the season under Mickey's management with a lineup that included the comedian Buster Shaver "and his two midgets," comedic dance duo May and Lou Seller, a "starlet singer" named Jerry Kruger, and a ballerina named Helene Denison. "The place is still Boston's finest show case and the site of the best revues in town," Dinneen wrote. "Mickey Redstone, who also operates the Mayfair, succeeds Lou Walters and will be as good a showman." Within a little more than a month, Mickey's Latin Quarter, despite being the most expensive of the city's nightclubs, with its $3 minimum, was drawing twelve hundred patrons on a Saturday night—the most of any club in the city.

*   *   *

Sagansky's other businesses were also flourishing. By then, he had become "perhaps the principal gambling racketeer in the New England area," according to FBI testimony before the Senate special committee on organized crime led by Tennessee senator Estes Kefauver in the early 1950s. And he was increasingly a player on the national scene. By 1942, he was speaking on the phone as many as six times a day to Frank Erickson, New York's biggest bookmaker, who had learned the trade as Arnold Rothstein's right-hand man and forged a lucrative partnership with New York mob boss Frank Costello. Along with Costello, Erickson—plump and bald with cartoonishly round features that made him look a bit like the Belgian comic strip character Tintin—pioneered a system of "laying off" bets, which let bookies all around the country minimize their risk through a system that worked essentially like reinsurance. If a large number of people placed a bet with long odds that, if it hit, would have required a large payout from the bookie, that bookie could hedge his risk by calling up a more powerful bookie, sometimes called a betting commissioner, and placing that same bet. That summer of 1942, Erickson was doing a lot of business as Sagansky's betting commissioner, collecting $13,520 ($200,000 in today's money) from him in July alone. Sagansky had similar relationships with betting commissioners from Houston to Chicago to Rhode Island, and business was booming. By the end of 1941, he had $1.1 million in the bank, and by the end of 1942, he had $1.3 million—nearly $20 million in today's dollars.

Mickey and Sagansky were riding the crest of a wave. But the good times would not last long.

*   *   *

It was a frigid Saturday night, November 28, 1942, and Boston's Conga Belt was buzzing. The undefeated Boston College football team had played Worcester's Holy Cross at Fenway Park that afternoon, and Boston College's victory party had been scheduled at the Cocoanut Grove. BC lost in an upset, but that didn't make the Grove any less the place to be that night. A Hollywood cowboy movie star visiting town, Buck Jones, had attended the game with Boston mayor Maurice Tobin and was due to make his own appearance at the nightclub, which had a special terraced area reserved for celebrities. Since Charles "King" Solomon's rubout, the club had been run by his lawyer, Barnett Welansky, who had installed a low-key efficiency to the operation, as well as some more respectability. Anyone who was anyone was going to be there, enjoying a slice of tropical island paradise amid a Boston winter.

By ten p.m., the club was packed with more than a thousand patrons, more than twice its legal capacity. Coats were stacked on the floor of the coatroom, and waiters had set up extra tables on the dance floor and in the hallways between rooms. Beneath columns disguised as palm trees, lighting fixtures dressed up as coconuts, and a ceiling draped with blue satin, patrons had to pass cocktails and oysters overhead to each other when waiters couldn't reach.

Downstairs, in the dimly lit Melody Lounge piano bar, a sailor and his date were getting intimate. Wanting a bit more privacy, the sailor reached into a fake palm tree and unscrewed the nearest lightbulb, leaving his corner of the lounge in complete darkness. Annoyed, a bartender asked a sixteen-year-old busboy to screw it back in. The busboy lit a match to better see what he was doing. The palm tree sparked, ignited, and then torched the reams of satin covering the ceiling. Panicked patrons soon found that many of the club's nearly dozen exits had been bolted shut to keep people from sneaking out without paying their bills. They stampeded for the revolving door through which they had entered, but only a few made it out onto the street before the stack of bodies lodged in the door rendered it useless.

Within less than a half an hour, 492 people had been killed or fatally wounded in the worst club fire in American history. The fire and toxic smoke had moved so fast that several patrons died with their drinks in their hands.

City officials launched a smattering of investigations, but they were all quickly subsumed by the one led by Attorney General Robert Bushnell, a crusading forty-six-year-old prosecutor who, but for the sweep of his cowlick and a bit of softness at the base of his mustache, bore an unfortunate resemblance to Adolf Hitler. Bushnell was a politically ambitious, New York–born Republican who sought to ride the same wave of reformist fervor that had propelled the similarly mustachioed Thomas Dewey from gang-busting prosecutor, best known for putting away Lucky Luciano, to the New York governor's mansion and presidential ticket.

He framed his Cocoanut Grove investigation as a story of political corruption, the almost-inevitable outcome of the too-cozy relationship between mob-affiliated nightclub owners and public officials. A neon lighting specialist testified in an earlier investigation that he had told Welansky that some lighting in a new wing of the club needed a city permit and supervision by a licensed electrician, and Welansky had replied that it wouldn't be needed because "Tobin and I fit. They owe me plenty." The quote became Bushnell's clarion call as he charged

Welansky and a handful of city officials with manslaughter. "The whole thing constitutes a trap in which lives were taken as a result of gross, wanton and willful acts and failures to act on the part of the defendants," Bushnell said at trial.

In the end, Welansky was the only one who went to jail, sentenced to twelve to fifteen years in Charlestown State Prison. In classic Boston fashion, he was pardoned, gravely ill with cancer, three and a half years later by Maurice Tobin, who had gone on to become governor.

Over the next year, Massachusetts tightened its fire safety codes, defining nightclubs and restaurants as places of public assembly for the first time, and therefore subject to stricter rules. And Boston, as well as other cities, began to enforce its already existing fire rules more forcefully. The Conga Belt would never be the same. The Latin Quarter had to yank down its sumptuous draperies to minimize potential fire hazards. Attendance suffered. Musicians went out of work while the city conducted its inspections. But that would turn out to be the least of the club owners' problems.

Most troublingly for Mickey and Sagansky, an emboldened attorney general now had a surge of popular support to crack down on the toxic cocktail of gangsterism, graft, and palm-greasing that had defined Boston's politics for a generation.

CHAPTER 3

"The Whole Situation"

J anuary 12, 1943, started out like any other Tuesday in Doc Sagan-sky's gambling empire. By ten a.m., his sales force had taken up their regular posts at the beauty shops, shoeshine parlors, and poolrooms of Boston's West End, North End, and Charlestown, ready to pick up the day's number pool plays and horse bets. In sparkling new cars, obtained the previous August despite the war's rationing of tires and limits on car sales, they made their rounds—once in the morning, once in the afternoon—before turning over the plays to the sales manager for their district as the midwinter sun set.

Normally, the sales managers would then take these plays to the syndicate's headquarters, disguised as a paper company inside a yellow brick and limestone building across the street from the Charlestown police station. But there had been a fire in the building a few weeks before, so for the last few days, Sagansky and his lieutenants were making do in the Back Bay apartment of a blond nightclub hostess. They were just converging here for the accounting hour, when the winning bets would be tallied and sent back out through the same network of managers and salesmen, when the door flew open.

At precisely 4:45 p.m., fifty-two state troopers and a handful of FBI agents simultaneously smashed through the doors of twelve apartments, homes, and offices suspected to be involved in Sagansky's sprawling gambling operation, including his palatial Brookline home and the headquarters that turned out to be owned by the city. Ominously for Sagansky, not a single Boston police officer was on hand for the raid.

A few of the gang tried to escape by diving out of windows, but the troopers, who had been methodically tracking the syndicate's routine for seven months, had covered all the exits. In the end, twenty-three people—including Sagansky; the hostess, Lee Goldblatt (who he would go on to marry several years later, after losing his wife to cancer); his wife's brother; and his wife's sister—were arrested and taken down to state police headquarters. The officers found so many adding machines, racing charts, and betting slips that it took two vans to cart all the evidence down to the station.

The *Boston Globe* ran Sagansky's mug shot on its front page the next day, his wire-rimmed glasses, crisp suit, and stoically pitying expression giving him more the look of the inconvenienced dentist he was than a criminal mastermind. Above it was an enormous headline painting him as the brains behind a $90 million gambling ring spanning Massachusetts, Rhode Island, and Connecticut that had defrauded the federal government of $1.5 million in taxes over the last eight years. A line of his compatriots in rumpled double-breasted suits marched by the news camera, hiding their faces with their fedoras. All twenty-three people were charged with conspiracy to set up and promote a lottery, but Sagansky's $25,000 bail (or about $350,000 in today's money) was more than twice anyone else's.

The paper touted the roundup as "the biggest raid of its kind in Massachusetts history," which, given the surge of illegal gambling throughout Massachusetts in the wake of Prohibition, spoke more to the priorities of local law enforcement than the ambition of these particular authorities. Indeed, a hint about those priorities would emerge the next day, when investigators rummaging through a locked closet in Sagansky's home found him named as the beneficiary on a $50,000 life insurance policy on Congressman James Michael Curley, the famously colorful and corrupt "Rascal King" of Boston's politics then passing a sojourn in Washington, D.C., between his third and fourth terms as Boston's mayor. Curley said the policy was collateral on an $8,500 loan from Sagansky and claimed he'd never met the bookie before borrowing the money. But his presence on Sagansky's client list was politically problematic nonetheless.

Curley had been mayor of Boston during Prohibition, when he would display his low opinion of the Eighteenth Amendment by attaching a corkscrew and bottle opener to the keys to the city that he gave visiting officials. The financial ties between Curley's Democratic machine and nightclub owners never fully dissolved after repeal. In the wake of the Cocoanut Grove fire, they became a liability for both sides. To top it all off, his involvement underscored the ugly appearance that the police were in on the whole thing. During Curley's term as governor in 1936, he had tapped his good friend Joseph Timilty, a tubby man with slicked-back, salt-and-pepper hair and bushy black eyebrows who was less of a lawman than a Democratic political operative, as Boston's police commissioner, despite loud protests over his lack of qualification.

Attorney General Robert Bushnell, who was probing the Cocoanut Grove fire, happened to also be the architect of the raid against Sagansky. And as was becoming increasingly clear, his true target was not so much Sagansky's gambling operation as his political relationships.

Within forty-eight hours of the raid, Bushnell went after Timilty directly, demanding that he hand over a "complete" record of the Boston police department's number pool, horse betting, and other gambling arrests and prosecutions over the last two years, ensuring the department's rank and file that they were "all right" because "for obvious reasons police officers of lower ranks are helpless when criminal syndicates are allowed to take over."

Bushnell was so bent on proving that Boston's police department, and indeed entire political establishment, was on the take from its underworld that he was not going to take any chances. Even as he pursued illegal gambling charges against Sagansky and his crew, Bushnell was also working with the Middlesex County district attorney on a new angle showing how Sagansky and his ilk bought off government officials. A week after Sagansky's brother bailed him out of jail, Sagansky was arrested a second time, this time for allegedly trying to bribe two aldermen from the Boston suburb of Malden to vote for a chairman who would grant him a license to run a game of beano, a variant of bingo played with beans. When Sagansky was indicted on bribery charges a few days later, Bushnell declared, "I am under no illusions as to what we are up against—undertaking to attack conditions which are deep-rooted and have existed for years."

*　　　*　　　*

Timilty's alliance with Sagansky had been in Bushnell's sights since the start of his term. One of his first acts as attorney general was to write the Boston police department about the complaints he had been receiving about the gambling rackets, particularly one "big shot" who controlled horses, numbers, and dice games. A Boston detective was assigned to investigate and came back naming the big shot—Harry "Doc Jasper" Sagansky—and giving the exact location of his headquarters. Police officials promised immediate action. But a year then passed, and nothing happened.

So in June 1942, having laid a paper trail revealing the police department's inaction, Bushnell assembled a team of investigators borrowed from state police, district attorneys, and federal authorities and launched his own investigation, quietly setting up an off-site location away from state police headquarters. For seven months, investigators filmed Sagansky's network making their rounds and picking up plays, occasionally posing as customers themselves to build trust. Again and again, they passed up opportunities to nab lower-level players in hopes that patience would lead them to Sagansky himself.

To most people reading about the gambling ring in the press— many of whom played the numbers themselves—none of the gang's crimes would have sounded particularly dastardly. So, with World War II raging in the background, the politically astute Bushnell emphasized not so much the gambling as the ration violations that enabled it. The American government had been rationing tires since 1941, when the Japanese took control of major rubber-producing regions in Southeast Asia, and by late 1942 it sought to further reduce wear and tear on tires by rationing gasoline. When Bushnell's investigators caught Sagansky's men on film pulling five-gallon gas cans out of the trunks of their cars and surreptitiously filling up, the attorney general knew he had the tinder for some political outrage. The same was true of Sagansky's men's ability to procure new cars, even though the government had shut down new car production the year before to free up factory space for the production of military vehicles. Even Sagansky's formidable phone bill of $5,160.75 for the first eleven months of 1943 was held up as evidence of a lack of public spiritedness, after the War Production Board banned phone companies in 1942 from expanding their lines so that the materials could go to the war effort.

But ultimately, it was the Cocoanut Grove fire—often described in newspapers of the day as a "holocaust"—that gave Bushnell the political capital he needed to throw the book at Sagansky and the Boston police. By February, he had convened a grand jury. When a reporter buttonholed him to ask what it had been called for—Sagansky, the Cocoanut Grove, or some new case—he replied, "Obviously, these things converge. It is on the whole situation."

By "the whole situation," Bushnell meant the way that, ever since Prohibition, Boston's entire city government, from the top of its police department to its mayoralty to its municipal courts, had been bought off by the mob, who used their interest in the nightclubs of the Conga Belt as their personal living rooms to entertain politicians and get a bit of money laundered in the process. As he painted it, beyond depriving the government of tax revenue and making a mockery of wartime rationing, their activities finally combusted in late November into a situation that killed nearly five hundred people.

As Bushnell built the two cases simultaneously, he emphasized their interlocking components. In the Cocoanut Grove investigation, he declared that everyone knew the club was "the product of the underworld." And as he unveiled his probe against Sagansky, he argued that it spanned not just the gambling element, but also "night life and entertainment promoters and certain public officials," as the *Globe* put it. The strength of "the whole situation" gave Bushnell license to do two unprecedented things. First, he decided to make an example of Sagansky and a few of his accomplices by charging them with operating a "fictitious lottery," a seldom-used felony charge dating back to Colonial times that meant Sagansky was facing hard time. Second, in a stunning and ultimately politically overreaching bit of corruption busting, Bushnell's grand jury indicted Timilty and a handful of his lieutenants for conspiring to permit the operation of gambling.

*   *   *

This was all very bad for Mickey Redstone.

The nightclub business had been so good to him that, by 1943, he and his family had moved into the sumptuous Copley Plaza Hotel, parlor of Boston's elite, just around the corner from the Conga Belt. But on the morning of February 4, 1943, all this was suddenly at risk, as he was forced to put on his best suit and make his way across Boston Common to the Suffolk County Courthouse to appear before Bushnell's grand jury. The proceedings laid out publicly for the first time that Mickey and Sagansky were partners in both the Mayfair and Latin Quarter, as well as in a lending company called Standish Finance alongside Charles "King" Solomon's former bootlegging lieutenant Louis Fox.

Louis Fox was a key member of Boston's Jewish mob and a shining example of how to turn bootlegging profits into legitimate business and social respectability. After he and associates like Hyman Abrams and Joe Linsey took over Solomon's bootlegging syndicate, they broadened it to gambling. Fox held a stake in the Wonderland Greyhound Park dog track, which Linsey would go on to take control of decades later, and in which Mickey remained invested until the 1980s. Once known as the "King of the North Shore" for his vast waterfront real estate holdings stretching from Boston to New Hampshire, Fox died in 1963 a millionaire, with most of his obituary taken up by his philanthropy to Boston College and Jewish charities. Only one small line was reserved for his being hauled in before the Massachusetts Crime Commission in 1957 and interviewed for five hours—during which he declined to answer any question except his birthday and would only repeat a single statement: "I am not now or have I ever been involved in anything to do with illegal gambling." During that testimony, he refused to answer questions about his role in Standish, though a few years later, his obituary listed him as having been the firm's president. During the same testimony, he also refused to answer a pointed question about whether he had ever visited Sagansky in prison. During the grand jury testimony in 1943, jurors learned that Sagansky held a stake in Standish and that its treasurer was Mickey Redstone. Details on Standish are scant, but one associate of Mickey's described it as a loan-sharking operation.

The optics of Bushnell's grand jury were not great for Mickey or his businesses, but his real headache would come from the probe into Sagansky's alleged attempts to "buy up" the city government of Malden in his quest for a beano license. Among Mickey's problems was that Club Mayfair was the scene of the alleged crime.

During the trial, two Malden aldermen testified that Sagansky had met with them at the Mayfair and offered them $1,000 up front and $100 a week if they voted for a chairman of the town's board of aldermen who would issue Sagansky a beano permit. Sagansky testified that those figures were mentioned but that he was describing how much money would go to the city, not the aldermen—and besides, it was his associate, not himself, who was seeking the beano permit. He added that Club Mayfair was "almost like home" to him, prompting the DA to crack, "No dental work there, except in the nature of extractions?" eliciting laughter from the courtroom.

Sagansky and his associate were found guilty of conspiracy to bribe the aldermen, and by February 20, they were being outfitted with gray trousers and coats to begin their two-year sentence in the Middlesex House of Correction. A month later, Sagansky was brought into court in handcuffs and pleaded guilty to conspiracy to violate the fictitious lottery law. He was sentenced to two and a half to three years in state prison and fined $5,000.

*   *   *

The episode didn't break up Mickey and Sagansky, but it imperiled their businesses enough that neither would ever again talk publicly about their partnership. Within a week of Sagansky's conviction, the authorities came for the nightclubs. Based on Sagansky's testimony that he was the assistant manager of and a stockholder in Club Mayfair, the Boston police recommended that the club's liquor license be suspended. Mickey was only able to get out of it by publicly breaking with Sagansky, writing him a $10,000 check to pay him back for the loan Sagansky had given him two years before and having Sagansky sign a witnessed affidavit severing all connection with the club. If Sagansky had some crazy idea in his head that their partnership went further than that, Mickey's lawyer testified, well, that was all a big misunderstanding. After the lawyer came up with evidence a few days later that Mickey had also gotten bank loans for the Mayfair, and thus was not completely dependent on Sagansky for funds, the liquor license was restored.

No sooner was the Mayfair out of trouble with the licensing board, however, than the Latin Quarter was in it. Barely a week after Sagansky was convicted the second time, one of the small fry rounded up in the raid on his gambling ring was shot, along with his friend, in an argument over a showgirl at the Latin Quarter, sending hundreds of terror-stricken patrons out onto the brick sidewalks of Bay Village in the wee morning hours of Friday, March 26, 1943. The police, mindful that they were vulnerable to appearing too cozy with the city's nightclub owners, recommended that the Latin Quarter be shut down, calling it a "menace to the patrons who frequent it."

This time, it was Bushnell who inadvertently saved Mickey's hide. The next day, Timilty and other police top brass were indicted and suspended from their jobs, and their replacements did not share their late-found zeal for shutting down the Latin Quarter.

*   *   *

While Mickey was being hauled in front of the licensing board to answer questions about his business partnership with a convicted criminal and ration violator, his son Sumner may as well have been on a different planet. He was in Arlington, Virginia, breaking Japanese codes for the war effort. It was a stroke of amazing good fortune that Mickey's darkest hour coincided with Sumner's first real stretch of total independence from his family.

When Sumner entered Harvard in 1940, he initially lived at home with his parents and brother in a rented apartment in Brighton. During the summers, he worked for his father, he said in his autobiography, though he is short on details on in what capacity. "I worked one summer selling hot dogs at the little shack of a refreshment stand at the Sunrise Drive-In," he wrote. "This was my introduction to the high-powered world of media and entertainment." During college, he only visited his father's nightclubs "on rare occasions." Despite finding Harvard disappointingly easy after the rigors of Boston Latin, he still studied all the time.

His maniacal study habits and facility with languages after having taken the required Latin and Greek at Boston Latin caught the attention of the college's administrators, who recommended that he take an intensive Japanese class from an elegant, charismatic professor named Edwin Reischauer, who had been raised in Japan by missionary parents. Sumner found the fast pace of the course and Reischauer's high standards exhilarating. In January 1943, with the war intensifying, Reischauer left Harvard to set up a school in a former girls' school of Arlington Hall to train Japanese translators and cryptanalysts for the U.S. Army Signal Corps. Sumner was one of about fifty to sixty (not two to three, as Sumner recalled it) of Reischauer's Harvard students he recruited to join him. These included some of the brightest minds of his generation, like future Supreme Court justice John Paul Stevens and Stanford Law School dean and the first president of the Council on Foreign Relations, Bayless Manning.

Sumner left Harvard without a degree and joined the army. Day in and day out, he scoured intercepted Japanese diplomatic cables. By the end of the war, codes he had helped break were being read to generals and colonels and helped play a role in battles like the one in the Gulf of Leyte where a Japanese fleet was nearly demolished. In 1944, he and his fellow code breakers were made second lieutenants, and he was later promoted to first lieutenant. Breaking the Japanese codes had been one of the crucial ways that the Allies won the war.

It all seemed a long way from the Conga Belt. Except that it wasn't.

After the war ended in September 1945, but before Sumner could muster out of the army, he was transferred to Special Services and charged with bringing entertainment to army hospitals. "Because my father was in the nightclub business I had met a few performers on the rare occasions during college when I had visited the clubs, so it seemed a natural assignment," he wrote. "I made some contacts and suddenly I was an expert on booking bands." He even got Benny Goodman to play for free. He was such a good impresario—and had access to such a powerful Rolodex—he received a commendation for his service from the army.

But there was no sign he wanted to follow in his father's footsteps. He had amassed enough credits before leaving for Arlington that Harvard allowed him to graduate at the end of the war, technically a member of the class of 1944. His Harvard yearbook of 1943–1944 shows him at twenty, slight and younger-looking than his classmates, filled with righteousness and idealism. With his concentration in classics and government, he intended to pursue a career in civil service.

If his father lived in the shadows, he would live in the light.

There was just one hint that this might not come to pass: he listed his home address as the Copley Plaza Hotel.

*   *   *

With Sagansky in prison, Mickey carried on with the show. He installed a new manager at the Mayfair and expertly spun his newfound inability to afford "name" talent at the Latin Quarter as a fresh approach to entertainment. Instead of stars, he offered novelty acts, like a circus-themed spectacle in August 1943 featuring a fake snake charmer, "Squatting Squaw, the daughter of Sitting Bull," and a man in a horse costume. "It was Mickey Redstone's idea, and it must have taken some courage to try it out, but the experiment proves that names do not necessarily make good entertainment," wrote Joseph Dinneen of the *Globe*. Boston was rooting for Mickey to get back on his feet.

Bushnell's crusade to eradicate corruption in Boston fell somewhat short of its goals. Timilty managed to get his indictment quashed and went back to work until the governor removed him later that year for another scandal entirely. He became what he called a "houseguest" of Joe Kennedy's, traveling with him, delivering threats to his political opponents, and acting as a beard for him when calling upon his girl-friends. The once-mighty police commissioner was reduced to tasks like delivering a bag of $12,000 in cash from Kennedy to Curley in 1946 in exchange for his decision not to run for a congressional seat that Kennedy thought his son Jack would be perfect for.

Bushnell never made it to the governor's mansion. He returned to private practice and died of a heart attack in 1949 in his hotel suite in New York, a workaholic till the end, his body surrounded by open law books.

In the end, Sagansky would have the last laugh. His two and a half years in state prison would turn out to be a mere blip in one of the longest and most successful illegal gambling careers in American history. He continued to have a role in the rackets and occasional run-ins with the law until he died of natural causes at the age of ninety-nine.

Even after power in the underworld shifted away from the Jewish and Irish mobs toward the Italian mafia, Sagansky remained part of the action. In the 1950s, the Senate committee investigating organized crime named him one of the top 150 bookmakers in the country. He would occasionally get busted—the Brookline police department caught him trying to stuff betting slips into a trapdoor in the floor of his office in 1954—but the charges almost never stuck. He kept his word, kept his friends, and didn't squeal. On his ninetieth birthday, he became the oldest federal inmate in the country for refusing to testify before a grand jury investigating organized crime.

By the end of his life, he had earned millions and given much of it away to Beth Israel Hospital, Tufts Dental School, Brandeis University, and Temple Ohabei Shalom. At his funeral, hundreds showed up to hail him as a "folk hero." And he still had enough left over to leave $9.5 million to his four children, according to probate documents obtained by the *Boston Herald*. His son told the *Herald* he was able to leave his children so much because "he sold all his interest in Redstone theaters years ago" and converted them into Treasury notes, mutual funds, and other investment vehicles.

But Mickey and Sagansky's partnership went beyond drive-ins, nightclubs, or even loan agencies. In the 1950s, as the mob was leveraging its gambling expertise to build a sparkling paradise of legal gaming on the Las Vegas Strip, Sagansky brought Mickey in with him as an investor in the Dunes Hotel, an Arabian-themed casino and hotel marked by a thirty-five-foot fiberglass sultan with a glinting car headlight playing the role of the jewel in his giant turban. The Dunes opened in 1955, quickly went out of business due to gambling losses, and changed hands. (Despite help from friends like Frank Sinatra, who performed at the opening wearing a turban and surrounded by a harem of scantily clad dancers, and interest from prospective buyers including Donald Trump, the resort struggled financially and was blown up in the 1990s to make way for properties like the Bellagio.)

Years later, as the FBI was investigating the assassination of President John F. Kennedy, its informants reported that some of Mickey and Sagansky's fellow investors had been front men for Raymond Patriarca, the Providence, Rhode Island–based boss of the Patriarca crime family, who controlled the New England rackets. According to the FBI files, some of Patriarca's associates were having trouble getting back even a portion of their original investment, but Mickey made $6,000.

* * *

After Sagansky got out of prison in 1945, his name would never again publicly appear alongside Mickey's, though there were signs that he was more than just a passive investor in their entertainment holdings. After the war, the focus of those holdings would shift back from nightclubs to the drive-ins. The nightclub business suffered from the lack of servicemen moving through Boston, as well as the growing fees that the "name" talents were demanding, and by 1949 Mickey handed over the keys to the Latin Quarter to new management. Meanwhile, the end of tire and gas rationing meant the drive-in boom that Mickey and Sagansky had once foreseen was now at hand.

By 1948, they had bought land bordering a marsh at the intersection of Routes 1 and 60 in Revere, in Boston's northern suburbs, and opened the Revere Drive-In with a swashbuckling adventure film *The Swordsman* starring Larry Parks. The same year, they opened a drive-in at the same location in Dedham that the community had so forcefully rejected in 1937.

But when they tried to take this expansion inside Boston city limits in 1949, with new theaters proposed in West Roxbury and Dorchester, they ran into problems. Drive-ins were no more popular with urban neighbors than they had been a decade earlier. Clergy in West Roxbury and Dorchester had appealed to Mayor Curley, then serving what would turn out to be his final term as mayor of Boston, not to approve the licenses for the theaters' construction, and they believed they had assurances from Curley that he would not.

But in the final weeks before the election, Curley, that old associate of Sagansky's, quietly approved the permits, setting off a firestorm of criticism from the local councilmen representing those neighborhoods. They threatened to work against his reelection.

In any other year, it would have been hot air, but in 1949, Bostonians were growing uneasy about their city's slipping stature. The port that had been the engine of industry for Boston was moribund, downtown was in seemingly permanent decline, the city's taxes were high, and its finances were a mess. Curley's strategy of "doing little things for little people" had helped him consolidate political power and votes among the city's downtrodden, but it had also kept the business community stagnant. Add to this that Curley had served part of his fourth mayoral term from prison for mail fraud, and the conditions were ripe for a city hall bureaucrat named John Hynes to pull off one of the great upsets in Boston political history by promising a "clean, honest and efficient administration."

Curley was not one to let an electoral loss keep him from doing a favor for a friend. The seventy-five-year-old spent the final hours of his mayoralty in a footrace with a female deputy sheriff who was trying to serve him with an injunction to restrain him from signing permits for the Dorchester and West Roxbury drive-ins. At five thirty p.m., he charged out of city hall with the deputy close on his heels, followed by what the *Globe* described as a "horde of angry taxpayers." Curley "managed to elude the deputy by racing down two flights of stairs and speeding off in his limousine," according to the *Globe*, but she caught up with him at his Jamaicaway home and served it to his maid.

On January 1, 1950, Hynes wrote Mickey, pledging to revoke all construction permits for the theaters, despite Redstone already having a bulldozer clearing the properties and a sign reading "New Drive-In Theatre Will Be Erected Here Soon." For weeks, the city council continued to rail about it. But when Hynes was sworn in, his corporation counsel informed him that he did not in fact have the authority to revoke the permits. The corrupt Curley era ended, but not before giving one last leg up to Mickey and Sagansky.

Still, Hynes had promised a "New Boston," and he was true to his word. In one of the most controversial acts in the history of American urban renewal, he set about wiping the West End from the face of the earth, bulldozing its tenements to make way for gleaming high-rises. The narrow streets were a fire hazard, he argued, the empty storefronts were blighted, and the new buildings and the upper-middle-class tenants that would inhabit them would bring more tax revenue to the city. But it was more than just that. The poor immigrants of the largely Italian and Jewish West End had voted for Curley. And, like New York's Lower East Side, the neighborhood's crowded streets had nurtured, in addition to artists and entrepreneurs and hardworking immigrants climbing into the middle class, generations of hustlers, gangsters, bookies, and prostitutes. By the time it was over, the streets where Mickey and Sagansky grew up no longer existed.

*   *   *

The 1950s brought a new era for Mickey and Sagansky, too. By 1949, Mickey's businesses were successful enough that he no longer needed to rely so heavily on his old partner. He headed into the new decade with a new partner: his son.

CHAPTER 4

The Next Generation

I t should have been a victory lap.

By April 1950, Mickey Redstone had largely prevailed in his closely watched fight to build the first drive-ins within Boston city limits. And so, for the first time, the middle-aged theater impresario sent his son out into the trade press to deliver the good news.

Edward Redstone was twenty-one years old, a year out of college, a taller, brown-eyed spitting image of his father. Since graduating from Colgate, he had been working part-time for his father while he waited for an acceptance letter from Harvard Business School, the credential that would finally put him on the same level of educational prestige as his elder brother, Sumner. An eager student who, unlike his brother, had always wanted to go into business, Eddie, as everyone called him, started out admirably enough, touting the beginning of construction of the controversial drive-ins at Neponset Circle in Boston's Dorchester neighborhood and along the VFW Parkway to the southwest in West Roxbury, and plans for further expansion to Natick, Massachusetts, and Bay Shore, Long Island.

But he couldn't quite stop at simple boasts about the company's growing footprint. Instead, he confessed to *Billboard* that box office revenue for the four-theater chain was down 15 percent in 1949, and that the Dedham and Revere drive-ins, which reopened in March, were "off in receipts." "This will be the year that will tell the tale in drive-ins," Eddie told *Billboard*. "It looks like the year of decision."

He was right. For all the frenzied building in the drive-in sector, the broader film industry was two years into a protracted slump that would cut theater attendance in half over a decade. Leading up to 1950, the industry was in free fall, with average weekly attendance dropping from ninety million per week in 1948 to sixty million per week by 1950. The decline would continue until the 1970s, when the first modern blockbusters (*The Godfather, Jaws,* and *Star Wars*) revived attendance somewhat, although as a percentage of population, moviegoing would never recover its postwar peak.

The cause was a perfect storm of demographic, technological, and regulatory change. Though television is often blamed, the decline began even before then, with the radical demographic shifts wrought by the post–World War II baby boom. Returning servicemen were starting families, buying houses, and signing up for college in record numbers thanks to programs like the G.I. Bill, leaving little time or money left over for leisure activities. And the houses that they were buying were increasingly located in far-flung suburbs, making traditional downtown movie houses inconvenient for a growing middle class.

Television then exacerbated the trend, beginning its definitive commercial expansion in 1948, when the number of television sets hit 172,000, up from 14,000 the previous year. By 1949, there were one million, and by the end of the 1950s, 90 percent of American households had one. Forgoing the movie theater for an evening on the couch, even if the fare was somewhat less entertaining, would prove to be an enduring temptation, particularly for families with young children.

Also, in May 1948, the Supreme Court handed down its landmark antitrust decision in *United States v. Paramount Pictures, Inc.,* which would ultimately force the major studios to sell off their theaters, marking the beginning of the end of the golden age of Hollywood. For decades leading up to the *Paramount* decision, the film industry was controlled by eight major studios, of which the most powerful Big Five—Paramount Pictures, Twentieth Century Fox, Warner Bros., RKO, and Loews, the parent company of Metro-Goldwyn-Mayer Studios—were fully vertically integrated, making the movies, distributing them, and showing them in chains of theaters that they owned, often in plum downtown locations. (The Little Three—Universal,

Columbia, and United Artists—were not meaningfully in the exhibition business but helped their larger brethren pad out their double features with cheaper fare.)

The majors operated as a cartel, giving preferential treatment to each other's movies at their best theaters, and forced independent theaters to buy large blocks of often mediocre films up front, sight unseen, in order to get access to the films with the biggest stars, practices called "block booking" and "blind bidding." With such a guaranteed pipeline to audiences, each of the majors (except for UA, which was only a distributor) produced between forty and sixty films a year—vastly more than their successors make today, when slates can be as small as a dozen films a year. Largely thanks to their ownership of prime first-run movie houses, by the mid-'40s the Big Five were sucking up roughly 70 percent of the country's box office receipts, even though they only owned or had interest in about a quarter of the country's movie theaters. In *Paramount*, the Supreme Court ruled that the Big Five were conspiring to monopolize exhibition. The decision put immediate limits on practices like block booking. Over the next several years, the Big Five sold off their movie theaters, which, combined with the rise of television, drastically reduced the number of films and the profits that the majors made. In the decade after *Paramount*, national film distributors cut the number of films they released annually from 448 to 352. Profits at the ten biggest companies dropped 74 percent to $32 million in the decade leading up to 1956. More than four thousand traditional indoor movie theaters shut down during this period.

Many of these trends, like the shift to the suburbs, were good for drive-ins. By 1951, 60 percent of American families owned a car, helping drive-ins to become, during these years, what second-generation drive-in operator Richard Smith called "a bright little spark [in an] otherwise terrible industry." Between 1948 and 1951, the number of indoor theaters contracted from eighteen thousand to fifteen thousand, but the number of drive-ins more than tripled from fewer than a thousand to thirty-six hundred.

The *Paramount* decision also theoretically opened doors to independent exhibitors like drive-ins by loosening the major studios' stranglehold on the exhibition business. But drive-ins would have to launch many more lawsuits before they got their hands on first-run product with any regularity. In the meantime, the *Paramount* decision's immediate fallout meant fewer decent movies to go around. And it was this dearth of product that Eddie Redstone was complaining about to *Billboard*. "Our problem," Eddie said, "is that drive-ins are being overtaxed by the distributor for the grade picture he is giving us." He went on to complain about the drive-in expansion he saw all around him, even though his own company was a major driver of it. "Everywhere I go, I see drive-ins," he said. "Some operators seem to forget that it is location that counts in this business."

It was an accurate diagnosis of the ills of the industry but utterly lacked the showman's boosterism that had so successfully marked Mickey's interactions with the press. While Mickey thought nothing of declaring his screens the world's largest or his neon signs Long Island's brightest, Eddie liked to tell the truth, at times to a fault.

"He wore his heart on his sleeve," said his widow, Madeline Redstone. "He wasn't a killer."

*   *   *

The reason that Sumner Redstone turned out to be "a killer" and Eddie did not can be partly explained by the five years that separate their births, five years that turned out to be a lifetime in terms of the Redstone family's socioeconomic ascent.

In his speeches, interviews, and writings later in life, Sumner frequently described himself as having grown up in poverty. "Our apartment in Charlesbank Homes in Boston's West End had no toilet; we had to walk down the corridor to use the pull-chain commode in the water closet we shared with the neighbors," he wrote in his autobiography. "That sort of living was all I knew and I never felt less privileged than anyone else."

Later, after the family had moved to Brighton, he described being beaten up by anti-Semitic Irish bullies on the way to school at the age of twelve. "The level of violence was not nearly as high then as it is now and I saw no knives, but I would get smacked around, and along with my bruises I'd hear a lot of threats and name-calling," he wrote.

Even after he tested into the prestigious, free public Boston Latin School, which he started in seventh grade—around the same time that Mickey and Sagansky opened their first drive-in—Sumner's memories are of poverty. "All I had going for me was an education. We certainly didn't have any money," he wrote. "The ten cents a day I spent on round-trip streetcar fare was a significant sacrifice for my family and I had to justify that sacrifice."

These reminiscences hit the Horatio Alger note a bit harder than the facts can support, given that his father started investing in real estate in Brighton by the time Sumner was two years old and his grandfather was running a successful bakery supply company and living in the fashionable suburb of Brookline before he turned ten. But the broad outlines of Sumner's conception of himself as having come up from the West End still held.

In contrast, by the time Eddie was born in 1928, the family had already bought property in Brighton, and the West End was a memory. "Eddie did not feel that he grew up poor," Madeline said. "The bathroom was not outside." Nor did he feel he experienced anti-Semitism as a child. "He had no childhood scars."

By the time Eddie was in high school, Mickey owned both the Sunrise Drive-In and the Mayfair and was living in the Copley Plaza Hotel. Rather than the hardscrabble Boston Latin, he went to Kimball Union Academy, one of the oldest private boarding schools in the country, nestled amid leafy splendor on a hilltop New Hampshire campus just down the road from Dartmouth College. He was the youngest student in his class. By most accounts, he was no less intelligent than Sumner, and he was accepted to Dartmouth. But because he was only sixteen, Dartmouth recommended that he go to Colgate for a year before matriculating. "He loved Colgate so much he stayed," Madeline said.

Upon graduating from Colgate in 1949, he went to work part-time

for his father, doing what he described as "everything from fixing septic fields to selling hot dogs, the whole gamut," with an eye toward a
career in the family business.

The acceptance letter to Harvard Business School did eventually
arrive, and in the fall of 1950, he enrolled. The next year, he got engaged to a striking, raven-haired beauty from a wealthy New York
family named Leila Warren. The only child of the president of the
Society Girl Corset Company, with homes in Manhattan and Westport, Connecticut, Leila was tall, fashionable, headstrong, and, ultimately, deeply troubled.

Eddie got his MBA in the spring of 1952, and by July, *Variety* was
reporting that he had joined his father's theater company "in charge
of daily operations of six ozoners," as the trade magazine called drive-
ins. At Eddie and Leila's wedding in October at the Plaza Hotel in
New York—the sister hotel to Boston's Copley Plaza—Sumner was
the best man. Despite their differences in temperament, the brothers
had always been close, in part because they had always been on such
divergent paths. Eddie was his father's heir apparent, and Sumner was
going to save the world.

*   *   *

For the first quarter of his life, through his marriage, early career,
and the birth of his two children, Sumner Redstone betrayed no hint
of interest in the media business. Though he worked at his father's
theaters in the summers like a dutiful son, he had higher aspirations
than the then-still-somewhat-déclassé world of theaters—a world that,
from the earliest movie moguls, was what corporate historian Bettye
Pruitt calls a "quintessential ethnic business" dominated by Eastern
European Jewish immigrants who saw opportunity in technological
change and often faced obstacles accessing more traditional enterprises. Sumner did not want to compete as a subset of anything. As
Doc Sagansky's daughter, Marilyn Riseman, once put it to *Vanity Fair*:
"You know what my father used to say about Sumner? 'If that man
weren't Jewish, he'd have been president.'"

In his autobiography, Sumner wrote that his rather grandiose sense of his own destiny was instilled in him by his mother, who was obsessed with his achievement.

To be the national best at any- and everything was my mother's goal for me. Second best was not an option as far as Belle was concerned. She was a very good-looking woman but I'm not sure how much fun she got out of life. There was only one number one and that had to be me. My brother, while he was smart and did extremely well in school, was not the target of her passion; I was. I was her pride and her focus.

One of Sumner's most-repeated stories is of his mother turning the clock back to trick him into practicing the piano or studying a half an hour longer. Eddie remembered her as cold and anxious. "I probably got along with her as well as anyone else got along with her," he said. "She was a nervous wreck." He added that "she didn't give of herself" to her children, and "probably didn't know how."

"My aunt Belle was a profoundly brittle, insecure woman," said Gary Snyder. "No doubt having a womanizing, magnetic husband with a presence that bounded beyond his skin did not help."

Sumner credits his mother's obsessive drive for propelling him into, and, more importantly through, Boston Latin School, which he called "the most rigorous and competitive experience I have ever had, and that includes business."

More than poverty, more than his mother's focused attention, it was Boston Latin School that shaped both Sumner's combativeness and his transcendent sense of his own potential—that made him, in essence, a killer. Even today, it is impossible to walk into the wood-paneled auditorium of the school without feeling a sense of awe, of history as a close and malleable thing, and, as many students of past generations would say, of dread. Founded in 1635, Boston Latin School is the oldest school in the United States—a year older than Harvard, nearly a century and a half older than the country itself. Five of the fifty-six signers of the Declaration of Independence were its students, and today their iconic names—among them John Hancock, Samuel Adams, and Benjamin Franklin, along with a host of governors, senators, congressmen, theologians, Nobel laureates, and cultural luminaries from Ralph Waldo Emerson to Leonard Bernstein—are engraved in gold lettering atop the auditorium's upper frieze, reserved for its most illustrious deceased alumni. The not-so-subtle message to students is that they ought to be gunning to get their own names up on that wall.

But the more direct message delivered to students of Sumner's generation is that they could expect the fight of their lives to make it to graduation. Students sitting in the auditorium on their first day were told, "Look to your left, look to your right, two of you are not going to make it," said Michael Contompasis, the former longtime headmaster of the school who said he barely graduated in 1957. "It was a survival issue. Half my class didn't graduate. It was probably worse when Sumner was here. . . . When I graduated this place and walked out the front door with my diploma, I vowed never to set foot in this place again."

From the beginning, the school's curriculum was anchored in Latin and Greek, with a tradition of Socratic argument and debate that includes, to this day, mandatory thrice-yearly "declamations" of memorized texts that must be delivered standing on a raised platform before one's entire English class. As a public school in a Boston that was absorbing wave after wave of immigrants in the early decades of the twentieth century, it was diverse and ruthlessly meritocratic— its then largely working-class student body got in, before the days of standardized tests, on the strength of their lower school transcripts— leaving little room for camaraderie. "I can name four people in my six years here that we had general conversations," Contompasis said. "It just didn't happen."

Sumner seems to have been both traumatized and fortified by the experience, which set patterns that would remain for his entire life. "I had no social life. I had no friends. I knew people only because I sat next to them in class or because they were my closest competitors for the school awards," he wrote in his autobiography. "I did nothing but study. Throughout high school, I don't remember eating. . . . The primary lesson I learned at Boston Latin was that life is rough, that tension is frequently crushing, and that the only hope that counts is the hope that lies within each individual."

His first year, he caught scarlet fever, which kept him out of school for weeks—a terrifying prospect. "I don't remember being scared of dying," he wrote. "I do remember being terrorized by the fact that I was missing classes." His mother, who had become close to his home-room teacher and the school's future headmaster, Wilfred O'Leary, brought him books, and he ended up winning the school's classics prize and modern prize for the year, and every year after that.

Over many decades of being profiled in the press, Sumner would repeat some version of the boast that he went on to graduate with the "highest grade point average in the three-hundred-year history of Boston Latin." As best it is possible to tell, this seems to be a hyperbolic flourish of the Mickey Redstone school of personal promotion. "When Sumner graduated, they did not keep grade point averages," Contompasis said. "What I can tell you is, he did have an outstanding academic record. It was probably in the top 1 percent of his class."

But he would get his name on the wall of the auditorium, albeit not (yet) on the upper frieze. "The lower wall is individuals who have made significant contributions, not only to their particular professions, but who have also given back to the school," Contompasis said. "Sumner was on the wall because he was a donor to the school."

Although Sumner maintained a nearly lifelong indifference to fancy (some might even say decent) clothes and developed a taste for grand houses only later in life, he would ultimately learn that money was an essential component to satisfying the craving for glory and power that Boston Latin had fostered in him. But before he came to this realization, he would set out into the world determined to satisfy it in what he believed was a more noble way, through public service. He had excelled at debate at Boston Latin, and entered Harvard, on scholarship, bound for its Debating Council and ultimately for Harvard

Law School, where he would follow in the footsteps of his mother's father and become a lawyer. When he passed the bar in September 1947, the *Boston Globe* ran a story mentioning him as one of several "sons of distinguished fathers"—including the son of a former governor of Maine—who were entering the legal profession that year. Although Mickey owned several drive-ins by that point, he was described as a "night club operator."

Immediately after taking the bar, Sumner married Phyllis Raphael, the petite, blond elder daughter of a department store founder living in Brookline, whom he had met during his freshman year at Harvard. Phyllis's parents had both been born in the old country, in different corners of the Russian Empire. Like the Rohtsteins, Phyllis's mother, the former Hilda Cherry, had come from a Jewish settlement in what is today Ukraine and passed through the West End. But Phyllis's father, Eli Raphael, had emigrated much more recently, in 1915, and his ascent was much faster. By 1921, he had founded a group of department stores in Everett Square in Boston's Dorchester neighborhood, and Phyllis grew up comfortably in the then largely Jewish suburbs of Mattapan and then Brookline. If young Sumner was driven and joyless, Phyllis was vivacious and carefree. Her only pet peeve, according to her high school yearbook, was when people tried to spell Phyllis "with one l and two s's." "She was an adorable girl who came from a lovely family," Marilyn Riseman told *Boston* magazine. "A pretty, lovely, bright, sparkly little girl."

Two years Sumner's junior, she was still at Brookline High School when she met him at a temple dance. Her parents were not thrilled about their daughter dating the son of a nightclub owner, even though Mickey's connections to Boston's underworld had not yet become front-page news, so they sent her to UCLA. "Her parents did not want the marriage," said one person close to the family. "They sent their daughter away."

After she graduated in 1946 with a degree in political science, she returned to Boston and enrolled in classes at Boston University while Sumner continued his pursuit. Belle Redstone approved of her son's choice, and by January 1947 they were engaged. They were married on July 4, 1947, and headed off immediately afterward to San Francisco, where Sumner had accepted a prestigious, if not lucrative, job as a clerk in the Ninth Circuit Court of Appeals for $43 a week. "I was not interested in either making a lot of money or limiting myself to academics," Sumner later wrote. "The postwar world was going in a million different directions and I wanted to make a difference."

After a year of clerking by day and teaching labor law at the University of San Francisco Law School at night, Sumner got his ticket to the corridors of national power in Washington, D.C., with a job on the staff of the Appellate Tax Division of the United States Attorney General. His hometown newspaper ran a story about the appointment, noting—no doubt at the nudging of some Redstone—that "he is one of the youngest lawyers ever appointed to this department."

On September 7, 1948, Sumner started his new job at the Department of Justice. The two and a half years he spent there were momentous ones for the department's shaping of the media industry. In the wake of the Supreme Court's decision in *Paramount*, Herbert Bergson, the department's assistant attorney general in charge of antitrust, continued to lead the government's fight against Paramount and the Big Eight's anticompetitive practices as they wended their way through the courts. Though Sumner was assigned to the tax division and largely occupied by other matters during these years, in 1950, when Bergson left the Justice Department with his second in command, Herbert Borkland, Sumner followed them into private practice.

"It was the best antitrust firm in the country," said Bergson's son Paul. A year after Bergson left the Department of Justice, Peyton Ford, the deputy attorney general, also joined the firm. Later in 1951, a twenty-eight-year-old Sumner would join him as partner of Ford, Bergson, Adams, Borkland & Redstone.

Bergson was the "face of the firm, a diplomat," said Borkland's son, also named Herbert. "Borky"—as his family called him—"was essentially the workhorse." One of the younger Borkland's earliest memories, in fact, was meeting Sumner when he came by the house to discuss a case. "As a very young boy, I was insane about cowboys," he said. "When he showed up, I insisted upon calling him Tonto, and this became a family joke" because Sumner was so clearly nobody's sidekick. "Even for a boy, he was distinctive, a straight-standing, well-spoken man. He made an impression, even on a child."

The media industry, still very much in antitrust officials' sights, was a critical part of the firm's client portfolio. United Paramount Theatres, the chain of movie theaters that Paramount was forced to spin off in 1949 as a result of the *Paramount* case that Bergson led at the Justice Department, became a client. Ford Bergson represented UPT before the Federal Communications Commission in its petition to merge with ABC. After that merger was approved in 1953, the merged entity would eventually change its name to ABC and remain a key client until the firm, later reorganized as Bergson Borkland, met its demise in the 1980s amid the Reagan administration's laissez-faire approach to antitrust. Sumner's years at the firm gave him invaluable experience in the legal and antitrust issues facing theater chains— knowledge that he was about to start using to enrich himself and his family in a whole new way.

*　　*　　*

The crowning achievement of Sumner's legal career was arguing a case before the Supreme Court for a hotel-owning couple who were in hot water with tax authorities for an unexplained surge in net worth. The court's decision on *Holland v. United States* was handed down on December 6, 1954. Although Sumner was unable to get the couple's conviction overturned, his argument that the government had the burden of proving that any suspicious increases in net worth were actually tax evasion did alter law, leading to the release of some prisoners.

In boasting about it years later, Sumner could not simply leave the story at that. He went on to say that, in the mid-1950s, while out in Las Vegas representing a group that was building the Dunes Hotel, he met a man who was working at the Flamingo Hotel whose brother had been one of the men released from Alcatraz as a result of the decision. Sumner claimed that this man then introduced him to Bugsy Siegel—the infamous Jewish mobster, partner of Meyer Lansky and Lucky Luciano, and architect of the Las Vegas Strip—who dangled untold riches in front of Sumner to entice him to come work his newly proven magic making unexplainable income untouchable by the tax man. "I wasn't tempted," Sumner wrote. "Money wasn't my vice and I saw life in a very different way." This story cannot be true, however, as Siegel rather famously got a pair of bullets in the head while sitting on his girlfriend's couch in Beverly Hills in 1947.

Sumner just got his mobsters mixed up. People close to the book project said that he had meant to say Gus Greenbaum, the associate of Meyer Lansky's who took over the Flamingo after Siegel's rubout and served as part of the inspiration for the character of Moe Greene in *The Godfather*.

Ironically, this story, probably unwittingly, revealed Sumner's connections to the mob. In his autobiography, he presents his work for the Dunes as the tail end of his Washington legal career. But he fails to mention that the group building the casino hotel included his father and Doc Sagansky, as well as some close associates of New England mob boss Raymond Patriarca.

By the middle of the 1950s, Sumner was more than ready to get his hands dirty.

*   *   *

Indeed, Sumner describes his decision to go work for his father's theater chain as a loss of innocence. Slowly, in the years since law school, it had dawned on him: "When you're practicing law it's just a business. It's not a crusade for humanity, it's a business. And when I reached that conclusion, I decided I was going into business for myself." That's an odd way of phrasing what he was doing because, by late 1954, the business he was talking about going into, then called the Northeast Theatre Corporation, had already become, in the hands of his father and brother, a rapidly growing chain of a dozen theaters.

In retelling the story in the subsequent decades, Sumner often min-
imized the size of the company that his father and brother had built
when he joined it. One front-page profile of him in the *Boston Globe*
in 1986 claims that, when he "assumed control" of the chain in 1954,
"it consisted of one drive-in theater in Worcester," though the words
are the reporter's, not his. In 1998, he told *Forbes*, "I started with two
drive-in theaters before people knew what a drive-in theater was." In
his autobiography, he calls it "a handful of drive-ins." In court testimony in 2009, he could only name two—Whitestone and Dedham—
that were operating when he joined and says he was unsure if the one
at Revere, which opened in 1948, had indeed preceded him.

By 1954, Mickey and Edward Redstone were riding the crest of a national wave of drive-in expansion. The company had opened the Sunrise
Drive-In in Valley Stream, Long Island, in 1938; the Dedham and Revere drive-ins in the Greater Boston area in 1948; the Whitestone Bridge
Drive-In in the Bronx in 1949; the Neponset Drive-In in Dorchester and
the Natick Drive-In, in partnership with fellow Boston theater chain
owner Phil Smith's Midwest Drive-In Theater Corp., in 1950; a drive-in
in Bay Shore, Long Island, which it opened in 1952 and sold in 1953;
and the long-awaited VFW Parkway Drive-In in Boston's West Roxbury neighborhood as well as the Lee Highway Drive-In in Merrifield,
Virginia, in 1954. By October 1955, they would be operating fourteen
across Massachusetts, New York, New Jersey, Virginia, and Florida.

These were family-friendly affairs, with free admission for children, playgrounds, and bottle warmers, almost always located at the
intersection of two major highways. Drive-in owners during this period felt that they were largely immune to the growing competition
from television that was hurting the indoor theaters, believing that
people wanted to get out into the air. They generally enjoyed a more
profitable business. In 1954, each dollar of payroll expense generated
$4.72 of gross revenue for indoor theaters but $5.34 for drive-ins.

Sumner said his father was skeptical of his decision to join the company since "he was not a risk taker" and the move meant reducing his

salary from more than $100,000 to $5,000. "But all I saw was opportunity," he wrote. In fact, Sumner entered the drive-in industry just as
it was peaking. In 1954, the average drive-in drew 93,100 admissions.
Four years later, it had dropped to 82,000. The industry had overbuilt,
and land prices were rising.

Sumner's exact role when he arrived at Northeast is somewhat
murky. He wrote that when he arrived, Edward handled "general operations" and he handled "both expansion and the film companies,"
but none of his examples of scouting for locations for building new
drive-ins quite hold up. Consider this story from his autobiography:

> *For instance, I flew into Louisville, Kentucky, drove around, saw sev-*
> *eral potential sites and finally found twenty acres of land at the inter-*
> *section of two highways that would be perfect. I wanted to buy it. So I*
> *found out who owned the land, visited them, called in a secretary and*
> *a notary, modified the contract form as necessary and left with the*
> *deal. We called it the Kenwood Drive-In. Done. I did the same thing*
> *in Cincinnati. How did I know these were good sites? I just knew it!*
> *I operated as my own lawyer. Having handled the zoning for several*
> *of my father's theaters, I knew the deals had to be conditioned on*
> *getting the planning and zoning permits. But you didn't have to be a*
> *zoning lawyer, you just had to know what you were doing.*

The Kenwood Drive-In opened, under that name, in 1949, and
Northeast's successor company, National Amusements, bought it in
1961 for $425,000. It might have been a good location, but Sumner
didn't scout it, build it, name it, or get its zoning permit. The same
was true in Cincinnati, where the Oakley Drive-In opened in 1956,
amid protests from residents, and Redstone Management/National
Amusements bought it in 1963.

For all of Sumner's talk of an immediate takeover, he kept a very
low profile for the next four years, leaving it to his father to boast about
opening six drive-ins in a single week in Greater Boston or his brother

to answer questions about rain slowing construction of new drive-ins in the Rochester, New York, area.

But as the broader film industry hurtled toward the catastrophically bad year of 1958, when the *Paramount*-wounded business as a whole lost $19 million, Sumner found himself in possession of two skills that the industry needed far more than a keen eye for drive-in locations: experience as a persuasive orator on the national stage and a sophisticated understanding of antitrust law.

In March 1958, Sumner Redstone flew out to his old stomping grounds in San Francisco for the first gathering of drive-in owners organized by the exhibitors trade group, the Theatre Owners of America. His official role as a moderator of a panel on ticket selling seemed almost laughably small, but when the press reported on what had happened there, it was as if he were the only one who had spoken. He pinned the woes of the industry on the *Paramount* decision. "Once the producers of pictures lost the houses in which to show their products, pretty soon there weren't enough good pictures on the market to keep exhibitors busy," he said.

The studios then made the situation worse by licensing their pre-*Paramount* movies to television instead of to movie theaters who desperately needed the extra product to pad out their bills. "It worked out," he continued, "that they were getting about $50,000 apiece for their films. Those films shown in privately owned theaters would have kept a lot of houses open and would have given the producer more money in the long run."

Attacking his mentor Bergson's handiwork yet further, he argued that the restrictions in *Paramount* that barred exhibitors from movie-making ought to be loosened. "Some way ought to be worked out to enable theater owners' chains to produce their own pictures if Hollywood does not supply them."

From his very first outing as a theater owner on the national stage, it was clear that Sumner Redstone wanted into the studio business. It was also clear that he had a future as an industry spokesman. By the time the Theatre Owners of America—a group that in previous years had lined up against drive-ins on a variety of issues from taxation to admission policies for children—had begun to organize its annual convention in Miami Beach in October, Sumner was named a cochairman of the event. And by July 1958, *Variety*, noting that the TOA had sent out a biography of Sumner to the press, was openly wondering: "Is Theatre Owners of America Giving Sumner M. Redstone the Big Buildup for an Important Post in the Organization?"

The answer, of course, was yes. At the convention at the Tisch brothers' newly built Americana Hotel in the then sleepy village of Bal Harbour, Sumner Redstone could not have been more in his element as he stood before his colleagues and pressed the assistant attorney general in charge of the antitrust division of the Department of Justice (his boss's old job) for changes to the *Paramount* consent decrees that barred exhibitors from making movies. "Do you think for one moment," Sumner said, "that we would have the poverty of motion pictures available for exhibition which confronts us today if producers of motion pictures had a vast stake in motion picture theatres throughout the United States?" He added that the film industry was in a unique position in American industrial life "where exhibitors, as suppliers of a product to the public, are restricted from correcting inadequacies of that supply by producing it themselves." He didn't do much persuading. The assistant attorney general said the DOJ was going to maintain its position for the time being. But Sumner did make an impression before his exhibitor colleagues. *Variety* noted that he looked "like a young man with a future in the TOA echelon."

Ironically, that same year, he filed a lawsuit for his father's company based on those same consent decrees, complaining that they hadn't been followed *enough*. The suit built a conspiracy antitrust case around the perennial ozoner's complaint that the Hollywood studios refused to give drive-ins first-run movies. In theory, the fallout from the *Paramount* decision had made this kind of discrimination illegal, but in practice, the major studios' position toward drive-ins was pretty well summed up by Andy Smith, vice president of sales for Twentieth Century Fox, in a 1950 column in *Variety*: "The proper place for the

Drive-In in the distribution system will have to be worked out, but we must always keep in mind our responsibility to the regular theatre, which shows our pictures day in and day out throughout the year. We shall continue to refuse Drive-In theatres first-run showings in any city or town that has adequate conventional first-run outlets." That same year, drive-ins won their most significant court victory, as a U.S. District Court ruled that the major studios had conspired to violate antitrust laws when they refused to allow an Allentown, Pennsylvania, drive-in owner named David Milgram to bid for first-run pictures on equal footing against the indoor theaters in his town. The majors appealed all the way to the Supreme Court, but the Supreme Court refused to hear the case, letting the Third Circuit Court of Appeals decision, which Milgram had won, stand. But as Sumner's case on the same issue eight years later showed, winning in court and changing market behavior are two different things. Ultimately, Sumner's antitrust suit against the Hollywood studios was settled. Northeast got the improved access to films it was seeking, but there was no broader impact on the drive-in industry. The experience showed the future media mogul just how effectively litigation could be used against business adversaries. *It wasn't a crusade for humanity. It was just business.*

Nonetheless, Sumner continued to speak out publicly against the ways that the major studios were stifling exhibitors' business. In March 1959, while emceeing a wild launch party for fellow Bostonian Joseph Levine's import of the French-Italian fantasy film *Hercules* through Warner Bros. at the Waldorf Astoria hotel in New York, complete with Hercules-engraved silver goblets at each table and floor-to-ceiling cut-outs of the muscle-bound hero throughout the ballroom, Sumner couldn't resist veering from the circuslike atmosphere for a moment to complain about the wonky issue of blind bidding. The room was packed with "many top members of the nation's exhibition fraternity," *Variety* noted, and Sumner played well to his audience. With this kind of national profile, those exhibitors might have been surprised to pick up a phone book the next time they were in Boston and discover Sumner listed as a mere vice president.

CHAPTER 5

National Amusements

The president, of course, was Mickey. At fifty-seven, Mickey, still handsome and square-jawed, was enjoying his role as a pillar of his industry and the wealth that came with it. Two years earlier, he had been elected "chief barker" of the Variety Club of New England, the showbiz social club and charity that used its drive-in screens and army of ushers to raise money for the Jimmy Fund for children's cancer research. He and Belle lived in a forty-two-hundred-square-foot, four-bedroom home, all modern glass and light, at 30 Goddard Circle, amid sprawling lawns in Brookline. His two sons were working for him, and the business was growing. On August 28, 1959, he decided to formalize this arrangement with a maneuver that, though simple enough on the surface, would provide fodder for more than a half century's worth of lawsuits.

By 1959, the Redstones found that their practice of holding the land, concessions, and operations of their theaters in separate corporations was limiting their ability to borrow to finance further expansion. So as they looked to add another drive-in in Maryland, they decided to consolidate all of the corporations into a single entity named National Amusements based in Maryland. Mickey put in $30,328 worth of stock, along with an extra $3,000 in cash. Sumner put in $17,845 in stock and Eddie put in $18,445 worth. And then, at its first meeting in Norwood, Massachusetts, on September 1, 1959, Mickey doled out 300 Class A shares of voting stock: 100 to himself, 100 to Eddie, and 100 to Sumner. In ownership, the three Redstones were equals, though the articles of incorporation made the hierarchy clear: Mickey was president, Sumner vice president, and Eddie secretary-treasurer.

Five years after his older brother arrived on the scene, Eddie was officially second fiddle. This tension—the sons' equality in ownership but inequality in daily operations and management decisions—would very nearly tear the family, and the business, apart.

But at the time, the move seemed largely administrative. The company used its newly consolidated heft to secure a $50 million line of credit from the Bank of New England and continued its expansion south and west. Meanwhile, across town, their rivals at Midwest Drive-In Theaters were forging a different path, taking their larger chain of drive-ins and indoor theaters public in 1960, listed at $5 million. Led by Phil Smith and his Harvard-trained son, Richard, the company bore striking similarities to the Northeast Theatre Corporation. Phil Smith, three years Mickey's senior, was the son of a Lithuanian Jew named Adolph Sandberg who changed the family name to Smith upon immigrating to the United States in 1885. Like Mickey, he opened his first drive-in in 1938, after having built a chain of indoor theaters throughout the Northeast and then having lost almost all of it in the Depression. Like Sumner, Phil's son, Richard, had grown up helping out at the theaters and then raced through Harvard in a little over two years during World War II. Like Eddie, Richard went to work for his father after school and was married in 1952. And like the Redstones, in 1959, the family consolidated its various holdings under a new name bespeaking its greater ambitions: General Drive-In Corporation.

But the Redstones and Smiths differed in their attitudes toward ownership and control. The Redstones bought the land under their drive-in theaters, which rose in value as America suburbanized and allowed them to transform their drive-ins into indoor theaters in the 1960s and '70s. By the late 1950s, the Smiths had determined that land values were too high to continue buying and building drive-ins, so they switched to a strategy of leasing land in shopping centers, which provided enough parking for a theater without having to invest in real estate. This let the Smiths expand their footprint rapidly, becoming the largest theater operator in the country, under the name General Cinema Corporation by 1973, and ultimately diversifying into

Harcourt Brace, Neiman Marcus, and Pepsi bottling. But by the time
the company went public in 1960, the Smiths owned just 35 percent
of General Drive-In, maintaining operational control through a long-
term contract with Smith Management. "I never felt I had to own all of
anything or even the largest or dominant interest in it," Richard Smith
told historian Bettye Pruitt. The Redstones, of course, felt differently.

In the Redstones' first major pitch for financing after forming National Amusements, Sumner drew an explicit contrast with the Smiths'
strategy. "While others were building theaters in shopping centers,"
Sumner told the bankers, "where someone else was responsible for the
development and planning of the area and might not respond to their
particular needs, we were buying and building on our own land. We
controlled our environment."

This approach would end up making all the difference. By 2000
General Cinema had joined many of its rivals in filing for bankruptcy
protection, while National Amusements carries on to this day. National Amusements' decision to keep all ownership within the family would prove a great strength—so long as that family could work
together.

*   *   *

For a while, the three Redstone men made a formidable team. They
opened their first indoor theater in Worcester, Massachusetts, in 1963
after a complete modernizing effort by William Riseman, a prolific
movie theater architect who had married Doc Sagansky's daughter,
Marilyn. Three generations of Redstones were on hand for the opening
of the first-run theater, including Sumner's eight-year-old daughter,
Shari, in her best dress. By 1965, they had opened their forty-second
theater and the chain's crown jewel, the thousand-seat Cleveland Circle indoor theater on the border of Boston and Brookline. Built in the
1940s and operated by a subsidiary of Paramount Pictures as a first-
and second-run theater, the Circle was the closest the Redstones had
come to the world of first-run, downtown theaters that had long been
out of reach for independent exhibitors. Riseman, who had designed

the Latin Quarter along with many other Redstone theaters over the years, redesigned the old theater into a modern landmark in shades of blue, green, and white with "front row vision from every seat."

On a clear, breezy November morning in 1965, Mickey, Sumner, Eddie, and Riseman feted the opening of their splashy new theater in classic Redstone fashion: with a luncheon at the Ritz-Carlton in Boston. There, they boasted that the new theater would "possess the most comfortable seating arrangements of any house in New England," with rocking chair–style seats and each row six inches higher than the one below. They had a gala opening planned, followed by a head-turning opening with *The Great Race*, a slapstick Warner Bros. comedy starring Jack Lemmon, Tony Curtis, Natalie Wood, and Keenan Wynn. It wasn't quite first-run, but it was close, just three months after the film was released. And it had been the most expensive comedy ever produced. At the luncheon, the four men stood in their dark suits around Riseman's rendering of the theater, smiling and pointing. But Sumner towered above them all.

*   *   *

As the '60s wore on, cracks formed in the Redstones' professional partnership. Sumner continued his ascent toward becoming the industry's most forceful and articulate spokesman. In September 1960, he sat on a panel titled "Pay TV: Beating the Menace" at the Theatre Owners of America's annual convention at the Ambassador Hotel in Los Angeles, though his hometown paper embroidered this role somewhat by reporting that he had delivered the keynote speech. The menace they were referring to was represented, not all that menacingly at the time, by Telemeter, an early experimental precursor to HBO and Showtime operated by sliding coins into a box connected to a television set. A lawsuit from a drive-in owner led the studios to cut off its film supply, and the technology limped along in Canada for decades before being shut down. Still, exhibitors were right to be afraid of the technological possibility it represented, and by May 1961, Sumner was holding forth at the Lions Club in Hartford, Connecticut, that "there is the ever present danger that, while pay television will most probably end in financial disaster, experimentation of the character involved in Hartford will deal the motion picture industry another critical blow from which it may or may not recover, without creating a new and enduring medium of entertainment." In 1964, he was elected president of the TOA, just as the organization was on the cusp of merging with its rival organization. Under Sumner, the two merged, and Sumner became the chairman of the newly formed National Association of Theatre Owners. Not lacking in grandiosity, they called it NATO.

While Sumner was off giving speeches near beaches and getting his picture taken with the likes of Julie Andrews, Eddie was cutting ribbons with local politicians in places like Milford, Connecticut, and fighting increasingly tedious battles with localities over the moral content of the movies. As the decade wore on, he was less and less able to mask his sarcasm. "I cannot be held responsible for the moral fiber of this community," an obviously exasperated Eddie quipped to *Variety* about a fight over a $1.4 million drive-in in Lansing, Michigan, where residents were raising concerns over "morality" that were identical to the ones that had bedeviled his father three decades earlier. Eddie also took on leadership roles in the industry, including president of the National Association of Concessionaires and president of the Theatre Owners of New England, though these roles were always a rung or two below his brother's. By the end of the decade, he was seeking opportunities beyond the family business, investing in real estate projects like a four-hundred-acre industrial park in Worcester, Massachusetts. As with other properties he had developed over the last two decades, it lay at the intersection of two highways.

Nevertheless, Mickey maintained the dream that he was going to pass his business down to both sons. He had begun to spend winters in Florida and more time playing golf, but in 1964 the whole family was given a wake-up call when he collapsed on the golf course of the Equinox Country Club in Vermont and was rushed to the hospital. It was a heart attack. Mickey got top-notch care from what the family referred to as "the president's doctor" and returned to work in such

strong form that his longtime secretary noted that he seemed reinvig-
orated and more engaged in the business. But the need to prepare for
the future was clear.

He began creating a plan to gradually retire from active involvement
in the family business, and on May 6, 1968, he put it into motion by
transferring half his stock to a trust set up for his grandchildren. The
gift tax return he filed with the Internal Revenue Service valued these
50 shares at $564,075, meaning all of National Amusements was
worth a little more than $3 million. In December of that year, Mickey
enacted the second stage in his retirement plan, exchanging his remaining 50 shares of common stock for nonvoting preferred stock.
By the end of the 1960s, the number of voting shares in National
Amusements had shrunk to 250, with Sumner and Eddie each owning 100 shares, and the Grandchildren's Trust—of which Sumner,
Eddie, Mickey, and Belle were the trustees—owning the remaining
50. The grandchildren would receive their shares outright when they
turned thirty-five.

*   *   *

The young cousins had all grown up within walking distance from
each other in the pleasant cocoon of Boston's affluent, heavily Jewish commuter suburb of Newton. Sumner's son, Brent, born on April
20, 1950, was the eldest and heavily doted on by his grandparents,
who lived in nearby Brookline. Sumner's and Eddie's daughters were
nearly twins: Sumner's second child, Shari Ellin Redstone, was born
on April 14, 1954, in the family's final months in Washington, D.C.,
while Eddie's eldest, Ruth Ann Redstone, was born on August 7 of
that year. Eddie's son was the baby, born December 23, 1957. Michael David Redstone was named after his two grandfathers, Michael
"Mickey" Redstone and David Warren, though the failure of these two
clans to merge much beyond his name would set the stage for his
troubled and unhappy life.

The tension had been there from the very beginning of Eddie and
Leila's marriage, which was a multiday affair of the "country club set"

that left a bad taste in the mouths of several Redstones. "Returning from Eddie's wedding, rather than happy and in a celebratory mood, Mickey and Belle felt something heretofore foreign to them—they felt less than," Gary Snyder said. "Leila presented herself as being from a prominent Westport family, and the Warrens were stepping out in 'their town' and in a manner that did not then, and does not today, fit our family well." She loved the opera, ballet, symphony, art, antiques, and designer clothes, while Eddie and Sumner would proudly shop at the middlebrow Filene's Basement well into their business careers. "Leila was not ever accepted by Uncle Mickey and Aunt Belle," Snyder said.

Despite their proximity, the cousins were not as close as one might expect. Sumner and Phyllis sent their children primarily to the Newton public schools, while Eddie and Leila sent theirs to single-sex private schools.

This tension grew worse when Michael began exhibiting serious behavioral problems as a very young child. "From the time he was about five he became very destructive," Eddie would testify years later. "And it progressively got worse, including such things as just going out and urinating on a sofa, a chair. He made Ruth Ann's life completely miserable. She couldn't study, she couldn't—she would do her homework, and he would run in and destroy it. We had great difficulties controlling him."

Without Eddie's knowledge, Leila took the five-year-old Michael to a psychiatrist named Stanley Walzer at the Judge Baker Children's Center, associated with Harvard Medical School. "She didn't want to upset me," Eddie said. She had also assumed, correctly, that taking her son to a psychiatrist would be anathema to her husband's family.

Michael's memory of the beginning of his treatment for mental problems is a bit different. "When I was four, I went to Children's Hospital with a broken collarbone, and my father told the doctor I was crazy, and they couldn't control me," Michael testified in the same case in 2004. When the lawyer asked how his collarbone came to be broken, Michael replied: "He kicked me."

People who knew Eddie and Michael strongly dispute this version of events. "Eddie would have no more kicked Michael than I would have," said Madeline Redstone, Eddie's second wife, who tried to get father and son to reconcile years later. One person close to Michael said he used to describe his earliest memory as being kicked in the face by his mother's pointy shoe.

According to his medical records, he was first seen by a psychiatrist at age seven for "uncontrollable aggressive behavior." Michael's presence in the home was putting a great strain on the family, so in 1967, when he was just nine years old, they sent him to boarding school at Fessenden, one of a small group of "junior boarding schools" that accept boarders before ninth grade. It was prestigious, with several alumni in the Kennedy clan, and located in West Newton, close to his family. But Michael regarded it as a betrayal and as an institutionalization. He was expelled on November 5, 1969.

Eddie and Leila were near the end of their rope. They enrolled him in another boarding school and began to discuss with Dr. Walzer what they could do to, in the words of one person close to the family, "try to get him straightened out." Their solution would trigger a series of events that would lead to the breakup of both the business and the family.

CHAPTER 6

"From One Catastrophe to Another"

ichael Redstone had not wanted to go to summer camp, but his parents insisted. He was twelve years old but already world-weary, well acquainted with principals' and psychiatrists' offices, and the thinking was that the brisk Maine air would do him good. In fact, it had been the recommendation of his psychiatrist, Stanley Walzer, who spent his summers as the doctor at Camp Powhatan, one of the oldest Jewish summer camps in Maine, that he give camping a try. But it was also simply what nice Jewish boys from places like Newton did in the summer—head north to the pristine forests of Vermont, New Hampshire, and especially Maine, to build "character" and form friendships that would help them succeed in society. In general, these camps had Jewish services and Jewish staff but rarely spent much energy on Jewishness; there was too much canoeing to do, too many sing-alongs. It was not Michael's cup of tea, however, so late one night in early July 1970, while the rest of the campers slept, he snuck out of his cabin and padded over to the recreation center, where he lit a fire and then took off into the night.

He didn't get far. Within two hours, he was captured and hauled back to camp, and his parents were called. They, in turn, called Dr. Walzer, who had a grim recommendation: it was time to have Michael committed. Eddie came up to meet with the camp director and then brought Michael back to Boston, where on July 11 he was admitted to McLean Hospital, the grand old mental hospital that had been treating Boston's elite since the early nineteenth century.

Being locked up in McLean put Michael in distinguished historical company. Founded in 1817 for an aristocratic clientele, the hospital's campus of brick mansions sprawled over 240 wooded acres, dotted with stables and orchards, that had been selected by Frederick Law Olmsted, himself a McLean patient. Early patients enjoyed private rooms with fireplaces, parlors, and private bathrooms, and the wards bear the names of Boston's great families. In the twentieth century, it became a kind of breeding ground for Pulitzer Prize–winning poets, with Robert Lowell, Sylvia Plath, and Anne Sexton all passing through its halls and writing about it. In one poem, Lowell described his fellow patients as "Mayflower screwballs" and "thoroughbred mental cases." But McLean would fully flood the American consciousness a year into Michael's stay there, when Plath's semiautobiographical novel *The Bell Jar,* which lightly fictionalized her treatment in McLean, was published in the United States and became a bestseller.

Michael's four years at McLean would contain none of this glamour. He was pumped full of Thorazine—he claimed at the "obscene" dose of 1,400 milligrams per day—and Mellaril, heavily sedating antipsychotic medications that today would be considered unthinkable to administer to an adolescent. He would later describe the experience to people close to him as an array of horrors, from being put in a wet straitjacket to being forced to room with people with violent pasts to being held in solitary confinement. "I was often locked in a room with nothing but a mattress for much of those four years," Michael said under oath decades later.

Mickey and Belle were horrified by Eddie and Leila's decision, which confirmed every suspicion they ever had about their moody, aloof daughter-in-law and undermined their confidence that Eddie had his child's best interest at heart. The grandparents were close to Michael and believed his problems stemmed mostly from conflict with his parents. They were also of the old, bootstrapping immigrant school that believed that calling upon psychiatrists brought shame upon the family. Joined by Sumner, they demanded that Eddie and Leila remove Michael from McLean, which bred deep resentment from Eddie and Leila regarding the intrusion into their personal lives. The cracks that had been creeping across the facade of family togetherness throughout the 1960s now broke open into a gulf.

"My grandparents didn't like my parents," Michael said of this period. "My parents didn't like my grandparents."

Eddie had toyed with the idea of leaving the family business for years, but his mother, father, or brother had always coaxed him back into the fold. But as he and Leila were preoccupied with Michael's mental health crisis, Eddie began to feel increasingly left out of big decisions at National Amusements. Things came to a head when Sumner hired Jerry Swedroe, a sideburns-sporting exhibition executive with a résumé stretching back to the 1940s, to run the operations that had previously been Eddie's job. Eddie was livid, and in June 1971, he quit.

He demanded his 100 shares, which were kept at National Amusements' headquarters in Dedham, but his father refused to hand over the stock certificates, arguing that National Amusements had the right of first refusal to buy back the shares. Mickey and his lawyers then invented a new reason why Eddie couldn't have his shares: that half of them had actually been held in an "oral trust" for Michael and Ruth Ann ever since Mickey doled them out in 1959. The oral trust argument was ingenious for several reasons. On its face, it rested on the at-least-somewhat-provable fact that Mickey had put in 48 percent of the stock at the time of National Amusements' founding but only received 33.3 percent of the shares, giving Mickey grounds for claiming he had additional say over what his sons did with "their" shares. Second, the lack of a paper trail—and there was none—does not disprove the existence of an oral trust. Third, the trust structure would let Mickey and Belle voice their reservations about Eddie's parenting choices. And fourth, since Sumner would become the trustee of these trusts, it would keep the assets under family control for longer, while ensuring that the transfer of wealth would completely bypass Leila, whom Mickey once called within Michael's earshot an "evil, scheming cunt."

Well aware that he was facing formidable adversaries, Eddie hired a well-respected Boston lawyer named James DeGiacomo to try to recover his shares, threatening that if his father and brother didn't give him a good price, he would sell them to an outsider—the ultimate act of war. For weeks, Eddie tried to entice his father and brother to sit down with him to negotiate, but National Amusements' lawyer, Lou Winer, refused.

"I have been disregarded, rejected, and devalued by Sumner and you," Eddie wrote his father on July 19, 1971. "Furthermore, it's very difficult, in fact impossible, for me to believe that you have the interests of my immediate family and me at heart."

Eddie, his heart ever on his sleeve, summed up his relationship with his father: "You know, Dad, whenever you and I have a difference of opinion, I talk 'apples' and you talk 'peaches,' so to speak." Hoping that DeGiacomo could open lines of communication that he alone could not, he added, "Do the family a service—meet with Jim prior to the institution of litigation. You've never respected my judgement [sic], and I urge you for once to do so." Throughout the letter, he repeated that he would do anything for his family, "but not at the expense of my self-respect."

Sumner has always been cagey about his role in the dispute. In his autobiography, he was open about how his father's decision to turn "the basic operation of the business to me" very quickly after he arrived "caused some tension between Edward and me." But he denied playing any role in pushing his brother out of the company. On the contrary, when Eddie began talking seriously about leaving the company to go into banking in later years, Sumner wrote, "I sat with my brother at a California hotel and pleaded with him, 'Eddie, don't leave. You have everything to gain by staying. You want to go into the banking business? Start doing that while you are at our company. It will provide you with a base of operations.'"

During his testimony in a lawsuit that his nephew, Michael, brought against him in 2006, Sumner repeated the story about begging Eddie to stay and said he didn't remember hiring anyone to replace him in

June 1971, adding, "My father would have probably made the decision." But in the next breath, when asked whether his father was still
making the principal decisions in the business in 1971 and 1972, he
replied, "I'm not sure that's true. At a certain point, my father got a
bag of golf clubs and started spending his time—with my blessing, of
course, because I thought it was good for him, he had worked hard all
his life—started playing a lot of golf. And at that point I pretty much
took over."

In his testimony, he characterized the fight as being between his
father and his brother. He was sympathetic to his brother's view that
he had no restrictions on his stock, but he also agreed with the general
thrust of his father's wish that Eddie set aside stock for his own children. "I myself had the sense that our company's heritage and culture
was that the stock went from generation to generation," he said.

Indeed, it was Sumner who led National Amusements' negotiations
for Eddie's exit, with Mickey only attending a few of the "numerous"
meetings with DeGiacomo in the six months following his hiring,
according to a memo DeGiacomo wrote the following June. The two
sides explored various options, including trying to keep Eddie on as
an employee or consultant or having Eddie sell back his 100 shares to
National Amusements. But Mickey would not sign on to a deal that
did not acknowledge the existence of an "oral trust" for the benefit
of Eddie's children. And so, by December 1971, they had reached an
impasse, and Eddie sued his father, his brother, and their family company in Massachusetts Superior Court.

Belle, excitable already, did not take the family infighting well. She
penned a desperate letter to her son, begging him to reconsider the
suit. The letter contained many of the tropes that successive generations of Redstones would use in their own infighting, including threats
to avoid family members' funerals and charges that the younger generation played no role in helping build aspects of the business. "Dad's
position is that when you were a youngster and still at school the stock
that he put in Nat'l like Sunrise, Whitestone, Dedham, Natick and Revere belongs to your children," she wrote. "You made NO contribution

to these theatres, and that he will move heaven and earth before he will turn it over to you to sell and to put money in your pocket. I scrubbed plenty of floors and did plenty of menial work to help Dad accomplish this and I can't see it either. All we want to do is protect your children. Don't you think this is reasonable? Eddie, it seems to me that you are going from one catastrophe to another. All you are going to accomplish is financial ruin for Sumner and your own family."

She ended the letter with a surreal, motherly nudge to call more often, before plunging the knife in where it hurt most: "P.S. Michael just called and sounded wonderful! As a matter of fact, the last few times I spoke to him, he sounded good. He said he might come down for the weekend. We are all excited. Why don't you come with him?"

Eddie, against his own better judgment, responded immediately. "Under all the laws of God, there is no justification for Sumner's and Dad's activities. For your position you only understand what has been told you. In addition to which, and I don't mean to be unkind, you are the result of years of receiving unbelievable cruelty from Dad. Knowing that which has occurred, no one, but no one, can expect anyone to believe that Sumner and Dad have my family's and my best interest at heart. The immorality of their activities is almost beyond belief."

While the increasingly adversarial litigation proceeded through the courts, the parties continued to negotiate, and by June 30, 1972, they had come to a settlement. Eddie would get $66^2/_3$ shares and agree to put the remaining $33^1/_3$ shares into a trust for his children. Eddie then agreed to sell his shares back to NAI for $5 million and to walk away from National Amusements forever. Most important, for the future of the company, Sumner was named the sole trustee of both of Eddie's children's trusts.

Years later, Eddie was at a loss to explain how he had left his children's trusts under Sumner's control. "I was under duress just to get out. Tremendous duress. And frankly I signed everything that would be put in front of me just to get away from them." Sumner may have urged him on occasion not to leave the business, Eddie said, but he "acted contrary to his words." "Sumner controlled my father until almost the very end. So you can't fight City Hall."

While Eddie was setting up the trusts for his children to settle litigation, Sumner voluntarily decided to set up parallel trusts for his own children, as a way of validating his father's claim that there had been oral trusts for these children all along. "I wanted to do the same thing as my brother did, only he did it as a result of litigation," Sumner testified in 2006. "I gave my kids a third of the stock voluntarily, not as the result of a lawsuit. In so doing, I did what I wanted and appeased my father too." (Sumner would come to regret these words, as the IRS used them to come after him for more than $15 million in unpaid gift tax and interest forty years after the fact.) Once again he made himself the sole trustee and gave himself similar powers over how, when, and at what price National Amusements shares in the trusts were redeemed.

By 1972, Sumner was firmly in charge, not just of the company's operations but of its shares. In addition to his direct ownership of $66^2/_3$ shares (or 36.4 percent of the company), he was the sole trustee of the Brent and Shari Trusts and the Ruth Ann and Michael Trusts, which together made up another $66^2/_3$ shares (or 36.4 percent of the company). He was also still one of the trustees on the Grandchildren's Trust, which contained 50 shares, or 27.2 percent interest.

The Ruth Ann, Michael, Brent, and Shari Trusts were written such that they would not have access to the money until they turned forty, giving Sumner a long and unencumbered runway to fly National Amusements to another altitude entirely.

* * *

A month after Eddie ended two years of bitter fighting over his role in the family business, his daughter entered her freshman year at Brandeis University. Ruth Ann was beautiful, with her mother's large eyes and bold brows, and long, honey-colored hair that she wore with a flower child's middle part. She had been deeply shaken by the shooting of unarmed college students protesting the Vietnam War at Kent State University two years earlier and found Brandeis full of kindred spirits. The small liberal arts college just outside of Boston had developed a reputation as a hotbed of radicalism by the early 1970s, thanks to the activities of both famous alumni, like Angela Davis and Abbie Hoffman, and less famous alumnae, like Susan Saxe and Kathy Power, the Brandeis roommates who spent twenty-three years on the run from the FBI for their role in a September 1970 bank robbery and murder of a police officer tied to an antiwar plot to arm the Black Panthers and overthrow the federal government. By late 1970, one student complained to the *Chicago Tribune*, "Brandeis has become a word like Chappaquiddick—standing for some mystical evil."

While Brandeis had its share of Marxist professors, student strikes against the war, and sit-ins for civil rights, it's debatable whether the idyllic New England campus really bred more radicals than any other university at that profoundly turbulent social moment. But Brandeis was unique in the freedom that it granted students. As the *Chicago Tribune* put it: "the place has almost no regulations. Upperclassmen have unlimited cuts. No one does bed checks at night. You can live off campus if you like—20 percent do. The kids say they respect two main rules—Be discreet, and wear shoes in the dining room."

Ruth Ann was ill-prepared for this kind of freedom. She had attended the Winsor School, formerly Miss Winsor's School, a small, prestigious, all-girls prep school founded in the nineteenth century. "She had been sheltered to an extent whereby it seemed, in conflict with her outward intelligence, her inner coding remained that of a girl entering an adult world of which she had little awareness," Gary Snyder said.

Around the same time that this idealistic girl was being let loose on a campus roiling with antiestablishment fervor, a band of self-described "Jesus freaks" were making their way east from California, stopping by antiwar rallies and college campuses targeting young hippies with their gospel that society was broken beyond repair. Children of God was founded in Huntington Beach, California, in 1968 by David Berg, the middle-aged son of Christian evangelists, who preached that his followers should prepare for the imminent apocalypse by emulating early Christians and dropping out of all secular occupations, surrendering all worldly possessions to the organization, living in communes, and devoting themselves full-time to evangelizing.

By 1970, having amassed hundreds of followers and grown a long, white beard, Berg withdrew into seclusion in Europe, thereafter communicating with his followers through thousands of profanity-laced epistles known as Moses Letters, or Mo Letters, after his name within the group, Moses David. But the withdrawal of Berg only made the group more popular. By 1971, it boasted sixteen hundred members, and parents of many of them had begun to organize an opposition, claiming their children had been brainwashed by a cult that taught them to hate their parents. By 1972, Children of God had communes, which it called "colonies," in 130 countries, but it was also feeling increasing heat from the authorities. In 1973, Berg instructed his followers to flee the United States and set up colonies around the world, predicting that the imminent arrival of the comet Kohoutek would bring about the destruction of America. Many of them fled to Latin America.

Ruth Ann was among them. She completed her first year at Brandeis, enrolled in a second—and then disappeared. "She took . . . off from Brandeis and she wandered with some friends," Eddie said in a deposition years later. "She originally went to South America." When asked how long she wandered, Eddie replied, "For the rest of her life."

People close to the family believe it's no coincidence that Ruth Ann joined an anticapitalist cult shortly after her family spent years fighting each other over money. According to a 1974 report by the New York Attorney General's Office (which called Children of God a "cult"), "members are required to give personal belongings such as car, tape recorder, T.V. sets, bank accounts, and cash to leaders of local communes who, in turn, purportedly transfer the same to Berg and his family." This "forsake-all doctrine," which was the group's initial primary source of money, also required new recruits to pledge all current and future income to the group.

The report also found that "virtually every" former Children of God member it interviewed said they were "constantly exposed" to the following Bible verse:

> *If any man come to me, and hate not his father, and mother, and wife, and children, and brethren, and sisters, yea and his own life also, he cannot be my disciple.*

LUKE 14:26

Berg's Mo Letter from January 1, 1971, drove home the point:

> *The parents have filled 'em so full of houses and cars and education and all that shit—it's like making them eat their father's dung!— And now the kids want to kill 'em for it! You can hardly blame 'em! I've felt that myself sometimes!*

But the reality of Children of God was far darker than a mere critique of materialism or authority. Around the time Ruth Ann joined, Berg began to introduce free-love themes into his teachings, proclaiming a "One Wife" doctrine that removed the requirement of fidelity within marriage and blessing "sexual sharing" between unmarried people as long as it was done to serve God. Then, in 1976, Berg sanctioned "flirty fishing," the practice of using sex to recruit new members. Berg called it "a radical way of witnessing and winning souls," but by 1977, he began instructing the group's women to charge for their services. "We can't afford to just continue supporting some kind of a religious brothel, ministering to men who don't pay their way," Berg wrote. "Happy Hookin'—but make it pay!"

Eddie and Leila were beside themselves, as were Mickey and Belle. Over the years, the family—including Sumner—spent huge sums on investigators and deprogrammers, attempting to bring Ruth Ann back into the fold, but she escaped and rejoined the cult, which, after

1978, was renamed The Family. Leila even became politically active, lobbying for anticult legislation that would require solicitors from religious organizations to carry identification cards and set up a task force to study fund-raising of religious groups. In the spring of 1980, Leila told the police that two well-dressed men accosted her and held a knife to her throat in a darkened parking garage in an attempt to pressure her to stop her lobbying. "They had that glazed look of somebody who's been in a cult," she told the *Boston Globe*. "They threatened my mother and my husband if I continued to work against their religious purposes." She told the paper that her daughter had been "deprogrammed" and had left home, but that seemed an optimistic spin on the situation. Leila and Eddie would never really get their daughter back.

Meanwhile, in 1973, Michael was transferred from McLean to the Menninger Clinic in Topeka, Kansas, the premier psychiatric hospital in the country. His family believed that his ongoing need for institutionalization was tied to Ruth Ann's disappearance. People close to Michael say that he worshipped his older sister, but he would have been insulated from the furor caused by her disappearance. He spent a little more than a year at Menninger, attending its accredited Southard School for emotionally disturbed adolescents, during which, he later testified, "nobody visited me."

Sometime after his seventeenth birthday, Michael managed an escape. "I had broken into an office and called an attorney and actually called the ACLU as well, and they agreed to take my case, went to court. They ordered my parents—custody removed from my parents, given temporarily to my attorney, and they assessed damages," Michael said. The lawyer that Michael found in the phone book in turn called a local lawyer named Ralph Skoog, who filed a suit to get Michael out of Menninger.

"He didn't want to be out there at the Menninger School, and didn't think that he belonged there, so we brought an action in the court to determine he was correct. They didn't have any power to keep him there against his wishes," Skoog said, adding, "We were in the transition at the time from when kids were supposed to do what their parents tell them to do until they finally got to this situation under the law that children had constitutional rights too."

The first person from Michael's family to arrive in Topeka for the trial was Mickey, followed by Sumner, who Skoog described as the "steady hand" behind the whole process of getting Michael on his feet. Eddie and Leila were not there, which was probably just as well. "I think we established at trial that Leila was probably mentally ill . . . and their two children ended up getting the brunt of it," Skoog said. As far as Eddie went, "He supported his wife instead of his children."

Michael ended up staying with Skoog, a father of five, for about six weeks, during which Skoog said he saw no signs of mental illness. "I don't know if there was anything wrong with him except that he was treated so strangely that he responded like kids do sometimes who are strong-willed. I never noticed that he had any difficulty, except that his response to things was different occasionally than my children's would have been."

Skoog said he does not remember what diagnosis, if any, Michael was given at Menninger, but he believed his parents put him there in part because "he, like a lot of youngsters, had smoked some pot." (Eddie, a New England curmudgeon who liked to drink and smoke to abandon at times, held a predictably dim view of the counterculture for his children's generation, telling the *Globe* in the midst of a kerfuffle over screenings of the documentary film *Woodstock*, "Personally, the concept of Woodstock to me is repulsive but I have no right to impose my views on other people.")

Michael believed he was in Menninger because his parents didn't want to deal with him. "He thought they were all involved with themselves, and their children were a burden, and they'd have the treatment first-class, but they wouldn't put up with it themselves," Skoog said. "Menninger was first-class."

After winning the case, Michael enrolled in Washburn University in Topeka for a semester. Skoog helped set him up with an apartment near campus and, with Sumner's help, got him a car and license.

Sumner began calling Michael regularly to check up on him. "Primarily, he was pushing me to get organized about going to school," Michael said. "It was about being in school and how my grades were and not to screw around and stuff like that. . . . Nobody had ever paid attention to me before, so . . . I was appreciative." These pep talks would continue through the next few years, as Michael moved to Florida to be near his grandparents, and then back to Boston to attend Northeastern University.

Skoog remained another lifelong mentor for Michael, attending his wedding and visiting Sumner and Mickey in their offices in Boston on occasion. But the thing that stuck in his mind the most from the whole episode was the few days Mickey spent hanging around his house before Sumner and their lawyers showed up for the trial. Perhaps put at ease by Skoog's plainspoken intelligence and midwestern drawl, the old man unburdened himself.

"He kept telling me, 'I just don't understand. We've got these two boys, and we've given them everything in the world. We made them rich. And it just doesn't help. They turn on you,'" Skoog said.

*   *   *

Some family members say Sumner nudged not only his brother but also his father aside before his father was truly ready, which might explain Mickey's lament about not just one but both sons turning on him. "I remember the sense that at the point where Mickey retired from active control of the business, that that was a difficult transition for him," said Russ Charif. "There has been all kinds of speculation about how Sumner pushed his father out."

CHAPTER 7

"Artful Dealings"

Contrary to popular assumption," Sumner wrote his fellow Harvard alumni at the end of the 1960s about his role at the helm of the exhibitors' trade group, "my primary function was not attending cocktail parties with famous stars and starlets (something my wife would have objected to anyhow)." But by the mid-1970s, that's exactly what he was doing—clutching a cigar and chatting up baby-faced Paramount Pictures chairman Barry Diller while a mustachioed Dustin Hoffman and white tunic–clad Marlo Thomas worked the room at the studio's sales convention in Los Angeles; lunching in Hollywood with Twentieth Century Fox chief executive Dennis Stanfill; dancing the hora at Paramount's president Frank Yablans's son's bar mitzvah; playing tennis with former Paramount chief-turned-producer Robert Evans amid the rose gardens, fountains, and four-hundred-year-old sycamore of his Beverly Hills estate. "He screams and argues about every point," Evans complained to *Forbes* about Sumner. "He's the single most competitive tennis player I've ever seen."

Sumner had always been close to the distributors that fed his family's theaters, ever since his father had divvied up the brothers' tasks and given him the crucial role of negotiating with the film companies. Over the years, some of the salesmen that he did daily battle with, like Yablans, climbed the corporate ladder, and Sumner remained close to them, cultivating a small circle of Hollywood insiders as intimates. Yablans, the son of a Brooklyn cabdriver with a high school education, had turned *Love Story* into a national phenomenon when he was running distribution at Paramount and was rewarded with the presidency of the studio in 1970. He shared Sumner's bluntness, street smarts, and caustic sense of humor, as well as the nagging sense that he was destined for national office. Yablans once told *New York* magazine he was planning a run for president, while Sumner's fund-raising work as the cochair of Senator Edmund Muskie's 1972 presidential campaign had his colleagues convinced he was headed for Washington, D.C., himself. "If Muskie would have been elected, he would have been attorney general," said longtime National Amusements executive Ed Knudson.

Sumner's friendship with Yablans grew out of his special relationship with Paramount. When corporate raider Herbert Siegel tried to take over Paramount in the 1960s, Sumner, as head of NATO, had been part of the management's resistance to the takeover, paving the way for the studio to be bought by the manic conglomerate assembler Charles Bluhdorn's Gulf + Western. Bluhdorn, a brilliant and impulsive corporate marauder with thick glasses and an even thicker Austrian accent, used the former auto parts company as a vessel to gobble up a dizzying array of unrelated businesses, but his bold moves at Paramount helped usher in a golden age. He plucked actor-turned-producer Robert Evans out of obscurity and placed him in charge of production at the studio, amid howls of protest from the rest of Hollywood, and Evans took Paramount from last place to number one, overseeing hits like *Chinatown*, *Love Story*, and *The Godfather*. Evans and Yablans, representing the creative and business sides of Paramount, both became Sumner's close friends.

In 1974, thirty-two-year-old Barry Diller, an urbane television prodigy, succeeded Yablans at Paramount, thus becoming the youngest-ever studio chief. He also inherited that special relationship with Sumner. "Shortly after I came to Paramount, I was confronted with 'Redstone issues,' which every leader of Paramount had been confronted with for the past ten, fifteen, twenty years," Diller said. These issues essentially consisted of Sumner's insistence that his theaters get a better cut of box office revenue from Paramount films than his rivals got. "The only exhibitor that I ever dealt with in that manner was Mr. Redstone, who always complained that he deserved a rebate for all his good work during the year." Diller chalked up Sumner's success in getting that rebate to "the tenacity of Sumner Redstone, plus very artful dealings with the distributor class."

Among the most useful assets that Sumner brought to these dealings was his photographic memory. "Sumner could tell you what a movie did six years ago in Toledo, Ohio," Knudson said. "Every gross he knew. You could not ever trick him." The obsessiveness he had inherited from his mother also helped. "I can remember booking meetings that would stretch from six thirty a.m. to almost noon because he was trying to figure out what two pictures to put together at a drive-in in Lansing, Michigan, that he thought would work well," Knudson said. These traits also made him something of a nightmare to work for. "He would call up in the middle of the night and say the time clock in the *Globe* was wrong," recalled Carol Aaron, who placed ads for the theaters in the 1970s. "He was very rude, very dismissive. He cut you off in mid-sentence."

National Amusements' early commitment to owning the real estate under its theaters also helped. With Sumner having completely consolidated power, the theater chain spent the 1970s and '80s building, turning its drive-ins into indoor theaters and its indoor theaters into increasingly sumptuous multiplexes—a term the company trademarked. Starting with 52 drive-ins and 41 indoor theater screens in the wake of Eddie's departure, Sumner had more than doubled the number of screens to 250 in less than a decade, becoming the tenth-largest theater chain in the country. The Redstone Theaters, as they were largely known in the industry, became famous for their comfortable, rocking chair–style seats, high-quality sound, and airy lobbies filled with framed film posters from Hollywood's golden age. "Our theaters were totally different than anybody else's," Knudson said. "They were very big, and they had free parking." Most important, the Redstone Theaters became known for having the very best first-run films in their markets.

The theaters were so successful getting the best movies that they began to draw complaints of monopoly from competitors—first in the press, then in the courts. In East Hartford, Connecticut, one grand old downtown theater owner said he had to switch to pornography—"not hard, not soft, but in between"—after the Redstone Theaters' ability to get big attractions like *The Exorcist* at its various suburban Showcase Cinema multiplexes made it impossible to compete. In New Haven, the downtown movie theaters were forced to drop their prices to 99 cents to try to lure moviegoers back from lining up on the highway exits to get into the first-run movies playing for $3.50 at the Redstones' Showcase Cinema V. "It is absurd to say that we control New Haven," Sumner told *BoxOffice* in response, not particularly believably. After five theaters in Connecticut shut down in one year, the operator of one chain laid it squarely at the Redstones' feet: "There is an extreme shortage of product. Redstone has been able to obtain the major films out of Hollywood on an exclusive basis and will not share play dates with the other theaters." In 1975, three small-time theater owners in the Quad Cities of Iowa and Illinois, where National Amusements owned six theaters, filed an $11.4 million lawsuit against National Amusements and nine of the biggest studios and distributors, alleging they had conspired to give National Amusements a "monopolistic position" in the market.

Sarge Dubinsky, a member of the film family behind AMC Theatres, was one of the small theater chain owners who sued. In the course of discovery for the lawsuit, he found out that the distributors were agreeing to take a significantly smaller percentage of the box office receipts from Redstone Theaters than from their competitors. While they might get a distributor to agree to take 50 to 60 percent of the gross from a successful movie the first week, he said National Amusements would somehow get the distributor to agree to only 40 percent. "I could never quite figure out why [the distributors] did it, but they did. It seemed to be a relationship that had been established over time. He worked it for what it was worth," Dubinsky said. "Sumner Redstone is a ferocious competitor, and a highly skilled one."

A. Alan Friedberg, an exhibitor whose career started in the Boston-based Sack Theaters in the 1950s and went on to include the chairmanship of the nine-hundred-screen Loews Theaters—the country's fifth-largest chain—by the late 1980s, competed against National Amusements for decades. "He was ruthless," Friedberg said. "He would do anything to win."

Dubinsky and his fellow plaintiffs capitalized on this perception, using a memo from a former National Amusements employee to allege that Sumner bribed Yablans to help his theaters get first crack at movies distributed by Paramount. The response from Sumner, National Amusements, and Yablans was swift and brutal—categorical denials and a barrage of countersuits, including a $10 million libel suit. The litigation was eventually settled, but for years afterward, the trade press was filled with retractions and apologies to Sumner and Yablans from one exhibitor or another connected to the case. "I have not discovered nor do I have any evidence substantiating any wrongdoing by Mr. Redstone or by Mr. Yablans," Grand Rapids exhibitor Robert Emmett Goodrich told *BoxOffice*, in one typical example. "I regretfully apologize for any embarrassment that the distribution of the memorandum has caused Mr. Redstone and Mr. Yablans." To top it all off, Goodrich was forced to donate $10,000 each to the Will Rogers Hospital in the name of Frank Yablans and to the National Association of Theatre Owners in the name of Sumner Redstone.

"That's the way Sumner operated: if you step on his toe, he'll smack you on the head," Dubinsky said. "If I could go back and stay out of his markets totally, that's what I would have done."

In an industry rife with litigation, Sumner stood out. His prominence as a trained lawyer made him both uniquely feared within and uniquely valuable to the exhibition business. As president of NATO, he used his legal chops and experience at the Department of Justice to lead the industry's fight against blind bidding, the film companies' practice of requiring theater owners to bid for the right to show a first-run film before they had the chance to see it. The DOJ put a few mild restrictions on the practice, but in 1968, the matter made it to federal court, where Sumner represented NATO personally, arguing that the practice was discriminatory since some big exhibitors with good relations with the film companies—he didn't say it, but like himself—

would always have an advantage over smaller players who remained in the dark about how good the movies they were buying were. The argument fell mostly on deaf ears, however, so Sumner continued to lead the fight at the state level, where NATO and other exhibitor groups were trying to get state legislatures to ban the practice. In April 1978, Sumner went before the New York State Assembly arguing that the practice was unfair because it deprived exhibitors of the right to exercise their business judgment about the merits of a movie. Pointing to *Exorcist II*, a Warner Bros. debacle that a BBC film critic declared "quite demonstrably the worst film ever made," Sumner said, "We put this trash on the screen, not only lost money, but had our customers criticizing us and holding us accountable for something we were contractually bound to and never saw." He argued that admission prices were being driven up to offset the huge advances that the "oligopoly" of the film companies were demanding. In June 1979, New York became the fifteenth state to ban blind bidding.

But if Sumner was playing the persuasive populist, trying to keep admission prices low and trash from the movie screen, he also had another reason to be incensed about the film companies' increasing restrictions on giving exhibitors advanced screenings of films. By the mid-1970s, Sumner had begun to invest in the film companies themselves, based on his own growing confidence in his ability to predict which films would perform well. Back then, most movie studios were independent public companies, not yet sucked up into the media behemoths that own them today, and their fortunes were tied directly to the box office. If Sumner saw a winner in previews, he'd call up his stockbroker, Madeline Sweetwood, and invest. (Sweetwood had taken over her late husband Ira's clients when he died of cancer in his thirties in order to support her three children and would go on years later to marry Eddie after he was widowed.) As with everything else in his life, he was obsessive. "I was on the phone with him from nine thirty a.m. until the markets closed," she said. "I had to have someone answer when I went to the ladies' room and everything." She remembers clearly the day in early 1977 that Sumner, just out of the *Star Wars* screening, called wanting to make a big play on Fox. In *Star Wars*, he saw instantly that "it was totally different than any movie that has ever been made. Everybody could go see this movie. It was the first film that was for everybody."

Under Sumner's direction, National Amusements eventually built up a 5 percent stake in Fox and made a killing on it, buying at $8 a share and selling at $60 when oilman Marvin Davis bought the company in 1981, resulting in a profit of at least $20 million. Sumner fared similarly well with Columbia Pictures, and positions in Warner Bros., Disney, Loews, and, later MGM/UA Home Entertainment Group. But in the late 1970s, as he was going around the country fighting blind bidding, none of those bets had yet paid off. All he had was his confidence in his ability to spot a great story.

*   *   *

No one is sure exactly when Sumner began his affair with the fiction writer Delsa Winer, but by the time she divorced her husband and the father of her four children in 1974, it was well under way. Delsa—who in the early years of their relationship went by her married last name, Weiner—was almost literally the girl next door, a doctor's wife who lived about four lawns away from the Redstones' hilltop home in Newton. According to Delsa's son, Winn Wittman, they met at the neighborhood social club, the Dudley Road Club.

Delsa was just a couple of years younger than Phyllis and arguably no more beautiful. But there was a sparkle to her brown eyes, a lack of apology in her close-cropped hair, an energy to her compact, tomboyish body. The protagonist of the novel she would later write described her dying mother's face with words that could have been written about Delsa's own mother, whom she closely resembled: "The aristocratic, slightly aquiline nose, a vertical crease above the bridge; high forehead; mischievous eyes. An almost feline quality. . . . A definitive face, only a scant trace of femininity. Density in the Russian-Jewish bones. Yet it is an elusive face." Delsa's own face was slimmer, infused with a kind of otherworldly, elfin beauty, but no less elusive.

While the Weiners' upper-middle-class suburban Jewish life resembled the Redstones' in many ways, Delsa's approach to it did not. She was a feminist and a free spirit, uninterested in convention or the roles that society had assigned her. She made few rules for her own children and encouraged all of them—even the girls—to put their own careers ahead of marriage or family, horrified that she had failed to earn a master's degree herself or find a way to make a proper living through her writing. She was ambitious, opinionated, intellectual, and brutally self-critical, not an object for Sumner so much as a foil. "They complemented each other," Wittman said. "I think some of Sumner's confidence wore off on my mother, who was an only child and naturally somewhat introverted." She, in turn, exposed him to culture. A passionate collector of art and books, Delsa sparred with Sumner over his taste in movies, which tended to run toward the blockbusters, and politics, particularly as his liberal views grew more conservative in his later years. Most important, as his profile rose over the decades they were together, she refused to flatter him. "She definitely stood up to him," Wittman said.

Delsa grew up the only child of a couple of Eastern European immigrants without college degrees who founded pharmacies and later nursing homes that made them a comfortable living in Brooklyn. "Self-educated, my mother made a million dollars investing in bonds, and at the same time prepared me for life as Emma Wodehouse was prepared—piano lessons, ballet, and horseback in Prospect Park," Delsa wrote in a biographical sketch in 1999. She spent summers at the iconic Grossinger's resort in the Catskills, one of the inspirations for the movie *Dirty Dancing*, performing excerpts from plays and self-written monologues and dating heartthrobs like the singer Eddie Fisher, who later married Elizabeth Taylor at the resort. Fisher was soon eclipsed by Albert Weiner, a handsome, Harvard-trained doctor and army captain just back from the war. After graduating from Syracuse University, where she studied drama, Delsa married Weiner and settled into the life of a 1950s suburban housewife. "For fifteen years or so I led a useful life like a pot holder, surreptitiously making words, nights while everyone slept," she wrote. "As the years passed my children noticed what was going on more than I thought they did. Each of them exploded in turn like wedding champagne left standing upright in the closet. I managed my problems alone until I acquired an ideal lover. My lover is faithful, busy and rich. *A woman must have money and a room of her own if she is to write fiction.*"

After her divorce, she threw herself into writing fiction full-time, and by the late 1970s her sophisticated short stories had begun to appear in publications like the *Boston Globe, Fiction,* and *Virginia Quarterly Review* and to win literary awards. Her protagonists were sometimes fiercely independent Boston women divorced from their doctor husbands and having affairs with high-powered corporate executives living in New York who couldn't ever quite manage to divorce their own wives.

Phyllis knew about it, of course, as did both Delsa's and Sumner's kids. In the difficult final years of Delsa's marriage, Albert had even known, at one point lashing out at Delsa that Wittman, their youngest child, born in 1964, might not even be his. (For years rumors circulated that Wittman was Sumner's, though his strong resemblance to Albert rebuts the argument.) The affair was the cause of domestic battles in both Newton homes, made all the more awkward because Shari and Brent were roughly the same ages as Delsa's elder children, and all of the children knew each other socially. Still, Sumner was not about to follow Delsa to divorce court. As much as Delsa was the love of Sumner's life, he was still emotionally bound to Phyllis, family friends say, in much the same way he had been emotionally bound to his own mother. Soon after Delsa's divorce, she and Sumner began to talk about getting a house together where they could live, essentially, as husband and wife, though it would be many years before they followed through. Delsa had no desire to get remarried—which made Sumner's own marital status less important—so they simply agreed that they would build a life together.

And so, since there were no outward signs beyond Delsa's divorce that anything was going on, Phyllis put up with it. Philandering was, to a certain extent, accepted and expected behavior. Mickey did it. Doc Sagansky did it. Why would Sumner be any different? "He always struck me as the guy who is going to cheat no matter what relationship he's in," Wittman said. The relationship was tolerated in part because it was private.

But that was about to change.

CHAPTER 8

Forged in Fire

E arly on the morning of March 28, 1979, the Three Mile Island nuclear reactor just south of Harrisburg, Pennsylvania, partially melted down, causing the worst nuclear disaster in American history and sewing panic in a nation already on edge from a decade of inflation and oil shocks. President Jimmy Carter would attempt to calm the country by touring the reactor, his feet swathed in yellow plastic booties, and a few months later diagnose its spiritual ills in a speech decrying America's "crisis of confidence."

But, amid the timeless limestone grandeur of Boston's old hotels, things proceeded very much the same way that they had for a generation. The Variety Club of New England, that same klatch of exhibitors that Mickey Redstone had led in the days of his first drive-ins, was hosting a luncheon at the Park Plaza Hotel to welcome the newest crop of distribution executives that the biggest Hollywood studios had sent to service the region. One of them was a rising, twenty-nine-year-old Warner Bros. branch manager named Roger Hill, who had been transferred to Boston from Jacksonville, Florida, the previous year. The purpose of such gatherings was clear enough: exhibitors lived and died by being able to get the best films into their theaters, so even as they were often suing distributors or complaining about them to the Justice Department, they were more often plying them with steak and martinis.

Nobody was better at this game than Sumner. As the day wore on, the festivities progressed two blocks down the street to the Copley Plaza Hotel, Mickey and Sumner's former residence, where Sumner was on hand to fete Hill a second time, this time at a Warner Bros.

movie premiere. Sumner seemed determined to show Hill a good time. He and Delsa decided to stay overnight in the hotel after the party, and they reserved a corner suite on the third floor that, according to one witness, adjoined the room where Hill was staying. Like Sumner, Hill was married. And like Sumner, the woman in the room with him that night was not his wife.

A little after midnight, they woke up to find smoke pouring under the door. In Sumner's telling in his autobiography, he said it was the smell of smoke that woke him up. But Wittman said his mother told him just before she died in 2013 that "they got a call in the room that there was a fire in the hotel." Delsa, naked, went for the window, but Sumner ran for the door. "Sumner, Sumner, don't go to the door!" she cried. But it was too late. He opened it, and flames engulfed him.

Delsa, being younger and more athletic, was able to climb out the window and onto a ledge, where she was rescued, suffering only smoke inhalation and minor injuries. "Only her right thumb was burned black," Wittman said. Sumner, meanwhile, was enveloped in flames. "The fire shot up my legs. The pain was searing. I was being burned alive," he wrote. In Sumner's version, which makes no mention of another person in the room, he opened a window and climbed out onto a tiny ledge, holding on to the window as the flames burned through his right hand and arm. By the time the fire department rescued him, he had burns on 45 percent of his body. Both were taken to Boston City Hospital. Delsa was listed in stable condition while Sumner was put on the "danger list."

The guest of honor that evening was not so lucky. Roger Hill's body was found in the hallway, along with the body of twenty-eight-year-old Patricia Mulcahy, a recent transfer to Boston from Warner Brothers' Minneapolis distribution office. Mulcahy had just quit her Warner Bros. job the week before for a better one traveling overseas but had been at the hotel that night because friends had called her and encouraged her to come to the premiere party. "I talked to her that evening, before she went the party, and she was so excited," said her mother, Virginia Mulcahy. "She said, 'Mom, I can't talk to you any longer because I'm going to this big party and the taxicab is going to come and pick me up.'"

Like Sumner, Hill had opened the door of his room and been overcome by flames. There was evidence that he had initially retreated to the bathroom to protect himself but was not able to get to a window, and so he was forced back out into the hallway, where he and Mulcahy succumbed to both the flames and smoke inhalation. He was taken to Massachusetts General Hospital with "serious burns" on more than 60 percent of his body, while she was taken to New England Medical Center and listed in serious condition. According to her mother, she had burns on over 40 percent of her body. She died five days later. Hill held on for nearly two months, seeming to improve shortly before he, too, succumbed to his injuries, on May 17, 1979.

The night Sumner arrived in the hospital, it looked like he was headed in the same direction. Sumner's doctors told his family that he wasn't expected to live through the night. His right wrist was sliced almost completely through, and his legs were so severely burned that the doctors assumed he would never walk again. But he was transferred to Massachusetts General Hospital's burn center, where he endured dozens of hours of painful surgery as doctors stripped skin from the healthy sections of his body and grafted it over the burns. By early June, the prognosis was good enough that Mickey sent a letter to the head of NATO, updating all of the people who had been flooding National Amusements' offices with letters and phone calls that Sumner was "already walking the corridors of the hospital." In his version of the fire story, traumatic amnesia papers over Delsa's presence. What happened between Sumner smelling smoke and opening the door was "unclear in his mind."

The fire roaring outside Sumner's room had been one of about a dozen set that night at both the Copley Plaza and nearby Sheraton Boston Hotels by a drunken eighteen-year-old who was angry about not being able to get his hotel dishwashing job back. The man, Julio Rodrigues, who later pleaded guilty to arson and manslaughter charges, had set fire to a couch in the third-floor hallway near Sumner's room—

the presence of which Sumner argued "violates every fire law that exists." Nearly two thousand people were evacuated and sixty-nine were treated for injuries, and the Copley Plaza's manager estimated that there was more than a million dollars' worth of damage. Boston's fire commissioner, George Paul, called it "potentially the most tragic fire situation in the City since the Cocoanut Grove fire."

Sumner and Phyllis jointly sued three corporations connected to the hotel for $12 million, alleging that Sumner suffered "great pain of body and anguish of mind" from his severe burns, and "his earning capacity has been impaired for a long period of time." Phyllis was asking for damages because "as a result of injuries sustained by her husband, she has been and will be deprived of her husband's services, society and comfort, companionship, relations, affection and consortium," according to the court documents. The fact that Sumner had been busy consorting with another woman that night—and in fact for the better part of the last decade—was immaterial. It would not be the last time that Phyllis had to look the other way from her husband's philandering, or that Delsa had to erase herself from her own life's story, for the sake of the millions that hung in the balance.

For a moment, it seemed like the fire might destroy the precarious balance between Sumner's two worlds. Sumner and Delsa's names appeared in the *Boston Globe*'s report of the injured the day after the fire, and local news footage showed them both climbing down the fireman's ladder. But Sumner's family barred Delsa from visiting him in the hospital, and within a few weeks, Mickey's version of Sumner waking alone to the smell of smoke had hardened into industry legend. The Redstones were so successful in writing Delsa out of the story that, more than two decades later, Sumner thought nothing of opening his autobiography with this partially fictional account. Her presence in the hotel room that night would not begin to come to light until a 2000 *Boston* magazine story, which assigned her a fake name, and would not fully emerge until after her death. Yet her debut novel, published in 2000, would leave little doubt that she had been involved. In it, her protagonist is burned beyond recognition in an accident that leaves her hand a gnarled claw—just like Sumner's. "There was still a lot of shame in the family" about the relationship in the wake of the fire, Wittman said. "Later on, everybody got over it."

For years afterward, Sumner rejected the easy narrative that the fire had transformed him, forging his iron will into a steel weapon of corporate conquest. But the fire *did* change him. His belief in his own abilities, always strong, became unshakable. "Determination, physical or any other kind, is the key to survival," he wrote in his autobiography. "If I hadn't learned that lesson before, I knew it well now." As soon as he could stand, he strapped a tennis racquet onto his mangled arm and got back on the tennis court. And almost as soon as he could speak, he flew to Los Angeles, against his doctor's recommendation, to deliver a blistering keynote address at NATO's annual October convention denouncing the "morally reprehensible and economically disastrous policy" of blind bidding. "If they won't terminate the practice, then I say fight!" he said. "I say fight in the courts—fight in the state and federal legislative bodies—and fight in the Department of Justice." NATO presented him an honorary award for his "inspiring courage," and the two thousand exhibitors crowded into the ballroom of the gleaming Bonaventure Hotel gave him a standing ovation.

But it was now painfully clear to him that this was not enough. Not long after the fire, he visited Delsa at her home, and they took stock of the future. He saw two paths before him: he could give up and spend the rest of his life running the theater chain, or he could go on to bigger and better things. Together, they decided to double down. As if to prove his point, Sumner sat down at the piano and played, despite the still-healing wound that would leave his hand like a claw. "When he got up," Wittman recalled, "the keys were covered in blood."

Delsa threw herself into her writing, and by 1981, she won a $3,000 Massachusetts Council on the Arts and Humanities fellowship that allowed her to buy her first computer, upon which she composed a half-dozen novels. Sumner, meanwhile, appeared for a moment to question his capitalist impulses and signed up to teach the Boston University Law School's first course in entertainment law. "If I had any talent and ability, I probably should have spent it in a more worth-while way," he told the *Boston Globe* in his first major newspaper pro-file in March 1981. But as the profile wore on, it became clear that Sumner's regrets were not about having been insufficiently philan-thropic. Rather, it was that he had spent so long stuck in the clunky caboose of the media train. Although his public persona came from his relentless warring against the studios, his true wish was to join them. "We sometimes wish we were they, and they were us," he said.

By then, of course, he was already on his way to taking control of the media industry's engine. He had already turned heads on Wall Street with the huge profit National Amusements made on its Fox stake and had amassed large positions in Warner Communications, MGM Films, Columbia Pictures, and Time Inc. "I don't see movie stocks as entertainment stocks," he told the *Boston Globe*. "Every time they pro-duce a picture, they produce an asset, which will outpace inflation in growth. The ancillary revenue from these pictures is escalating." And so was his stake in the studios. Over the course of 1981, he ramped up his stake in Columbia to nearly 10 percent. When Coca-Cola Com-pany agreed to buy the company in January 1982, his shares were worth $48 million, giving him a profit of about $26 million. That year, Sumner appeared on *Forbes*'s list of the four hundred richest Americans for the first time, at number 316.

This milestone came as Sumner was, rather curiously, doling out increasingly dour predictions about the prospects of his own indus-try. As early as 1981, he saw the future of the five-hundred-channel cable package, as well as the threat it augured for movie theater own-ers. "Despite what others have said, the fact remains that the aver-age person will, before too long, be able to punch out one of perhaps 100 possibilities on his television set, which also will be different in terms of size and resolution. And this fact will have to affect exhi-bition, perhaps drastically. There's an enormous revolution going on today, and I don't know if most theatre-owners are as aware of it as they should be," he wrote in *Film Journal International* in November 1981, just as he was upping his Columbia stake. He added, "And let's face it: if distributors begin a policy of simultaneous release of major films to home markets along with theatre, then theatres are *through, over and out.*" In a *Boston Globe* profile of his rival exhibitor A. Alan Friedberg, in 1982, he was even more blunt. "The theater industry is a non-growth industry," Sumner said. "It's going down."

Nevertheless, he continued to build ever-larger multiplexes and unveil them with ever-grander displays of pomp. In the summer of 1982, he lit up the sky over Revere with fireworks celebrating the opening of what he claimed—in true Redstone fashion—was the largest indoor movie complex in New England, Showcase Cinemas 1–10, built atop the demolished remains of Mickey's Revere Drive-In. The next year, he performed the same trick on the Whitestone Drive-In, converting it into a ten-screen multiplex, with an entire room dedicated to nothing but popping popcorn around the clock. By then, the eleven-theater multiplex built on the site of the former Sunrise Drive-In, which he had demolished in 1979, was, he claimed, "the world's largest-grossing theater complex." If he delivered a mixed message on indoor theaters, on drive-ins, his naysaying was not for show. He told *Newsweek* in 1983 that "drive-ins are rapidly becoming part of our nostalgic past—I foresee their extinction by the end of the decade," and set about unsentimentally hastening that reality.

In 1983, Sumner turned sixty, the age at which another man in his position at such a closely held family company might have begun to turn his attention to succession. Had it been given, such attention might have been rewarded: Brent and Shari were model Redstone offspring. Both were attorneys who, in 1980, married other attorneys. Brent had followed in his father's footsteps to Harvard, followed by a law degree from Syracuse University in 1976. By the early 1980s he was working as an assistant district attorney in Boston, prosecuting murder cases, and had married Anne Vanderwerken, a graduate of Rochester Institute of Technology from upstate New York. Yet not a word of their marriage ever appeared in the press, in contrast to Shari, whose announcement of her engagement to Rabbi Ira Korff, the scion of a prominent family of Boston rabbis, filled half a column in the *New*

York Times. It had to be long just to list all of the degrees that she and her fiancé had racked up in their barely three decades on the earth.

In adulthood, as in childhood, Shari was Sumner's favorite child, the one most like him and the one he most liked to brag about. "He always spoke more admiringly about Shari than about Brent," Wittman said. She inherited his auburn hair, blue eyes, intelligence, combativeness, and obsessive streak. Like Sumner, Shari was impatient to get to the next thing. In middle school, she attended a special program that let students work at their own rate, and by her junior year she was taking all senior-level and AP courses. Like many teenagers of her generation, she fell for the books of Ayn Rand and Rand's objectivist philosophy that a person's primary moral duty was to her own happiness. But she was also pulled toward public service and working with children. She volunteered at Boston Children's Hospital and spent her free periods in high school helping teach kindergartners and second graders. After she graduated from Newton South High School and enrolled in Tufts University, she thought she might go into education. Instead, she studied psychiatry before switching to English, writing her thesis on police discrimination and discretion in arrest procedure. The research gave her a taste of legal work, and after graduating from Tufts in 1975, she went on to receive a JD degree from Boston University Law School in 1978.

But her ambition was never to join a high-powered law firm. She had a job teaching constitutional law at METCO (Metropolitan Council for Educational Opportunity), the pioneering voluntary school desegregation program, when she ran into Mark Shub, the nephew of Mickey and Sumner's longtime secretary, Tilly Berman, at a funeral. Berman was a kind of mother figure to Shari, mentoring her on how to navigate the male-dominated world of exhibition and typing up her papers for her when she was at school. Shub's law firm, Salon, Silver, Heffernan & Shub, was looking for an associate. The firm did some criminal defense work, and Shari had enjoyed her criminal procedure professor in law school, so she took the job. She worked alongside partner Stephen Salon on at least one criminal case, records show, and otherwise enjoyed the convivial culture of a firm where the associates went out drinking together after work and she learned to play cards and backgammon. "We enjoyed life," Shub said. But over time, she found that the partner she really wanted to work with was Shub, who did business transactional work, which required a sophisticated understanding of tax law. So she decided to enroll in the same master's program in tax law that he had attended at Boston University.

It was there, in the dubiously romantic setting of a tax law lecture, that she met her future husband. A slight man with intense brown eyes and an air of great confidence, he was sitting a few seats down the row. She moved to sit next to him, and they struck up a conversation. She was surprised to find that he had no idea who she was, but they soon discovered that their grandfathers had been close.

Korff was the grandson of Grand Rabbi Jacob Korff, a direct descendant of the founder of the Hasidic movement; he had been elected the last rabbi in Zvhil, a Ukrainian town near Kiev that was a center of the movement. When a pogrom tore through Ukraine in 1919, the family of the grand rabbi, who was in Boston at the time, was targeted. His wife attempted to flee her home carrying her infant son—Ira's father, Nathan Korff—with her three other young children behind her. A bullet went through Nathan's foot and killed his mother, but the children survived and immigrated to Boston. There the grand rabbi and his family welcomed waves of refugees, becoming prominent pillars of Boston's Jewish community. All three of his sons also became rabbis, the most famous of whom was "Nixon's rabbi," Baruch Korff, a close adviser to the president who controversially defended him during the Watergate scandal.

The Korffs came from the tradition in which rabbis chose not to make a living from their rabbinical work and so always needed a second—or in Ira's case, third or fourth—profession to support them. By the time Ira met Shari, he had a formidable résumé across both the spiritual and secular worlds, including a BJE degree from Hebrew College, a BA from Columbia University, a JD from Brooklyn Law School, an MA in international relations, another MA in international law and diplomacy, and a PhD in international law and politics from Tufts University's Fletcher School of Law and Diplomacy. By the time he was married, in 1980, he had worked in Boston's DA's office and with the Massachusetts attorney general and was then serving as a consultant in international law and relations and working in business. As if that weren't enough, he was also serving as chaplain of the City of Boston and had been the rabbi of Temple Aliyah of Needham since 1975.

Sumner saw a great deal of himself in his eloquent, ambitious son-in-law. Like Sumner, Korff spent much of his thirties giving speeches, on everything from "President Reagan's Foreign Policy" to "World Current Events," and Sumner was always bragging about his résumé. Shari's engagement announcement notes that "in 1973, at the age of 24, Dr. Korff was selected by the Chamber of Commerce as one of the ten outstanding young men in America"—the kind of thing that only Sumner would have included in an engagement announcement. Sumner was overjoyed when Shari and Ira had a daughter, Kimberlee, the year after they were married. (As Sumner put it to a profiler a few years later, "I have a 3-year-old granddaughter, Kimberly [*sic*], who recently said to me: 'We should spend some time alone.' That's more important to me than building 315 theaters.") By this point, Ira had joined the Boston law firm of Berman & Lewenberg and brought Shari on board, briefly naming the firm Berman, Lewenberg, Redstone & Korff. Shari did a bit of legal work for her husband's clients, but as their family grew she decided that a legal career was incompatible with the kind of mother she wanted to be, the kind that baked cookies and, as Tilly Berman once put it, made "seventy different kinds of chicken, each more delicious than the last." She kept her law license but focused on her family.

With the next generation out of professional school, married, and ready to take on the world, this was just like the point in Mickey's life when he had begun grooming Eddie and then Sumner to run the business one day. But Sumner showed few signs of preparing to hand over the reins to his own children. Brent, who always had the more difficult relationship with his father, made clear early on that he wanted nothing to do with it, and his father had concluded that he lacked the pugilistic instinct that exhibition required. Shari would often say later in life that she had never imagined going into the family business, and indeed her only apprenticeship growing up was a summer between college semesters spent interning on the Paramount lot, mostly as a way to visit California. For a while, this was fine by Sumner, who honestly believed after living through the fire that he would live forever.

But as his fire-forged ambition made him grow ever more restless with what he saw as the dead-end business of exhibition, he began trying to persuade his son-in-law to step into the role as potential successor, a trusted insider who could hold down the fort at home as he prepared for bigger things. One day he took Korff for the proverbial walk in the woods, telling him, "I don't have a son," meaning that he didn't have the kind of son he felt could take over the business. "What if something happens to me? Even if you decide you want to sell the company, you have to be in it to understand the value." He suggested Korff come in and try it out, just one day a week. Sumner of course had no intention of selling the business, but the guilt trip worked, and by the mid-1980s, Korff joined National Amusements as executive vice president, the title Sumner had once held under his father.

Meanwhile, Sumner focused on completing his consolidation of control of National Amusements. "Sumner wanted to buy Michael out," said a person close to the family. He had given Michael a job at National Amusements, it hadn't worked out, and he somehow convinced Michael that it was he who wanted to cash out, not the other way around, the person said.

Beginning in 1982, Sumner began preparing to redeem all of the National Amusements stock he was holding as the sole trustee of the Ruth Ann and Michael Trusts and as trustee of the Grandchildren's Trust, according to court documents later filed by Michael. He directed the company's accountant, Sam Rosen, to prepare a valuation of the company and then hired Jim DeGiacomo—the same lawyer who had represented Eddie in his settlement—to help with the redemption.

By 1984, Michael, now twenty-seven, had stabilized and moved back to Boston, where he was attending Northeastern University. But he "was struggling," according to one person who knew him, and "chafing" against the many hoops he had to jump through to get at the money that had been set aside for him. He wanted to cash out. Sumner was only too happy to oblige. On March 8, 1984, he drew up an agreement to have National Amusements redeem all $83^{1}/_{3}$ shares of National Amusements stock held in the three trusts for $21.4 million, based on Rosen's valuation. As trustee of the trusts and president of National Amusements, Sumner was, as Michael would complain, both buyer and seller in the transaction.

Michael got $7.5 million. Ruth Ann, still at large somewhere in South America and not in communication with her family, theoretically got the same, though she would never lay a finger on it. Brent and Shari each got $3.2 million from the redemption of the Grandchildren's Trust but held on to their own trusts, together owning $33^{1}/_{3}$ shares in NAI. That left Sumner with $66^{2}/_{3}$ shares—clear, overwhelming control. As a hint of what he planned to do with that control, six weeks after the redemption, he amended National Amusements' articles of organization to authorize it to engage in either cash or margin transactions in commodities and securities.

Years later, both Michael and Brent would accuse Sumner of lowballing the trusts for his own benefit. Michael complained that Rosen made National Amusements appear far less valuable than it was by using financial information that was more than two years old and failing to count National Amusements' substantial investment income, treating it as a nonrecurring event even though the company had been investing in media stocks since the mid-1970s. Perhaps more deviously, the valuation included all of Sumner's naysaying about the state of the theater industry, raising "serious concerns about [the company's] future ability to continue its past performance" because the motion picture industry had been "flat" for nearly two decades and faced a "serious and potentially devastating threat."

What Rosen failed to mention, amid all the corporate boilerplate, was that Sumner had a plan for how to fight that threat. But he would need total control to carry it out.

Years later, Brent would claim that Sumner justified seizing that control—in a maneuver that, in redeeming the Grandchildren's Trust, would end up costing his own children millions—by telling Brent and Shari that they would manage and control the company. He just didn't say when.

Phyllis wanted no part of this journey. On August 23, 1984, she filed for divorce, citing cruel and abusive treatment. By this point, she and Sumner were living separately, she at 98 Baldpate Road in Newton and he at his parents' former condominium at 180 Beacon Street in Boston. A family friend told *Boston* magazine that Delsa was named a codefendant in the suit, which has since been sealed. Their relationship had been rocky from the beginning, and Delsa was hardly Sumner's first dalliance. Phyllis was "verbally and physically and financially abused by him every day of her life," Shari wrote in an email in 2014, and the fighting was constant. For his part, Sumner complained bitterly to colleagues that Phyllis would not even get out of bed to get him a cup of coffee, and her tendency to run late made him apoplectic. But Doc Sagansky's daughter, Marilyn Riseman, said it was Sumner's Hollywood dreams that turned Phyllis off. "I think she's a simple person, and she just wanted her simple husband," Riseman told *Boston* magazine. "She doesn't understand the bigness." Because Massachusetts divorce law allowed her to potentially walk away with half of his assets, the suit threatened his careful designs on the control of National Amusements. He begged Phyllis to stay, and on January 8, 1985, she withdrew the suit.

With control of National Amusements even more firmly in his grasp, Sumner began to pursue his extracurricular studio investments with new fervor. In 1981, MGM, one of the original Big Five major studios known for epics like *Gone with the Wind* and *Ben-Hur*, bought United Artists, the near-bankrupt Little Three studio. The newly merged company then spun off its Home Entertainment division into a separate company set up to exploit its library of forty-six hundred movies—the largest in the industry—across home video, pay-TV, and other nontheatrical markets and sold 15 percent of that company to the public. Sumner, keenly aware that the growth of cable was going to open up vast expanses of open airtime that would make these old movies newly valuable, bought up about half of that outstanding stock, calling it "the most effective way of participating in the exploding home entertainment market."

But two years later, MGM/UA decided it wanted to buy back the Home Entertainment division, which turned out to be one of the best-performing parts of an otherwise beleaguered media company. Because it owned 85 percent of the shares of Home Entertainment, it could vote to accept any price the parent offered. Sumner found the price that they did offer "insultingly low," so he sued in federal court, charging the parent company's management and board of directors with fraud, misrepresentation, and violation of securities. The company raised its offer several times, and eventually the two sides settled at a price that meant an extra $10 million for Sumner.

Sumner held up the episode as an example of how litigation is sometimes necessary. But perhaps more important, it showed him that not only could he profit from bets on Hollywood but he could remake its business practices. The same take-no-prisoners, scorched-earth approach he'd used to pry the best movies out of studios could be used to shape the Hollywood dream machine itself.

CHAPTER 9

Defeating the Viacomese

As one might expect from a fledgling cable outfit built on rock videos, MTV Networks always threw wild parties. But one particular company retreat, held at Gurney's seaside resort in Montauk in the fall of 1985, took an especially depraved turn. The senior management, led by thirty-two-year-old Bob Pittman, had committed themselves to tequila for the evening, having just lost out on their attempts to buy the company in a leveraged buyout. His colleagues started throwing bottles, then chairs, then fish from the aquariums, and, eventually, six-foot potted palm trees through the windows. One enterprising inebriate threw a giant jar of Red Hots down the stairs. "We kind of destroyed the place," said Tom Freston, general manager of MTV and VH1 who, at age forty, was by far the eldest of the executives. "If MTV can still go back to Gurney's I'd be shocked," said Pittman. "We were very poorly behaved," agreed Geraldine Laybourne, a former schoolteacher then running the children's channel Nickelodeon, herself "ancient" compared to her colleagues at thirty-five. "It was really kind of frustrated adolescence misbehaving."

They had good reason to be frustrated. MTV Networks was exploding with promise. In less than five years, its flagship MTV had become the driver of America's youth culture. Dire Straits' hit song "Money for Nothing," with Sting's falsetto "I want my MTV," was the number one song in the country. The previous year, 1984, MTV had made more advertising revenue than any other channel on cable, and by 1985 it was the most profitable and fastest-growing of all the cable channels. Meanwhile, the broader company, which also included Nickelodeon and newcomer VH1, was on track to make $144 million in revenue in 1985, nearly 50 percent more than the previous year. And yet the company's beleaguered and mismatched parents, Warner Communications and American Express, wanted out. They had formed Warner-Amex Satellite Entertainment Corp. (WASEC) in 1979 based on a vision of the future that was accurate but ahead of its time: that our lives would one day revolve around screens attached to telecommunications lines that we would use to consume entertainment and buy things. But by the mid-'80s, as it became apparent that cable television—particularly a channel featuring men in leather pants and pink lipstick—was not going to be a vehicle for selling financial products, Amex was eager for an exit. Warner, meanwhile, needed cash in the wake of the implosion of its Atari video game business, so they put MTV Networks on the block.

In an attempt to control their own destinies, Pittman, Freston, and other MTV Networks senior executives tried to acquire the company themselves through a leveraged buyout backed by Forstmann Little, a New York private equity firm. For weeks, it seemed like Warner Communications, which by then had agreed to buy out American Express, was going to accept Forstmann Little's offer of first $470 million and then $500 million, but in the final days of August 1985, the deal fell apart. Instead, MTV Networks and Warner-Amex's 50 percent stake in its sister company, Showtime/The Movie Channel, went as part of a broader $667.5 million deal to a bunch of financial guys from a company called Viacom—then pronounced Vee-uh-com—whom the snarky MTV executives began to derisively refer to as the "Viacomese."

Viacom International Inc. was created in 1971, after new federal rules barring the Big Three networks from syndicating their programming forced CBS Inc. to spin out its cable television and television rerun distribution business into a separate public company. Starting with a base of old CBS library shows like *Gunsmoke, The Andy Griffith Show,* and *I Love Lucy,* Viacom had grown by the mid-'80s into a diversified media conglomerate spanning four television stations; eight radio stations; a stake in the Lifetime cable network; a stake in Showtime/The Movie Channel, the tenth-largest cable system operator; a television production company that made shows like *Matlock*; and a television and film syndication arm that, most crucially, had the syndication rights to *The Cosby Show*, then the top-rated show on television. It was led by Terry Elkes, a bespectacled, Bronx-born, City College–educated lawyer and former paper mill executive who had won Wall Street's admiration with the company's 23 percent compound growth rate in its first fourteen years but was nobody's idea of a creative visionary—not even his own. As he told the *Wall Street Journal* in 1985, "The company that was spun off from CBS had a distribution and marketing mentality and not a production mentality and it's taken us a long time to understand what to do."

But his aggressive bidding for MTV Networks and the rest of Showtime was undeniably savvy, transforming Viacom overnight into a cable-programming powerhouse just as cable deregulation was loosening the belt that until 1984 had kept cable fees low and thus cable bundles slim. Elkes correctly predicted that the new cable legislation would prompt cable operators to create a new "basic" service in which they would offer more programs—including movies now available on a subscription basis—for a higher price than the $9 to $12 a month their customers were currently paying, creating a massive new demand for cable programming. His only mistake was to underestimate the extent of the change. He mused to the *Los Angeles Times* that the new rules might allow the emergence of a new basic cable TV service for around $25, or $57 in today's dollars. In 2016, the average cable bill was about $100.

But what Terry Elkes did not take into account was just how much these hooligans from MTV Networks—now the fastest-growing unit and strategic core of the company—would grow to hate the Viacomese. This opinion was solidified the morning after their mournful bacchanal, when a bunch of hungover mostly twentysomethings dragged themselves into a luncheon to meet their new owners. Elkes arrived by helicopter, like the corporate conqueror that he was, and delivered a stiff welcome to his new underlings that fell entirely flat. "The Viacom guys were essentially deal people and distribution people; they didn't know how to talk to creative people," Pittman said. "They were just so out of their element. And, I think, they were just sort of dorky."

The young leadership of MTV Networks at the time was, meanwhile, the epitome of cool. The tone was set by Pittman, a former long-haired radio programing prodigy from Brookhaven, Mississippi, who had started his broadcasting career at age fifteen and once gone by the DJ name "The Mississippi Hippie." Pittman had climbed to head of programming at WNBC in New York when he was just twenty-three years old and joined WASEC in 1979 to apply his programming expertise to The Movie Channel, WASEC's challenger to HBO. When Warner-Amex executive John Lack came up with the idea for MTV, he tapped Pittman to lead it. The idea was deceptively simple: take the free promotional videos that bands were making to help sell their albums and string them together on a television channel aimed at twelve- to thirty-four-year-olds, a demographic that mainstream television executives more or less ignored at the time. MTV launched on August 1, 1981, with the Buggles' paean to disruptive innovation, "Video Killed the Radio Star."

One of Pittman's first hires was Freston. Tall and wild-haired with deep-set blue eyes, Freston arrived at the countercultural idea factory of MTV with the least traditional background of all, having spent most of the last decade running a clothing company in Afghanistan and India. Freston had grown up in Rowayton, Connecticut, and after graduating first in his class from New York University's Stern School of Business, he had started out in advertising before finding that hawking G.I. Joe dolls at the height of the Vietnam War was more than he could stomach. He left to travel the world, eventually settling down in Afghanistan, which at the time was "very safe and enchanting and exotic," to start his business. The Communist coup in 1978 and changing Indian trade policies did it in, and he returned to the United States at the age of thirty-four, half a million dollars in debt. His record executive brother told him Lack was looking for people without television experience to work on a new music channel. Freston, a passionate music fan, was interested. Lack hired him on the spot in March 1980 to run marketing, despite suspecting that Freston's talk of being in the "import-export business in India" was a code for something less legal. "I think he thought I was a hashish dealer or something," Freston recalled.

Freston shared an office with John Sykes, a twenty-four-year-old former Epic Records promoter buzzing with true-believing music fanboy energy, who headed up promotions for the channel. In the early years, Freston and Sykes would go out to cable markets like Tulsa and Syracuse in search of evidence that MTV was actually helping bands sell records. "You selling any Buggles? Are you selling any Police records? Are you selling Duran Duran records?" they would ask, according to Sykes. When they found a store that had suddenly sold a bunch of Duran Duran records, they'd rush back to New York and make an ad for *Billboard* about it. Their hustle paid off.

"MTV took off like a rocket," Laybourne recalls, dragging its sibling, Nickelodeon, along for the ride. As the first channel devoted completely to children, Nickelodeon was a revolutionary idea that won piles of programming awards, but it took longer to start making money. (Today, Nickelodeon is Viacom's most valuable channel.) "I used to joke that MTV had a bigger Communicar bill than our programming budget," she said, referring to the limousine service. The small budgets in the early years were tolerated because they came with great autonomy set by Warner Communications chief Steve Ross. "We were really just a creative company that wanted to make great stuff," Laybourne said. "Bob Pittman was not a big spender, but he was excited about brave ideas."

Pittman, now short-haired and most often spotted in a suit, initially signed on to serve the new regime as president and chief executive of MTV Networks, largely out of loyalty to Ross, his mentor. But it didn't last long. "I chafed under the fact that we tried to buy the company and now I'm working for these guys," he said. Within a few months, he left to start a new venture with MCA, and Freston was named copresident in a power-sharing arrangement with an ad sales executive named Bob Roganti. The Viacomese "didn't trust Tom with the ad sales or business side," Laybourne explained. Meanwhile, more founding executives like Sykes followed Pittman out the door, while those who stayed grew increasingly frustrated. "They didn't pay any attention to us, and they didn't let us spend any money," Laybourne said.

* * *

Little did they know that in March 1985, six months before their failed leveraged buyout, a Boston theater chain owner in his sixties had begun quietly buying up Viacom stock as a hedge against the lack of growth in his own industry. By now Sumner Redstone was an icon in Boston and the exhibition industry and a respected figure among his fellow investors, but virtually unknown beyond these realms. But an interview with the *Boston Globe* that spring suggested he was not content to keep it this way. "What has really driven me, though, is the desire to do whatever I do better than anyone else," he said. "I enjoy recognition."

Nearly a year later, in May 1986, a corporate raider who *was* a household name, Carl Icahn, made what at first appeared to be a play for Viacom, buying up a 17 percent stake in the company and saying he'd be willing to buy the whole thing. In the end, Icahn's move turned out to be merely "greenmail," meaning he was willing to go away after the company bought back his shares at a higher price than he bought them for. So when Sumner, Mickey, Korff, and National Amusements ramped up their holdings in Viacom to 8.7 percent over the course of the summer of 1986, most of Wall Street wrote it off as just another greenmail attempt. "Although Viacom has been widely recognized as a takeover target, National Amusements isn't a likely suitor," the *Wall Street Journal* wrote soothingly. "Mr. Redstone frequently makes sizable investments in entertainment companies, and in most cases has cordial relationships with management."

Terry Elkes, however, wasn't taking any chances. Sumner's growing stake and the Icahn greenmail spooked him, so he and other top managers put together a $2.7 billion bid to take Viacom private through a leveraged buyout. Sumner woke up on the morning of September 17,

1986, and read about it in the *New York Times*—and hit the roof. The bid was only about $5 a share above Viacom stock's trading price of $35 a share, which Sumner felt was far too low given the potential that lay within the content engines of MTV and Showtime.

"He thought, 'They were trying to steal the company away. I don't like it. I think it's worth a lot more,'" recalled Philippe Dauman, then a young associate at Shearman & Sterling whom Sumner had hired that summer to help with the regulatory paperwork required when investors cross the 5 percent threshold of ownership in a public company, during a 2016 interview.

The son of French immigrants and raised in Manhattan, Dauman was dark-eyed, diminutive, and coolly formal, with a penchant for elegant European tailoring and a raw intellectual brilliance that rivaled Sumner's own. He had skipped directly from kindergarten to third grade, scored a perfect score on his SATs at age thirteen, and entered Yale at sixteen. Like Sumner, he didn't find the Ivy League undergraduate experience much of a challenge, so he spent most of his time playing poker and backgammon, honing a love for craftily separating his peers from their money that he would bring into his professional life as a mergers and acquisitions lawyer. A youth spent surrounded by classmates much older and taller also instilled a quality that would endear him to Redstone, who was then used to underlings quaking before him as if he were an angry volcano: Dauman was utterly unafraid.

"It was obvious from the beginning that Philippe and Sumner had an affinity," recalled Steve Volk, Dauman's boss at Shearman & Sterling. "Sumner listened to him, threw a lot of questions at him, and liked the way Philippe answered them. There was just a chemistry between them."

Even though Dauman was just thirty-two years old and not yet a partner, Sumner requested to deal directly with him, and soon they were on the phone multiple times a day, beginning with a routine call from Sumner to Dauman's home each day at five a.m. Dauman, trained to work through the night on big deals, had gotten good at faking an alert voice even when summoned from slumber and appeared to Sumner to be keeping the same hours as his restless client. Eventually, Dauman told Sumner that he was waking up his wife, and Sumner agreed to put off the calls until seven a.m.

Within twenty-four hours of reading of management's buyout attempt, Sumner had decided to go to war, with Dauman at his side. He immediately bought more stock and hired Merrill Lynch—the one major banking outfit that the Viacom management had not tied up with its own bid—to explore how he would go about financing a takeover. No one, including Sumner, was quite sure of his intentions, but as he continued to ramp up his holdings, Viacom's stock price soared above management's initial offer, forcing them to sweeten it. Meanwhile, Sumner put on his best country bumpkin routine, a pose he would employ frequently in the ensuing years to ensure his rivals underestimated him. "It's a whole new world," he marveled to the *New York Times*. "It was not long ago that all I knew about leveraged buyouts was that they were referred to as L.B.O.'s. I'm much more educated now." On October 17, 1985, he made one last effort to convince management to keep Viacom a public company, but when the board voted the next day to approve management's sweetened bid, the battle lines were set. Management owned just 5 percent of the company's equity—far less than Sumner owned—and was having to rely on high-interest junk bonds to finance their bid. "He said, 'These guys are going to take over the company for less money than we already have invested in the stock. Why don't we think about doing it?'" recalled one person close to National Amusements.

And so he essentially moved into a one-bedroom room at the Carlyle Hotel in New York and hunkered down with Dauman, Merrill Lynch's Ken Miller, and the rest of his advisers for round-the-clock negotiations with bankers. It took months, during which Sumner came to rely ever more heavily on Dauman, who could both authoritatively explain concepts like "poison pill"—an antitakeover measure that Viacom's board had adopted that would dilute shares if any investor went over 20 percent—and happily deliver papers to his hotel room in the middle of the night that Sumner would sign in his bathrobe. On Christmas morning, long before the age of cell phones, Sumner even managed to track Dauman down at his in-laws' house, despite Dauman never having mentioned his wife's maiden name to Sumner. Convinced that some catastrophe had happened with the deal, Dauman ran to the phone. "He just wanted to talk," Dauman recalled. "He must have called ten or eleven people to find out where I was."

On February 2, 1987, Sumner offered to buy Viacom for $49.25 a share—an offer, he argued, that was not just higher than the management's offer but more secure. Viacom's management's reliance on junk bonds would almost certainly require selling off and cutting huge pieces of the company to make the interest payments, were they to succeed. Sumner's offer would be funded by $400 million in cash and Viacom stock that National Amusements already owned, along with $2.25 billion in bank loans. Nevertheless, Viacom's board rejected it, claiming it was worried about the time it would take Redstone to clear regulatory hurdles. Sumner wanted to go higher, but he needed more information about the inner workings of the company. He requested it from Viacom's board but for a long time got nothing. So he resorted to other methods.

*   *   *

By now, Bob Pittman was well-ensconced in his new offices in Rockefeller Plaza, where he was subletting space from his former bosses at Warner Communications while he got his new company, Quantum Media, backed by MCA, off the ground. He had left on reasonably good terms, and Viacom was pitching in with launching a record label for the new company. But in truth there was no love lost between Pittman and the Viacomese, who had nickeled-and-dimed him on his way out the door. Sumner asked him for some insight into Viacom. Pittman was only too happy to give the Bostonian insurgent his take: MTV Networks executives hated their new overlords, and talent was streaming out the door. Sumner was impressed by Pittman and asked him for entrée into MTV Networks. Pittman immediately called Freston and Laybourne, arguing, "You are right now the bastard stepchild of Viacom. But if you help Sumner and he gets the company, you are going to be the crown jewel."

"I didn't know Sumner Redstone from Adam," Freston recalled. "None of us did. I was just told there's this cranky old guy from Boston who is taking positions, and if any of you talk to him, you're going to be fired." But Pittman was persuasive. A dinner was arranged at the Carlyle.

Knowing nothing about Sumner beyond the thickness of his Kennedyesque Boston accent, Freston arrived at the Carlyle expecting something out of Camelot. The elegant Upper East Side residential hotel had become famous as JFK's "New York White House," thanks in part to its warren of tunnels that let the president discreetly smuggle in his mistresses, including, the legend goes, Marilyn Monroe. He was surprised to find a relatively modest single rented room—Sumner had not yet rented an apartment there—with Phyllis's cotton underwear drying on a line over the bathtub. *She's doing her own laundry in a single room,* he marveled to himself.

But Sumner proved a charming dining companion, full of questions about the young MTV Networks. "I got him very excited about the company," Freston recalled. "I would trade this guy, the devil I don't know, for the devil I know, which were these guys who didn't seem to have a vision that was on par with what we wanted to do with the company." Sumner wanted to know if they would leave if he bought the company and fired Elkes and the other managers who were behind the LBO. "We said, 'Hell, no,'" recalled Laybourne. "We would see it as a chance to really take control of our businesses." They invited him to come see their offices, which were located at 1775 Broadway, a healthy walk north from Viacom's headquarters in 1211 Avenue of the Americas. If the Viacomese found out, they'd be fired, but they figured they could slip him in.

Early the next morning, he showed up in the lobby with a rumpled sport coat, mismatched pants, a checked shirt, and a dab of shaving cream on his ear. "I thought, 'Look, he's like an old man,'" Freston said. But Sumner was intoxicated by the chaotic scene that greeted him—music blaring, kids with long hair, quarter-inch and one-inch tapes stacked everywhere. "There were other things, too, that he liked about Viacom, but it was MTV Networks that really sold him," Freston said. "He thought that was the sexiest part."

He returned to his war room in the Carlyle determined to win the company. He raised his bid several more times, and management matched it each time. Sumner, near the limits of his financing capacity, took a deep breath and asked Dauman and Ken Miller for a gut check: Should he really risk everything by going higher? "He turned to me and Ken and said, 'I'm not going to do the deal unless you say yes,'" Dauman said. "That's an unusual position for an outside lawyer."

Dauman and Miller agreed, and Sumner raised the bid again, to $3.4 billion. This time, he added a Redstonian flourish: threatening to sue Viacom's board of directors. "To be frank, at the time I thought it was a questionable tactic," recalled Miller. "You finally had to get the approval of the people you were suing. But he threatened their net worth, and that turned out to be fairly effective in a clinch."

Dauman, though concerned, was more open to the maneuver. He and Sumner penned the subtly but definitively threatening letter to the chairman of the subcommittee of Viacom's board evaluating the bids. The kicker was clear enough: "The management must have the sense that it need not have the best offer in order to win. Neither we nor, we believe, the shareholders will stand for such a result." Watching Sumner and Dauman go for the jugular in the courtly language of the law was a thing to behold, recalled Volk. "It was like Leonard Bernstein and Stephen Sondheim writing *West Side Story*."

The performance was a hit. On March 4, 1987, following a twelve-hour meeting at the financial district offices of the lawyers for the special committee, the Viacom board announced that they were rejecting management's last-minute, junk bond–financed $3.3 billion bid. National Amusements had won the day and was now poised to swallow a company with five times its own revenue.

At sixty-three, Sumner Redstone was suddenly a media mogul. He was ebullient. "This could add another 10 years to my life," he crowed to the *Wall Street Journal*. The financial press, by and large, was indulging but skeptical—suspicious that he had overpaid, unsure that he'd be able to handle the massive debt, and even less sure that he'd know what to do with Viacom's sprawling operations after a lifetime of autocratically running a theater chain that the *Journal* called "a lean operation with practically no corporate staff." Even at the height of the takeover battle, he had never stopped his habit of checking the theaters' grosses each morning. But Sumner said all the right things, telling the *New York Times*, "I am going to have to change my management style now."

In truth, he already had. As his passion had drifted away from exhibition through the mid-'80s, he had delegated more and more responsibility to his son-in-law, who had begun to use his international connections to put his own stamp on the company. The same month that Sumner seized Viacom, news began to dribble out that National Amusements was about to make its first expansion overseas with a multiplex in Nottingham, England. The move was Korff's idea, built on relationships he had forged at the Fletcher School of Law and Diplomacy—where he became friends with elite British figures like Michael Dobbs, the author of *House of Cards*—and in his work as an international mediator. Under Korff's leadership, National would go on to become the dominant multiplex theater chain in the UK.

Korff was also a close adviser to Sumner through the Viacom takeover, flying frequently to New York for negotiations at the Carlyle, and helping Sumner track a worst-case scenario in which, even if Viacom went belly-up, National would still have its real estate holdings anchoring its value. But Sumner's own children remained far from the fray. The *Journal* noted that both were lawyers "who aren't currently involved in the family business." With three young children at home—including a one-year-old—Shari was focusing on being a full-time mom. Brent continued to work at the Boston DA's office, with two young children of his own, Keryn and Lauren, known as Lee Lee.

This was a triumphant moment for the family business, and yet

Sumner had no blood relative to share it with. One month to the day after National won the bidding for Viacom, but months before the deal officially closed, Mickey died suddenly at the age of eighty-five in Florida. He'd been sharp up until the end, warily complying with Sumner's demands in recent years that he shed his often colorful longtime partners in various subsidiaries and help him consolidate control. He did not especially appreciate Sumner's more recent tours in the press, claiming he was a self-made man who grew up in a tenement. "It's a good thing I was born before him, because he would take credit for that, too," Mickey once quipped to a family member. But he was proud of his son and supported his decision to go after Viacom. The *Boston Globe* heralded him as "a prominent theater and night club owner," pioneer of drive-ins, and important philanthropist, but his obituary in the *New York Times* was only three paragraphs long. No mention was made of Viacom.

Death stalked the Redstones for the rest of the year. Three weeks after Mickey died, Eddie and Leila, then living on Martha's Vineyard where Eddie had recently purchased control of the local bank, got a call from the Japanese consulate. The consulate informed them that their daughter, Ruth Ann, had died on April 21 in Kashiwa, a Tokyo suburb, and then asked, "What should we do with the child?" Eddie and Leila were dumbfounded. They had had no idea that she was in Japan, let alone that she had a three-year-old son. They immediately boarded a plane to Japan to collect her body and their grandson, where they were greeted with new horrors. They discovered that during her pregnancy in Brazil, Ruth Ann had suffered from eclampsia, a blood pressure disorder that put her into a coma upon delivery and resulted in the amputation of most of her toes. Eddie and Leila ordered an autopsy and discovered that their thirty-two-year-old daughter had died of pneumonia, made fatal by a case of full-blown AIDS. Family members say she contracted AIDS from a blood transfusion from her health crisis in Brazil, but the cult, which by then had changed its name to The Family, was shaken by the implications of her disease for their free-love lifestyle.

"The discovery sent shock waves through the Family," wrote Ed Priebe, a former Family member, about the incident in 2002. "As much as they believed God was blessing them, as much as they felt that He would spare them from 'the plagues of the Egyptians,' they had to come face to face with grim reality: they weren't immune to AIDS. What made it so serious was that the woman had had sex with members of Berg's personal household."

Eddie and Leila brought their grandson, a beautiful, dark-haired boy named Gabriel Adam Redstone, back to Massachusetts to raise as their own son. It was a chance at redemption after their relationships with their own two children had gone so horribly wrong. Although Ruth Ann was in her thirties and thus eligible for disbursements from her trust, she had never touched any of her money, and so the $7.5 million she had gotten for her 16.7 percent stake in National Amusements in 1984 went into a trust for her son, whom the Redstones would call Adam.

On July 1, Belle followed her husband into the grave, as if unsure of what to do with herself without him. "When she was in her late 70s, Belle still sighed and fussed over Michael like a teenager; until the day he died, and despite his numerous infidelities, Belle was madly in love with him," wrote Belle's great-niece Judith Newman in *Vanity Fair*. Sumner was grateful for all that his mother had pushed him to do, but his relationship with her had always been complicated, and her death brought both pain and relief. "One of the great regrets of my life is that neither my mother nor my father lived to see what I finally accomplished," Sumner wrote.

In the end, Leila would not get a second chance to be a successful parent. On December 1, she "dropped dead," as Eddie would later put it, of a heart attack, leaving him alone on the island with a young child.

The Viacom takeover simultaneously imprisoned and liberated Sumner in his love life. Just before he made his play for Viacom, he had finally decided, after fifteen years of talking about it, to leave Phyllis and make a new, public life with Delsa. On June 17, 1986, he filed for divorce, citing irretrievable breakdown and listing separate addresses for him and Phyllis in the paperwork, according to *Boston* magazine. But Viacom's management's lowball LBO offer in September pushed him to consider his own takeover, which would require National Amusements' full financial force. Sumner could not risk losing half his assets in a divorce. Before making his counteroffer, Sumner withdrew his divorce suit on January 9, 1987. On paper at least, the corporate takeover that made Sumner also sealed him into an unhappy marriage.

Once the Viacom takeover was complete, however, he felt financially strong enough to live the life he wanted with Delsa, regardless of his marital status. They picked out a gracious mid-century modern four-bedroom home on seventeen wooded acres in Lincoln, Massachusetts, and on August 24, 1988, a trust administered by George Abrams bought it for $1.75 million. Sumner moved in, and Delsa built a writer's studio on the property. Sumner and Delsa threw dinner parties, attended weddings and bar mitzvahs together, took her children on vacations to places like the Caribbean and the Arizona desert, and filled photo albums like any other family. Sometimes her children even came along to events like the U.S. Open or MTV Video Music Awards, flown out on the Viacom private plane. Other times, Sumner would tell Phyllis that he was going out to dinner with Dauman and his wife when he wanted to go out with Delsa, knowing Dauman would cover for him. But just as often, Delsa had to stay home from Sumner's most high-profile events, as much as she would have liked accompanying him to the Oscars or a Democratic convention. "I despair of ever being able to live in peace and happiness with Sumner," Delsa wrote in her diary not long after moving to Lincoln. "We are too different. Understanding is missing. When I met him, I was someone else, I let him choose me. Myself, I didn't know how to choose, just to be chosen." Nonetheless, they lived as a family for many years, with Sumner providing Delsa the money she needed to live on. He was close to her children, particularly the younger two, Harte Weiner and Winn, helping them financially when they needed it. He brought Winn to stay with him at Bob Evans's house, where

Evans, upon hearing that Winn wanted to be an architect, showed him his first Fabergé egg and offered the counsel that "lighting is very important." He especially bonded with Harte, whom he respected for having attended Harvard and earned multiple graduate degrees, and mentored her academic career, going so far as to fly her out to Stanford for graduate school. When she decided to have a child on her own with in vitro fertilization, she gave the child "Sumner" as a middle name. One day, as they were all coming back from Delsa's father's funeral in the early '90s, Sumner turned to Winn and said, "Winn, I fucked up. I should have married your mother."

*   *   *

Shortly after the Viacom deal closed that summer, Viacom held a retreat for its employees in Alpine, New Jersey. Buses carted everyone out to play softball, volleyball, and tennis and lie around the pool. Sumner made an appearance, but by mid-afternoon he had had enough and took the first bus back to the office, which was mostly empty on summer afternoons. Henry Schleiff, who had just been hired from HBO to run Viacom's entertainment and broadcast groups, also returned early, and at around four o'clock, he got a call from Sumner in his office.

"Henry, it's Sumner. Are you busy?"

"No, I'm not."

"Could you come down? I'd like to talk to you."

Henry, still in shorts and sneakers, a bit sweaty from playing tennis, went down to Sumner's office, where he held court from his Barcalounger. Sumner swiveled around to look at him.

"Can I ask you a question?" Sumner asked.

"Sure," Schleiff said, expecting another of Sumner's Socratic interrogations of why affiliates pay cable programmers money.

"Do you think we are alone in this world?"

Schleiff looked at Sumner, unsure how to respond. Trying to inject some levity, he quipped, "You mean aliens?"

Sumner gave Schleiff a look that said, *No, you idiot.*

"No," Sumner said. "Family. People. Do you think you're alone?"

Schleiff frantically grasped for something soothing to say. "No, Sumner, we have our parents, we have our wives and loved ones, our kids. You have your family."

Sumner scanned the room, paused, then looked directly at Schleiff. "No," he said. "I think we are alone in this world."

CHAPTER 10

Scaling Paramount

From the beginning, Sumner spoke about Viacom in the language of love. "I have a great feeling for the company," he told the *Wall Street Journal* in the flush of his 1987 takeover victory. "It's on the cutting edge of so many growth businesses." But he admitted that this feeling, though expansive, was also rather vague. "I didn't really know the full difference between a basic channel and a pay channel," he told a crowd of exhibitors that year. Viacom's top management was on its way out, and Sumner knew that he needed a seasoned professional chief executive to run his new prize. During a three-day retreat on Martha's Vineyard to plan the transition of power, Viacom's outgoing management suggested to Sumner a list that included former HBO chief executive Frank Biondi.

Biondi, forty-two, had left HBO amid a power struggle a few years before and gone on to lead the television division of Coca-Cola, which had gotten into the entertainment business after buying Columbia Pictures studio in 1981. A child of the New Jersey suburbs, he had an impeccable East Coast résumé, with a degree from Princeton, a Harvard MBA, and time on Wall Street before going into television. He would know what to do with the beleaguered Showtime, the thinking went, and had the financial chops to help Viacom with its substantial debt. With neatly parted hair and staid suits, there was nothing Hollywood about him, but his intelligence and candor charmed Wall Street analysts and the press alike. Many of the other people Sumner spoke to agreed he was the right person for the job. There was just one problem: Biondi had just sold his house in the tony northern Bronx neighborhood of Riverdale and bought a new one in Beverly Hills after Coke had asked him to move to their Burbank headquarters. His kids were already enrolled in new schools in Los Angeles. The moving van was coming in a week.

Nevertheless, late one Friday in July, Sumner called Biondi at his office and told him, "Some guys in Hollywood told me that you would be the ideal person to run Viacom." Biondi, whose straightforwardness would one day rub Redstone the wrong way, didn't play too hard to get. "It would be better than where I am going," he said. "But I'm moving in seven days."

"I get up at four a.m.," Sumner replied. "Anytime after six a.m. come over to the hotel. We'll get it done in a day." Biondi arrived at the Carlyle by eight a.m., and by noon, they had a handshake agreement. Sumner had Dauman draw up the paperwork: a five-year contract starting at $600,000 a year, plus stock that Sumner told Biondi would be worth $15 million in five years, according to the *New Yorker*. Sumner called Biondi's wife, Carol, congratulated her, and told her to unpack.

Biondi's friends were aghast at the move. "Everybody said, 'Don't do it. He's a nasty man,'" Biondi recalled. One person he'd asked for advice had a relative who had been gravely injured in the Copley Plaza fire and sent to Massachusetts General Hospital, where they had overheard screaming among the family members in Sumner's room. Other industry colleagues simply warned him to watch his back.

But the laid-back Biondi wasn't worried about working for a big personality, and he was quietly confident he knew what to do with Viacom, having competed against its various assets for years. His first order of business was to get rid of a layer of the corporate old guard. A few were spared, including Tom Dooley, a young finance executive that Terry Elkes's number two, Ken Gorman, had mentored. Biondi also quickly elevated Tom Freston to president and chief executive of the MTV Networks unit, telling him over breakfast at the Dorset Hotel that he was giving him a three-year deal and a $250,000 salary. "It seemed like an obscene amount of money," Freston recalled. Best of all, from Freston's perspective, Biondi told him to get rid of his copresident. Freston's early loyalty to Sumner was rewarded.

But in general, Sumner did not get involved in operations. He attended the division heads' regular Tuesday morning meeting but rarely spoke up. "He would sit there for hours and not say a thing," Freston said. "He could tell you the number of tiles in the bathrooms at any one of his theaters, but he really knew nothing about the cable business, or pay-TV business," Biondi said. "He said, 'All I want to do is be involved in deals.'" Nevertheless, he was determined to learn, even if that meant asking "stupid" questions. That first summer, he'd often call Henry Schleiff into his office and grill him on the basics of the industry: Why do people advertise on television? What's CPM (the industry acronym for the cost per one thousand advertising impressions)? Why is that the measure? How do you know people are influenced by it? "As you gave the answers, you gave the given wisdom, but because he pressed like a good lawyer, you began to question the given wisdom," Schleiff said. He began to think of it as Sumner's "Columbo" routine, feigning ignorance to draw out truth. "He even had the raincoat."

In the beginning, Sumner's Viacom—which he had renamed VIE-uh-com during the first board meeting, in a nod to his fighting spirit—couldn't take a lot of chances with $2.5 billion of debt hanging over its head. The banks wanted them to sell assets, preferably MTV or Showtime. But Sumner was committed to content and blessed with luck. Chuck Dolan, the founder of Cablevision Systems Corporation, was so hungry for Viacom's cable systems on Long Island and suburban Cleveland that he agreed to pay an eye-popping $550 million for them. On top of that, reruns of *The Cosby Show* ended up fetching far more in the marketplace—a record $515 million—than the previous management had expected. Combined with some debt refinancing, these moves gave Viacom breathing room without having to sacrifice core assets.

Meanwhile, the strategic heart of Viacom, MTV Networks, was just beginning to hit its stride. Although the channels were "barely profit-able" when Biondi took over and Nickelodeon had only just started to take advertising, "it was pretty clear those were incredibly hot chan-nels," Biondi said. Once Freston finished staffing the unit, it began to grow at between 25 percent and 30 percent a year. The group had strong management, willing to take creative risks on projects like the addictively demented original animation series *Ren and Stimpy*, but it also had massive macroeconomic tailwinds. "From 1987 to 2010, basic cable networks were the best business in the U.S. media landscape," Biondi said.

Altogether, these moves meant Sumner was richly and quickly rewarded for his great gamble. A little over a year after taking over Viacom, the 83 percent stake that National Amusements had paid $420 million for had almost tripled in value to $1.25 billion, thanks to the surge in Viacom's stock price. The company was still operating at a loss, due to debt servicing, but revenues were up and Wall Street clearly believed the company had a bright future. For the first time, Sumner joined fellow newbies Donald Trump and Rupert Murdoch in *Forbes*'s elite billionaires club with estimated assets of $1.4 billion. The *Boston Globe* figured the Redstones were now the richest family in Boston. By 1989, *Forbes* pegged him as the third-richest man in America. "What happened is that we risked our lives in Viacom, and it quintupled in two years," Sumner told the *Boston Globe*. "But it's all funny money. I work harder than ever, 16, 18 hours a day, and I live in the same house in Newton that I bought 35 years ago."

It was around this time that Sumner latched on to the catchphrase he would use for decades to explain his strategy and his success: "content is king." Against the backdrop of the growing power of John Malone, the feared "cable cowboy" who had built Tele-Communications Inc., or TCI, into the biggest cable company in the country, Sumner wanted to deliver a pep talk to the Viacom employees about why they were on the right side of the battle between content and distribution. Tom Dooley, the young finance executive with the gift of gab who had quickly be-come one of Sumner's most trusted advisers, suggested he tell the troops that "content is king," meaning the creative product (or, as they call it today, intellectual property) will always have the upper hand in negotiations over distribution platforms. Sumner quickly made it a permanent part of his stump speech.

More than just the fantastic wealth, Viacom brought Sumner the political relevance he had always craved. During the 1992 presidential election, MTV tried its hand at politics for the first time as part of its "Choose or Lose" campaign, which combined nonpartisan get-out-the-vote public service announcements by the likes of Aerosmith with political news coverage led by twenty-five-year-old Tabitha Soren. The real get, though, was coaxing then governor Bill Clinton onto the channel to answer young people's questions. This was accomplished by former Warner-Amex executive Ken Lerer's PR firm, Robinson, Lake, Lerer & Montgomery, which had been working more or less continuously for MTV almost since its inception. Lerer provided corporate strategy advice to the suits in New York but tapped a young PR journeyman in the firm's Washington office named Mike McCurry to woo Clinton and the other candidates onto MTV's airwaves. "Clinton was doing these forthright, bite-the-lower-lip answers," McCurry said. "He was pretty good at it." More young people turned out to vote in 1992 than in any other election of the past two decades, helping put Clinton in the White House. MTV threw a massive inaugural ball—hosted, somewhat controversially, by Freston and Lerer—and the Clintons stopped by. Over deafening screams, President Clinton shouted his thanks. "I think everybody here knows that MTV had a lot to do with a Clinton-Gore victory."

*   *   *

And yet, for all the wealth and power, something was missing. Ever since his teenage years selling popcorn at his father's drive-ins, Sumner had been enamored of the movies and would never truly be happy until he owned the means of making them. Even amid the glow of his victory in the Viacom takeover, he told his fellow exhibitors that "it's the motion picture industry and the world of motion picture entertainment that captured my heart some decades ago, and that love affair will never end." The instant that Viacom's corset of debt loosened enough to breathe, he began saying it all over town: "The only thing we lack is a studio."

In many ways, it was the most natural thing in the world. Hollywood was built by exhibitors, a cadre of largely Eastern European Jewish immigrants like Adolph Zukor, Louis Mayer, Carl Laemmle, the Warner brothers, and William Fox who in the early years of the twentieth century climbed from the fur and garment trades to owning nickelodeons and projecting films to founding Paramount Pictures, Metro-Goldwyn-Mayer, Universal Pictures, Warner Bros., and Twentieth Century Fox. In the model of these original movie moguls, exhibition was merely a rung on a ladder to controlling intellectual property. The Supreme Court's *Paramount* decision kicked down this ladder, and for more than a generation, exhibitors stayed in their place. But just as he was making his move on Viacom, the Reagan-era Justice Department, with its lax approach to antitrust matters, was beginning to openly question the relevance of the *Paramount*-era consent decrees amid the rise of home videos and cable television. "From our standpoint, the decrees have outlived their usefulness," Charles F. Rule, the assistant attorney general in charge of the antitrust division, told the *New York Times* in 1987, as Hollywood studios began buying up movie theater chains. "Vertical integration does not necessarily have any anti-competitive effect."

Indeed, vertical integration was increasingly seen as imperative. In 1989, Time Inc., the publisher of *Time, People,* and *Fortune* magazines as well as the owner of HBO, agreed to merge with Warner Communications Inc., the parent of Warner Bros. studio and Warner Music, to create the largest media and entertainment company in the world. The deal was presented as largely defensive, a way of finding equal footing with global giants like the German conglomerate Bertelsmann, Sony Corp. (which had recently bought CBS Records and Columbia Pictures), and Rupert Murdoch's News Corp. "There will emerge on a worldwide basis, six, seven, eight vertically integrated entertainment conglomerates," Time Inc. president N. J. (Nick) Nicholas Jr. told the Sunday *Times* of London. "At least one will be Japanese, probably two. We think two will be European. There will be a couple of American-led enterprises, and we think Time is going to be one." Very soon afterward, reporters started asking Sumner where Viacom fit on this consolidating chessboard.

From the moment he seized Viacom, Sumner had had his eye on Paramount Pictures, the studio he had been closest to as an exhibitor. Paramount was not just the last major Hollywood studio not snapped up by some global conglomerate; it was in some ways the most intact vestige of the old Hollywood that Sumner had first fallen in love with. Paramount had been the first truly dominant Hollywood studio, as its father, Adolph Zukor, had invented the much-mimicked business model that turned the American movie industry into an economic powerhouse.

A Hungarian immigrant born in 1873 and orphaned by the age of eight, Zukor had made his first fortune selling furs before getting into the penny arcades that showed early motion picture travelogues shortly after the turn of the century. He soon realized that longer, more coherent films would be required to popularize the medium, and he set about procuring filmed versions of stage plays. In 1912, he and his partners formed the Famous Players Film Company, which he then merged with a competitor and a distributor named Paramount and took over. Zukor quickly built his dominance by signing rich, exclusive contracts with stars like Mary Pickford—represented by the arch of stars over the mountain in the Paramount logo—and amortizing his costs over a vast international distribution system.

By 1921, Paramount was the largest maker and distributor of films in the world, producing commercially successful epics like Cecil B. DeMille's *The Ten Commandments* in 1923 and winning the first-ever Oscar for Best Picture for *Wings* in 1929. Within a decade, after a buying spree of deluxe movie palaces, it would also own the largest theater chain in the United States. Toward the end of the 1920s, Zukor erected a monument to this achievement in Times Square, its crowning clock tower encircled in the same stars that surround the mountain in the Paramount logo. He maintained an office on the top floor of the Paramount Building—today best known for the Hard Rock Cafe on the ground floor—until his death in 1976 at the age of 103.

Luckily for Sumner, he had an in at Paramount that few could rival. Back in 1965, when he had helped Paramount beat back a hostile takeover from corporate raider Herb Siegel, he had been invited to do so by a young marketing executive named Martin Davis. Together, they had helped deliver Paramount into the hands of Charles Bluhdorn's Gulf + Western, and they had stayed in touch ever since. Davis, a thin, fierce Bronx native who never finished college and came up through movie publicity, became Bluhdorn's right-hand man, and when the fifty-six-year-old Bluhdorn died suddenly of a heart attack aboard his private jet in 1983, Davis ascended to his throne. Davis then set about unmaking the multibillion-dollar hodgepodge that Bluhdorn had assembled, slimming down Gulf + Western into a media company consisting of the Paramount film studio, a television division that made shows like *Cheers* and *Star Trek: The Next Generation*, Simon & Schuster, Madison Square Garden, the New York Knicks and New York Rangers, a handful of television stations, and some theaters and theme parks. When he was done, he renamed it Paramount Communications.

But despite renaming the company he ran after a Hollywood studio, Davis was not beloved by Hollywood. When Bluhdorn died, Davis inherited one of the most legendary studio management teams in Hollywood history: Barry Diller, chairman and chief executive; Michael Eisner, president and chief executive; and Jeffrey Katzenberg, head of production. Together, Diller and the "Killer Dillers" he mentored were responsible for one of the studio's most successful periods, with films like *Beverly Hills Cop, Saturday Night Fever,* and *Raiders of the Lost Ark*. But Davis had little tolerance for the way successful executives had been treated at Paramount. "He was acting like the goddamn protected species at the company," Davis, who died in 1999, told *Vanity Fair* of Diller. "I was sick of it." Diller left to go run Fox, and Eisner and Katzenberg left for the top two jobs at Disney. These men have many friends in the industry and went on to great success; Davis earned a reputation as a cold, heartless New York suit. "He was a distasteful man," Diller said.

Davis knew that the slimmed-down Paramount was vulnerable to a takeover, and he spent much of the late '80s and early '90s holding talks with a dizzying array of merger partners, from Sony to Gannett to AT&T, hoping to eat before he was eaten. Sumner and Davis held some preliminary talks in 1989 brokered by Herb Allen of the media bankers Allen & Company, but at that point Davis was not ready to give up control. The picture had shifted by early 1993, however. The studio had suffered a series of flops and lost market share over the previous five years, weakening Davis's negotiating leverage. Worse still, there were rumors that Davis's nemesis, Diller, was plotting a run at the company.

Smelling blood, Sumner summoned Dauman, his deal-making consigliere, from his partner's perch at Shearman & Sterling and offered him a job in-house as Viacom's senior vice president and general counsel. Dauman had been rewarded for his help in the Viacom takeover with a seat on the board but had remained at the law firm in the intervening years, serving as Sumner's personal lawyer on his estate planning, executor of his will, and even trustee of his family trusts. Dauman had been part of earlier rounds of secret talks between Sumner and Davis over the years that not even Biondi knew about—Sumner felt Biondi had "loose lips" and was a poor negotiator—and Sumner trusted Dauman implicitly. By February 1993, he had his own office near Sumner's on the fifty-second floor of Viacom's Times Square headquarters. Another war room was taking shape.

The next time an investment banker came knocking, offering to play matchmaker between Sumner and Davis, Sumner was ready. This time it wasn't Herb Allen but Robert Greenhill, president of Morgan Stanley, who had gotten to know Sumner by inviting him to a tennis camp in Carmel, California, a few years before. In April 1993, Sumner and Dauman meticulously prepared for the dinner, making a plan that Sumner would not bring up price, only the question of control. As Sumner and Davis settled in for their leisurely meal in the private dining room of Morgan Stanley, Sumner was surprised to find that Davis had already made up his mind to hand over control. Davis had calculated that it was better to give up control to someone he trusted than to risk a hostile attack from someone he didn't. Paramount was slightly larger than Viacom, with a market capitalization of $6.8 billion, compared to Viacom's value of $5.2 billion once its massive debt was taken into account. But Davis was not a significant owner of Paramount, while Sumner owned almost all of Viacom. In a merged company, Sumner would still keep control. At the dinner, they agreed that Viacom would control the board, Davis would keep his role as CEO, and the merged company—in a nod to Paramount's superior brand, if not superior economics—would be called Paramount Viacom International.

From that evening onward, Dauman took the lead in the negotiations with Davis's number two, Donald Oresman. The secret haggling stretched on for months, with Viacom unable to justify offering much over $60 a share and Davis insisting on an offer "with a seven." Eventually, Sumner got up to $69.14 a share, within spitting distance of the "seven" that Davis craved. To seal the deal, Sumner invited Davis to dine with him and Phyllis at his apartment at the Carlyle. "You know, Sumner," Davis said, surveying the view of the city from the Carlyle, according to Sumner's autobiography, "when this deal gets done, they'll build a big statue of you in the middle of Central Park and I'll be forgotten." "No, Martin," Sumner replied, "they'll build statues of both of us and I will be looking up to you in admiration."

At seven forty-five a.m. on Sunday morning, September 12, 1993, Sumner walked up to the Midtown Manhattan headquarters of Shearman & Sterling, where his board was meeting to approve the Paramount deal. The off-site location had been selected to preserve the secrecy of the talks, but as Sumner approached, he ran into the *New York Times*'s lead reporter on the media beat, Geraldine Fabrikant, and happily submitted to an interview. "I feel great," he gushed. "Tired but great." As the hour for voting approached, the board members inside were getting restless, and Dauman dispatched his deputy, Michael Fricklas, to track down Sumner. Fricklas found him, posing for the *Times*'s photographer, in no hurry to wind up his interview. "I don't think they are going to start without me," he told Fricklas. The deal was announced that day. It was almost too easy.

The next day, wearing a wide, wildly patterned black-and-gold tie and a maniacally wide grin, Sumner stood next to Davis in front of Viacom's seventh-floor conference room and declared that the merger was "an act of destiny" that would create "the single most powerful entertainment and communications company in the world." It was the biggest media deal since the Time-Warner merger in 1990, and Wall Street's early response was positive. Although many of the questions at the press conference were about Diller, analysts thought the deal was generally solid, the $8.2 billion sale price giving Paramount shareholders a respectable premium to the stock's previous trading price of $61 a share. "They made the price high enough that it's a preemptive bid," Lisbeth R. Barron, an analyst at S. G. Warren, told the *Los Angeles Times*. Sumner declared: "This marriage will never be torn asunder. It will be the age of Paramount and Viacom. It is an age that some have likened to the Industrial Revolution of the past. An age which will witness a sweeping transformation of technology . . . providing programs for the superhighway of the home."

Biondi was less enthusiastic. At the press conference, where his future role at the company was pointedly undefined, he didn't even try to mask his annoyance, quipping to the *Los Angeles Times*, "What about the mandatory retirement policy?" His reservations about the deal went far beyond his displeasure at having to give up the CEO title for a few years until the sixty-six-year-old Davis retired. For him, and much of the top management at Viacom, the deal lacked industrial logic and, worse, precluded more interesting opportunities. "There wasn't a lot of support in-house for it," Biondi said. "It seemed to be a fairly unwieldy thing." Biondi believed Sumner's interest in Paramount was purely emotional. "What you've got to understand about Sumner is, this was the Yankee bat boy growing up to buy the Yankees." Sumner knew that some of his most trusted lieutenants, including Freston, were cool to the idea, but he argued his side to Geraldine Laybourne, who was on a work trip in Asia, over the phone. "I really want to do this," he told her. "I want to be Louis B. Mayer."

CHAPTER 11

Killer Diller

For a brief moment, Sumner got to imagine himself as the owner of Paramount, the seizer of his destiny, the gold letters of his name bound for both the Hollywood Walk of Fame and the upper frieze of the Boston Latin School auditorium. But the euphoria did not last long. The day after his bombastic press conference, the *Wall Street Journal* reported that National Amusements' purchases of Viacom stock had helped send its price soaring 26 percent in July and August, inflating the currency that Viacom was using to pay for Paramount. The story raised questions about the ethics of these stock purchases at a time when Sumner had inside information about a material event in Viacom's future. Viacom argued that the purchases were routine, but the damage was done. Viacom's stock price dropped enough that day to lower the value of its Paramount offer to $7.9 billion and soon dropped further to $7.5 billion. Suddenly, Sumner's bid seemed a lot less preemptive.

It didn't take Barry Diller long to exploit the opening. As Martin Davis had feared, Sumner wasn't the only mogul who believed Paramount was his destiny. Diller was a creature of Hollywood with a golden touch for programming and the kind of restless ambition and combativeness that Sumner respected. Compact and immaculately dressed, with an impish gap-toothed grin and a fearsome prematurely bald dome that fueled rumors that he was the model for Mr. Burns of *The Simpsons*, Diller had grown up the son of a wealthy real estate developer in Beverly Hills, dropped out of the University of California at Los Angeles to work in the mail room at the William Morris Agency, and risen quickly at ABC, where he was credited with inventing the

miniseries and made-for-TV movie. His youthful tour as the chairman of Paramount during its wildly successful decade from 1974
made him an icon. In the wake of Bluhdorn's death and his clashes
with Davis, he left for Fox in 1984. There, he defied all expectations
and created the first new broadcast network in decades, launching pop
cultural phenomena like *The Simpsons, Married . . . with Children,* and
In Living Color that changed the face of television. When he left Fox
in 1992, unhappy that he would always be an employee and never an
owner in Rupert Murdoch's empire, the *Washington Post* declared him
"one of the few individuals in Hollywood with the talent and background to attract enough capital to buy a studio or even a network if
he chose."

Instead, he set off on a technological spirit quest, toting his laptop across the country and picking the brains of luminaries like Bill
Gates as well as Sumner, in search of a business of his own to run.
He shocked the industry by settling on QVC, the home shopping network best known for hawking cubic zirconium. But QVC had some
very smart money behind it: Comcast's Roberts family and TCI's John
Malone. Between them, they owned 35 percent of QVC. TCI had just
announced that it had the digital compression technology to provide
its subscribers more than five hundred channels by 1994, and Diller
was expected to preside over a brave new media future where the cable box became an "interactive" portal for ordering on-demand movies, buying luxury products, and even banking. Diller invested $25
million, giving him 3 percent equity, but Malone and the Robertses
agreed to give him the right to vote their shares and the title of chairman. Malone and the Robertses were essentially giving the original
"Killer Diller" a tank to drive wherever he wished.

Four days after announcing his purchase of Paramount, Sumner
opened up the *Journal* to learn that Diller and QVC had hired Herb
Allen to explore a rival bid for the company. Sumner had been worried
enough about Allen—who was more than a little displeased to see his
megadeal closed by another banker—that he'd sent Allen a check for
$1 million after he sealed his Paramount deal, but he had ominously

returned the check. Now the most influential media banker in New York, the host of the famous annual Allen & Co. media confab in Sun Valley, was not just angry at Sumner; he was working for the other side.

As for Diller, Sumner wasn't exactly surprised, but he did feel betrayed by the man he called "my best friend on the West Coast." He and Diller had been bouncing ideas off each other for years. As Sumner pursued and captured Viacom, Diller was one of the industry luminaries whose counsel he most often sought. "I probably knew more about television than most people that Mr. Redstone dealt with or knew," Diller said. When the formal bid came on September 20, eight days after Viacom's board voted to buy Paramount, a messenger delivered a copy to Sumner at the Carlyle with a handwritten note from Diller saying he hoped it wouldn't affect their friendship.

But how could it not? The bid was overwhelming: QVC was offering $80 a share, or $9.5 billion—$2 billion more than Viacom's offer, at current stock prices—with more than three times the amount of cash contained in Viacom's offer. QVC could afford such a rich offer thanks to a $1 billion commitment from Malone and Comcast. Comcast president Brian Roberts, who had been the one to recruit Diller to QVC in the first place, declared that Diller was "uniquely qualified to run Paramount," adding, "From the moment Diller came to QVC we knew we were going to build a major media company."

Davis was horrified but careful. Any hint that he was dragging his feet in evaluating QVC's bid could open his board up to shareholder lawsuits. Paramount put out a statement that it still believed Viacom was the "best fit" but would "evaluate the QVC proposal." Paramount shareholders, meanwhile, were delighted to watch a full-scale bidding war unfold. As Mario Gabelli, whose Gabelli Funds made up one of Paramount's biggest shareholders, put it: "Let the auction begin!" Paramount's stock price climbed as Wall Street licked its lips awaiting Viacom's higher bid.

The clash of the business titans that ensued dominated the business press for the next six months and turned Sumner into a household name. At age seventy, he was at the top of his game, squaring off

against the biggest names in the industry—Diller, Roberts, Malone—
and bringing the full force of his decades of ruthless legal and negotiating experience to bear. As a media mogul, he might still be
learning, but as a deal brawler, nobody was better. This occasionally
caused tensions with Frank Biondi. When the *Journal* called up Biondi
asking if Viacom planned to sweeten its bid, he said he couldn't rule it
out, but Sumner, in the same story, was unequivocal: "Maybe Frank is
not as precise or articulate as I am, but there has absolutely not been
any discussion or contemplation of increasing our bid."

This was Sumner's battle and, as such, would be fought with
Sumner's favorite weapon. Three days after QVC made its bid, Viacom
filed an antitrust lawsuit in the U.S. District Court for the Southern
District of New York against TCI, alleging that QVC's bid for Paramount was "one more step in John Malone's conspiracy to monopolize" the cable industry. The charge came as the media industry and
regulators were growing increasingly worried about Malone's growing
clout. Through TCI and its spin-off, Liberty Media Corporation, he
now controlled 20 percent of the country's cable subscribers, making
him the de facto gatekeeper for which cable channels lived and died.
Altogether, his market power combined with his hardball tactics—he
was not above using his leverage over distribution to get better terms
on a programming acquisition—led then senator Al Gore to dub him
"Darth Vader" and the leader of the "cable Cosa Nostra."

Given Malone's power over Viacom's channels, Viacom's management was terrified at the prospect of suing their biggest customer.
A few days before filing the suit, Sumner gathered them and the
company's legal team in a conference room at Viacom to lay out his
plan. Several of them begged him to reconsider, worried that Malone
would retaliate by kicking channels like MTV and Nickelodeon off
TCI. Tom Freston voiced some of these concerns. But Sumner was
not swayed. "Nobody shits in my mouth!" he bellowed, red-faced. The
blood drained from Freston's face. The suit progressed, and Sumner's
gamble paid off: MTV and Nickelodeon were indeed too popular for
TCI to kick off its service.

In the meantime, Sumner tried to dampen the enthusiasm for Diller, who was being portrayed on Wall Street and in the press as a maestro who could conduct the orchestra of the interactive media future. "I don't care if the shopping channel is the best shopping channel in a zillion places, it is what it is," Sumner told the *Los Angeles Times*. "Interaction: you mean a bunch of telephones? . . . I guess that's the interactivity. Somebody calls you up and orders some jewelry. Right? That's great interactivity." He added, lest anyone was unclear: "Short of a bullet going through me, this merger is going to take place."

Behind the tough talk, Sumner's team, led by Dauman and Greenhill, was frantically trying to assemble more backers so they could raise their bid. They wooed Blockbuster Entertainment and Nynex, the telecom that later became Verizon, to put up $1.8 billion between them. Meanwhile, Sumner's play to knock out Diller's biggest backer yielded results. Just as whispers were coming up from Washington, D.C., that the Federal Trade Commission was going after QVC's Paramount bid, Malone dropped the bombshell that TCI was merging with Bell Atlantic Corp.—a much bigger deal that would keep him from being much help to Diller with Paramount. Sumner, who had testified before the Senate as part of his fight that "Mr. Malone decides what people can hear and see in the United States," was happy to claim credit for sidelining his rival.

But the victory was temporary. Cox Enterprises and the Newhouse family's Advance Publications stepped in to help finance the deal for QVC, and the battle wore on.

Meanwhile, Diller's side had launched a legal attack of its own in Delaware, where a judge blocked Viacom's friendly merger, criticizing Paramount's board for improperly rejecting QVC's higher bid. Paramount's board members were shocked. Davis was devastated. After losing their appeal, Paramount had no choice but to put itself up for auction.

The haggling between Sumner and Diller pushed the price of Paramount past $10.5 billion. Analysts started to complain that whoever won would be overpaying by several billion dollars. "We're in a bit of

a tulip craze now," one investment banker told the *Wall Street Journal.*
Sumner didn't care; he was intent on winning. But he was also out of
money. When Diller raised his bid again, it looked like he would win
the day, until Sumner agreed in the heat of battle to merge Viacom
with Blockbuster, thereby getting the extra cash he needed to raise
his bid.

Wall Street hated the Viacom-Blockbuster merger. They thought
the Florida-based Blockbuster was a village under a volcano, its home
video rental business about to be wiped out by on-demand cable systems. Viacom's stock dropped. But Viacom looked at the hundreds of
millions in annual cash flow and saw a sound way to service the debt
it was going to rack up to pay for its Paramount deal, as well as more
gunpowder for the battle at hand. Sumner would keep control of 61
percent of the new company, Viacom-Blockbuster Inc.

Blockbuster chairman Wayne Huizenga was the kind of entrepreneur Sumner could relate to, if never entirely trust. After turning a
Florida garbage-hauling business into the world's largest disposal
company, Waste Management, he branched into everything from por-
table toilets to pest control before entering the video rental business.
He took Blockbuster from nineteen video stores to more than thirty-
six hundred, creating a workaholic culture that mirrored his own:
come in early, stay late, go ahead and come in on Saturday. Although
he saw the writing on the technological wall years before and began
diversifying into content with investments like a controlling stake in
Beverly Hills 90210 maker Spelling Entertainment Group, analysts
interpreted the merger as a "beautiful bailout" for Huizenga, going
out at the top of his game before his 50 percent quarterly earnings
increases drooped.

The Blockbuster merger would cause no end of headaches for
Sumner and Viacom down the road, but for now, it gave Sumner the
ammunition he needed. The auction continued. As the February 1
deadline for bids loomed, Viacom made one last tweak to its bid, adding $800 million in additional cash and stock and a partial guaran-
tee, or "collar," that it would make up the difference if its stock fell

below a minimum price. Both its and QVC's bids were worth roughly $10.4 billion, but Viacom's seemed like more of a sure thing. "On the surface, Barry's bid is higher, but Sumner's bid has more cash and the back end has a little more certitude," Gabelli told the *Los Angeles Times*. Diller raised his bid a bit before the deadline but did not add the protections against a stock price drop that Viacom added. That would prove definitive. Viacom won the day.

"It was painful," recalled Diller. "After staring at a wall and realizing that it had gone as far as we wanted it to go, we knew that if we did not make a bid, we would lose it. We didn't." For years afterward, Diller thought he had made a mistake. "I was too new at this large-scale mergers and acquisitions business, I had never been in that position before. I should have raised the bid. The truth is, I'd let an opportunity go by."

For Sumner, news of his victory arrived on an auspicious day, February 14, 1994, Phyllis's birthday. A few months earlier, in the midst of the bidding, she had filed for divorce yet again. This surprised few Viacom executives, who witnessed Sumner and Phyllis's constant fighting aboard the company plane. And yet as much as Phyllis hated Sumner by this point, she also admired and loved him. "She used to tell me, 'We fight like cats and dogs, but afterwards the sex is amazing,'" said one former Viacom executive. "They lived to fight. It's just what they did." As in past incidences, she had withdrawn the suit after a few weeks, but her point was made. As the *Wall Street Journal* wrote, "Her action raises questions about whether Mr. Redstone could ultimately lose control of his cable-TV empire in a divorce proceeding." It would not be the last time the question would become an issue for Sumner during a merger.

But on this evening, that all seemed a distant memory. As the final shares were being tendered, Sumner was strangely serene. He left the office mid-afternoon to play tennis with a pro, then attended the opening of a Nickelodeon boutique at FAO Schwarz. That evening, he hosted a small birthday party for Phyllis at the hypermasculine deal den "21," a wood-paneled New York institution just two years younger than Paramount. Dauman, Tom Dooley, and Frank Biondi were all in attendance when the call came around eight thirty p.m. to tell them that they had won. Sumner picked up a glass of champagne and said, "Here's to us who won." He then turned to his wife and joked, "Don't say I never bought you anything for your birthday."

The high-profile battle had not just brought the warring spouses together. It had also finally piqued Shari's interest in her father's media empire. She happened to be in his office the day that he and his team worked out the structure of the Blockbuster merger. The world of business, which she had always regarded as dry and boring, could, she realized, actually be quite thrilling.

CHAPTER 12

Immortality

If buying Viacom in 1987 had made Sumner feel ten years younger, winning Paramount seven years later proved twice as rejuvenating. People around him marveled that he seemed twenty years younger since he closed the deal. The universe had bent to his will once again. It was increasingly hard for him to imagine that it would not continue to do so. But at seventy-one, he was also not taking any chances. Always a health nut, he continued to rise before dawn each morning and run three miles on the treadmill or play tennis. He became increasingly obsessed with his diet, monitoring his intake with clinical precision. Sugar was out, protein was in. Lunch often consisted of a single slab of dried corned beef. Waiters were berated for bringing baskets of bread to the table. Those dining with him who dared order dessert could expect a wry smile of disapproval. "I'm one of those people," he told the *Boston Globe*, "who would like not to die."

Living forever was worth the trouble because Paramount had given him, now, finally, in his eighth decade, the life he had always wanted. Days after the deal was done, he flew to Los Angeles to deliver the requisite call for corporate synergy to his new employees gathered in one of Paramount's theaters. But the real treat for Sumner was sitting down with Paramount Motion Picture Group chairman Sherry Lansing, first in the conference room outside her office on the Paramount lot and later at a candlelight dinner at The Ivy, the celebrity-packed, paparazzi-encircled fishbowl of a West Hollywood restaurant. Lansing, a raven-haired former actress whose mother had narrowly escaped the Nazis as a teenager, had become Fox's first female studio chief at age thirty-five and become chair of Paramount in 1992. Two years into her tenure, she was still rebuilding the studio's slate, but as she laid out her philosophy of focusing on scripts instead of talent-driven "packages," Sumner brought up a project in Paramount's pipeline that he thought could change all that. "At some point, he said, 'So tell me about this movie *Forrest Gump*.' That was extraordinary to me because we never mentioned any of our movies" at that stage, Lansing recalled. "I said, 'How do you know about that?'" Sumner clearly had his own sources in Hollywood and had gotten wind that this quirky, episodic film that had been slowly grinding its way through the gears of the industry for the better part of a decade had promise. "That's going to be a big movie," he said. He was right. A few months later, *Forrest Gump*, the subject of a financial fight that had capped its budget at $55 million, became an instant cultural phenomenon, racking up more than $660 million globally and winning six Oscars including Best Picture. It was the beginning of another golden decade for Paramount, with hits like *Braveheart*, *Titanic*, *Saving Private Ryan*, and *Mission Impossible*. Lansing described Sumner as an ideal boss who gave her and her business-side partner, Jonathan Dolgen, whom Sumner made chairman of the Viacom Entertainment Group, both autonomy and support. "What I think made him so good—and he was just brilliant—was that he was a fan, and he loved movies."

Such glory came at a steep price. The Paramount fight left Viacom $10 billion in debt, forcing it to sell off assets like Madison Square Garden and its cable systems. In order to service this debt, it had had to acquire Blockbuster, well past its sell-by date, which turned a company of about seven thousand employees focused largely on content into a content-and-distribution behemoth of more than seventy thousand, blurring Sumner's investment thesis considerably. The deal also significantly diluted National Amusements' ownership interest in Viacom, though it maintained control through super-voting shares. While some executives at the company in those days argue that the Paramount acquisition paid for itself with well-negotiated subsequent asset sales—the bulk of Simon & Schuster's assets went to the UK's

Pearson for the rich price of $4.6 billion in cash—many others believe buying Paramount was a mistake. "The fact that they needed this film studio ended up taking so much value out of the company, because in order to get the studio, they had to overpay for Blockbuster, which they sold basically for scrap metal years later," said John Sykes, who returned to Viacom in the 1990s to lead VH1. "The real value was the growth of the cable business," Biondi agreed. "If he had just stayed with the original company, he would have been richer than Bill Gates. It turns out, motion picture companies are not a growth business. They are able to grow their top line, but they end up giving most of it back to talent."

Most challengingly for Sumner, buying Paramount forced him to publicize his succession plans. As part of Nynex's negotiations to fund Viacom's campaign for Paramount, Nynex wanted assurances that the company would not be sold or otherwise destabilized after Sumner's death. Sumner agreed to show Nynex his estate plan, which named Dauman as chairman in the event of his death, assuring Nynex that his trusted consigliere knew enough about both his estate and Viacom's operations that he could block a family attempt to sell or otherwise dismantle the company after his death. As the word began to circulate among more executives, Dooley recommended that Sumner make a wider disclosure of this plan. When the *New Yorker* brought this arrangement to light a year later, Wall Street was stunned. "I would have thought that Biondi would have been named," one Wall Street analyst told *USA Today*. Another agreed. "Biondi is integral to the success of Viacom." (One family associate said, "Sumner had no intention of naming a successor. As long as he had control, he could have named the Man in the Moon and then taken it back.") But in some ways, the real news was that Sumner had passed over his own children, who were then in their forties, both lawyers, both on the board of Viacom, and both actively working in the family business. Indeed, Shari and Dauman were exactly the same age.

*   *   *

Brent was the first Redstone of his generation to join Viacom, becoming a director in November 1991, one month after leaving a fourteen-year career prosecuting murderers and rapists as an assistant district attorney in Boston. His cases in Suffolk County were often grisly and emotionally wrenching. Early in his career, he won a conviction for an eighteen-year-old who had raped a seven-year-old girl, though the rapist only got half the sentence Brent asked for. Toward the end, he prosecuted a man for fatally whipping his girlfriend's three-year-old 277 times with an electrical cord. The man was charged with first-degree murder but was ultimately convicted of a lesser charge of manslaughter because the defense had successfully argued that cocaine had driven him temporarily insane. Brent was drawn to the work, according to his daughter Keryn, because of his own difficult childhood, during which he had watched his father routinely reduce his mother to tears. "My dad wanted to do something of service to humanity," she said. "He was going to put people away."

Brent inherited his father's height but his mother's disposition, with none of the ruthlessness that Sumner so valued in his closest colleagues. His curly hair and full, pink cheeks gave him a benign, cherubic air—like Sumner, but plumper—while his thick glasses made him appear harmless. He was, as one former Viacom executive put it, "a really nice guy not up to Sumner's demand." He was ethical almost to a fault, loved animals, rarely expressed his emotions, and sometimes seemed to inhabit a world all his own. During one sales trip to Vail in the 1990s, he brought his family and tried skiing for the first time. The first day he loved it, Biondi recalled—"rosy cheeks, smiling from ear to ear"—but the second day he complained his feet hurt. When Biondi looked down, he identified Brent's problem. "He had the boots on the wrong feet. He can be that absentminded."

He had also always had tense relations with his father. During one family vacation to the Korffs' place in Plymouth, Massachusetts, toward the end of his prosecutorial career, Brent and Sumner got in a fight and Sumner told him "to go fuck himself," Keryn recalled. Brent exploded and declared that his family was leaving. "Everyone was like,

Brent, ignore it. They sent all the kids outside to play on the beach in front of the house" while the adults argued. In 1993, he left the Boston area for good, moving to Evergreen, Colorado, where he and his wife, Annie, eventually built their dream home on a six-hundred-acre ranch. When people would ask him later why he moved to Colorado, he would reply, "Because there are no direct flights from Boston."

Nonetheless, Brent went along with the plan when Sumner decided that, as part of his estate planning, he wanted to bring his children onto the board of Viacom. (Ironically, Dauman had been the one to suggest to Sumner that he bring his children aboard, arguing that it would be better for Sumner's ultimate goal of never having his companies sold if they were engaged in the business.) "My dad felt it was better to know what was going on," Keryn said. "He felt like there needed to be some voice of reason there." Brent worked for Viacom briefly at Showtime's office in Denver—the early mecca of the cable industry— and did work for National Amusements setting up its Latin American theaters. By the late '90s, he worked in the legal department at MTV, trying to head off incidents like the time a mother sued Viacom after her five-year-old burned down her trailer after watching *Beavis and Butthead*. When he heard that Dauman was named in his father's will as his successor, Brent was livid. "During the last year that we were in Dover [a suburb of Boston near Dedham], there was a lot of aggressive language about Philippe," Keryn recalled. "'Philippe's a fraud.' 'Philippe is a piece of shit.' 'Philippe is exploiting the situation. . . . Philippe's a yes man, and that's why he's in this position.'"

Shari had even more reason to feel uncomfortable with Dauman's ascent. Just before Viacom's battle for Paramount, her marriage ended, and Sumner, wanting to avoid any entanglement with a breakup that was also going to deprive him of the executive running National Amusements, tapped Dauman to quietly keep Korff in the fold. Sumner had come to rely on Korff to run the theater chain and expand it to new overseas markets while he was busy chasing the latest corporate megamerger, and when he heard the news about their plans to divorce, his first response was, "Does that mean Ira's going to leave the company?" Shari wanted her ex-husband out of the business. In May 1994, just after the dust had settled from the Paramount fight, Korff resigned his positions as president and director of National Amusements, though he retained a long-term consulting contract that he would ultimately keep renewing for the next decade and a half as he remained a close adviser to Sumner—a relationship that greatly angered Shari. "Ira remains a member of my family and the father of my grandchildren," Sumner told the *Los Angeles Times* at the time of his departure. "Neither his business nor personal relationship with me has been affected by the divorce."

But, from the outside, Korff himself appeared greatly changed. In 1990, the year before his marriage fell apart, he acquired the *Jewish Advocate*, one of the country's most venerable Jewish newspapers, founded eighty-eight years before in Boston by the Zionist leader Jacob de Haas, which made Korff an important player in Boston's Jewish community. Then, a couple of years later, his uncle, Baruch Korff, "Nixon's rabbi," received a terminal cancer diagnosis and summoned Korff to tell him he wanted him to assume the mantle of a Hasidic rebbe, or grand rabbi, that his grandfather had once held. Korff agreed and began to go by the title Grand Rabbi Y. A. (Yitzhak Aharon) Korff. Once a clean-shaven business executive who was so competitive that Biondi said he "always had the look like Al Pacino after a long day," Korff grew his beard long, donned the flowing black garments of Hasidism, and politely instructed people how to properly refer to him in the third person. Although Korff had always been a traditionally minded practicing rabbi who kept kosher and proudly proclaimed his direct lineage to the founder of Hasidism, some corners of Boston's Jewish community found the transformation bizarre. "None of us in our lifetime has watched a conservative rabbi become a rebbe," said one member of Boston's Jewish community. "It doesn't happen."

Sumner and Phyllis respected Korff's traditionalism, making their house kosher for him and the children. But sometimes it caused awkwardness. During one Rosh Hashanah service at his synagogue in Dover in 1993, after the divorce was finalized, he shocked the congregation by delivering a sermon railing against the vulgar influence of MTV and shows like *"Beavis and Butt*—I can't even say it in a synagogue" on American popular culture while Sumner sat a few feet away in the front row, according to people who were there. Several members of the congregation of about thirty people were aghast, but none of the Redstones seemed to mind. Shari and Phyllis, who were seated in the separate women's section, stayed for the whole service.

Shari, who had once been so supportive of her husband's rabbinical work that she helped organize bus service from the neighborhood of the struggling synagogue he had built in Dover, where they lived, to Boston's Jewish day schools a half an hour away in an effort to draw more observant Jews to the area, had meanwhile become less religious. Friends say she remained committed to Judaism but was just not particularly interested in Hasidism.

As she was trying to figure out what to do with the next chapter of her life, a friend suggested she talk with Paula Stahl, founder of Children's Charter, a clinic for abused children in Waltham, Massachusetts. Stahl's work inspired her and crystallized her decision to enroll in the master's degree program at Boston University's School of Social Work. "She was very much intuitively drawn to helping children," Stahl said.

And yet, in 1993, a newly single Shari was approached again by her father, with his classic maneuver of suggesting she try coming in for a couple of days a week. "Someone in the family needs to know how to run the business," he said. (Some Redstone observers believe it is not a coincidence that this overture came the same year that Brent defected for Colorado.) She took a leave of absence from social work school and within six months was working full-time for a salary of $200,000. She joined the board of National Amusements, still as Shari Korff, alongside her parents and brother. By 1994, she had dropped her ex-husband's name and joined the Viacom board, and by

the next year, National Amusements named her executive vice president, the same title her father held for much of his rise to power.
"This is something I never anticipated doing," she told *BoxOffice* in
her first big profile as a National Amusements executive in 1995. In
the photo, she wore a red double-breasted blazer with *Working Girl*
shoulder pads, a curling-ironed pouf of auburn hair, and a fearless
expression.

Exhibition was an overwhelmingly male industry, and National
Amusements had been run by a cadre of mostly the same male executives for decades. Sumner set up regular Monday management
meetings as a way for her to learn about the business. For a year, she
mostly kept her mouth shut and listened, occasionally suggesting wild
ideas that were dismissed, like serving coffee in the theaters. After
one meeting she had convened to prepare a presentation to National's
board, she walked out of the room and heard the door close behind
her, as the men in the room circled to talk about her behind her back.
Tilly Berman, recognizing what was going on, told Shari to walk right
back into the room, which she did. The men met later without her
anyway, but the episode showed that she was not going to tolerate being isolated from her team. She befriended Nikki Rocco, the head of
distribution for Universal, in part because they were the only women
anyone could think of who did what they did. "As a woman in the
business, you have to go the extra mile to get along with men," Rocco
said. "You have to be very tough, and you have to be able to take your
lumps because that's what happens in this business. There's no room
for weakness."

Shari attacked her role at National with Redstonian zeal. Learning at the feet of the graybeards who had been running National for
Sumner for decades, she got up to speed quickly and carried forward
a massive building spree, planning to expand the 850 screens in the
United States and Britain deeper into Europe and South America. In
the meantime, she quickly began to fill her father's shoes at NATO
events, holding forth on the state of the industry.

Yet, strangely, throughout it all, her father was largely silent about her role at National. As she began to be cast as her father's second in command in the press, he seemed to bristle. As she recounted to *Forbes* in 1994, he normally beat her at tennis, but one recent day she had beat him for a change. "I said, 'Dad, doesn't it make you feel good that here I am, your daughter, and we played tennis together, and I did really well?'" Shari told the magazine. "He looked at me and said, 'No, it doesn't.'"

CHAPTER 13

"Remember, I'm in Control!"

Far from wanting to cultivate a successor, Sumner had become convinced he could run the entire show himself. Frank Biondi's laid-back style had begun to annoy him. "Sumner didn't like Frank because Frank would leave at five," Tom Freston said. "Frank would not want to go out to meals with him. Frank was a no-bullshit guy. He had a family, and he drove a regular car to work from the Bronx. He would write his own checks for his houses. He'd pay the plumber. Any time I'd go into his office he was always writing checks to somebody." For MTV Networks, which enjoyed one hundred quarters of double-digit growth, this hands-off approach was just what the doctor ordered, allowing its channels to keep their quirky, authentic voices and unshakable connections to their audiences. But Sumner believed that other divisions of Viacom, especially Paramount and Blockbuster, needed more of a swashbuckling, Murdoch-style CEO, ready to swoop into problem areas and fix them himself. He was eager for the role.

On the afternoon of Wednesday, January 17, 1996, Sumner nervously padded across the few feet of plush carpet that separated his office from Biondi's at Viacom's Times Square headquarters with a press release announcing Biondi's departure in his hand. He told Biondi that it was time to make a change, he was tired of sharing the credit, and he wanted to run the company himself. "I said, 'I think you are making a big mistake,'" Biondi recalled.

Biondi was surprised because, by most objective measures, he was performing well. Viacom was the toast of the media industry, its decision to focus on content—and, specifically, meaningful brands like MTV and Nickelodeon—rather than distribution seeming ever smarter against the backdrop of the rise of the Internet. Analysts expected the company to outgrow competitors such as Disney, Time Warner, and News Corp by at least 10 percent over the next several years. "I cannot find anyone who has anything bad to say about the management at Viacom," Keith Benjamin, a media analyst for Robertson Stephens, told *Wired* in April 1995. In the nine years that Biondi had been at the helm, the company that Sumner had bought for $3.4 billion had grown to be worth nearly $30 billion.

But over the past few months, the bloom had begun to come off the rose. The stock was down 27 percent from $54 as recently as September. Just two weeks before Biondi's ouster, it dropped 8.6 percent in a single day when analysts cut their cash-flow forecasts for Blockbuster and Paramount. The real issue was the variable common rights, or VCRs, that Viacom had issued as part of the Blockbuster purchase. Those securities were to convert into Viacom Class B stock if its closing price didn't reach $52 a share by the end of the previous September, leaving the company vulnerable to having to issue as many as 39 million new shares, a massive dilution to its stock price. So Biondi and his team pulled out all the stops to keep the stock price up and in the end only had to issue 6.4 million shares to VCR holders. "But the rosy prospects that Mr. Biondi and his team painted for the company, which helped drive the stock price up, haven't fully materialized," the *Wall Street Journal* noted. As a result, Viacom investor Mario Gabelli explained that Sumner "had to shoot someone."

Sumner's own explanations of his actions mentioned almost none of this. He did complain about the performance of Paramount, where the flop of Christmas-season Harrison Ford vehicle *Sabrina* capped a dismal year. Viacom executives told the *New York Times* that Sumner was frustrated that Biondi didn't tighten control over the studio, despite his request that he do so. But Sumner had just renewed the contracts of Jonathan Dolgen and Sherry Lansing, the two executives who were running the studio. Several other Viacom executives mentioned he blamed Biondi for the departure of Geraldine Laybourne, one of his favorite executives, for Disney. In his autobiography, Sumner wrote that the last straw was Biondi's lack of enthusiasm about flying to meet personally with European broadcaster Leo Kirch's company to seal a $1.2 billion deal to license Paramount content in Germany. Philippe Dauman and Tom Dooley had already gone to Europe for a round of talks, and Sumner thought he and Biondi should go to finish the transaction. In the wake of Biondi's firing, he told the *New Yorker*, "Frank is not an aggressive person."

Many Viacom executives working with both men at the time said it was an earlier article in the *New Yorker*, which dubbed Biondi "Redstone's Secret Weapon," that was the beginning of the end for Biondi. Up to that point, he had gotten relatively little press, but in 1995 he was the subject of a series of laudatory profiles. According to a subsequent *New Yorker* article, when *Wired* wanted to put Biondi on its cover, the PR shop at Viacom insisted that Redstone be included as well.

Biondi perhaps should have known this was a risk. In the wake of the Paramount takeover, Sumner ostensibly decided he wanted to get rid of Richard Snyder, the revered head of Simon & Schuster, because Snyder was not enthusiastic about sharing his division's financial information with his new bosses, and his use of a chauffeur struck Viacom's executives as signaling a dangerous profligacy. (Snyder said the notion that there was anything optional about sharing financial information was preposterous. "He didn't want to share the podium and the press," he said, adding that multiple Viacom directors told him "you were dead from the first day this deal was done.") But Sumner didn't want to be the one to do the deed, Biondi said, because Snyder was a legend in the press. "Oh no, why don't you and Philippe do it," he told them. After they did, and got some press for it, Biondi said, "He was pissed because he's not mentioned." As one person who was part of the discussions to fire Biondi put it, "He had to be fired because Sumner couldn't be in the same room with him anymore."

Instead, Sumner increasingly preferred to be in the same room with Dauman and Dooley. Dubbed by some executives as "double D," they were both promoted to deputy chairmen in the wake of Biondi's ouster. Sumner responded to queries about whether he, at age seventy-two, was too old to be CEO by pointing to the candidacy of Bob Dole. "If Dole thinks he can run the country at 72, then I can run Viacom."

*   *   *

Wall Street, which loved Biondi for his competence, directness, and good humor, was doubtful, sending Viacom's stock tumbling on the news of his shocking departure. That hunch turned out to be correct. Sumner was no better at solving the fundamental structural problems of the Paramount and Blockbuster deals than Biondi was.

He got off to a strong start, forgoing a salary and immediately hopping on a plane to Germany to seal a ten-year, $1.7 billion deal with the Kirch Group that more than tripled what Viacom had been getting out of the market previously. He sold Viacom's cable networks in what he called the "nick of time," and Dolgen and Lansing began to turn Paramount around by slashing its film slate and revamping marketing.

But a year into his tenure as CEO, Sumner still faced a disintegrating mess at Blockbuster. Viacom had to take a staggering $100 million write-down in the fourth quarter of 1995 to cover the costs of closing more than fifty failing Blockbuster music stores and then dealt analysts another unpleasant surprise three months later when it further revised down its cash-flow estimates for the video rental giant to a decline of 15 percent. "I was shocked when I got the numbers so soon that were so different than the numbers we had been given," Sumner told the *New York Times*, sounding every bit like the dog had eaten his homework. The stock had dropped even further, to $27—half of what it had been six months before—prompting the *Times* to declare that "the financial community is skeptical of Mr. Redstone's stewardship."

Viacom was forced to pump money into Blockbuster immediately to buy many more copies of hit movies after realizing that many of Blockbuster's customers were leaving stores empty-handed. But none of the grand synergies that were promised—turning Showtime into the "Blockbuster Channel," a new chain of Blockbuster-launched Viacom stores selling Star Trek watches and "MTV Party to Go" CDs, MTV executives using their juice in the music industry to help Blockbuster's music stores—materialized. Most troublingly, the *Wall Street Journal* reported that Viacom changed Blockbuster's accounting after it acquired the video rental giant, writing down the cost of its videotape inventory to the tune of $318 million, effectively goosing its earnings over the course of the next crucial year when it was trying to keep its stock price high to avoid having to pay out on its VCRs. Blockbuster was revealed as the veritable sick patient it was, an aging sugar daddy whose medical bills were piling up.

But the worst blow for the press-obsessed Sumner landed in a *Businessweek* cover story, published on March 2, 1997. The story, titled "Sumner's Last Stand," argued that he had "trouble articulating a comprehensible strategy for the company," was too far down in the weeds to ably manage his executives, and, worse still, was failing by the only metric he ever cared about, Viacom's stock price. The stock had lost half its value since 1993, meaning that his stake, worth $6 billion just before the Paramount and Blockbuster mergers, was now worth just $3.5 billion, including shares he had bought recently for $250 million. Sumner had been expecting a positive profile in the magazine and nearly lost his equilibrium. "I could hardly sleep at night," he wrote in his autobiography. "I saw my whole life not just slipping away but being pulled out from under me. In a way it was like a second fire."

But rather than hand off the CEO role to a more experienced executive, Sumner doubled down. He ousted Bill Fields, the former Wal-Mart chief he had just recruited to turn around Blockbuster, and he, Phyllis, Dooley, and a new recruit from Booz Allen Hamilton named Bob Bakish flew down to the company's half-empty Dallas headquarters to fix it themselves. They nixed Fields's general-retail strategy, which had been an attempt to make up for declines in the video rental business by hawking cheap candy and sodas near the checkout counter, along with its vague "One World, One Word: Blockbuster" tagline. "We are out of the retail business," Sumner told analysts on an earnings call. "We are not selling underwear." When a Blockbuster executive explained to Sumner that sales were declining because they were in the business of "managed dissatisfaction," meaning convincing people who had walked into the store to rent the new Tom Cruise movie to walk out with a five-year-old Tom Clancy movie instead because the Cruise flick was sold out, Sumner blew his top. "I thought Sumner was going to have a stroke," recalled one executive in the room. "He started screaming at the guy, '*What do you mean, managed dissatisfaction?*'" He came up with a plan to get more copies of the new movies for less by negotiating revenue-sharing deals with the studios, and then did much of the negotiating himself. He hired Taco Bell CEO John Antioco to be Blockbuster's CEO and business picked up. Meanwhile, Viacom chipped away at its debt with the sale of its half of USA Networks and Simon & Schuster's educational, professional, and reference book units.

Within a year, the stock was back up to $56, and Sumner was gleefully crowing about his managerial skills to the *Los Angeles Times*. "I don't think anybody has a passion for a company more than I do for Viacom," he said. "I love what I'm doing, and I know I'm good at it. When the day comes, and I will know it, that I don't feel I can contribute as much as I should to Viacom, somebody else will have the job of CEO." When the interviewer asked the seventy-four-year-old if he'd like his successor to be within his family, he demurred. "I have two highly qualified kids. I guess kids is not the right word for people in their 40s. But management will come from the present managers of this company." In the same interview, he said, "We are not, not, not interested in buying CBS."

Neither of those last two statements turned out to be true.

*   *   *

Mel Karmazin had been ruthlessly chewing his way up through the floors of corporate suites for much of the 1990s until arriving atop CBS with an enormous Wall Street fan club. With a helmet of prematurely white hair, bushy black eyebrows, and a tan that suggested a leisure life that he did not, by most accounts, actually have, he came up through the business of radio advertising sales, where budgets were lean, salaries were low, and commission-based salesmen had to eat what they killed.

The son of Eastern European immigrants, he grew up in a Queens housing project and entered the advertising business out of high school, earning his college degree at Pace College at night. After seven years at an agency, he went to do ad sales at WCBS-AM, and later at WNEW-AM and WNEW-FM. In 1981, he cofounded Infinity Broadcasting, the radio station group, and by 1987 he was its president. Under Karmazin, Infinity became the country's biggest independent radio company, as he bought poorly performing stations in major markets and turned them around. In 1992, Infinity went public and its stock climbed an average of 58 percent each year—powered by stars like Howard Stern and Don Imus, as well as Karmazin's obsession with bottom-line results—until Westinghouse bought it in 1996. "I was driven by opening up the paper and seeing my stock price every day," the famously press-shy Karmazin told *Fortune* in a rare interview in 1997. "I truly got off on that." Along the way, Karmazin got results by focusing on driving ad sales. "He'd walk into a sales office where there'd be a bunch of salesmen sitting around," one longtime associate told the *Los Angeles Times*. "He'd say, 'You, you and you are fired and the rest of you are all on commission.'"

His success building Infinity and selling it to Westinghouse brought Karmazin, then regarded as the smartest manager in radio, into the executive and shareholder fold of Westinghouse Electric Corporation, a century-old Pittsburgh-based manufacturing company that, in 1995, had acquired CBS for $5.4 billion as part of a bid by CEO Michael Jordan to reinvent itself as a media company. By 1997, Westinghouse had sold off its defense and technology assets and renamed itself CBS Corporation, and Karmazin, the company's largest shareholder, was fast climbing its executive ranks. He went from running the combined Westinghouse/CBS radio group to chief executive of its TV station group (in a move the *Wall Street Journal* described as a "boardroom putsch") to president and chief operating officer of the company. When CBS announced near the end of 1998 that Jordan would retire three years earlier than expected and Karmazin would take over as chairman and CEO at the start of the year, CBS shares jumped 10 percent.

Karmazin was not about to stop there. For a couple of years, he had been eyeing Viacom, going so far as to say publicly that he wanted to buy it. Sumner rebuffed his attempts to meet, but in August 1999, the bureaucrats at the Federal Communications Commission gave him an in. They loosened rules limiting how many television stations a company could own in a single market, allowing "duopolies" in certain markets for the first time. That gave Karmazin, who controlled fifteen stations, an excuse to reach out to Sumner, who controlled seventeen, to see what they could do together. In the third week of August, Sumner invited Karmazin to lunch at Viacom, and Karmazin laid out his pitch: What if we combined our stations in markets like Boston, Dallas, and Miami, where we both own one, so we could get the benefits of duopolies? Or what if we swapped our cable networks for your television stations? Or, actually, what if we merged?

Sumner was hesitant to buy a broadcast network after telling the world so loudly that he did not want one. Disney's purchase of Capital Cities/ABC in 1996 had been challenging, and the networks were all losing audience to cable. But Karmazin urged him to look past the network to the TV stations, radio stations (the biggest group of them in the country), outdoor billboards, and syndication holdings and to see the total package as an advertising behemoth. "He began to turn me on and then overnight we entered into very serious discussions," Sumner later told the *Wall Street Journal*. Karmazin returned to Viacom for another meeting a few days later, this time with double D, Dauman and Dooley, who urged Sumner to consider the merger. Soon the negotiations got so intense that they had to be moved from Viacom's headquarters, where they were making executives like Freston start to ask questions, to Karmazin's apartment in Trump Tower, which just happened to be the former headquarters of Paramount. On a rainy Tuesday, August 24, they came to a deal, and over Labor Day weekend, Viacom's board approved it.

On another rainy Tuesday, September 7, seventy-six-year-old Sumner and fifty-six-year-old Karmazin stood together at a podium and announced the biggest media merger of the twentieth century. Viacom would acquire CBS Corporation for $37.3 billion, creating the second-largest media company after Time Warner. Sumner would keep control, with a majority of board seats on the merged board, as well as his now largely ceremonial CEO title, but Karmazin would run it, with all executives reporting to him under the title of president and chief operating officer.

Wall Street loved the deal, which sent both stocks up in heavy trading. Strategically, a deal that combined Viacom's programming assets with CBS's distribution holdings struck analysts as making a great deal of sense, as did one that offered advertisers a single place to reach all stages of life from watchers of *Rugrats* to fans of *60 Minutes*. Everyone else was bulking up, from Disney's purchase of Capital Cities/ABC to Time Warner's purchase of Turner Broadcasting, so the combination had a sense of inevitability. There was also a certain poetry to the notion that Viacom, cleaved off from CBS in the 1970s with an uncertain future, was now returning as the victorious buyer. But among the most important advantages of the deal for many Viacom watchers was that it finally gave Sumner an heir apparent. As part of the deal, Karmazin wanted Dauman and Dooley gone. They were sent packing with golden parachutes of $150 million each, though Dauman stayed on the board. "We felt it was important to the deal," a pale and tired Dooley told the *Journal* the day the deal was announced.

"This is the deal I have wanted to make from the time I was bar-mitzvahed," Karmazin declared. But as he was launching into his strategic vision for the merged CBS and Viacom on national television, Sumner couldn't help blurting out, "I'm in control! Remember—I'm in control!"

Except, of course, as his wife of fifty-two years was about to demonstrate, he was not. One week after the Viacom-CBS merger was announced, Phyllis filed for divorce again, alleging adultery and cruelty and demanding half of his $6 billion fortune. If she got the full $3 billion she was asking for, the *New York Post* noted, it would be the biggest divorce settlement on record. It could also very easily force the breakup of Sumner's media empire, since nearly all of his wealth was wrapped up in Viacom stock. Phyllis had learned a thing or two from half a century married to a master negotiator and had picked a point of maximum leverage.

"The previous two times, Mr. Redstone talked her into dropping proceedings for the sake of the family," her lawyer, Irving Helman, of Boston's Nutter, McClennen & Fish, told the *Post*. "But she doesn't care anymore."

This time, Phyllis had photos.

Phyllis had put up with Sumner's philandering for most of her life, but after Sumner bought Paramount, he took it to a whole new level. Movie openings became opportunities to meet bright young things. Paramount executives introduced him to girls whom they thought he might like. He began to dye his hair ever-wilder shades of orange. And then, a few years into Sumner's ownership of Paramount, his old friend Bob Evans, who had a production deal with the studio but whose films had been few and far between in the decade before Viacom bought Paramount, had his deal come up for renewal. Evans sent his business partner, a high-cheekboned, model-esque blonde named Christine Peters—the ex-wife of former Columbia Pictures cochairman Jon Peters—to do the presentation for him and to meet Sumner. Peters presented the films they had in development, including the promising romantic comedy *How to Lose a Guy in 10 Days*, which went on to be a hit for the studio. Evans's deal was renewed, and Sumner was smitten. Here were beauty, brains, and Hollywood hustle, rolled up in a single package. When Evans suffered a series of strokes in 1998, Sumner flew to his bedside every week, encouraging him to fight to get his old self back. While he was in town, he courted Peters, pressuring her to marry him.

Phyllis knew about it, of course, but knowing was not what made it intolerable; it was the public humiliation. The fame Sumner had garnered in the Paramount battle meant that his personal life was tabloid fodder.

When Sumner vacationed with Peters in the summer of 1998 on the Mediterranean island of Sardinia, word got to a *Daily News* gossip columnist, who phoned Sumner, only to have him respond that Phyllis was "in the next room!" and he and Peters had only had "one dinner together, in Los Angeles." By the next February, when Sumner and Phyllis were visiting Brent's family in Colorado for Phyllis's birthday, tensions were already boiling over. Sumner abruptly left in the middle of the visit to fly to California, despite Phyllis complaining that she didn't feel well. "I remember them fighting about it," Keryn Redstone recalls. "'Don't go to California! I know what you are doing. I know you are seeing that whore.' She was convinced that he was building a house with Christine Peters." Sumner went anyway, and Phyllis ended up in the hospital with an emergency appendectomy.

Phyllis would not have to wait long for her revenge. She hired a private detective, who on May 20 tracked down Sumner and Peters in Paris and snapped a photo of them walking hand in hand. Just outside the frame of the photo were Peters's two daughters and mother, whom she was traveling with on a museum-hopping tour of Paris and her native Holland when Sumner swooped in on the private Viacom plane to take them all out to dinner. But the chaperoned context hardly mattered. Phyllis had the evidence she needed, and it soon appeared on the front page of the *New York Post*.

Instantly, analysts began to fret about what the divorce meant for the CBS deal, and Viacom was forced to put out a statement that same day to placate them: "The Redstone family interests in Viacom's parent company, National Amusements Inc., are structured in such a way that the personal matters between Mr. and Mrs. Redstone will not affect the ownership, control or management of Viacom, nor will they affect the merger with CBS." Then, George Abrams, Sumner's personal lawyer who served on the boards of both Viacom and National, delivered the shot across Phyllis's bow: "In the interest of his family,

Mr. Redstone chooses not to reply publicly to any allegations, no matter how false or misleading they may be. This is a personal matter which Mr. Redstone intends to resolve in a private way. Mr. Redstone and both his children are united on all matters affecting the family's business interests."

The statement was a bluff, but it revealed Sumner's weakness. As the owner of two-thirds of the voting shares of National Amusements, he effectively had control, but he did not own all of it. The other third was split between his children, Brent and Shari. Because Sumner did not know how the divorce was going to turn out, he suddenly needed his children in a way that he never had before.

CHAPTER 14

The Hotshot

O n a balmy December evening in 1999 not long after Phyllis filed for divorce, Sumner and Shari dined together overlooking the Pacific Ocean at the Ritz-Carlton in Newport Beach, California. Their companion for the evening was Paul Heth, a blue-eyed, baby-faced exhibitor buzzing with earnest, optimistic energy who had opened the first successful American-style movie theater in post-Soviet Russia. After talking for a few years, Heth and Shari had decided to go into business together—making Heth the first partner for the partner-averse Redstones since Mickey's old bootlegging and bookmaking buddies. But Shari wanted Sumner's blessing.

Heth was nervous as dinner got under way, but he relaxed a bit when he discovered that the outfit he had chosen for dinner with the man who had just announced the biggest media deal in history—a turtleneck and blazer—matched Sumner's own. Determined to follow his mother's advice to "just be yourself," he started the meal in the way to which he had become accustomed since moving to Moscow: with a vodka cranberry. Sumner, inspired by his choice, ordered his old favorite, a vodka martini. (Shari, poetically, ordered a sherry.) Sumner proved a charming dining companion, grilling Heth on the status of the ruble and Boris Yeltsin's latest antics. When Heth, whose grandfather revered entrepreneurship so much that he kept a collection of business cards with Henry Ford's on top, asked Sumner who he thought was the best entrepreneur in America, Sumner replied, only half-jokingly, "You mean present company excluded?" and went on to say, "I believe I'm the best corporate lawyer, or one of the best corporate lawyers, in modern American history."

But when the drinks arrived, Sumner—by now notorious for his impatience with waitstaff—was displeased. Settling into full professorial mode, he informed Heth that he was going to teach him a business lesson and called over the waiter. "I knew Bill Marriott, I've been eating at the Ritz-Carlton since the 1950s, and this drink is made wrong," he said. The waiter called the manager, who called the maître d', and then another manager. A disagreement ensued, and someone fetched a mix book. Sure enough, they found they had made it wrong (or said they did) and sent him another. "Paul, that's a little demonstration that I believe in my convictions," Sumner said. "So if you believe in Russia, or whatever you are going to do, you have to stand by your convictions."

Heth passed muster, and he and Shari formed CineBridge Ventures to explore upscale movie theater features such as assigned seating that he had tested in Russia. Heth, whose financial contribution to the venture ran in the "tens of thousands," was named president. Shari, who contributed most of the money through National Amusements, became, for the first time in her life, a chairman and CEO. (Although she'd been working at National Amusements for eight years and had been president, running its 1,350-screen theater chain, for the last four, her seventy-seven-year-old father still got the grosses faxed to him each morning and still claimed the CEO title there.) "Shari and I wanted to change how people do movie theaters," Heth said. They visited boutique hotels to study their bars and lobbies and hired an interior designer from the pages of *Vanity Fair* to outfit their creation in sophisticated muted tones like "sand," far from the garish red-and-black template of the typical movie theater. In 2001, they opened The Bridge, a seventeen-screen multiplex theater in a shopping center near the San Diego Freeway; it offered valet parking, assigned seating, a concierge, cocktails, and live entertainment—all for $9.95, a little less than twice the national average ticket price at the time. "We had flowers and jazz in the restrooms," Heth said. "Really it was ahead of its time."

The posh theater wasn't quite as replicable as Shari and Heth had hoped, having promised "openings in selected cities in the U.S. with expansion to continue to European countries" in their launch press release. Only one other Bridge opened, in Philadelphia, though many of its features were rolled out across the United States in National Amusements' "Cinema de Lux" brand. Still, The Bridge's ambitious concept turned heads in an industry enduring one of its darkest periods, as National Amusements' rivals, staggering under debt from a building spree of expensive suburban "megaplexes" they couldn't fill, were going bankrupt right and left.

In some ways, Shari's greatest victory at National Amusements was not in what she built but in what she didn't. When she settled into her full-time role as the executive vice president of National Amusements in early 1995, the movie exhibition industry was in a building frenzy. The previous year, 1.3 billion tickets were sold, the most in thirty-five years, and the industry grossed a record $5.4 billion, lulling exhibitors into believing that rising competition from cable channels and home videos was not the threat that it had first appeared to be. In a way, they were right: all these new "windows" to see movies in gave the movie business new revenue streams, which in turn gave Hollywood studios the incentive to make more of them. A "tidal wave" of films, as the *New York Times* put it, flooded the market, inspiring theater owners to build more venues.

They didn't just build more, they built bigger. The biggest national chains, like AMC Entertainment, Regal Cinemas, and Carmike Cinemas, pushed past the multiplex to so-called megaplexes, defined as theaters with fifteen screens or more, that allowed hourly showtimes and so many choices that people could drive up to the theater without having made up their minds about what movie to watch. The extra theaters were great when blockbusters like 1996's *Independence Day*, which grossed $306 million domestically, were selling out theaters, but a few exhibitors worried that they would turn into "expensive white elephants" during Hollywood's inevitable next creative slump.

Shari was among the wary. "Overall box office is not necessarily increased by adding a megaplex to the market," she told *Film Journal International*, emphasizing that they are only a good idea if they are built in truly underserved areas.

True to her word, one of the first theaters she built was a fourteen-screen multiplex in East New York, a poor and largely African American neighborhood in Brooklyn that did not even have a major grocery store at the time, let alone a movie theater. (The neighborhood's city councilwoman said she and her constituents were "screaming" with delight when they heard the news about the $30 million theater, saying, "I'm excited about the fact that, for once, it looks like people are coming back.") National Amusements owns it to this day. Shari continued to build modestly through the late 1990s, opening a seven-screen multiplex in Worcester, Massachusetts. At the opening, she spoke of remembering when National opened its first Worcester theater in 1963, saying, "I grew up with this . . . it's in the blood." She also built a twelve-screen multiplex in Hicksville, Long Island, and announced a twenty-screen theater outside Cincinnati, Ohio, on the site of one of the company's former drive-ins, but the project fell through in the end.

But she focused on overseas markets, largely because nobody else at National Amusements was. "I got involved in acquisitions, development and strategy planning, probably because my father is so very focused on film," she told *Film Journal International*. "It allowed me to find my own place in the company." She picked up where her ex-husband left off on National's UK expansion and began the company's first push into South America with a fourteen-screen multiplex in Santiago, Chile, in 1998, where staff baked cookies in the lobby and moviegoers could order frozen yogurt with fresh fruit. By 1997, she had 360 screens in development in five countries, including Argentina and Brazil. From the time she joined National Amusements to 2002, she nearly doubled the number of screens, to 1,400.

But while she was building, her competitors were building even more. From 1988 to 2001, the number of screens in the United States rose from 23,129 to 37,185, a 61 percent rise, according to NATO. But theater admissions only rose about 36 percent, to 1.47 billion during the same period. *Forbes* estimated that, by the end, the average theater was only 12 percent full.

Shari's seat on the Viacom board gave her special insight into the folly of this strategy. She was privy to Viacom's efforts to get Paramount to cut its film slate and rein in costs. "It's interesting that while everybody talks about megaplexes, and focuses on making theaters bigger and bigger and bigger, the studios are announcing that they're cutting back on production," she told *Film Journal International*. By 1998, Shari was sounding the alarm about the industry's overbuilding. "Once this frantic expansion activity subsides, there'll be a lull while circuits assess the effect on the marketplace. Then you'll begin to see the fall-out—consolidations and some closings."

Sure enough, the drumbeat of bankruptcies started in 2000. All of the big guys—AMC Entertainment, General Cinemas, Regal Cinemas, Loews, and United Artists—as well as smaller ones like Carmike Cinemas and Edwards Cinemas, either filed for Chapter 11 bankruptcy protection or warned investors they were mulling it. And the consolidation happened. AMC bought General Cinemas, Loews, and, eventually, Carmike. Bankrupt Regal merged with United Artists and Edwards. Theaters shut down across the country. National Amusements weathered the storm, in part thanks to the ballast of its real estate holdings. Although Shari strayed at times from her grandfather's strategy of buying rather than leasing the land under their theaters and made a few bad bets on theater locations in the UK, by and large, she had successfully captained the ship through rough waters.

Her father, finally, took notice. "She exceeded my highest expectations," he told *Forbes* in May 2002. "In a very difficult period of time, she did better than anyone else in the industry." It was the first time that Sumner had ever publicly praised Shari, and in true Sumner fashion, he took it over the top. "Nobody in the entertainment industry is rising as fast as Shari," he declared. "It's like father, like daughter. She has no major weaknesses. She is a great businesswoman."

Shari's rise in her father's estimation coincided with the decline of his relationship with Mel Karmazin. This surprised precisely no one. From the moment the Viacom-CBS deal was announced, the *Wall Street Journal* predicted that the "Mel and Sumner show" would be filled with debilitating drama. For Sumner, running Viacom was a social experience, filled with dinners with top executives at the Four Seasons Pool Room, Paramount movie premieres, and MTV events where he and Phyllis met stars like Bono and Puff Daddy. Reporters adored him for his fearless willingness to give good quote. Karmazin's idea of a good time was grabbing a slice of pizza at the corner stand near his Manhattan apartment, and he avoided the press like the plague. "Mel and Sumner were like oil and water," Tom Freston said. Like Frank Biondi before him, Karmazin "didn't want to hang out with Sumner at all. Mel was another guy who went home at five o'clock at night," though the workaholic Karmazin showed up at the office at the crack of dawn.

Karmazin made some key acquisitions, overseeing the purchase of BET in 2001 and buying the rest of Comedy Central from partner AOL–Time Warner in 2003, and Sumner appreciated his obsession with Viacom's stock price. But Karmazin's cheapness at times exasperated him. A little over a year into their corporate marriage, Karmazin proposed nixing the company holiday party for top Viacom executives as a cost-cutting measure. Sumner responded by paying for the lavish affair at Sotheby's himself, bringing his personal friend Tony Bennett in for the entertainment. Karmazin made a brief appearance but, according to the *New York Times*, left before dinner.

Karmazin had an even worse relationship with Sumner's children. Shari had been opposed to the role that Karmazin carved out for himself in the Viacom-CBS merger. "She felt that Sumner was giving up too much control to Mel," said one former Viacom executive. "Sumner overruled her." (Other Viacom board members said these concerns were widely held on the board as it mulled the CBS merger but that ultimately the chance to acquire CBS with no premium was too good to pass up.) In the wake of the Viacom-CBS merger, Karmazin returned the favor, requesting that Shari and Brent stop attending Viacom operating meetings. When Sumner brought Shari around the executive offices one day, Karmazin "went down and said to Sumner, 'Is this take-your-daughter-to-work day?'" Freston said. Sumner began referring to him behind his back as "Karma-fuck."

Shari, meanwhile, was making the case for greater involvement at Viacom. From the moment she got to National Amusements, she was constantly seeking synergy, suggesting that the movie chain partner with Blockbuster to open "Block Party" adult entertainment centers with video stores, movie theaters, virtual reality arcades, and retail stores on National Amusements properties. She proposed Paramount commissaries in the movie theaters, joking that "we're looking into a Klingon take-out service." She even posed holding a bag of cross-branded popcorn between two monsters, Krumm and Ickis, from Nickelodeon's show *Aaahh!!! Real Monsters* to highlight a promotional campaign for the show inside National's theaters. She attended Viacom management retreats and grew friendly with the executives, particularly at MTV Networks. With teenagers at home, she had a connection to the channels as well as to its management. "She liked us, and we liked her a lot," said Mark Rosenthal, chief operating officer of MTV Networks at the time. "She was always very careful not to be intrusive."

Yet she was also not shy about voicing her desire to shape the future of the company. Even if she had "absolutely no desire" to be chief executive—the role that was promised to Karmazin in his contract should her father die—she told *Forbes* that, as a board member, she'd like to see Viacom make more content acquisitions. "Viacom is an extremely significant asset of National Amusements," she said. "I'd like to take a larger role."

She would soon get one. A month after the piece was published, Shari and Heth announced a new joint venture to build the first American-style multiplexes in Russia. They called it "Rising Star Media," after a line in the *Forbes* story calling Shari a "rising star." Their first theater, an eleven-screen multiplex in Moscow in a development anchored by IKEA, was set to open by the end of the year under the name Kinostar, making National Amusements the first major American theater chain to enter the Russian market.

One month later, Sumner and Phyllis finalized their divorce. In a lawsuit a few years later, Brent, who had always been protective of his mother, accused Shari of cozying up to her father during the divorce, in exchange for his "extreme favoritism." He alleged that a panicked Sumner, having promised investors that the surprise divorce would not alter his absolute control over National Amusements, pressured both of his children to sign over their voting rights to him in the form of an irrevocable voting trust. "If [Phyllis] were to get one-half of his two-thirds, she could go to court with him and force the sale of Viacom," Keryn Redstone said. When Brent refused, Sumner went to Shari and offered her a revocable voting trust, which she signed. Ever since, Brent charged, Sumner had retaliated against him. In 2003, Sumner removed Brent from the Viacom board.

Sumner's deal with Shari helped him get a divorce settlement that assured his continuing control of National Amusements and, therefore, of Viacom. In essence, instead of getting half of Sumner's assets, Phyllis agreed to take half of the income from them. As part of the settlement, Sumner agreed on June 28, 2002, to put his two-thirds stake in National Amusements into a new trust, the Sumner M. Redstone National Amusements Trust, overseen by seven trustees: Sumner, Phyllis, Dauman, George Abrams, David Andelman (Sumner's tax lawyer and a director of National Amusements and Viacom), Norman Jacobs (Sumner's divorce lawyer), and Leonard Lewin (Phyllis's divorce lawyer). During Sumner's lifetime, he would be the sole beneficiary, though if he took any disbursements, he had to give half of the after-tax amount to Phyllis. If he died while Phyllis was still alive, half of the shares would go into a section of the trust for Phyllis's benefit, while the other half would go into a section (the General Trust) for the benefit of Brent, Shari, and their children. After Phyllis died, the remainder of the National shares would go into the General Trust, which would be overseen by two family trustees and five nonfamily trustees. Initially, the two family trustees were to be Brent and Shari, and the nonfamily trustees the same as above. (Brent's seat would change several times in future rounds of family infighting.) But from the outset, Shari had a more prominent role than her brother in the trust. So long as she was still a director of both National and Viacom at the time of her father's death, the trust stated, "Shari shall succeed [Sumner] to the Chairmanships" of both National Amusements and Viacom and hold them "for at least a three year period." The idea was to give Phyllis some comfort that her interests would be looked after at the main source of the family's wealth after Sumner died.

*   *   *

While Shari was solidifying her role as her father's successor as chairman and Brent was starting to come to terms with the new world order, Karmazin was having an increasingly hard time securing his promised position as the successor to Sumner's role as CEO. In public, Sumner tortured Karmazin by refusing to commit to renewing his three-year contract when it was due to expire at the end of 2003, or to ceding his title of CEO. It got so bad that Viacom's board at one point had to tell Sumner and Karmazin to stop fighting and run the company.

Sumner, meanwhile, had become a holy terror to the people around him. He was known to throw a steak across the room that he found not cooked to his liking, and he was banned from Le Cirque and Elio's in New York for his rudeness to the waitstaff. Once, aboard a company plane, he threw a turkey leg at a flight attendant's head after learning that it had not come from the iconic Nate'n Al Delicatessen in Beverly Hills.

People close to him theorized that some of his orneriness during these years came from his personal life. The end of his marriage to Phyllis had not brought the liberation he had craved. Instead, the photos her private investigator snapped of Sumner strolling around Paris hand in hand with Peters had come as a shock to Delsa, who had always assumed they had a relationship of mutual trust. She felt betrayed by his cheating, and even further betrayed when he asked her to do whatever it took to keep any mention of their relationship out of the press during his divorce proceedings from Phyllis, lest it be used against him to deprive him of control of Viacom. On top of it all, she was appalled to learn during Thanksgiving dinner of 2000 that Sumner, a lifelong, self-proclaimed "liberal Democrat," had voted for George W. Bush. (Some say it was because of his plans to roll back the estate tax, while others say it was more a matter of foreign policy.) After three decades together, Sumner and Delsa broke up. According to people close to both Delsa and Sumner, the fact that Delsa, despite being four years younger than Sumner, was nonetheless now in her early seventies and beginning to look her age had a lot to do with it. As Sumner once put it to one of the much, *much* younger girls he would later date, "Would *you* date someone your own age?"

Paula Fortunato was in her late thirties—nearly a decade younger than Shari—when she was set up with Sumner in 2001 by his stockbroker, Steven Sweetwood, Madeline Redstone's son. Like many people who worked closely with Sumner, Sweetwood suspected his step uncle might be happier—not to mention less of a trying curmudgeon—if he had a woman in his life. Sumner thought so, too. He was always trying to convince Christine Peters to marry him, and proposed to another striking, cosmopolitan blonde from a well-to-do Jewish Argentinian family named Manuela Herzer around the same time, bringing her to his company-owned apartment in the Pierre hotel in New York with her child and nanny in 2000. But both the blondes rebuffed his offer.

Paula, an elementary school teacher who had never married, was a completely different species than the Hollywood sophisticates Sumner had been spotting squiring around Los Angeles in the previous few years. A trim, tan brunette with dark eyes and a Julia Roberts smile, she grew up a doctor's daughter in New Jersey and bounced around to various jobs after college before finding her passion in teaching in her late twenties. When Sweetwood called about the date, she had no idea who Sumner Redstone was. "He's not a parent at the school, is he?" she told *Vanity Fair* that she asked at the time. "Because I don't date parents at the school." She reluctantly agreed to meet Sumner at Il Postino. Immediately, there were sparks. The next day, Sumner messengered over a pile of his press clippings so she would understand who he was. Soon he was picking her up from school in his limo and whisking her to dinner in Los Angeles on his private plane. After a nearly two-year courtship, they were engaged in August 2002, a month after his divorce was finalized, and married on a chilly April day in 2003 at the grand Reform Temple Emanu-El on Fifth Avenue. The bride wore a demure long-sleeved cloak over a white brocade gown, while the seventy-nine-year-old groom wore a black yarmulke, improbably bright blond hair, and a schoolboy's grin.

Of course there was a prenup. Sumner told the *New York Times* that the marriage "does not affect anything on my economic life, and Paula has made it clear she wants nothing from me." His assets after death would go to the children of his first marriage. Nevertheless, Shari was less than thrilled, not least because the marriage was soon followed by Sumner's move to Los Angeles. After all these years of earning her way into the building, the minute she got there, he decamped for the other coast with his new bride.

Sumner had actually bought the Mediterranean-style mansion in the exclusive enclave of Beverly Park, high atop the craggy hills overlooking Beverly Hills, from neighbor Sylvester Stallone before he had proposed to Paula. At one point, he even tried to convince Delsa to move to the West Coast with him, according to one person close to the family, though she demurred. Her health began to decline soon after, and she eventually moved into an assisted-living facility. But Sumner never forgot about her. He called from time to time, and every birthday or Valentine's Day, he sent her embarrassingly large bouquets of roses. Delsa would usually feign annoyance. As late as 2011, when the flowers came, Delsa's son, Winn Wittman, recalled, she opened the card and said, "Sumner, who's this guy?"

Sumner moved into the mansion with Paula and began a new life of daily nude swims in his private pool, feeding his vast collection of saltwater fish, and running his empire via phone from a soft chair in his study with a dog in his lap as CNBC blinked in the background. In the evenings, Paula, whose fit frame looked Oscar-party worthy in an evening dress, accompanied him everywhere. For a while, it seemed like he might be able to enjoy a life less consumed by conflict and conquest.

But the move to LA also separated Sumner from his roots, the Boston circles that had known his father, his cadre of lawyers, his children, most of his grandchildren, Delsa, her children, and even Phyllis, whom he had befriended again shortly after his divorce. Suddenly he was removed from anyone who could tell him no. Out there, he was just a mogul in a city full of moguls. There was nothing to do but spend his money and enjoy himself, which, in retrospect, was a very dangerous position for someone like Sumner Redstone to be in.

Within a year, he began to grow restless. It was not so much being removed from the buzzing energy of Viacom's tourist-thronged Times Square headquarters; he quite liked his placid koi ponds and Zeus's-eye view over the canyons of Los Angeles. It was the stock. For the better part of two decades, Sumner had measured his self-worth by Viacom's stock price and needed to constantly buy back Viacom shares in the way that other people needed to breathe. In February 2004, Viacom decided to rid itself of the ailing Blockbuster, whose business was being hammered by the rise of cheap DVDs. It took a $1.3 billion write-down on the business and announced a tax-free split-off, which prevented Sumner from buying back Viacom shares for much of the year. Colleagues point to this prohibition to explain Sumner's otherwise baffling decision to begin a slow-motion takeover of a beleaguered video game company that hadn't turned a profit in five years: Midway Games. As one former Viacom executive put it, "He had time on his hands."

As the company that brought the seminal Space Invaders to the United States in 1978, Midway had a venerable pedigree in a fast-growing industry that was increasingly being blamed for television's stalled ratings. But by 2004, it was still best known for its 1990s-era ultraviolent fighting game Mortal Kombat, had no titles on the list of top 20 bestsellers, and had suffered seventeen straight quarters of losses. Sumner, however, knew the management well, as he had been investing in its former parent, WMS Industries, since 1983—WMS's pinball machines were in National Amusements' movie theaters— and was convinced the company was in the midst of a turnaround. So in March 2004, he began to push his holding past 30 percent, a few percentage points at a time; by May that same year, he had control and overhauled its board. Among the first two directors he placed on the board was his daughter.

From the outside, his approach was similar to the way he initially approached Viacom, and his reasoning (when he gave it) was similar: he wanted to be in the business that he feared was killing the business he was currently in. But if his approach to buying Viacom had confused analysts in the early months, his Midway attack positively confounded them. Nobody could figure out what this wildly successful media mogul was doing with this demonstrably doomed video game company, especially if, as he claimed, he had no intention of merging it with Viacom. Even Shari, whom he soon elevated to vice chairman, seemed at a loss to explain it. "My father was originally fascinated with the company," she told the *Chicago Tribune*. "It's something that stemmed from him. I don't know what the future holds, but we have enormous confidence in Midway." To understand it better, she bought herself a PlayStation and got hooked on Psi-Ops: The Mindgate Conspiracy, a shooter game where players use psychic powers like "mind drain" and "mind control" to fight terrorists trying to take over the world. "He bought it as a plaything, and tried to manipulate the stock," said a former Viacom executive.

Some Viacom executives thought Shari was engaging in some "psi-ops" of her own when she bought an apartment overlooking Central Park in late April and told the *New York Times* that she planned to start spending a third of her time at Viacom in the fall. "It was always my intention that when the kids were grown, I would spend more time and play a more significant role at Viacom," she said. "Next year is the year I intend to start attending meetings more regularly." Sumner downplayed the significance of the move, which he had requested, emphasizing that Shari would not have an operating role. "She's doing something extremely important," he told the *Times*. "She is building relationships and building knowledge. And she is assisting Viacom." He stopped short of saying she would be named chairman, saying, "No decision has been made," but he was still in full praise mode about her running of the theaters. "If she were not doing the right job, she would not be there. She was not there a year before I could see that she was a hotshot."

If the writing was not yet etched on this particular wall, then it was in boldface on the stock price. Karmazin's arrival atop Viacom had been greeted with cheers on Wall Street, but soon after the merger with CBS transformed the company into the biggest advertising player in the country, the United States slid into a prolonged advertising recession. Viacom missed its earnings targets from 2001 to 2003, and its stock price remained stalled for three years. By June 2004, the price had declined 20 percent over the past year, dragged down by the slowing ad sales in its radio division, which was most closely associated with Karmazin. The people who worked under Karmazin described him as a good boss and a straight shooter, with a wisecracking fearlessness that endeared him to his troops, but Sumner had grown to loathe him.

Against this backdrop, the *Times* story caused a sensation. Nine days after it was published, Viacom held its annual shareholders meeting, and Sumner spent much of it fending off questions about his relationship with Karmazin. After the meeting, Karmazin told a few board members he wanted to leave. The next day, after attending an "up-front" advertiser presentation for Viacom's struggling homegrown television network, the United Paramount Network, at Madison Square Garden, Karmazin walked back to his office, called his lawyer, and told him to tell Viacom that he was resigning. Karmazin walked away with a $30 million exit package and never had to have the awkward conversation with Sumner. He would later explain his decision as a response to the constant speculation about his future there, telling *USA Today*, "I didn't want another summer of Sumner and Mel." But he also admitted that questions about the role that Shari would play were "part of the stuff that was going on," adding, "Sumner has control and can do anything he wants." As long as Sumner was the controlling shareholder, he told the *Journal*, "there is never going to be a succession."

As predictable as Karmazin's exit was, its exact timing came as a surprise, and Viacom executives asked Karmazin to keep his exit under his hat until they could come up with a succession plan. Immediately after word had begun to leak out from the board that Karmazin was planning to leave, Sumner summoned Freston to his apartment at the Carlyle to deliver the bombshell: "Karmafuck is going to go, and I want you to be the CEO of the company." Freston wasn't sure what to say.

"At every point in my life, I've always done exactly what I wanted to do, and I somehow fell into this thing on MTV Networks, which was everything I loved and cared about," Freston said. "It was a creative business. We were building stuff. It wasn't like pulling corporate levers. I'd been around enough to see what a public company CEO did. I didn't want to get farther away from the creative process and put up there."

His mind was racing. Sumner, who could be exceedingly charming when he wanted to be, laid it on thick, praising Freston as the guy who had delivered for Viacom. As chairman and CEO of MTV Networks, Freston had long been responsible for the largest and fastest-growing profit engine in the company. The numbers were extraordinary: MTV Networks had revenue of roughly $100 million when Sumner took over in 1987 and elevated Freston; it now brought in more than $3.5 billion from a sprawling global network of channels and merchandising deals. He was the rare executive who was both respected and beloved in the industry, harnessing the power of the growth of pay television in the United States to nurture a creative culture that had shaped American society. Through it all, he maintained his countercultural credentials, spending his free time hanging out with the likes of the Flaming Lips and organizing music festivals in Senegal.

Freston felt flattered but cornered. "Let me think about it and be back to you tomorrow," Freston told Sumner.

Sumner, who abided waiting so little that his dining companions felt pressured to have their orders already queued up in their minds before sitting down to dinner with him, was not about to give Freston the requested twenty-four hours. Annoyed that Freston didn't leap at the chance to be CEO, he turned around that same day and offered the job to Leslie Moonves, the highly competitive, politically savvy chairman and chief executive of CBS.

A former actor with a deep tan and a salesman's smile, Moonves approached programming as a showman, lifting the CBS network from third to first place, thanks to hits like *CSI* and *Survivor*. He grew up middle class in Valley Stream, Long Island, the son of a psychiatric nurse and the owner of a group of gas stations. He started out studying premed at Bucknell University but decided instead that he wanted to be an actor, moving to Greenwich Village and supporting himself as a bartender while auditioning for parts.

After landing parts in shows like *The Six Million Dollar Man*, he moved into the business side of television, rising steadily through the ranks of Twentieth Century Fox, Lorimar Television, and Warner Bros. Television, where he developed megahits like *Friends* and *ER*. In 1995, he took over the CBS network, then in last place with the oldest audience on television. Using his considerable programming instincts, he turned it around and in the process earned a reputation as "the man with the golden gut," as superagent Ari Emanuel put it. But behind the scenes, Moonves was a meticulous workaholic, even a bit of a micromanager, sending emails at all hours and showing up to casting calls for CBS shows.

Moonves, naturally, accepted immediately. The next day, as Moonves was performing his annual boasting ritual at the CBS up-front sales presentations for advertisers at Carnegie Hall ("Make no mistake about it," Moonves declared from the podium. "We at CBS show across-the-board growth; everyone else is down in all categories!"), Freston called Sumner to accept the job. Sumner told him he'd already offered it to

Moonves. "I told you to give me a day, for God's sake!" Freston said. "A day's not even up yet." Freston had been like a son to Sumner, so Sumner decided to split the baby, making them co-COOs.

Freston and Moonves carved up the company between them. Freston got to add Paramount and Simon & Schuster to his portfolio at MTV Networks, while Moonves added the radio and billboard businesses to his CBS TV holdings. Among other things, the arrangement meant that Paramount's Jonathan Dolgen, the financially savvy, innovative cost-cutter to whom Sumner spoke by phone multiple times a day, would leave the company. Sumner said he would break the news to Dolgen but failed to do so, leaving it to Freston to awkwardly explain why Dolgen's name was left out of the press release announcing the changes.

In late May 2004, Viacom executives worked out an announcement knowing that it would shock Wall Street. It was to be released just after Memorial Day weekend: Karmazin had resigned as president and chief operating officer, Freston and Moonves were promoted to share those titles, and Sumner had agreed that he would hand over his CEO post by 2007. But just as Sumner was busy carving up his empire and laying out a new succession plan in the same fast-and-loose manner he'd done in so many of his previous business maneuvers, tragedy struck.

CHAPTER 15

"Sumner in a Skirt"

Adam Redstone's life was just beginning to turn around. The toddler who had been left behind when Sumner's estranged niece, Ruth Ann, had died in Japan had spent his teenage years in and out of the best drug treatment programs that his grandparents' money could buy—Hazelden, Betty Ford Clinic, Gray Wolf Ranch—as well as the occasional jail cell. But by age twenty, he had gotten sober, enrolled in community college in Los Angeles, and, a few weeks before his twenty-first birthday, been accepted at the Otis College of Art and Design, where he hoped that the large canvases he had been painting to hang in his friend's warehouse would set the path toward a career as an artist. "He'd lend a friend bail if they got caught smoking weed, but he never talked about having money," said Charmaine Reroma, who met Adam at a yacht party and dated him for about a year. With a surfer's drawl that belied his privileged Yankee upbringing at schools like Milton Academy, gym-tended muscles, and a swoop of brown hair, he was popular with the ladies, whom he liked to take on high-speed joyrides down the Sunset Strip in his Ford F-150.

But his real love, outside of painting, was motorcycles. On May 24, 2004, he was heading toward the California State College, Northridge, campus on his yellow Ducati when a drunk driver pulled out of an El Pollo Loco and hit him, knocking him off his bike and crushing his rib cage.

Eddie and Madeline were asleep when the call came from the hospital. Madeline immediately knew something was wrong when she looked at the clock: eleven thirty p.m. "No one calls us that late," she would later say. A woman from Northridge Hospital explained that

Adam had been in an accident. Madeline started to scream, "We'll be there, we'll be there!" But Eddie already knew it was too late. "He started to collapse," Madeline later recounted. For her part, Madeline had to wait for the voice on the other end to say it before it sunk in: "He didn't survive."

While Madeline snapped into action mode, talking to the coroner's office and making arrangements, "Eddie was just comatose," Madeline recalled. "He lost his daughter and now he lost her son." Adam had been Eddie's second chance at parenthood, and Eddie had been determined to correct the mistakes he had made with his own children, when he had been too busy with National Amusements to be a truly present father. He had left the isolation of his beloved Martha's Vineyard for Concord so that Adam might have a chance at a "normal" childhood. They took him on skiing trips and on safari, and Madeline—the more athletically inclined of the couple—coached his football and baseball teams. When they began to suspect that his wealthy friends at Milton Academy had introduced him to drugs, they begged the school to drug-test him, and when he was later expelled, they whisked him to Hazelden, beginning a long odyssey of drug treatment programs. Even when those difficult years forced them to adopt "tough love" tactics, they never stopped believing he was a talented, good-hearted kid, eventually adopting him in 2002. His early years with the cult had left their imprint. He was afraid of men in suits and would speak of being locked in rooms and exposed to dogfights. But Eddie and Madeline were sure they could overcome any of this. "We were inseparable," Eddie said. "I mean emotionally inseparable."

Adam's death was more than just an emotional problem for the family. When Ruth Ann died, her untouched trust passed down to her son, but when he suddenly died with no heirs or estate, the documents were somewhat unclear about where, exactly, the money—by now worth nearly $25 million across three trusts—was supposed to go. A significant portion of it was due to go to Ruth Ann's brother, Michael, whose toxic relationship with his father had never really improved.

On Thursday, May 27, Eddie and Madeline flew back to Boston with

Adam's body, where they sat shivah for five days at their home in the Four Seasons Residences, the swank residential tower overlooking Boston Public Garden. Friends and family flew in from all over the country to comfort and feed them. By Sunday, the day of the funeral, even the oft-warring Redstone clan had gathered in its near entirety at Adam's graveside in the verdant, historic Temple Israel Cemetery in Wakefield, Massachusetts, near Congregation Kerem Shalom, the synagogue in Concord where Adam had been bar mitzvahed: Sumner and Paula; Phyllis, her sister, Cecelie, and brother-in-law, Ralph; Brent and Annie and their children, Keryn and Lee Lee; Shari and her children, Kim, Brandon, and Tyler; Madeline and Eddie and Madeline's three children from her first marriage. The only person missing was Michael, who later explained that his son had his college graduation that day in Worcester. Madeline and Eddie were furious at his absence.

A month later, they filed a lawsuit to block some of the money from Adam's trusts from going to Michael, asking to first be paid back for some of the expenses they had incurred while raising Adam. "They had been paying Adam's expenses because he was their son, and they wanted to keep the money [in the trust] for Adam to have. But once the money was no longer going to Adam, then they wanted to be reimbursed before it was absorbed back into all the other trusts," explained Howard Castleman, Madeline and Eddie's lawyer. The lawsuit wound on for years, roping in many members of the Redstone family and resulting in only a partial victory. Along the way, the discovery process dredged up documents revealing to younger generations the settlement that Sumner and Eddie had made when Eddie left National Amusements in 1972, and details about how Sumner went about buying out Michael's and Ruth Ann's National Amusements stakes in 1984. Those files would lay the foundation for future lawsuits that would threaten Sumner's control of his empire and sunder his relationship with every member of the next generation of his family, except for his daughter, Shari.

*   *   *

After the family threw dirt on Adam's grave, Sumner and Paula ducked out early, skipping the reception back at the Four Seasons. Sumner had work to do. Two days later, he was on the phone with analysts, trying to soothe their shock at the sudden departure of Karmazin. "Nobody asked for Mel's resignation," he said. Freston and Moonves, who were friends, vowed that their bake-off would be a "partnership," not an episode of *The Apprentice*. The performance worked, and Wall Street mostly shrugged at the drama, sending Viacom's stock down only a few cents, to $36.50.

The problem was that it then barely budged for nearly a year—and that price was well below the $46.30 a share that Viacom was trading at on the day after the CBS deal was announced. "There are an awful lot of people here whose stock options are underwater," one executive whispered to the *New York Times*. The biggest media merger of the twentieth century had destroyed shareholder value.

A growing chorus within the building argued there was nothing left to do but undo it. Its leader was Bob Bakish, the former consultant who had been promoted from overseeing ad sales at MTV Networks to executive vice president with responsibilities for strategic planning in the reshuffle that followed Freston's elevation. He was joined by an army of investment bankers from Morgan Stanley, Bear Stearns, Citibank, and Lazard, who argued that the best way to "unlock shareholder value," as the corporate cliché goes, was to separate the high-growth assets like MTV Networks from the slow-growth assets like radio and the CBS broadcast network. This tidy plan had the benefit of sparing Sumner the unpleasant task of having to choose between Freston and Moonves. Each would get his own public company to run as CEO, and Sumner would remain controlling shareholder and chairman of both. One analyst dubbed the companies ViaGrow and ViaSlow.

Bakish's team mapped out which assets belonged on which side of the divide based on their growth rate. That meant that Simon & Schuster, which had been under Freston but was growing at the modest rate of a "mature" business, got handed over to Moonves. Ditto Showtime. This decision left more than a few analysts scratching their heads,

since a movie-filled premium cable network had more obvious synergies with Freston's cable channels and Paramount. Freston got Paramount's film studio on the strength of his pitch that he would make
movies out of MTV Networks' intellectual property, but Paramount
TV went to Moonves. Moonves put a positive spin on the situation,
saying his slower-growing, cash-rich businesses would allow him to
pay out more dividends, but privately he fumed at the characterization
of his side of the company as a "value" stock.

Sometimes it seemed like Moonves couldn't catch a break. When it
came time to divvy up the company's two Bombardier Global Express
private planes—identical save that one was old and the other brand-
new with a five-year warranty—both wanted the new plane, which
was worth about $2 million more. They decided to flip a coin. Freston
won the new plane.

*   *   *

With the split, finally, came a legitimate succession plan. The same
day the Viacom board voted to cleave off CBS from the company, it
voted to make Shari nonexecutive vice chairman of both Viacom and
CBS. Rumors swirled that she had refused to bless the split until she
was guaranteed such a post, but in fact Sumner had been pressing
her to take the vice chairman role for years. Shari, wary of titles and
the commitment to half a dozen board meetings a year in New York
while still feeling she needed to be home to cook dinner every night
for her kids back in Boston, had balked in the past, going so far as to
suggest having the conversation over dinner at Blu at the Ritz-Carlton
in Boston, in hopes that being in a public place would make him
less likely to make a scene when told no. But by 2005, with her kids
out of the house, her father playing the newlywed out in California,
and Karmazin's star on the wane, she had already begun spending
about half her time in New York. She was ready to take on the mantle, and her father finally seemed ready to give it to her. After years
of hemming and hawing about how the matter "has not even been
discussed," Sumner began stating openly that when—not *if*—he died,

Shari would take over his role as controlling shareholder. "Sooner or later, no matter how good I look and how good my vital signs are, I'm gonna die and control of the company is likely to pass to Shari," he told the *Los Angeles Times*. It was at this moment that Shari, with her auburn hair, Boston accent, and fierce negotiating style, was given a nickname by a former Viacom executive in the *Wall Street Journal* that stuck: "Sumner in a skirt."

*   *   *

Once she had the vice chairman's megaphone, she was not afraid to use it to disagree with her father. But she would learn that her dissenting opinions held little weight. It was the people who agreed with Sumner who got the power. Within a month of her becoming vice chairman, Viacom's loss of MySpace to archrival Rupert Murdoch would deliver an object lesson in this dynamic, with disastrous consequences for the future of both the company and her family.

It wasn't necessarily a given that MTV Networks would lose its young audience to the Internet. In early 1999, a year before the transformational AOL–Time Warner merger put all media companies on notice that they needed an aggressive online strategy, Freston gathered his channel chiefs and digital executives together to discuss the online future. "He believed that the Internet wasn't just a transitory medium and that it was really going to be a powerful medium for the whole entertainment industry, especially in the music space," Nicholas Butterworth, president of the MTVi Group, a division combining the online presences of channels like MTV with recent digital acquisition SonicNet, told *MediaWeek* in 2000. Despite the major challenge of the record companies' reluctance to give MTV the digital rights to their music videos, Freston had some reason to be optimistic: MTV.com was the top music entertainment site on the Internet, VH1 showed up in the top 10 less than a year after it was launched, and pageviews for the group had tripled over the past year.

With an eye toward the soaring valuations of online companies, MTVi filed paperwork that February for a $10 million initial public offering, projecting it would double its revenue to $40 million over the next year, even as its losses were widening. But just as they were starting out on their road show, the dot-com bubble burst. MTVi pulled its IPO and soon fired a quarter of its four-hundred-person staff. "We had, like, four different people reviewing the Nelly album," explained a Viacom spokesman.

The crash, followed by the apocalyptic collapse of the AOL–Time Warner merger, spooked Viacom, as well as many of its competitors, from the online space for years. The company woke up in 2004 realizing it didn't have a digital strategy.

At the same moment, as chronicled in Julia Angwin's *Stealing MySpace*, MTV Networks executives began to notice that fans of its shows were hanging out on MySpace, which had just surpassed Friendster as the largest social network by pageviews. In July 2004, MTV Networks digital executive Nick Lehman walked into his boss Jason Hirschhorn's office and showed him that one of the most popular areas of MySpace was devoted to the MTV show *Laguna Beach*. He explained how social networks worked and told his boss that he believed they were the future home of MTV's audience.

Hirschhorn agreed. "MTV of the future needed to be the platform where the audience told each other what was cool," he said. When Freston and Moonves held a "digital show-and-tell" in August 2004 for all the divisions of Viacom to present their ideas for the company's digital strategy, Hirschhorn included MySpace, as well as the gaming website IGN, on the list of companies he wanted to buy. Freston, who had declared he wanted 15 percent of the company's revenues coming from digital in five years, told him to go for it. In early December, Hirschhorn called up MySpace cofounder Chris DeWolfe and requested a meeting. Soon a parade of MTV executives were tromping through MySpace's hip Santa Monica offices, waxing nostalgic about how much it reminded them of the funky chaos of MTV's early days. Like pre-Redstone MTV Networks, MySpace hated their corporate overlords at Intermix Media, a bizarre grab bag of a marketing company whose biggest winners included wrinkle cream and diet pills.

For MTV Networks, it seemed like the perfect match. MySpace wasn't just the biggest social network; it was a cultural fit. While Friendster had the feel of an earnest dating profile and still-emerging Facebook was born in a nerd's Harvard dorm, MySpace was heavily used by bands, and its open code that allowed people to customize their pages with seizure-inducing animation and music gave the whole site a nightclub vibe.

But Viacom's legal department, led by Michael Fricklas, had qualms. They worried that the company might be sued for copyright infringement for the remixes that people were posting to their profiles. They feared that advertisers would balk at placing ads next to user-generated content they didn't control. And most of all, after New York attorney general Eliot Spitzer filed a lawsuit in April 2005 against Intermix, alleging it had installed spyware on its users' computers without their knowledge, they worried that a lot of MySpace's eye-popping traffic was bogus. Although Intermix settled with Spitzer by June, according to one person familiar with Viacom's view, "that investigation raised a question about whether a lot of the so-called traffic was really spyware or malware sitting on people's computers generating traffic."

Nevertheless, Viacom, recognizing that Intermix controlled MySpace, decided to pursue a deal with Intermix, flying a team including executive vice president of operations Bob Bakish out to California for an initial due diligence meeting on July 7, 2005. Viacom had no idea that Intermix, wary that the closeness between MTV and MySpace might prompt Viacom to make a bid for the social network alone without its parent company, had given the same pitch a week before to Rupert Murdoch's News Corp.

Sumner had long regarded Murdoch as his biggest rival. In part, it was because they were so similar. Each had taken his father's regional media business and built it into a global media and entertainment colossus, all the while maintaining absolute control long into old age. Both by then had considerably younger wives. And both were grooming their children to take over their empires, though Murdoch seemed far more dedicated to this last point than Sumner ever did.

What Sumner most envied about Murdoch's family was not the way that he successfully prepared his children for operating roles in his companies but that his mother was still alive to see her son's glory. "The thing that used to drive him crazy was Murdoch's mother walking around, lucid," said one former Viacom executive. (Dame Elisabeth Murdoch died in 2012 at the age of 103.) The only thing that drove him crazier was losing a deal to Murdoch.

Over a frantic two weeks in early July, both Viacom and News Corp pursued Intermix, with Viacom never knowing that News Corp's new digital strategist, Ross Levinsohn, had gotten a few days' jump on them. On July 12, 2005, News Corp beat Viacom to the punch with an "exploding" offer of $580 million in cash, meaning the terms would only hold until the end of the week. Intermix CEO Richard Rosenblatt called Freston, who was on vacation at the Four Seasons Resort in Maui, to alert him to the offer, thinking he was starting an auction. But Freston didn't take the bait. Viacom's deals team was still in the final stages of doing due diligence and planned to make an offer after the company's board meeting in the middle of the following week. He didn't believe that Murdoch could really get the deal done by the end of the week, since it was in Intermix's interest to have multiple bidders. What Freston and the rest of Viacom did not know was that Intermix had an obscure clause in its arrangement with MySpace that gave it an incentive to take the first offer that came along, lest it risk triggering MySpace's right to go sell itself directly. On Monday, July 18, 2005, News Corp announced that it had agreed to purchase MySpace owner Intermix for a 20 percent premium over its stock price. MTV Networks executives were stunned. "He came in on a weekend, no due diligence, and just bought it for $580 million," Freston recalls. "Just bought it." (A person familiar with News Corp said they did do due diligence.)

Two days later, Freston and his fellow MTV Networks executives went before Viacom's board to beg Sumner to counterbid. Freston noted that there was plenty of room to keep bidding as MTV Networks' internal valuations were as high as $810 million. "What took so long?" Shari said, according to Angwin. "We should have had this already." She said she supported a counterbid. Alan "Ace" Greenberg, one of Sumner's most trusted investment banking advisers, also supported a counterbid, but Sumner did not. "Rupert is not afraid of overpaying," he said. "He doesn't care about the market, and he will outbid us." Dauman agreed, and that was the end of it.

A few months later, the whole painful episode repeated itself when News Corp swooped in and snatched IGN, the unprofitable gaming media company that had been on Hirschhorn's wish list, for $650 million. This time, Freston went to Sumner to personally apologize and explained the structural problem of not having Viacom's deals team reporting to him. Sumner said he would just have to wait until he got his own CEO title in January, when the companies split.

A few years later, News Corp would off-load both of these purchases in a fire sale, each for under $100 million, but people close to Viacom's deal-making say MySpace's descent into tawdry, ad-choked irrelevance was not inevitable. "MySpace under Tom Freston would have been a home run," said one senior Viacom official.

Again and again, Viacom showed that it had the tuned-in talent to identify where media was going in the Internet age but not the corporate nimbleness to execute deals at the speed that age required. It did make a few small digital purchases, but the misses outweighed the hits. As infamous as the MySpace miss would soon become, the biggest miss of all was yet to come.

By Thanksgiving of 2005, MTV Networks was intent on buying Facebook. Earlier in the year, MTV strategy chief Denmark West had informally offered to buy the not-yet-two-year-old site for $75 million, which was rejected, and in the process had gotten word that Facebook founder Mark Zuckerberg only wanted to deal with other CEOs. So Freston welcomed Zuckerberg—in flip-flops, in February, in New York—and pitched him on the overlap between MTV's and Facebook's audiences. According to David Kirkpatrick's *The Facebook Effect*, Freston even suggested he could help Facebook develop content for his platform, an idea Zuckerberg dismissed, saying, "We think of ourselves as a utility." One Viacom executive described it as a "no-thank-you meeting." But MTV Networks' new president, Michael Wolf, formerly a well-known media industry consultant, was not about to give up. He had seen the data from MTV's focus groups of college students, who talked constantly about Facebook, and took to IM'ing Zuckerberg to set up dinners near Facebook's headquarters in Palo Alto, which he would then fly out to attend. Wanting to get a sustained stretch of the young CEO's attention, he devised a plan to offer him a ride home for the holidays on the Viacom plane, which Zuckerberg accepted. Before Zuckerberg's parents picked him up at the Westchester County Airport in their minivan, Wolf and Zuckerberg talked about just how much Facebook's audience loved MTV shows like *Laguna Beach*. Zuckerberg had told Wolf he believed his company, which was projecting $20 million in revenues for 2006 and essentially no profit, was worth $2 billion.

Soon after, Viacom made a bona fide offer to buy Facebook for $1.5 billion—a little over half up front and the rest earn-out. As Kirkpatrick noted, "It was by far the most serious and concrete offer Facebook had ever received." MTV and Facebook's deal teams negotiated for weeks. Zuckerberg wanted more cash up front. Wolf got the number up to $800 million but couldn't justify going beyond that for a company with no revenue. As the talks faded, Facebook announced it had raised a $25 million round of venture capital and that it had never been for sale.

Freston did bag one critical deal for his side of the company before stepping out into the glare of the Wall Street spotlight. As confident as he was about his ability to run MTV Networks, which brought in most of the revenue and nearly all the profits on his side of the company, he was worried about Paramount, which was in a slump. Earlier in the year, at media magnate David Geffen's suggestion, he had surprised Hollywood insiders by tapping Brad Grey to run the studio. Grey was the talent manager of clients like Brad Pitt and Jennifer Aniston, and he had helped bring groundbreaking shows like *The Sopranos* to television. He had a reputation as a savvy deal maker but lacked studio experience. His mandate was a top-to-bottom overhaul of the studio, but that would take time. In the near term, they needed films, and fast. When Grey caught wind that DreamWorks SKG, the studio that Geffen cofounded with Steven Spielberg and Jeffrey Katzenberg, had run into a snag in its talks to sell itself to General Electric's NBC Universal, he took the opportunity to Freston, who approved a plan for Viacom to try to buy it.

Around midnight on December 8, 2005, Freston secretly boarded a private plane to Los Angeles with the aim of swooping in with a last-minute offer to buy DreamWorks. Over sandwiches at Spielberg's house overlooking the Pacific Ocean, he made a successful pitch, and two days later the companies announced that DreamWorks would be sold to Viacom for $774 million, plus the assumption of $840 million in debt. (Sumner worried about the size of the deal, so Freston rounded up outside investors to fund $1 billion of the $1.6 billion.) Viacom might get beaten on the tech pitch, but here in the halls of old media, where relationships and deference to talent are everything, GE's obtuse number crunching had nothing on Freston's charm. The deal included an agreement for Spielberg and Geffen to produce four to six movies a year, a godsend to bolster Paramount's thin slate.

*   *   *

Shari, too, was preparing for the split, recruiting independent directors for the boards of newly separate Viacom and CBS, including significantly more women and Robert Kraft, a friend and owner of her beloved New England Patriots. But before she could formally assume her roles in the new companies, she would have to do a more unpleasant bit of family empire housekeeping.

Since beginning to ramp up his share two years earlier, Sumner had grown increasingly obsessed with Midway Games. All through 2005, he continued to buy the stock until he owned 89 percent of the company, pushing the stock price up 81 percent in the process. "The prime reason for the stock's run has been Redstone," said one analyst. "There are few other buyers of the stock." The Redstones wanted to replace unprofitable Midway's management, but before they could, Sumner ran into debt problems. He had borrowed $425 million from Citicorp to buy Midway stock using National Amusements stock as collateral, and as Midway delivered a series of disappointing earnings in 2005, Citicorp issued a margin call, which meant Citicorp could have seized Sumner's shares of National Amusements. Sumner asked National Amusements to bail him out by buying the stock. Shari, as a minority owner of National Amusements, agreed to do the deal on the provision that she be given full control of National's Midway holdings and National never again be put in a position where it had to buy Midway stock. In a document filed with the Security and Exchange Commission at the end of 2005, Sumner and Shari agreed that if Sumner wanted to buy more Midway stock, he'd have to do it with his own money, not the family fortune. Sumner abruptly stopped buying, and Midway's share price plummeted 50 percent in the next two months.

While Sumner was watching the more than $500 million he had pumped into his plaything evaporate, his broader empire was hit with its most serious blow to date. Out of the blue, Brent, armed with the documents unearthed in Eddie and Madeline's lawsuit, sued his father, alleging a campaign to freeze him out of the empire and demanding that his father's $8 billion media empire be dissolved so that he might be able to walk away with his one-sixth share. Brent's list of grievances against his father was long, including kicking him off the Viacom board, failing to give him adequate information about National Amusements' business so he was forced to abstain when voting on issues, and failing to ever declare a dividend "despite monumental profits." He complained about Sumner's favoritism to both Shari and her ex, accusing Sumner of self-dealing when he "caused NAI to gratuitously award a severance package worth millions of dollars to Ira Korff." High on the list was the Midway debacle. Brent again accused his father of self-dealing when he borrowed $425 million from Citigroup "and then arranged an NAI bailout of his loan and repayment of his debt in exchange for stock, much of which he had acquired with the loan proceeds."

Among the most interesting aspects of the complaint was its straightforward declaration that Sumner had "repeatedly" told Brent and Shari that they would "run the company." The documents from Eddie and Madeline's lawsuit had only strengthened this sense of birthright: Mickey had set up the Grandchildren's Trust clearly wanting the company to be passed down from one generation to the next. "Plaintiff shared these expectations."

Brent did not succeed in breaking up his family's media empire, but he would eventually walk away with a $240 million settlement. He would never speak to his father again.

CHAPTER 16

"This Is Crazy!"

On Tuesday, August 22, 2006, Tom Freston, now a public company CEO, was taxiing onto the Van Nuys runway in Los Angeles in his new Global Express when his flip phone rang. The stunned voice of Carole Robinson, his head of communications, informed him that Sumner had just given an impromptu interview to the *Wall Street Journal* declaring that Paramount was firing Tom Cruise, its biggest star, over concerns that his increasingly erratic behavior had dampened the box office for *Mission Impossible III*. "It's nothing to do with his acting ability," Sumner told the *Journal*. "But we don't think that someone who effectuates creative suicide and costs the company revenue should be on the lot." Freston, livid, called Sumner.

"This is crazy!" he said. "First of all, you can't fire Tom Cruise, because he doesn't work for us. And even if he did work for us, and if we were going to fire him, it should be done by Brad Grey who runs the studio, not by you, not by me." Cruise was the cornerstone of the Paramount library—why would Sumner want to diminish him? Sumner countered that he controlled the company and could do anything he wanted to do. Freston started pacing up and down the aisle, yelling, "You can't do this! This is bullshit! This is crazy!"

It was their first screaming fight in twenty years of working together, and it was a doozy. Sumner was famous for bellowing at underlings, but he had an almost paternal relationship with Freston, with whom he dined often and considered one of his dearest friends. Back in the 1990s, during Sumner's first trip to Asia, Freston had even, at Sumner's request, taken Sumner and Delsa around the sex clubs of

Bangkok. (The sight of a naked, fornicating couple descending from the ceiling atop a Harley-Davidson would be Sumner's first taste of commercial sex but not his last.) But Freston was now in the most famously dangerous job in media: CEO of Sumner Redstone's Viacom.

It wasn't going especially well. After all the talk of how Freston's side of the company was going to grow fast while Moonves's was going to crawl, the opposite had happened: CBS's stock was up almost 8 percent since the start of the year, while Viacom's, battered by a sector-wide cable advertising slowdown, was down almost 12 percent. Freston now walked into his office every morning to a stack of angry faxes from Sumner, wanting to know why the stock was down a few cents. His first quarterly earnings surprised investors with a 10 percent decline in profit, in part due to the loss of an advertiser in Germany that Wall Street wasn't expecting, leaving analysts grumbling that Freston could have communicated with them better. And the annual spring "up-front" advertising sales season was soft, stoking fears that MTV was losing its youth marketing mojo to upstarts like YouTube. By July, just six months into his tenure, analyst Rich Greenfield declared, "If Mr. Freston cannot swiftly reorient Viacom, Sumner Redstone and the board need to find a new CEO." To top it all off, Rupert Murdoch had appeared on the cover of July's *Wired* magazine in a pinstripe suit behind the giant word "MySpace." The title of the largely laudatory piece? "His Space."

Freston wasn't the only one who thought firing Tom Cruise was crazy. For decades, Cruise had been a money-minting machine for Paramount, hauling in some $3 billion from films like *Top Gun, The Firm*, and the Mission Impossible franchise. He was paid handsomely for it: Paramount paid him and his business partner, Paula Wagner, up to $10 million a year to develop films, and he got an enormous 20 percent cut of gross box office revenues from his movies, not to mention a substantial portion of DVD sales. But over the past year, his fiercely disciplined facade had begun to slip. He became more outspoken in his promotion of Scientology, went on the *Today* show and criticized Brooke Shields for using antidepressants for her postpartum depression, and became an object of Internet mockery when a clip of him jumping on Oprah Winfrey's couch declaring his love for Katie Holmes became a viral sensation.

Sumner said it was his wife Paula who had first understood the impact this behavior was having on Viacom's bottom line. "Paula, like women everywhere, had come to hate him," he told *Vanity Fair*. He claimed the nearly $400 million box office haul from *Mission Impossible III* would have been $100 million higher had Cruise not alienated female fans. In fact, Paramount already had been working on a more graceful way to lower its Cruise-related costs, putting a lowball offer of around $2 million on the table as the deadline to renew his production deal loomed. When his production company didn't respond, it seemed like Cruise would exit the lot quietly. (Indeed, Wagner said later that they weren't fired but quit.) But then Sumner went public in a massive breach of Hollywood protocol that undercut both Grey and Freston. The news shot through Hollywood like a bolt of lightning, confirming the suspicions of the growing number of entertainment industry players who had lately spotted the octogenarian tottering into walls or wandering disoriented into the kitchens of posh Beverly Hills eateries. As Hollywood's best-sourced and most savage chronicler, Nikki Finke, put it: "If I were a Viacom shareholder, I'd be asking Ol' Sumner right now: Are you nuts?"

Little did Freston know when he was arguing with Sumner on the tarmac that he was already toast. A week before, Sumner had offered Freston's job to Dauman. Sumner would later claim that the decision was the result of weeks of deliberation at the board, where they weighed Freston's strengths and weaknesses against Dauman's. But other board members remember no such deliberation, only a hastily arranged conference call at five p.m. on Labor Day during which the board voted to buy out Freston's $60 million contract.

Freston truly didn't see it coming. An hour after the board vote, Sumner called Freston and asked him to come to his house in Beverly Park but got voice mail. Freston was busy enjoying the final hours of summer playing tennis with Yahoo! CEO Terry Semel at Bob Evans's

estate. When Freston did finally call Sumner back, Sumner asked him
to come by the mansion. When he got there, Sumner was waiting in
the living room with a press release, near tears. "Sit down," Sumner
said. "I've got really bad news for the both of us. The board of directors
has decided that you have to go." The implication was that the decision was somehow outside of Sumner's hands. "*Firing* me?" Freston
said, stunned. It had only been eight months. Just six weeks earlier,
Sumner had told the *Wall Street Journal* that it would take at least a
year to evaluate the success of the split and that there was "no circumstance" in which he could see himself ousting Freston.

Freston got up calmly and left without looking at the press release, so Viacom spokesman Carl Folta had to call him later to go
over whether he wanted to say he quit or was fired. They went with
"resigned," and Freston contributed a classy, if implausible, kicker
quote: "I have worked closely with Philippe Dauman and Tom Dooley
over the years and have the highest respect for their abilities. I have
every confidence that Viacom is well positioned to prosper under
Philippe's leadership." The sting of this final indignity was soothed
by an $85 million severance.

The press release that went out the next morning announcing Dauman and Dooley's return from the wilderness to become Viacom's
chief executive and chief administrative officer was a masterwork of
corporate propaganda, but it did contain one revealing comment from
Sumner praising them as the executives "with whom I shared the
most productive and successful period in Viacom's history." Sumner
desperately missed the late '90s, those go-go years when Viacom's
stock price tripled, powered by the juggernaut of MTV Networks. In
an effort to reclaim them, he had split the company. But the rise in
pay-TV subscribership that had fueled that growth—from 56 percent
of American households in 1990 to 83 percent by 2000—had already
begun to reverse by 2004.

Despite Sumner's nostalgic note, the regime change was sold as a
remedy to the perception that Viacom was losing on the digital front.
"We have to be more plugged in," Dauman told analysts. There was

truth to the criticism. MTV still claimed eighty-two million monthly viewers on television, but online, the four million monthly unique visitors who came to its MTV Overdrive video site were a fraction of the fifty-five million stopping by MySpace each month. But Sumner's digital beef seemed more personal than industrial. "Before Rupert got into the act, MySpace was sitting there for $500 million. Tom never took it," he told Charlie Rose. "It was a humiliating experience."

Sumner suggested that Dauman and Dooley's time as private equity investors gave them "important insights that will enable us to better navigate the digital transition and prudently capture the enormous opportunities that are clearly out there." But their firm, DND Capital Partners, was mostly known for investing in start-up cable television channels like the Tennis Channel. It soon became clear that the most important word in Sumner's previous phrase was "prudently": he had no intention of opening his wallet for a transformational digital deal. "I would not consider Facebook because we looked at it, it's a great company, [but] we thought the price was too high," he told Charlie Rose not long afterward. "We are not going to overpay! . . . We are very financially disciplined." Six months before, Facebook had done a fundraising round at a valuation of $500 million. Today, its market capitalization is around $500 billion, thirty-seven times the size of Viacom.

If the news of Tom Cruise's firing was like a bolt of lightning through Hollywood, Tom Freston's firing was an atom bomb. It's hard to overstate how beloved and respected Freston was in every corner of the media industry, and even harder to find someone in a position of power in the business who does not claim to be his friend. In the wake of his firing, Oprah, Bono, Steve Jobs, Bill Gates, and Rupert Murdoch all beat a path to his door. At a previously scheduled roast of Freston a few weeks later, News Corp president Peter Chernin joked, "How bad it must feel for Tom to be screwed over by a man so old that he needed a little blue pill to do it."

Wall Street wasn't impressed, either. Viacom's stock dropped 6 percent on the news of Freston's ouster, as analysts took the move as evidence that Tom Cruise wasn't the only one walking around the

Paramount lot exhibiting some erratic behavior. Merrill Lynch analyst Jessica Reif Cohen downgraded Viacom's stock, citing the new management team's lack of operational experience and unwelcome impression that this was "an attempt by Mr. Redstone to reassert himself in an operating role." Bruce Greenwald, a finance professor at Columbia University, summed up the overall response to the *New York Times*: "I think that Sumner has just lost it."

Privately, Sumner expressed reservations at the time to some of his closest advisers about naming Dauman to the CEO job. "He said, 'I don't have a first choice. I don't have a best choice. I would prefer to have somebody who is reliable that I can lean on to the unknown.' He saw that there were reservations there," said one family adviser.

But the full extent of Sumner's mistake was not apparent until Thursday, Freston's last day in the office. As he emerged from the elevator into the lobby for the last time, he was greeted by a mob of more than a thousand employees, jamming the lobby so full they had to spill out onto the Times Square sidewalk, cheering, crying, and chanting his name. He stopped, said a few words, and received many hugs. "People were weeping, screaming," one MTV staffer told *Broadcasting & Cable*. "I've never experienced anything like that at the workplace." The man who had turned MTV into the defining cultural voice of several generations and shaped MTV Networks into the most successful cable television business on earth, who had built and greased and tuned up the profit engine of Viacom, was gone. Analysts fretted that his deeply loyal employees would follow him out the door, and the stock kept falling.

But Dauman was used to being underestimated. He and Dooley set forth on a charm offensive, wooing Freston's most important lieutenants, Judy McGrath and Brad Grey, and convincing them to stay. Grey, as Freston's hire, was seen as particularly vulnerable, since he was heading into his second year atop the studio still in last place. But minutes after Freston was fired, Dauman was on the phone with Grey, reassuring Grey that he wanted him to stay. Dauman was similarly complimentary about McGrath, Freston's protégée, whom Freston had selected to be CEO of MTV Networks and to whom MTV Networks executives and employees were fiercely devoted.

Gradually, as Dauman and Dooley talked analysts down from the ledge they had fled to after hearing Sumner's rage about MySpace and interpreting that as plans for a big acquisition, the stock recovered. Dauman and Dooley pledged no big changes in strategy, and certainly no big acquisitions, and by the end of the year the stock was back to where it had been at the beginning.

*   *   *

Instead of buying the next hot online media property, Dauman kicked off his tenure by suing one. YouTube was exploding in popularity among the same teenage audience that MTV had long dominated. By the summer of 2006, it had hit twenty million monthly unique visitors, its rate of growth far outstripping MySpace's. But YouTube had a problem: much of that traffic was people watching copyrighted clips of *The Daily Show* and *South Park* that users were uploading illegally, not to mention homemade music videos with copyrighted sound tracks. According to the Digital Millennium Copyright Act of 1998, Internet companies were not liable for such copyright violations so long as they took them down as soon as the content owners asked them to, but this protection only held so long as they didn't profit from the violation. That meant YouTube couldn't put ads on a lot of the videos on its site. To solve this problem, YouTube had been trying to negotiate licensing deals with the big media companies, to some success. But as YouTube grew, so did its tensions with media companies. Despite the audience overlap, Sumner declared in October that he did not see it as an acquisition target because of the legal liability involved, though it would later emerge that Viacom had been a suitor. Google had no such compunction, and in October 2006, it bought YouTube for $1.65 billion.

Hours after that announcement, Google CEO Eric Schmidt sat down with executives from Viacom, whose deal from the previous year with YouTube to distribute video from MTV Networks over the Web had lapsed. Trying to defuse growing tensions, he made the case that Google was a friend to content owners and was working on a digital "fingerprinting" system to identify copyrighted content that had been posted to YouTube. He even floated the idea that Google might be willing to guarantee Viacom as much as $500 million in advertising revenue over the next few years as part of a deal that would indemnify it from copyright litigation. Viacom thought the number should be closer to $1 billion. Over these and other technical questions, the talks stalled by the end of the year. In February, Viacom ordered YouTube to pull down one hundred thousand clips of Viacom content and then sued YouTube for $1 billion, alleging "massive intentional copyright infringement."

It was a stunning move, the first time a media company challenged YouTube in court. Of course, it was also classically Redstonian, using the courts as a way of shifting the leverage at a negotiating table. But the Internet was a different arena than the antitrust playing field of old. Many Viacom executives worried that their channel brands would become irrelevant if they vanished from the kids' favorite online hangout. Dauman had also misjudged the case before him. The litigation dragged on for six years and the parties ultimately settled out of court with no money changing hands. In the meantime, Viacom licensed its video instead to also-rans like Joost and watched much of the online video revolution pass it by.

*   *   *

The full extent of the error would only be apparent in hindsight, however, and in the moment, Dauman was making good on his pledge to double the company's digital revenue to $500 million by the end of 2007 by launching more than three hundred websites, mostly overseas. Sumner had no reason to worry. Caught up in his marriage to Paula—they bragged to friends they had sex as many as four times a day, fueled by an obsession with cruciferous vegetables that he credited with his longevity—he was becoming more isolated from the business back in New York. Were he to get hit by a bus tomorrow, he told *Newsweek*, he would be quite comfortable knowing that Dauman was in charge of his empire.

But just as Sumner was feeling at ease with his consigliere at the controls, his empire was hit with yet another broadside from a disgruntled blood relative. This time it was his nephew, Michael, who on November 3, 2006, sued both Sumner and his own father, Eddie, for allegedly depriving him of his rightful stake in the Redstone media empire. Using documents dredged up by Eddie and Madeline's suit, Michael alleged that both National Amusements' 1972 buyout of Eddie's stake and its 1984 buyout of Michael's and Ruth Ann's stakes had shortchanged him and the other Redstone descendants. He wanted $4 billion, half the value of the empire. Like so many times before, Sumner's control over Viacom and CBS was threatened by a member of his own family.

Sumner was enraged. "This suit is particularly troubling considering the important role Sumner Redstone has played in helping Michael overcome serious obstacles throughout his life," a National Amusements spokeswoman said. "Mr. Redstone essentially rescued Michael from a difficult family environment, removed him from a mental institution, paid for his education and gave him a job at NAI. It is unfortunate that this is how Michael has chosen to repay Sumner Redstone's care and generosity."

Painting Michael as crazy while also bragging about having employed him was a delicate balance, but people who knew Michael say he continued to have profound emotional problems until his death, alone, at age fifty-six, from what the coroner ruled a toxic combination of fentanyl, oxycodone, and temazepam. "He was a recluse," said one person who knew him at the time of the case. But he had inherited the intelligence, as well as some of the resilience, that ran in the Redstone family, and he managed to piece together a surprisingly normal adult life. He earned his GED while still at the Menninger Clinic in Topeka, then returned to Boston to enter Northeastern University, where he earned a bachelor's degree in public administration. He continued to seek mental health treatment on his own and was diagnosed at twenty-one with post-traumatic stress disorder (PTSD), he later said in court. While at Northeastern, he met his first wife, Shelley, with whom he had three children. In 1988, he got his MBA from Bentley University in Boston, and after working an array of jobs including at his father's development company, he came to work at National Amusements in 1994 in what he described as international business development. "My duties range," he said. "He kind of went in and futzed around the office for a while," said one person who knew him.

Tall, blue-eyed, and auburn-haired, with more than a dab of his grandfather's movie star looks, Michael had trouble reading social cues but pursued his interests in aviation and the natural landscape of Colorado, where he later moved. He was devoted to his children but feuded bitterly with his own father his entire life. He and Shelley had wanted to adopt Adam initially when he arrived from Tokyo because, as he said in a deposition in 2004, "we knew that once my parents took him, that he was going to have a horrible life. And I knew that because I had lived part of it when I wasn't in the hospital, and I saw what happened to my sister. And when he died, I mean, I wasn't that surprised." In the same lawsuit, Eddie declared, "My son is manipulative and he's a liar and has serious mental problems."

During Eddie and Madeline's 2004 litigation, Michael learned about the 1959 trust that his grandfather had set up for his benefit. He also learned, for the first time, of the "oral trust" that his grandfather had directed his father to keep half of his National Amusements shares in for his grandchildren. According to Michael's complaint, Eddie's settlement had effectively reduced his and Ruth Ann's stakes in National Amusements from 50 shares to $33^1/_3$ shares, without their having any say in the matter. Worse still, he alleged, was Sumner's handling of the 1984 buyout of his and his sister's stakes in National Amusements. "Sumner was effectively both the buyer and the seller in the transaction, signing the agreement as president of National Amusements on one hand and as trustee of the trusts on the other hand," his complaint alleged. As a result, he argued, the trusts sold out for bargain-basement prices: $21.4 million for shares representing 45 percent of the company, despite the fact that National Amusements' real estate by itself was worth more than $150 million.

A judge ruled that the statute of limitations had passed and threw out most of the case, but Michael would ultimately get his revenge, if not his money. The fight over the meaning of the term "oral trust" went on for years, hauling Sumner onto the witness stand. While up there, Sumner unwisely claimed that, while Eddie had been forced by the settlement to put his shares aside for his children, he had given his shares to his children as a gift. Seizing on these words, the IRS later successfully sued Sumner for unpaid gift taxes that, over forty years of compound interest, added up by some estimates to more than $16 million. "Somebody compiled all the papers for the Michael litigation and wrapped them up in a bow and delivered them to the IRS under the whistle-blower statute," said one person familiar with the case. In little ways, here and there, Sumner's ruthless willingness to push aside his own family members to maintain absolute control of National Amusements was starting to catch up with him. So was his age. On the witness stand, "it wasn't the old Sumner," said one person close to the family. "There were some gaps there."

CHAPTER 17

"Good Governance"

By the time Shari became vice chair of Viacom in 2004, she was accustomed to being the only woman in the room. She was often the only woman at meetings for the theater circuit, the only woman at National Amusements' board meetings, and now the only female director of the second-largest media company in the country. But as that company prepared to split, she helped recruit a new crop of independent board members to ensure that, for the public companies at least, this would no longer be the case. Viacom had long been notorious for overpaying its executives, a characteristic typical of controlled companies with their often clubby, homogenous boards, but with the stock stalled, there was pressure for change. After Sumner, Freston, and Moonves took home nearly $160 million between them in 2004, a year the stock dropped 18 percent, shareholders sued Viacom's board. Under the banner of "good corporate governance," Shari wanted to ensure that the new Viacom and CBS boards would resemble royal courts somewhat less than Viacom's had in the past. This ultimately did not sit well with the king.

Things started out promisingly enough. Of the seven new independent board members she helped recruit for the two companies, three were women, and one was African American. She recruited Bob Kraft, owner of her beloved New England Patriots, to be her ally and chair Viacom's compensation committee, with the goal of tying pay more closely to performance. Sumner was such a Patriots fanatic that once, while spending the holidays with Paula's family in New Jersey, he forced Teterboro Airport employees to work on Christmas so that he could watch the Patriots play from his grounded private plane as a way of bypassing the NFL's blackout rules. Shortly after Freston's ouster, Viacom cut Sumner's compensation in half, to $10.5 million, and made more of it contingent on the company's performance. When CBS followed suit a few months later amid ongoing settlement talks with the shareholders who sued, Sumner declared, "The pay-for-performance model is one I have long championed." But by then, all three of the newly recruited female independent directors had resigned.

Shari and Sumner had been fighting about his pay for years. Shortly after she arrived at National Amusements, Sumner wanted to increase his salary there, as he did not yet take a salary from Viacom (that would only come during the Karmazin years). Shari voted against it, stunning her father and the rest of the National Amusements board with her chutzpah. In the ensuing years, directors and executives at Viacom and CBS heard Sumner use the "c-word" to refer to her on multiple occasions. They fought about the use of the Viacom plane. They fought about the future of the theater business. Most people chalked it up to two passionate personalities clashing. "I never took any of the fights seriously," said Sherry Lansing, who was close to both of them, as well as to Phyllis. "I just thought, 'Oh well, they will be back together next week.'" Shari still wrote him poems on his birthday and signed them, "Love, Shari."

But by late 2006, the strain was starting to show publicly. In an interview with recently retired Disney CEO Michael Eisner in October, Sumner was candid about their disagreement on the theater business: he wanted to sell the theaters, while she wanted to keep expanding. "I don't have to agree with her because she's my daughter," he said. "It's not a growth business." But it was what he said after Eisner prodded him on why he wasn't planning to name Shari CEO of National Amusements that everybody remembered. "You want to give away what you have to your family, be my guest. . . . I am still very active. I work very hard and travel around the world for Viacom. I'm not about to give up control. . . . My wife is closer to me these days than my daughter." The studio audience laughed, like he was joking.

But the thing that truly broke their relationship was Midway Games. In early 2007, despite his promises at the end of 2005 to never again put National Amusements at risk with his Midway obsession, Sumner wanted National Amusements to buy more of his Midway shares. Shari vehemently opposed the idea, but she was outnumbered by Dauman, Abrams, and Andelman. In February, National Amusements bought another 12.4 million shares from Sumner for roughly $85 million, bringing National's stake to 74.3 percent and Sumner's personal stake to 13.6 percent. Shari was stunned that these men, savvy lawyers all, who all knew perfectly well that Midway was a dog, would allow this madness to continue. The moment crystallized for her the impossibility of her situation: so long as these men were on the board of National Amusements, her 20 percent stake would always be meaningless. In her view, they were more interested in sucking up to Sumner than representing the fiduciary interests of National Amusements and protecting her family's legacy.

The break over Midway was profound enough to prompt Sumner to begin maneuvering to undermine her right to succeed him as chairman. "Unfortunately I have come to believe that Shari does not have the requisite business judgment to serve as chairman of the three companies," he wrote to the trustees of the trust on February 8, 2007. Because Congress had passed the Sarbanes-Oxley Act tightening regulations on public company accounting since the trust was signed in 2002, he argued, "I believe it may not be wise for the trustees of the NA Trust to impose on the independent directors of CBS and Viacom the obligation to have Shari appointed as chairman of the board of each company." He suggested, instead, that the boards should "have the discretion to independently judge whether to appoint Shari as chairman." In the letter, which only came to light in litigation a decade later, he also seemed to suggest that because Dauman was back working at the company—and in fact was CEO—he no longer needed Shari as a successor. But of course, the whole reason he agreed to make Shari chairman during the divorce was so that Phyllis could have assurances that someone loyal to her, not one of Sumner's lackeys, would have oversight of the empire after Sumner died.

Shari had had enough. She wanted out. She hired lawyers, and negotiations began on her possible exit from the empire.

Meanwhile, the tensions spilled into public view again in April 2007, after Sumner pledged $105 million to three medical institutions. When Sumner asked that National Amusements pay the first installment of his pledge, Shari objected, arguing that National Amusements, not Sumner, should then get credit for the gift. Again, Dauman, Abrams, and Andelman sided with Sumner. Andelman told the *Boston Globe* that the gifts were "modest and highly tax-advantaged" and in the best interest of National Amusements.

Then Sumner took off the gloves.

On July 20, 2007, Sumner sent an open letter to *Forbes* lashing out at his daughter, throwing her talk about "good corporate governance" back in her face. "While my daughter talks of good governance, she apparently ignores the cardinal rule of good governance that the boards of the two public companies, Viacom and CBS, should select my successor." He said he would allow Shari to be bought out, "as long as the price is acceptable," and ended with a vicious kicker: "It must be remembered that I gave to my children their stock; and it is I, with little or no contribution on their part, who built these great media companies with the help of the boards of both companies."

For Shari, who had spent more than a decade running the theater chain, trying to balance full-time work with motherhood, taking the Delta Shuttle down to New York for Viacom board meetings and then back in time for dinner, only to return again the next morning, it was a devastating blow. It was also revisionist history. Her spokeswoman shot back that Shari had received her first shares in National Amusements in 1959 from her grandfather Mickey and suggested that the chairman title was not her aim. In a dig meant to highlight Sumner's obsession with clinging to the CEO title, she added, "Anyone who knows Shari Redstone knows she is the one Redstone family member who does not aspire to power or covet titles." But she did say that Shari would be willing to consider selling her 20 percent stake of her father's empire for $1.6 billion, using the same valuation that Brent had used in his lawsuit.

Dauman was once again tapped to help out with one of Shari's divorces, only this time he represented Sumner in talks, as *Fortune* put it, "about reducing her influence in the affairs of CBS and Viacom." It was a curious role for him to be playing, as the chief executive of Viacom, but people who know the family say he was always Sumner's fixer first. They discussed Sumner buying her voting stock or offering her the theaters in exchange for voting stock, but in the end, according to her spokeswoman, she had "no intention of leaving the board."

By the end of the year, the feud appeared to have blown over when Sumner named Shari chairman of Midway Games. "I fully support the election of Shari as chair and I am totally confident of Midway's success," Sumner said in a statement, despite the stock being down 60 percent for the year. In fact, Shari's ascension to the chairmanship of Midway was just another stop on its downward spiral. The previous chairman, Ken Cron, had left in frustration after Sumner refused a $300 million offer for the troubled company. A large part of Phyllis's divorce settlement had been in Midway shares, and Shari felt duty-bound to try to right the ship. But Sumner didn't let Shari run Midway any more than he had let Cron.

And then, in the early morning hours of September 15, 2008, Lehman Brothers collapsed, triggering the nightmare scenario that had long kept Shari up at night: the debt from Sumner's Midway Games purchases suddenly threatened National Amusements. As global markets went into free fall over the next three weeks, the value of CBS was cut in half, while Viacom dropped nearly 40 percent. Unbeknownst to Viacom and CBS investors, National Amusements owed $1.6 billion in bank debt that, while unsecured, had covenants linked to the value of National Amusements holdings. As that value plunged, National

Amusements was forced to sell $233 million's worth of nonvoting shares of CBS and Viacom to avoid breaching covenants on the loan.

Sumner tried to get out in front of the story, sending his allies to whisper to the press that the $1.6 billion loan had been used for expanding the theater chain, prompting Shari to put out an on-the-record denial. "The implication that this stock sale was required by the operation and expansion of the company's theater circuit is not accurate," National Amusements said in a statement the day after the sale. The real reason for the loan was a combination of Midway Games stock purchases, retrofitting National's old theaters, expanding the theater chain, and Brent's settlement. Investors began to panic that Sumner would be forced to sell his voting stakes in CBS and Viacom, and perhaps even the companies themselves. Sumner tried to calm them, telling the *Wall Street Journal* that there was "not a chance" he would sell any more shares of the companies.

But the money had to come from somewhere. Not surprisingly, Sumner came for the theaters first, proposing to the bankers that he sell the family's entire fifteen-hundred-screen chain to help restructure the debt. But Shari, whom he tapped to lead the negotiations with lenders, pushed back. She hired her own financial adviser from the Blackstone Group, and talk resurfaced that she might exit the family media empire altogether as part of the restructuring. But the situation was dire enough that those talks had to take a backseat to saving National Amusements. The *New York Times* speculated that, with his debt so high and the value of his assets so depressed, Sumner might not even be a billionaire anymore.

Instead, Midway was the first to go. At the start of December, National Amusements sold its 87 percent stake in Midway to an investor named Mark Thomas for the fire-sale price of $100,000, a stunning loss for a company that Sumner had pumped nearly $800 million into. The sale wasn't part of National's talks with banks, but it did improve the company's financial picture. Sumner's lawyers looked at the sale as a tax maneuver—National could count the loss against its income from the year. But the sale doomed Midway by triggering change-of-control provisions that let its bondholders demand full repayment of some $240 million's worth of debt. Two months after the sale, Midway filed for Chapter 11.

The theaters were next. Although Shari was leading the negotiations, she was part of a three-person special committee of National Amusements directors, along with Andelman and Abrams, and by late December she had been outvoted on selling off the theaters. The situation grew so tense by then that Shari and Sumner were only communicating by fax. By February, the Redstones struck a deal with the banks to repay the $1.46 billion it now owed by the end of the year, and put together a prospectus to sell some of its 118 theaters, which analysts estimated were worth between $500 million and $700 million. In October 2009, National Amusements sold $1 billion in nonvoting stock in Viacom and CBS to pay off its debt, which kept it from having to sell off the entire theater chain. A few months later, it sold thirty-five theaters, including The Bridge in Los Angeles. The company that Mickey had envisioned as a national chain had been pared back to its roots in the Northeast. Shari blamed her father for destroying her grandfather's legacy.

Shari was so upset that she came very close to following in her brother's footsteps and suing her father. In 2009, her lawyer, Betsy Burnett of Mintz Levin, delivered an explosive eighty-page draft complaint to Sumner and Dauman, outlining a host of grievances, including the Midway affair and years of mistreatment from her father, threatening to file it the next day. Negotiations followed, and Shari ended up with a settlement that gave her the Russian theaters, a lifetime employment contract at National Amusements, charitable donations, and $5 million with which she would go on to start a venture capital fund. As part of the settlement, she agreed to give up all legal claims on these issues. While she had tried to get the language promising her the chairmanship of Viacom and CBS made less ambiguous, the old, ambiguous language remained. As far as the outside world knew, Shari was still her father's possible successor, but within the family, their bonds were broken. "Sumner hated Shari at that point," said one person familiar with the negotiations.

Amid these crises, Sumner and Paula amicably divorced. She felt isolated in LA and was seen in a few nasty public blowups with Sumner at premieres and Dan Tana's. His empire in shambles, Sumner was now alone.

CHAPTER 18

Strange World

One summer evening in 2011, the five members of the raunchy, ostensibly bisexual all-girl band the Electric Barbarellas spilled out of a black SUV onto a West Hollywood sidewalk. Drunk and dressed for clubbing, they were in high spirits, shrieking like teenagers and playfully calling each other "whore!" At one point, the ringleader, a towering, willowy blonde in dark glasses, faced the paparazzi and declared, "One of the Barbarellas has lost her virginity tonight!" Their antics were meant to stir up buzz for their eponymous reality show, which had recently debuted on MTV. Taking the hint, the others turned to the cameras and continued to riff. "In the butt!" added one. "These guys told me that they were going to put it in her butt tonight, and she said, 'OK, for $500.'" Another, remembering that one of the show's narratives was supposed to be that they were constantly sleeping with each other, chimed in, "It was me!"

But none of this salaciousness had been on display a few weeks earlier, when the band had made its network television debut on CBS's *The Late Late Show with Craig Ferguson*. Dressed, in the words of one Web commenter, like "10-cent hookers," they woodenly plodded through a middling pop song from their album *Strange World*, candy-colored deer in headlights, more off-key than on, their stripper heels so tall they could barely dance.

By then, everyone in the industry knew that this awkward performance had been mandated from the top. A little over a year earlier, the band's leader, a twenty-nine-year-old named Heather Naylor, had been spotted at Dan Tana's with Sumner, Moonves, and Moonves's wife. Sumner wanted Naylor to pitch her show to the CW network, which was partly owned by CBS. Someone tipped off *Daily Beast* reporter Peter Lauria, who wrote a bombshell story that Sumner had taken a shine to Naylor, flying her and her bandmates by private jet out to New York to convince MTV's extremely reluctant executives to give them a show. The tensions got so bad that Judy McGrath—a woman who wore Chuck Taylors, had won Peabodys, and spent her adult life fiercely guarding the authenticity of the MTV brand—considered resigning. Viacom spokesman Carl Folta didn't even try to deny what was going on. "He loves the concept of the show, believes the women are extremely talented, and thinks there's a very good chance this could become a major hit," he said.

Sumner got his way but was determined to plug the leak. A few weeks after the story appeared, Sumner, whose favorite film was *The Godfather*, left Lauria a menacing voice mail that would have made Don Corleone proud. He offered financial rewards if Lauria coughed up his source. "We are not going to kill him," he said. "We just want to talk to him." After all those years of trying to shed his father's underworld associations, here, as old age closed in, was Mickey Redstone's son.

The voice mail only made matters worse by causing a sensation, and soon it emerged that Sumner had given Naylor, a former MTV production assistant, $150,000 worth of Viacom stock. Another of Sumner's girlfriends would later claim he gave Naylor some $21 million before it was all over. (People familiar with Ms. Naylor's thinking say the $150,000 was payment to dissolve a contract in connection with her show, and that while Sumner did financially invest in her band and show, she was not given $21 million.) Naylor was just one of many beautiful young women upon whom Sumner lavished riches in the years following his divorce from Paula. If he didn't pluck them from some corner of his media empire, as he did with Malia Andelin, the flight attendant on CBS's corporate jet, then he hooked them up with jobs in it, as he did with Rohini Singh, the thirty-year-old party girl he demanded Showtime executives employ. Both got $18 million, according to the later girlfriend's lawyers. Company executives referred to the period as "Sumner's third mid-life crisis."

Sumner met some of these women through his grandson Brandon Korff, who had moved to Los Angeles in 2009 at age twenty-four to work at MTV. Of all his siblings, Brandon was the one with showbiz most in his veins. A natty dresser with a smoldering stare who had moved to LA "to be rich and famous," as one person who knew him put it, Brandon's first job after graduating from the George Washington University in 2006 was at Eminem's record label, Shady Records. By 2008 he had joined the family business, as manager of corporate development at National Amusements—essentially the same job that Michael Redstone had once held—overseeing the launch of the Showcase Live music venue at Patriot Place, near the home of the New England Patriots. After a year, he moved in with his grandfather and then got a place near Beverly Park, while still returning to his grandfather's estate to watch sports with "Grumpy" in the fish room or to escort him to events. Meanwhile, he also had a hedonistic streak, driving a Bentley, producing a well-regarded documentary on the Electric Daisy Carnival electronic dance festival, and hanging out with gorgeous women. Some he introduced to his grandfather, who would date them and lavish them with gifts. Once he brought a beautiful woman to an MTV event who ended up going with Sumner.

Sumner had good reason to feel frisky. Since beating prostate cancer in 2004—a feat he credited to his doctor, celebrity oncologist Dr. David Agus—he had become more convinced than ever of his immortality and devoted to his regime of daily exercise and "eating every antioxidant known to man." He kept bowls of dried goji berries and apricots nearby at all times, had red wine with meals, and was such a believer in the acai-berry drink MonaVie that he became a distributor. "I have the vital statistics of a 20-year-old man," he bragged to Larry King at the Milken Institute in 2009. "I'm not going anywhere else. I like it here." Part of why he liked it was that he had not slowed down sexually, he said, thanks to what he called "drugs for men." He began work on a memoir titled *How to Live Forever.*

For the mogul who had long claimed "Viacom is me," Viacom's improving performance bolstered Sumner's sense of invincibility. By

2010, the economy was climbing out of the financial crisis, and Viacom was climbing with it. The crash had not been all bad for Viacom. It gave Dauman cover to cut about three thousand of Viacom's thirteen thousand jobs—nearly one thousand of them at Paramount—and leveled the media playing field. While Viacom's stock had consistently traded at lower multiples than its peers before the crisis—due in some part to the "Redstone discount" caused by his overwhelming control—after the crisis the gap eased. MTV had its first bona fide hit of the Dauman era in *Jersey Shore*, a reality show celebrating the self-proclaimed "guido" lifestyle of a bunch of deeply tanned, Italian American twentysomethings. It drew an astonishing eight million viewers at its peak and turned stars like Snooki into household names. Along with other grittier reality fare like *Teen Mom*, the show helped MTV's ratings grow by double digits over the next several years.

Things were even turning around at long-suffering Paramount, where Grey's strategy of nearly halving the studio's slate to about a dozen films a year produced record profits. Although Paramount's marriage to DreamWorks had ended in divorce in 2008 after Grey clashed with its leadership and Dauman referred to cofounder Steven Spielberg as "immaterial," DreamWorks had left behind the crucial Transformers franchise, which delivered a blockbuster sequel in 2010. Combined with the breakout performance of the low-budget horror flick *Paranormal Activity*—which was made for $15,000 and brought in $107 million at the box office—Paramount was suddenly a profit maker after years in last place at the box office. Meanwhile, Viacom's top brass promised Wall Street they'd make no big acquisitions and focus instead on buying back stock, a favorite technique across the industry for goosing a company's stock price. By the end of 2010, Viacom's stock was trading at $40, more than twice what it had been at the nadir of the crisis, and Dauman had taken home $85 million, making him the highest-paid CEO in America.

But, even as Viacom's financial performance was improving, some of the deals Dauman was making during this period threw the future of the business into question. In 2009, MTV Networks signed a deal to put old seasons of popular shows like *South Park* and *Sponge-Bob SquarePants* on Netflix. At the time, Netflix was a still-emerging streaming service with just ten million subscribers, a fraction of the roughly hundred million households that subscribed to pay television, and many media executives saw streaming deals as found money. But some worried that they were helping build a dangerous competitor that trained viewers to wait until they could watch their favorite shows in a sleek, easy-to-use environment without ads, for a fraction of the price of traditional pay-TV. Dauman was not one of these worrywarts. In 2010, Viacom strengthened Netflix's offerings even further when it signed a five-year, $1 billion deal to make Paramount movies available on the service through its pay-TV service Epix. "When satellite came along as a new form of distribution, that was a very good thing for a content owner," he told the *Wall Street Journal*. "And in the same way, whether it's Netflix, whether it's Hulu, whether it's other services that are developing models that are based on distributing professionally produced content, that's a very positive development for us."

While Wall Street may have found Viacom's lack of acquisitive appetite soothing, it meant Viacom missed some big opportunities. In 2009, Marvel Entertainment, the comic book empire that created Spider-Man, Captain America, and Iron Man, came up for sale. Paramount already had a deal with Marvel to distribute films, and would have made sense as a dance partner, but Dauman had ruled out big purchases. Instead, Disney bought Marvel for $4 billion. Analysts initially believed Disney overpaid for Marvel but began to sing a different tune after *The Avengers*—which Paramount had originally been contracted to distribute—made $207 million domestically during its opening weekend in 2012. Today the deal is considered one of the smartest moves Disney CEO Bob Iger ever made, part of a series of acquisitions, including Pixar and Lucasfilm, that helped the company become roughly twice as valuable as its closest competitor.

Sometimes Viacom missed out on hits because of Dauman's cool relationship with talent. While Freston would drive over to *South Park* creators Matt Stone and Trey Parker's studio to hang out for hours,

Dauman never visited. And when the duo was developing their Broadway musical *The Book of Mormon*, Dauman initially agreed to have Viacom invest $1 million, which would have given the company the rights to tack *Comedy Central Presents* onto the show's title. But he changed his mind the day the check was due, approving half as much and giving up the naming rights. The musical, which raised $10 million for its launch in 2011, has gone on to gross more than $1 billion.

One of Dauman's first moves as CEO had been to unwind a joint venture with Vice Media, the Brooklyn-based gonzo journalism outfit that had been one of the first movers in online video. Started as a free zine in Montreal in 1994, *Vice* had been transferring the feral spirit of its magazine into video travel reports like "The Radioactive Beasts of Chernobyl," which caught the attention of a Viacom executive named Jeff Yapp. In 2007, Viacom and Vice launched VBS.tv, a joint venture that featured reporting from places such as an illegal arms market in Pakistan. "It scared Viacom to death," Yapp said. It also led to a friendship between Vice CEO Shane Smith and Tom Freston, another globe-trotter with a taste for thrill-seeking. When Freston was fired just as VBS.tv was launching, Vice decided they wanted out. Viacom had loaned Vice $3 million with warrants to buy equity, and in the end, they decided not to exercise the warrants. Vice paid Viacom back its $3 million and went on its way.

As much as MTV's and Vice's audiences seemed a perfect match, Smith was glad to be out of post-Freston Viacom. "I used to take the elevator there, and everyone would shit-talk their own company," he said. "It was a toxic environment." Instead, Smith and Freston, who now had a lot of time on his hands, started hanging out, traveling to exotic locales. Freston recognized the same spark in Vice that he had seen in early MTV, and he was entertained by Smith's audaciousness. He joined Vice as an adviser and opened up his Rolodex of rich and powerful friends. Today, with investment from companies like Twenty-First Century Fox and Disney, Vice is valued at $5.7 billion, making it the most valuable new media company. (Vice has since missed some revenue targets and had to apologize for its "boys club" atmosphere after a *New York Times* report revealed several settlements for sexual misconduct among its employees and a culture of male entitlement.)

It took years for Dauman to fully rid MTV Networks of the influence of Freston and his band of merry, profit-making pranksters, but if there was a single inflection point, it came on Thursday, May 5, 2011, the day after *The Electric Barbarellas* premiered on MTV. That was the day that Judy McGrath, the woman who more than anybody else there made MTV look like, sound like, and mean what it did, announced her resignation. Dauman was gracious, calling her a creative force "that has defined and fueled a great deal of our creative and business success" and joking that "filling Judy's Chuck Taylors will be a big task." But he had no intention of filling them. He had her direct reports begin reporting to him and, in a symbolic but telling move, he changed the name of the once-autonomous MTV Networks to Viacom Media Networks. Viacom's cable channels would never again reach the audiences or wield the influence they did when McGrath was in the building.

As Dauman tightened control, creative executives headed for the exits. The contract negotiations he led the next year with Comedy Central stars Jon Stewart and Stephen Colbert—comedians at the peak of their powers and the center of American discourse—were so nasty that they laid the foundation for both stars leaving the company two years later, part of a broader exodus of top *Daily Show* alumni, including John Oliver and Samantha Bee, to other networks. "I don't think Philippe in any way saw what we do as special," Stewart said in Chris Smith's *The Daily Show: An Oral History.* "As far as he was concerned the star is the real estate, and whether or not we are the ones who carved out that real estate and made it valuable is not important to him."

*   *   *

All this—and Sumner wasn't paying a great deal of attention. By late 2010, his tawdry skirt-chasing had become a corporate liability. Brandon, who had grown tired of introducing his grandfather to girls and the payouts that often followed, decided his grandfather needed a steadier, classier girlfriend, and he hired Patti Stanger, host of *The Millionaire Matchmaker* on Bravo, to set him up. "He was looking for a quality girl he could have a serious relationship with," Stanger said. "He tended toward the brunette side, but was open to anything." He signed on for a year's membership to her Millionaire's Club for $120,000, which gave him the right to sample unlimited girls. Initially, "Sumner wanted to eat every single thing on the smorgasbord," Stanger said. But eventually, he zeroed in on a forty-year-old brunette with feline, turquoise eyes and a caustic sense of humor named Sydney Holland.

Born Sydney Stanger (no relation to Patti), she grew up the daughter of a cosmetic dentist and a social worker–turned–star interventionist in La Jolla, an affluent beach town north of San Diego, where high school girls would often date surfer dudes in their mid- to late twenties. "Girls around here just go around with people who are a lot older," a teenage Sydney told the *Los Angeles Times* after a friend of hers was in an accident with a twenty-four-year-old boyfriend. "It's just the way it is around here. We're more life-wise smart."

After graduating from La Jolla Country Day School, Sydney decided to forgo college to go into the fashion business, helping market luxury brands and eventually starting her own lines of lingerie and eco-friendly sportswear. Her father, who died suddenly of a massive heart attack when she was twenty, had always told her that she was a natural saleswoman and ought to consider becoming an entrepreneur. People who know her say his untimely death probably contributed to her taste for older men.

In 2000, she married Cecil Holland, a general contractor and former Hugo Boss model sixteen years her senior. They divorced three years later. By 2004, she appeared under her birth name in an ad with a business partner for a new business, the Inner Circle VIP Social Club. "New Matchmakers in town!" the ad declared. "A first-class dating service for exclusive gentlemen and exquisite ladies who seek to meet the love of their life!" She and her partner planned to use the service as the basis for a reality show, but it didn't work out. Sydney fell into debt and went into recovery for alcoholism.

But while attending Alcoholics Anonymous meetings in 2009, she met a rich, older man who looked like he was going to fix her financial troubles. Bruce Parker was fifty-three and divorced, a gifted salesman whose career at Callaway Golf—where he backed edgy ideas like using Alice Cooper to sell golf clubs—had made him a millionaire. Parker also liked the taste of cocaine and the company of beautiful women, according to his sister, Susie Parker, though he had gone into recovery. He and Sydney hit it off immediately, and after one month of dating, she moved into his Wilshire Boulevard condo. Being the woman in Parker's life typically came with financial perks. "He used to send his girlfriends on shopping sprees," his sister said. "That's what he did. He was very generous." But on the night of October 24, 2009, Parker snorted cocaine and dropped dead of a heart attack, leaving Sydney suddenly without a benefactor. She refused to leave the condo or give up the Mercedes he had leased for her, forcing Parker's estate to sue her to get the condo back. "It wasn't until Bruce died that her true colors showed up," Susie said. After several months, Parker's family agreed to pay her around $60,000 to walk away, according to two people with knowledge of the deal.

A few months later, in the fall of 2010, Sydney, thirty-nine, met Sumner, eighty-seven. In court papers, Sydney described their whirl-wind romance: long drives down the Malibu coast listening to Tony Bennett and Frank Sinatra, sharing "Sumner's favorite dessert" of chocolate mousse at restaurants, accompanying him to charity events, movie premieres, and parties celebrating the mogul. Even though he was dating other women at the time, it was Sydney he wanted to take him to the dentist as he gradually had his teeth replaced. "Before they knew it," her lawyers wrote, "they were spending nearly every waking moment with each other." Sumner was, by his own lawyer's description, "infatuated with Holland."

By early 2011, he asked her to move in with him. She says he also proposed around this time, buying her a nine-carat canary yellow en-gagement ring. Sydney became his constant companion, organizing his life and carrying out his wishes with the efficiency of a personal assistant. This often meant helping him maintain relationships with other women. She was the one who ordered flowers or gifts for Delsa on special occasions or called ahead to Dan Tana's to arrange to pick up dinner for Paula, with whom Sumner remained on friendly terms. According to Sumner's lawyers, Sydney also "arranged for other women to visit" Sumner during this period, though people close to Sydney say she merely tolerated visits that the strong-willed mogul arranged on his own. She handled Sumner's correspondence with the Viacom and CBS top brass, even organizing a board meeting at the mansion at one point; arranged his regular Sunday movie-viewing parties; and managed his social calendar. And most important, she oversaw his medical care.

She was well compensated for her efforts. By March 31, 2011, Sumner had updated his will to give Sydney $500,000. By May, he had bought her a $1.8 million house. By the end of the summer, her payout in the will had climbed to $3 million, according to his lawyers. He began to fund her next business, a film production company called Rich Hippie Productions.

All of this, according to Stanger, was classic Sumner. "He leads with money," she said. "What he does is, he mentors women and says, 'I'm going to put you in business.' That was his style. You can't call the kettle black if you lead with money. He liked women needing him."

Around this time, according to emails leaked to the *New York Post*, Sydney emailed with her lawyer about how she was getting a "gorgeous diamond ring" and was "up to" $3 million in the will. They discussed the idea of marriage, but Sydney said she doubted Sumner "will ever marry me." When the lawyer said that, together with her house and bonds, she had probably racked up between $9 million and $10 million from Sumner, he wrote, "Starting to get some comfort?" Sydney responded, "20 would be best!!! Just saying." When the emails leaked in 2015, her lawyer said Sydney believed they were fake.

*　　*　　*

While Sydney was growing closer to Sumner, Shari was trying to forge her own path beyond his shadow. In 2009, when she unveiled a Cinema De Lux multiplex and luxury shopping complex, complete with an Apple Store, on the site of her grandfather's original Dedham Drive-In, her speech christening "Legacy Place" pointedly omitted any reference to her father. "My grandfather was a visionary," Shari said, adding that it was his foresight to buy the land under the theaters that had made the acquisition of Viacom and CBS possible.

This same year, Shari began thinking about legacy in a different way, holding late-night brainstorming sessions with her son-in-law, Jason Ostheimer, about investing in media and technology start-ups. Jason met Shari's daughter, Kim, at the University of Pennsylvania, from which they both graduated in 2004. They were married in the garden of the InterContinental Boston in 2007, with a lavish reception attended by the likes of Patriots owners Bob and Myra Kraft and Australian media mogul James Packer, finished off by blasts of heart-shaped fireworks over Boston Harbor. Kim, a classic beauty, worked as a lawyer at the Legal Aid Society until deciding, like her mother had, to stay home with her kids. Jason worked in private equity at the Blackstone Group but had always had an entrepreneurial itch.

Shari got interested in the idea of investing in early-stage media and tech start-ups after a Viacom board meeting in 2009, just as *Jersey Shore* was becoming a phenomenon. "I asked, 'Do we know who's watching *Jersey Shore*'?" she said in an interview in 2015. "The answer was a mixed answer. No disrespect to Viacom, but this was a real opportunity." The measurement company Nielsen had been tracking TV viewership for generations, but as viewership started to drift onto online platforms, it was having trouble keeping up. The kind of instant data that websites are used to having about their readers was simply not available for traditional television at the time. Shari felt there was an opportunity to invest in the next generation of what she and Ostheimer called "tools for the CMO," or chief marketing officer, to track audiences in the digital age. They also shared an interest in emerging online video players, digital publishers, e-sports, and virtual reality companies.

In June 2011, Shari and her partners decided to sell Rising Star

Media, the Russian movie theater chain that she had gotten in her settlement with her father in 2009, to Russia's largest exhibitor for $190 million. Two months later, she took some of the $5 million she got in the settlement and, with Ostheimer, launched Advancit Capital, a venture capital firm focused on early-stage investments in media, entertainment, and technology. The first fund was modest, just $3.2 million. After a year, they recruited a third partner, veteran digital executive Jon Miller, the former chief of News Corp's digital business and chief executive of AOL, and launched a $25 million fund. A third fund would aim to raise $40 million. Over the years, they invested in companies like Percolate, a marketing technology company; NewsCred, a content marketing company; Mic, a millennial-focused digital media company; and Maker Studios, a multichannel network of online videos that was bought by Disney. Shari retained the title of president at National Amusements, but it was ceremonial. She had decided to reinvent herself as a skinny jeans–wearing, Apple Watch–sporting VC. "I'm going to leave my day job, and this is what I'm going to do," she said to herself. "It just seemed like the world was changing really quickly, and I thought, 'What's the best way that I could add value to National Amusements and Viacom and CBS? Really understanding the future.'"

*   *   *

Just as Shari was launching Advancit, the first signs began to appear that Dauman might not have had such a great handle on the digital media ecosystem himself. In August 2011, Netflix launched a new feature called "Just for Kids," which let kids browse the site by clicking on images of characters like SpongeBob SquarePants or Dora the Explorer. Almost immediately, Nickelodeon's ratings tanked. Analysts who had fretted that licensing content to streaming services like Netflix would kill the golden goose of pay television seized upon the episode as confirming their fears. It certainly appeared that, when given the opportunity to watch old *SpongeBob* episodes on Netflix without commercials, kids were tuning into Nickelodeon a lot less. "This is pretty close to a smoking gun," Todd Juenger, an analyst at Sanford C. Bernstein, told the *Wall Street Journal*.

Dauman rejected this narrative, arguing during a tense earnings call that Netflix could not be blamed because the number of "content streams" that Netflix reported to Viacom was "pretty much the same" in both the fall quarter and the summer, before the ratings drop. He chalked up the drop to competing shows on the Disney Channel and a glitch in Nielsen's new measurement sample. But when ratings sank 25 percent in the next quarter, analysts began asking bigger questions about the strategy of Nickelodeon and Viacom in general. *SpongeBob*, which debuted in 1999 and was the network's biggest hit, had accounted for 40 percent of Nickelodeon's airtime in 2011. They were running the sprockets off a sure thing, eroding its value, without investing in new hits to replace it. Anticipating this criticism, Dauman emphasized that the company was planning more *SpongeBob* episodes as part of a push to make five hundred episodes of new programming in 2012, a third more than the previous year. But the investment that spoke loudest was the buyback. The company said it spent $700 million buying back its own stock in the last quarter of 2011 and planned to continue at the same brisk pace in early 2012. At the time of this announcement, the stock was trading at around $48 a share.

Theoretically, media companies ought to have been able to move their television shows and movies onto new platforms like laptops, iPads, cell phones, and Roku boxes without totally blowing up their business models. After all, the new places to watch TV only increased the amount of TV that people watched. But during these crucial early years when the country's broadband and wireless infrastructure was finally robust enough to let people watch live television anywhere, an obtuse standoff between channel owners, like Viacom, and their distributors, like Comcast, ensured that the lucrative, high-margin pay-TV business that fed both of them would fall to the barbarians from Silicon Valley.

The pay-TV industry's name for its counterattack was the optimistically titled "TV Everywhere," coined during an early experiment between Time Warner Inc. and Comcast. In this early version, Time Warner agreed to give the digital rights to its channels like CNN, TNT, and Cartoon Network to Comcast, which then built a digital player for its subscribers to be able to watch the channels they were already pay-ing for on their digital devices. There was just one deeply annoying catch: the subscribers had to type in a password to prove they were current on their Comcast bill that month. It wasn't perfect, but it was a good start against the incursions of Netflix, which executives like Time Warner CEO Jeff Bewkes argued was appealing not so much because of what it offered (it was still, at this stage, mostly serving the warmed-over leftovers of the rest of the media industry) but how it offered it. Time Warner's vision also had a key component: it offered these digital rights to its distribution partners free of charge. The idea was to encourage the Comcasts of the world to invest in the technol-ogy to make Time Warner's channels available on more platforms.

But the nature of the relations between television programmers and distributors is that nothing gets done unless it is part of one of the big, long-term distribution deals they negotiate every few years. And so many TV programmers, eager as they were to do TV Everywhere, found themselves having to wait many years until their deal with a certain distributor was ready for renewal before they could make their channels work on iPads or Roku boxes. That's how Viacom, which was one of the first to attempt to do TV Everywhere with a service called "Entitlement" on Time Warner Cable back in 2008, ended up being one of the last media companies to have its channels function on dig-ital platforms. And while they didn't explicitly charge distributors for the digital rights to their channels, they did use them as a sweetener for overall price hikes, further slowing the evolution of the ecosystem. Meanwhile, the long-promised advertising business on distributors' video-on-demand services never materialized—it was too technically difficult to swap out old ads for more current ones and simply not worth the effort for the tiny audiences that watched.

"The operators just sat there and let Netflix and Hulu and the other platforms take away the digital share of their business," said one media company executive. They never invested in the infrastructure that would make pay-TV as pleasing to use as Netflix because they didn't have to—they could just exit the TV business altogether and focus instead on selling broadband, using TV as a mere glue to hold together bundles of telecom services rather than as the main attraction. The fact that programming costs were going up sharply every year— eating into distributors' margins unless they raised prices—made it an easy strategic decision for distributors to make. "I think the distributors could care less," the executive said. "They are thriving on their broadband business. Their TV business was secondary." So while TV Everywhere continued its glacially slow rollout, Netflix relentlessly increased its market share to a majority of U.S. households, teaching a whole generation to expect television without advertising. Still, Dauman was sanguine about it, often joking to colleagues in later years that Viacom made more money from Netflix, Amazon, and Hulu than any of those companies had, with their emphasis on growth over profits.

Viacom stock kept going up, and earnings per share, the ultimate Wall Street report card, went up even faster, boosted by the company's constant buybacks. By the time Paramount celebrated its centennial in the summer of 2012, earnings per share had more than doubled since Dauman became chief executive, and the fixer who once delighted in flying under the radar was profiled in the *New York Times* in a piece titled "The Man Who Would Be Redstone." "I can't say what will happen after I'm gone—which will be never," Sumner told the *Times*. "But everyone understands, I think, that Philippe will be my successor."

Behind the scenes, though, Dauman and Shari were playing tug-of-war. Two weeks after the *Times* story, Sumner gave an interview to the *Wall Street Journal* clarifying that "it hasn't been decided yet who will be my successor. And Philippe knows it. He knows Shari might be my successor and it's not a competitive race between them. We have to see what happens." But then he said that it was likely that Dauman would inherit the chairman role at Viacom and Moonves would inherit it at CBS. There was reason for him to say this: both Dauman and Moonves had provisions in their contracts that allowed them to walk away with big payouts if they had to report to anyone other than Sumner.

The real fight, however, was not over the boards of CBS and Viacom but over the trust that would one day control them both. And increasingly, Shari was starting to feel like she would have to one day sue Dauman to protect her family's empire. A month after the *Journal* story, she wrote her father a draft letter to complain about changes to his estate planning that she felt disadvantaged her, and she sent it to Sydney for advice. "This is nothing more than a calculated move by Philippe to oust me from the company, and limit my role going forward," Shari wrote her father. "Having grown up with you as my mentor, and having learned from watching you at work, I am sure you understand why I will not give in to a bully." And then, to Sydney, she wrote, "In the meantime, every email my father sends to me will be used against me in court if I ever have to take Philippe on."

*   *   *

By early 2013, as Sumner headed toward his ninetieth birthday, he had grown weak enough to need overnight nursing care, and Sydney was exhausted. He demanded her constant presence; if she stepped into another room or went out to run an errand, he would call her phone over and over. (Keryn Redstone once joked to Sydney that Sumner ought to just go ahead and get her a shock collar, so agitated did he become when she was not in his line of sight.) So Sydney was grateful when a longtime female friend of Sumner's, Manuela Herzer, decided to move into the mansion while her house was being renovated.

Manuela, a blond Argentina-born beauty who had dated Sumner before he had married Paula, was seven years older than Sydney and more worldly. Born in Buenos Aires to a wealthy Jewish family, she immigrated to the United States with her parents and four brothers when she was a small child. Fluent in French, Spanish, and English, she attended college in Paris, where she met and married her first husband, Eric Chamchoum, son of a wealthy Lebanese family with business interests in Nigeria, when she was twenty-one. They had two children, Bryan and Christina, before going through a bitter divorce. With a subsequent boyfriend, Manuela had a third child, Kathrine Herzer, who plays the daughter of the secretary of state in CBS's *Madam Secretary.*

Like Christine Peters, Manuela had met Sumner through Bob Evans, Hollywood's indefatigable ladies' man. They were both taking tennis lessons at his estate and were introduced by tennis pro Darryl Goldman. They went on to date for two years. Sumner proposed marriage, but she did not want to marry again. Instead, she settled into the role of friend and confidante, particularly when it came to Sumner's relationships with other women, and he grew close to her children. In 2009, he bought her a $3.85 million house in Beverly Hills, according to *Fortune,* and by 2010, she says he told her he was setting aside money for her and her children. Not long after Sumner met Sydney, he invited Manuela and her son, Bryan, over to dinner to meet her. Two years later, when renovations on Manuela's house were dragging on and she tired of renting, Sumner invited her and her daughter Kathrine to move into the mansion. She moved in in April 2013.

And so began one of the stranger partnerships in the history of the Redstone family. Sydney and Manuela, who in any normal circumstance might see each other as rivals, became a team. Together, they made the mansion accessible for people with disabilities and managed Sumner's increasingly complex health care needs. And together, they began to receive increasingly large portions of Sumner's personal estate in his estate planning. By the time he turned ninety, his lawyers say they were each due to receive $15 million in Sumner's will.

CHAPTER 19

"Our Family"

For Sumner's ninetieth birthday, Sydney and Manuela threw him a surprise party worthy of the "King of Hollywood" he had long claimed to be. Tom Cruise, Mark Wahlberg, David Letterman, Danny DeVito, and Al Gore all strode down the red carpet they had installed leading up to his Beverly Park mansion beneath a movie marquee. They erected a stage in the backyard under a tent, where a four-course dinner was served, and the entertainment was provided by Sumner's good friend Tony Bennett, who thanked Sumner for "putting me on MTV and making me a bigger star than I ever was." Dauman, Moonves, and Grey were there, as were old friends Bob Evans, Sherry Lansing, Jeffrey Katzenberg, Michael Milken, and Michael Eisner. Shari and her children came, and so did ex-wife Phyllis. Every one of them, alongside Sydney, Manuela, and Manuela's kids, took part in an elaborate birthday video in Sumner's honor, "created with love by Sydney and Manuela." Sydney, sitting next to a giant teddy bear with a white toy poodle on her lap, made it clear that she thought of herself as Sumner's family, saying, "I'm so excited to be spending your birthday with all our family and friends." Manuela's message was even more overt. "There are not enough ways to express how grateful and blessed we are to be a part of your family, yesterday, today, and tomorrow—and for the rest of our lives."

It was an odd thing to say in front of Sumner's actual family. But, according to Manuela's legal filings, that's how they talked about each other: he called her "family," and she returned the sentiment. She and her children celebrated birthdays and holidays with him, and he attended her son Bryan's graduation from the University of Southern

California in 2012. Sydney had recently decided to become a mother herself, hiring a surrogate (with Sumner's financial help) to bear her a child in June 2013. By the time the red-haired, blue-eyed baby, who was named Alexandra Red, was brought into the mansion, Manuela's and Sydney's respective hauls in Sumner's estate had been raised to $22.5 million, according to his lawyers. By all accounts, Sumner adored the baby, and Sydney claims he wrote her into his will in 2015.

Shari saw the baby as a ploy for Sydney to increase her influence over her father. In April 2013, she wrote her sons, "Sydney has a contract for a baby to be delivered in the summer. Grumpy is not planning to adopt the baby, but of course [the] baby will be living there. I'm done." Still worried that Sumner might indeed adopt the child, she followed up saying, "If I go May 27 that will be it. I am not going to that home with Sydney's baby living there."

Shari wasn't the only one concerned about Sydney and Manuela's growing sway over Sumner. While Sydney was in San Diego picking up her baby on June 12, 2013, Heather Naylor came by the house to have lunch with Sumner. According to later legal filings, Naylor appeared to be on a mission to reveal to Sumner that Sydney was a gold digger. Naylor sat Sumner down and showed him printouts of compromising photos of Sydney and emails between Sydney and her lawyer strategizing about how to get more money from him. Manuela witnessed the exchange and, according to *Fortune*, interrupted it by downplaying the materials' significance. Sydney fired back by suing Naylor for $1 million, accusing Naylor of stealing her laptop—which she believed to be the source of the materials—in 2011 and demanding that it be returned and the materials destroyed. Naylor denied having the laptop and countersued, accusing Sydney of convincing Sumner that her band was "talentless," contributing to MTV's canceling her show and the disintegration of her relationship with Sumner. She also alleged that Sydney had Sumner on lockdown, going so far as to change his phone number to keep potential rivals away so she could "control" Sumner "for her own economic advantage." Sydney denied these claims.

In the wake of this dustup, Sumner's lawyers claim Sydney and Manuela overhauled the house staff, firing long-serving staffers and even cutting ties with Sumner's longtime doctor, Dr. David Agus. They hired new staff that reported to them and hired a new doctor, Dr. Richard Gold. (People close to Sydney think Sumner made these decisions, though Sydney did, at his request, hire the new staff.) Agus says that's baloney. "The decision to bring in Dr. Gold was one hundred percent made by Sydney Holland and Manuela Herzer," he said. "As soon as they left the picture, I resumed my friendship with Mr. Redstone." Friends who did visit during this time were shocked to see the man who had been such a health nut and never taken much medication suddenly taking sleeping and antianxiety pills. Sumner's lawyers alleged that Sydney and Manuela asked the nurses to administer the antianxiety drug Ativan to calm Sumner when they wanted him to sign documents. (People familiar with Sydney's thinking vehemently deny this.)

One longtime friend said that during this period, Sumner was often so disoriented that he would ask what the women were doing in his house and would express surprise when told that they lived there. "The last time he called me, he had me on speed dial. [After that] all the speed dial numbers got taken out of his phone," the friend said. "He said, 'Help, they are finally gone. Can you come up here?' Somewhere in the back of his mind, he knew."

The person added: "He wasn't there. Since 2011. And they all knew it."

*   *   *

Concerned friends expected that Sumner's family would intercede but didn't realize that his family was feeling increasingly cut off. From Sydney and Manuela's perspective, the estrangement between Sumner and Shari was simply the continuation of tensions that had been racking the family for years. "I just can't deal with LA and Grumpy for four days," Shari wrote to her son Tyler on December 27, 2012. "I can't even begin to describe what it does to me mentally and physically."

By early 2014, tensions had grown worse. Sumner considered Shari's behavior too "erratic" to become his successor, according to people close to the mogul, and so Dauman, George Abrams, and David Andelman began plotting a way to buy Shari out of the company. National Amusements formed a special committee to explore buying out her 20 percent stake. Moonves, whose fear of a post-Sumner future reporting to Dauman made him a natural ally of Shari's, got wind of this effort in its early stages and tipped Shari off. "If my father wants me to drop dead, he doesn't need to do anything else," Shari wrote her children, her mother, Andelman, and Leah Bishop, an estate planning attorney at the firm Loeb & Loeb, on June 3. "He has made how he feels about me perfectly clear." Shari spent much of the year in negotiations over the buyout proposal but was ultimately able to beat it back. Dauman, meanwhile, assured Sydney that he would help her if Shari came after her gifts when Sumner was gone.

In later litigation, Sumner's lawyers alleged that Sydney and Manuela blocked his family's calls, barred them from visiting, and then told him that they hated him because they never called or visited. (Sydney and Manuela have denied blocking Shari or her family from visiting the mansion or talking to Sumner, and in legal filings both pointed to the long history of tension between Shari and Sumner.) Still, several people close to the family believe the women helped widen the gulf between father and daughter. One longtime friend said that Sumner may have griped about Shari over the years and not wanted her running the business, but "he never hated Shari like that, not like they made it to be."

*   *   *

By 2014, life in Beverly Park had settled into a rhythm of daily deliveries of bags of $100 bills and millions charged to Sumner's credit cards at stores like Yves Saint Laurent, Chanel, and Barneys, according to Sumner's lawyers. But as his ninety-first birthday approached, Sumner's lawyers alleged that Sydney and Manuela began to worry that Shari and her family would challenge the gifts Sumner had made to them in his will, and they hired an estate planning attorney to explore ways for him to transfer more of his wealth to them while he was still alive. (People familiar with Sydney's thinking say it was Sumner who instructed them to hire the attorney because he was worried about what Shari would do.) While almost all of his net worth was tied up in National Amusements' share of Viacom and CBS, he did have various stock options and other forms of compensation from the companies that could be converted to cash without threatening his control. On May 19, 2014, Sumner startled investors by exercising his options and selling stock worth about $236 million, or about $100 million after taxes, which he essentially split in half and gave to Sydney and Manuela. Each got $45 million the same day. According to Sumner's lawyers, because the women had emptied his bank accounts, he had to borrow $100 million from National Amusements to pay the generation-skipping taxes on the gift. At the same moment, Sumner's will was changed to split the remaining $150 million of his estate—everything that existed outside the trust—between the women, and they were named co-agents of his health care.

Up to this point, Sumner's longtime personal attorney, David Andelman, had signed off on all his gifts to the women. But Andelman had recently begun expressing concerns to Sumner that the women were, as Andelman put it in a sworn declaration, "exercising immoderate influence" over him, particularly after Sumner fired his longtime caretaker and house manager, Carlos Martinez, in early 2014. So, according to Sumner's lawyers, the women recruited Leah Bishop to work with Sumner on these and all future bequests. Keryn Redstone said Bishop once introduced herself to her at a party as "one of the good guys who is going to protect your grandfather from Shari." It was an understandable position given her knowledge of the situation. During this period, Sumner referred to Shari alternately as a "bitch" or a "fucking bitch" and was adamant that he wanted Sydney and Manuela to get everything. To protect the gifts against future challenges, Bishop had a geriatric psychiatrist test and sign-off on Sumner's mental capacity whenever he made any estate planning decisions, according to Andelman.

It was all more than Shari could take. On May 26, 2014, a week after her father's $45 million gifts, she emailed her children saying, "I am reviewing legal options. I am going to go after them regardless of the strength of the case. Enough is enough. Sydney believes that she can keep doing this and we will never act. The time has come."

With this maneuvering in the background, Sumner's ninety-first birthday party was a smaller, tenser affair than his ninetieth. Organized by Manuela and Sydney in a private room at Nobu in Malibu, a couple of dozen guests gathered from the warring camps. One of them was Keryn Redstone, by then a thirty-year-old law school graduate whom Sydney and Manuela had been cultivating, knowing that Keryn had bad blood with her aunt Shari. As Brent's daughter, Keryn had grown up amid a fair amount of Redstone family tensions, but she and Shari had become mortal enemies in recent years in the course of a fight over the health care of Phyllis's childless sister, Cecelie Gordon, who had dementia and with whom Keryn had been close. Keryn petitioned to be named her aunt Cece's guardian, Shari opposed it, and eventually Keryn withdrew her petition after the court named an independent guardian. Not long afterward, in 2013, David Andelman removed Keryn as a future trustee on Sumner's trust, replacing her with Shari's son Tyler. The move effectively left Brent's side of the family without representation on a trust that was still held for the benefit of all five of Sumner's grandchildren.

Keryn wouldn't find out about the change for another year, but that night at Nobu, there was no doubt that Shari was on a war footing. Sumner had been having trouble swallowing, and he asked Keryn to sit down next to him to help him eat. Shari asked that Keryn switch seats with her, so that she could sit next to her father. When Keryn refused, she claimed, "Shari erupted and threatened to kill me." (Shari's spokeswoman, Nancy Sterling, denied all of Keryn's claims when she filed them in court in 2016.)

Over the summer of 2014, worried that Shari was going to sue Manuela and Sydney for unduly influencing Sumner, Sumner hired four different legal teams to protect them, according to Sydney's legal filings. As Sumner and Shari continued their negotiations on her buyout from the company, a new element of the deal took shape: according to a term sheet that circulated that year, in exchange for $1 billion, tax-free, she would relinquish her 20 percent stake in National Amusements and her claim to the chairmanships of Viacom and CBS and walk away with a handful of movie theaters that she had built, so long as she agreed to sign legal releases promising not to go after Sydney and Manuela's gifts from Sumner.

Shari refused to sign, so Sumner, Sydney, and Manuela tried a different tack: on July 7, 2014, Sumner made burial instructions that stated that, in the event of any challenge to his estate plan, the family cemetery plots in Sharon Memorial Park in Dedham would be given to Manuela and Sydney. Still, Shari refused to sign the releases.

*　　*　　*

As this private battle raged in 2014, Sumner's public leadership of his media empire had atrophied to mumbled introductions at the start of earnings calls—where he recited a familiar script calling Dauman the "wisest man I've ever known" and praising Moonves as a "genius"—and perfunctory appearances at the CBS and Viacom annual meetings. Nevertheless, at its annual meeting in March, Viacom shareholders voted to boost his salary for fiscal 2014, which ended in September, citing his "vision and leadership." CBS held its annual meeting two months later. Before the event, two large men carried Sumner out onto the stage behind a curtain. When the curtain was pulled back, Sumner, in what the *Journal* described as a "strong but slurred voice," welcomed the crowd and introduced Moonves as a "super genius." As soon as the meeting was over, the curtain was closed. CBS did not hike his pay for that year, but it did continue to pay him a $1.75 million salary and a $9 million bonus, among other forms of compensation. Shareholders would never see him in person again.

In July, Viacom's stock hit an all-time high: $88.36 a share. Almost immediately afterward, Sumner suffered a series of health scares that put him in the hospital three times in quick succession. The hospitalization and subsequent health decline would mirror the beginning of a long slide in Viacom's stock price. They would also bring about the beginning of the end of the women.

CHAPTER 20

"Sharp as a Tack"

I n September 2014, Sumner lay in a hospital bed in a private room at Cedars-Sinai Medical Center in Los Angeles, recovering from yet another brush with death. His swallowing problems had gotten worse, and he had inhaled food into his lungs, causing aspiration pneumonia that had sent him to the intensive care unit. It was his third trip to the hospital that summer, but this time his condition was bad enough that his family had been called in from the East Coast. The hospital stabilized him and transferred him to his own room, where Sydney was waiting with two nurses for his family to arrive. The doctors did not want Sumner to risk another episode by continuing to eat solid food, so he was receiving nutrients through a tube in his nose. That made Sumner even more ornery than usual. He asked his nurses to move him to a reclining chair, and as they did, he began arguing with Sydney.

"I want my $45 million back," Sumner told Sydney, according to the sworn declaration of one of the nurses, Giovanni Paz. (A person close to Sydney denied that he named a specific figure and said he was simply screaming deliriously about money.)

Sydney tried to change the subject, Paz said, but Sumner was insistent.

"I will give you your money back, but let's not talk about this now, let's talk about this another time," Sydney told him, according to Paz. "Your family is coming. Please don't do this to me."

Sydney stepped away from the nurses to call Manuela, who was in New York, according Sumner's lawyers' filings. She came back into the room and, according to Paz, told Sumner's nurses, "We have to put him to sleep." (People close to Sydney's thinking say she never made that last statement, and argue that it is ridiculous to suggest that anyone but hospital staff had control over the medications administered to Sumner in the hospital.) A few minutes later, a nurse from the hospital came to the room and administered a sedative. Sumner relaxed and grew quiet. By the time his grandson Brandon arrived, he was almost asleep.

Paz was uncomfortable and alerted Brandon later to what he had seen. It was the first in what would turn out to be a series of actions by Sumner's nurses over the next several months to warn Shari and her family about aspects of the women's treatment of Sumner that worried them. In later litigation, Sumner's lawyers would characterize the nurses as concerned whistle-blowers, while Sydney's and Manuela's lawyers would paint them as a spy ring paid by Shari and her allies. Manuela would eventually go so far as to file a federal RICO case— the kind designed to put away mobsters—against Shari, her children, and the nurses, alleging they were part of a conspiracy that included illegal recording. Manuela later dropped the nurses from her suit, but Sydney continued to go after them. "Holland is not going to be able to prove her claims," said Bonita Moore, the lawyer for Octaviano and Jagiello. Shari and Tyler deny charges they were directing the nurses to record.

Paz turned out not to be much help to Shari, as Manuela and Sydney fired him a few days later, telling him he lacked the necessary medical qualifications. In the wake of his firing, Shari paid him a month's salary, according to emails that emerged in later litigation. But another nurse, Joseph Octaviano, turned out to be very helpful indeed. A few days later, he pulled Shari aside at the hospital and told her that the women were constantly telling Sumner that she and her children were liars, that they hated him, and that they never wanted to visit. He said they often berated Sumner, frequently reducing him to tears, and offered to tell Shari what he was seeing in the mansion, even though he knew he risked meeting the same fate as Paz.

Sumner's health crisis brought the long-simmering tensions between Sumner's family and his live-in companions into open warfare for the first time. Because Sydney and Manuela, and not his own family, were designated as his health care agents, health care decisions sparked screaming fights. One of them was overheard by Keryn, who was coming down the hallway toward Sumner's hospital room when she heard Shari, her daughter, Kim, and Sydney arguing about what she later learned was the doctor's recommendation to move the temporary feeding tube in his nose to a permanent one in his stomach. "Listen to the doctor," Sydney said, according to Keryn. "This is what the doctor is saying." Shari replied, "That's not kosher!" (In later court filings, Manuela alleged that Shari had opposed the permanent feeding tube, but Shari has denied opposing it. In an email to his family at the time, Tyler advised that "if there is no other possible way to provide nutrition, then a feeding tube may be necessary," adding, "If he's deemed competent to make a decision, it's not our call." It was ultimately installed.) Sumner, agitated, could only grunt his objection to their fighting, according to Keryn, saying, "Stop it! Stop it! I'm alive!"

*   *   *

Sumner returned to Beverly Park a shadow of his former self. He could not walk or stand on his own. He required a catheter. He would never eat another meal again. And perhaps worst of all, for the silver-tongued crusader whose way with words had been his ticket to success ever since he stood on the raised floorboards of Boston Latin School and delivered his declamations, the aspiration had, according to Manuela, caused brain damage that left him barely able to speak. What speech he had was limited almost entirely to monosyllabic grunts. He was more dependent upon Manuela and Sydney than ever, and Shari's hostility to them only made him push her farther away. "I just called to tell him that I love him and that I would be there tomorrow and all he kept saying was leave Sydney and Manuela alone," Shari wrote her children on September 15. "He said it 100 times. He was not interested in the fact that I loved him or that Tyler and I were coming out."

The next day, Shari and Tyler came to visit Sumner at his mansion

while Sydney and Manuela were out. Things quickly got tense, and
Sydney called the house, telling Sumner to ask his family to leave.
He did. Octaviano wrote Shari an email later that day saying the incident was typical of the way he had seen the women treat Sumner in
the past. "I witnessed verbal abuse almost every day," he said. "One
time Manuela told your Dad that none of his family loves him, except
them."

Shari thanked him and asked him to update her son Tyler going
forward. At twenty-eight, Tyler was the baby of the family, sharing
his mother's enthusiasm about the latest technology but also steeped
in the religious and mediation traditions of his father's family. Like
his father, he was both a lawyer and a rabbi, following in his father's
footsteps to earn his JD at Brooklyn Law School while simultaneously
studying for his rabbinical degree from Yeshiva Rabbi Chaim Berlin.
After college, he started his own legal practice, focusing on corporate
transactional work. He joined his friends' technology start-up, Bug-
Replay, as CEO and later cofounded another called tvParty, but starting in 2013, he also began bearing the responsibilities of a much older
man, joining the boards of both Brooklyn Law School and National
Amusements. At National, he served on the special committee created
to evaluate his mother's potential buyout in 2014, alongside David Andelman and George Abrams.

A pragmatic peacemaker by nature, Tyler was worried about his
mother's intention to sue the women. As negotiations for that potential buyout dragged into the fall, he became frustrated that his mother
still refused to consider signing the releases. "To not even consider the
releases is a mistake," he wrote in an email on September 30. "She's
going to be suing the women (and getting no money back), she's going to be suing Philippe (who supposedly says he won't enforce the
agreement naming her chairman), she's going to be suing NAI over
the redemption which she claims is a dividend to which she is entitled
to 20 percent—and that's a minimum."

As the missives ostensibly from Sumner ratcheted up the pressure, begging Shari to sign the releases to give him "peace of mind,"

Shari dug in. "And why would I ever give SMR his dying wish of peace when he never gave me any peace during my whole life?" she wrote to Tyler on October 1. "Going after those [women] will give me peace. They should get what they deserve." She hired a private investigator to research their pasts and told Tyler in an October 5 email that she was pleased with the initial results. "In one week we sure have them pegged based on background." A week later, her anger with her father was palpable. "He could not go to any stronger lengths to ensure we are all left with nothing and that his little sluts get it all with no interference by us," she wrote in an email. "And of course that David and George and Philippe are 100 percent protected and I can be dumped."

*   *   *

On November 14, 2014, Wall Street analysts dialing into Viacom's quarterly earnings call could just make out the words as Sumner opened the call in a faint voice: "Good morning, everyone. Here's my wise friend, Philippe." It would be the last time they would hear his voice.

Viacom had performed better than analysts expected, due to the surprise success of Paramount's latest Transformers movie. But beneath the quarter's performance lay some deep cracks in the core business. The cable networks were in free fall, with double-digit ratings declines across all the biggest networks. BET was down 34 percent for the season, Nickelodeon down 28 percent, and MTV down 27 percent in their target demographics. Dauman blamed the declines on Nielsen, which was not yet able to measure viewing on mobile devices. "We are at a transitional moment where the existing measurement services have not caught up to the marketplace," he said. Nielsen took his critique seriously enough to respond that same day, ensuring that it was "committed to delivering comprehensive measurement," but in general the rest of the industry interpreted Dauman's argument as—as one media executive derisively put it—"The dog ate my homework." Dauman announced a new plan to try to boost the amount of advertising revenue that was "non-Nielsen dependent" in the future, suggesting that no one should expect ratings improvements, or measurement improvements, anytime soon. Even more potentially dangerous, over the summer, two small distributors, Suddenlink Communications and Cable One, had dropped Viacom's entire package of two dozen channels and lived to tell about it. Between them, they only accounted for a little more than two million subscribers, but analysts worried that they might signal the beginning of the end of Viacom's distribution dominance.

For years Viacom had used the leverage of Nickelodeon's pole position among kids' channels and must-have shows like *The Daily Show* to force cable and satellite companies to take its entire package of twenty-two channels, increasing their fees every few years when the distribution contracts were set to expire. But with every media company doing some version of this, the average cable bill was rapidly approaching $100 a month, a wholly unsustainable price point in a world filled with appealing $8 alternatives like Netflix. Everyone knew the dam was going to break, and soon. Viacom's distribution troubles seemed like they might be the breaking point. Analysts openly fretted that Dish Network, with its roughly thirteen million subscribers and mercurial, poker-playing CEO Charlie Ergen, could be next. But on the call Dauman assured the analysts that Suddenlink and Cable One were "isolated incidents."

Two months later, Dauman's contract was extended for another two years. "Philippe has been my long-term partner in building Viacom into the global entertainment powerhouse that it is today," Sumner said in a statement. "He has been an extraordinary CEO over more than eight years, and his strategic vision and creative leadership have delivered outstanding operational and financial results."

A week later, the company revealed that Dauman's compensation had risen 19 percent in the previous fiscal year to $44.3 million, even though the company's share price had fallen 8 percent during that time.

*   *   *

Three days later, on January 29, 2015, a number of Sumner's nurses and household staff, including Octaviano, filed a report with Los Angeles County Adult Protective Services, alleging that Sydney and Manuela had been mentally and financially abusing Sumner, according to Sumner's lawyers. January had been a brutal month in Beverly Park, filled with crying and screaming from Sumner, as the fight to get Shari, her mother, and her children to sign releases protecting Sydney and Manuela reached its climax—a letter from Sumner to Shari and her children threatening to bar them from his funeral unless she signed. Through it all, Octaviano's emails provided Tyler a behind-the-scenes look at how the correspondence coming to them from Sumner came to be, and why family members were having trouble getting through to Sumner. On January 8, for example, the day that Shari's family received the threatening letter, Sydney met with estate planning attorney Leah Bishop and Sumner in the fish room at around eleven a.m. By eleven thirty, Octaviano wrote, he could overhear Sumner crying during the meeting. A while later, Sydney came by to tell Octaviano that Sumner was not to receive phone calls from the family, "especially Shari and Kim," though Steven Sweetwood, his stockbroker and step-nephew, and Keryn Redstone could be put through.

A few days later, on January 12, Kim finally got through and spoke to her grandfather on the phone. When Sumner told Sydney that he had told Kim that she and her two young children were welcome to visit anytime, Sydney got angry, telling Sumner that Kim was a liar just like the rest of the family, Octaviano reported. Sumner replied by screaming, "I love Kim!" prompting more screaming from Sydney.

These incidents fit into a broader pattern of abuse outlined by nurses Jeremy Jagiello, Octaviano, and Paz in sworn declarations for later litigation. In their telling, Sydney and Manuela spent a great deal of time coaching Sumner on what to say to Bishop, sometimes writing a script in large letters on a notepad so that he could memorize his lines before estate planning meetings. They woke him up to have him sign cash withdrawal forms or legal documents when he was groggy. And during sensitive meetings with the women about money, the nurses were sent from the room but often overheard Sumner crying; when the meeting was over, they would come back in to find Sumner had gotten so upset that he had soiled himself and had been sitting like that for at least a half an hour. Jagiello reported that putting through calls from Sumner's family around this time was a "fireable offense."

Sydney believes these anecdotes are fabrications by nurses who were on Shari's payroll. In Manuela's legal filings, she argues that after Paz got $10,000 from Shari, the other nurses expected similar largesse to side with her, or at least job security. In one email between Octaviano and Shari in Sydney's legal filings, he responds to her question about what she could do for him by telling her that he would like to buy a house.

Adult Protective Services sent an investigator to the house to visit with Sumner, but Sydney, who was out of town, instructed staff not to let them in, and instead to ask them to make an appointment for later, according to Jagiello's declaration. When the appointment came a few days later, the investigator walked in to find Sumner surrounded by the women and lawyers, including Robert Shapiro, best known as a onetime member of O.J. Simpson's legal "dream team," one of the big legal guns that Sumner had encouraged Sydney and Manuela to hire to protect them from Shari. The investigator only spoke to Sumner, the women, and the lawyers, but not to any of the nurses, staff, or family, according to Jagiello, who was at the house that day. Adult Protective Services never took any action on that complaint, or on another one filed in August of that year. Manuela's lawyers claim that the abuse complaints were bogus.

Undeterred, Shari and Tyler continued to gather information about what was going on inside the house. At times, the nurses' communications to them suggested that some nurses were not merely listening, but secretly recording conversations between Sumner, the women, and their lawyers—a crime in the state of California.

*　　*　　*

Ultimately, though, it was not Shari's manipulations but Sydney and Manuela's fear of what Shari would do to them after Sumner died that led to their downfall. In the spring of 2015, Sydney and Manuela decided to go public with their relationship with Sumner by participating in a *Vanity Fair* profile by veteran investigative business reporter William D. Cohan. They saw the profile as a chance to show the world Sumner's love for them and contempt for Shari, and thus create a bulwark against the likely challenge to their inheritance. Viacom spokesman Carl Folta thought it unwise, but he was overruled. Manuela and Sydney hired powerful spinmeister Mike Sitrick, founder of the preeminent LA crisis PR firm Sitrick & Co., and sat for formal portraits for the piece in red carpet–worthy evening gowns.

Given Sumner's extreme difficulties speaking, Cohan would not be allowed to visit or interview him, but there would be an emailed question-and-answer portion that Shari knew Folta and Bishop were crafting Sumner's answers for. Shari worried that they were "all out to do a major trashing of me in the story," she wrote Tyler. "I don't know what your grandfather will say. Probably whatever the women tell him to say." If she didn't have her lawyer and spokeswoman to protect her, she felt that she wouldn't survive, she said, adding, "Because this is war."

Shari's instincts were right. Octaviano got a peek at a draft of the questions and answers a few days later and reported back to Shari that they were not favorable to her. They said that the only family member who visited him was Keryn and that Sumner regretted giving Shari power at the company. He also reported seeing Sydney write notes for Sumner to read to Bishop over the phone about the article or dictate a sentence to him—"I kicked Shari out of the house"—that he repeated over and over again, preparing to tell it to Bishop. (People close to Sydney said this is not true.)

Ultimately, however, Bishop did not think that responses to the magazine criticizing Shari were a good idea. On April 9, a lawyer named Adam Streisand, who had worked with Bishop at Loeb & Loeb and had recently jumped to Sheppard Mullin, where he began representing

Sydney and Manuela, sent an email to the women recommending that Sumner refrain from antagonizing Shari in his emailed interview. "The main concern by Viacom/Leah et al. is that if Sumner shames Shari publicly then Shari will seek to establish a conservatorship over Sumner," he wrote. "If she does that, then his current condition will become public, and Viacom will have to remove Sumner as an officer/director and stop paying him compensation."

When the email leaked a year later, Shari denied having ever considered conservatorship of her father. But the email stands as probably the single most damning piece of evidence that the people around Sumner—including Dauman, Tom Dooley, Shari, and Andelman, who were all on the boards of the public companies that Sumner controlled—likely knew that Sumner was unfit to serve on these boards nearly a year before he stepped down as the salary-drawing executive chairman of Viacom and CBS. At least two of these people—Dauman and Andelman—were among the trustees with the power to determine whether Sumner lacked the capacity to remain in control of the trust that held all National Amusements shares. According to the terms of Sumner's trust, Sumner could be deemed "mentally incapacitated" only if he was judged "incompetent" by a court of proper jurisdiction, or if three doctors sent the trustees certification that he was "unable to manage his affairs in a competent manner." And yet they never did it. So long as Dauman and his supporters, like George Abrams, were on the trust, Shari had no incentive to trigger it, since she would likely be outvoted in exactly the same way she had been on the Midway fiasco. And so long as Sumner kept signing off on ever-larger pay packages for Dauman, he had no incentive to take action, either. In the next couple of years, both Dauman and Shari would file lawsuits alleging that Sumner lacked mental capacity or was subject to manipulation. But for now, Sumner continued to pass the mental capacity tests that Bishop arranged, and the status quo rolled on.

In the end, calmer heads prevailed, and the *Vanity Fair* article—titled "Who Controls Sumner Redstone?"—did not contain any quotes from Sumner attacking Shari. But it was a meticulously reported bombshell nonetheless. Folta and Dooley went on the record for the first time about his health. "He's lost some of his mobility in his jaw," Dooley told Cohan, but he had been making strides working with a speech therapist. Folta added that "he can't run out of a building," confirming reports that he could not walk, but refusing to confirm rumors of his still-secret feeding tube. When the topic turned to Sumner's mind, Dooley said, "He's sharp as a tack."

The most astonishing aspect of the story, however, came out of the mouth of Manuela, discussing how she and Sydney regarded their financial arrangement with Sumner. She told Cohan that when Sumner dies, she expects to be taken care of. "It's such a fine line when you talk about money," she said. "He considers me family and my children family. I mean, that's his whole thing. He's like, 'You're my family.' You don't pick your family in life, but Sumner Redstone does. He just does. He wants who he wants in his life." She said he told her that he wants her to run his foundation when he dies, and she made clear she expects gifts in his will, for both herself and Sydney. "I have to tell you, would she be there if he wasn't doing something for her? Probably not. But does she love him? Absolutely. I don't have a doubt in my mind," Manuela said of Sydney. Sydney was "a good girl and she has his best interests at heart. For her, it's a job almost, it's a job." (Sydney never looked at the relationship as a job, according to people close to her.)

Among the people shocked by the article was a forty-nine-year-old former actor and ex-con named George Pilgrim, who had been carrying on an affair with Sydney for nearly a year. Blessed with hunky good looks that helped him land roles on *Guiding Light* and Showtime's erotic thriller *Red Shoe Diaries*, Pilgrim had had what he called an "extremely colorful" life, having served more than two years in prison, from 2006 to 2008, for his involvement in an advertising fraud scheme. From the beginning, he had known that Sydney was Sumner's live-in girlfriend, having reached out to her on Facebook after reading a story in the Hollywood trade press in the spring of 2014 about her lawsuit against Naylor. Pilgrim had also been battling Naylor over her refusal to release her assistant from her contract so that she might join a reality show that Pilgrim was pitching, and Pilgrim thought he and Sydney could join forces. He sent his phone number, she called him, and by mid-2014, they were dating. She was so taken with his bad boy backstory that she optioned the autobiography he was writing, *Citizen Pilgrim*, for her production company, Rich Hippie Productions. She bought a $3.5 million house in Sedona, Arizona, where he had been paroled to his parents' house, and he soon moved into it. They joined a country club together, flew back and forth by private jet, sent each other sexually explicit texts, and talked of marriage. In late 2014, Pilgrim sent her emojis of a family, a ring, and a bride, and then called her to propose. He later texted, "Is that yes?" and she replied "yes yes," followed by a string of heart emojis. Around this time, Sydney asked him to donate his sperm and tried to get pregnant via in vitro fertilization. A devotee of New Age spirituality, she arranged black tourmaline crystals around the Sedona house to ward off bad luck. They must have worked: at one point, Jim Elroy, the former FBI agent whom Shari had hired to investigate the women, called the house, but Shari never took any action to expose Sydney.

Meanwhile, Sydney told Pilgrim that her relationship with Sumner was not romantic. He was her "mentor," she said, and she was in charge of his health care. When Pilgrim got impatient, texting her to run away with him, Sydney replied, "Yes please." "Waiting for a man to die!!! Fuck that we can be explorers travel the world Indiana jones stuff," Pilgrim texted. "I know," Sydney responded. "It sucks for both of us I am sorry." To make sure she got her inheritance, she told Pilgrim that she had to be vigilant about not leaving Sumner alone with his family. "Listen I can barely leave the house," she told him, later adding that "he is old and crying all the time," but Sumner's family "won't be able to do much I will be here the whole time and so will pitbull," Sydney and Pilgrim's nickname for Manuela. When Kim came to visit, Sydney snapped a photo of her watching television with Sumner and texted it to Pilgrim, saying, "It's so fake and phony, she is such a little spy and I am not leaving this room."

Given Pilgrim's assumptions about their relationship, when the

Vanity Fair story came out quoting Sydney rhapsodizing about how Sumner has "this beautiful hair" and "the most beautiful skin I've ever seen in my life," Pilgrim flew into a jealous rage. He was drinking heavily, and by May 2015, Sydney had convinced him to check himself into a rehab facility outside Austin, Texas, with her mother as his sponsor. While he was in there, she kicked him out of the Sedona house. When he found out about that, he broke out of rehab, flagged down a taxicab, and talked the cabdriver into driving him eighteen hours back to Sedona. They broke up, and soon lawyers got involved. Sydney wanted Pilgrim's silence, and Pilgrim wanted Sydney's millions. Their lawyers batted dollar figures back and forth, and by August, a $10 million settlement was on the table that would have given Pilgrim a share of the proceeds from the Sedona house and a chunk of Sydney's inheritance from Sumner, so long as he and the people close to him signed nondisclosure agreements.

But in late August 2015, Pilgrim, who is bipolar, had grown impatient with the talks. One night he and his former girlfriend, with whom he had gotten back together after he and Sydney broke up, wandered into the posh Beverly Hills wine bar Wally's, which was owned by a group of investors that included the family of Manuela's daughter Christy's boyfriend, Matt Marciano, the son of Guess? Jeans cofounder Georges Marciano. They found themselves seated next to Manuela, her son, her daughter Christy, and Marciano. Pilgrim knew who they were, but they didn't know he existed. As he listened to their banter, he began to wonder whether he was doing the right thing. A week later—two days before his settlement was supposed to go through—he was invited to a party at Wally's where he saw Marciano again. This time, he decided to blow it all up. He introduced himself to Marciano as Sydney Holland's fiancé, and showed the photos on his phone as proof. Word got back to Manuela, who was angry at having been kept in the dark about Pilgrim, and everyone involved decided that Sydney had to come clean. On August 30, 2015, Sydney and her high-profile attorney, Patty Glaser (who is Robert Shapiro's law partner), sat Sumner down and told him about Pilgrim. By the end, both

Sydney and Sumner were in tears. Within forty-eight hours, she and Alexandra were gone.

Manuela consolidated power immediately. On September 3, Sumner called in Bishop, wrote Sydney out of his will, and boosted Manuela's bequests in the will to $50 million in addition to his Beverly Park mansion, worth an estimated $20 million. (Sumner had already made Manuela the joint tenant on his $3.75 million Carlyle Hotel apartment so she would inherit it when he died.) He also removed Sydney as his health care agent, so that now Manuela held the role alone. Dauman was named as the alternate. In court documents, Manuela held up the fact that Sumner did not choose members of his own family for this role as evidence of Sumner's estrangement from Shari. To make sure the changes stuck, Bishop called in geriatric psychiatrist Dr. James Spar to administer a mental capacity exam, which Sumner passed. She later told the *Wall Street Journal* that this was done "to safeguard against meritless challenges."

Manuela knew she would need backup for her new role. The day after Sydney left, she called Keryn, who for months had been discussing moving from Colorado to Los Angeles, and told her to move immediately. Keryn's presence in the house meant that, among other things, Manuela couldn't be accused of barring Sumner's family from seeing him. But Keryn was a safe ally for Manuela because she might have been the one person on earth who hated Shari more than she did. Keryn had been fighting with her own parents, Brent and Annie, over the trust that they set up for her, and she had not yet passed the bar, so she needed financial help with the move. Sumner agreed to loan her his credit card for moving expenses, hotels, and food, she said in court documents. Soon after she arrived, on September 9, Sumner set up a $1 million trust in her name, with Manuela as the trustee. She wasn't allowed to touch the principal for twenty years, but she could live off the income. To help her through her immediate financial problems, Sumner agreed to give her $15,000 in 2015 and $15,000 in 2016 and told her, according to Keryn, "You can have any job you want."

When she first got to LA, Keryn found Sumner agitated and angry, obsessed with seeing pictures of George Pilgrim and bulking up his mansion's security after Manuela told him that Pilgrim and Sydney were plotting to kill him. But he also just cried a lot. Soon he became obsessed with a woman named Terry Holbrook, a sixty-year-old former Ford model and Dallas Cowboy cheerleader whom he had known since 2010. Holbrook said he had been sponsoring her two show horses for years, adding, "He's been a savior in my life." Manuela claimed Holbrook had received some $7 million from Sumner since 2010, including a house and monthly payments of $4,500, which Sumner's driver would leave for her at the Beverly Park guard gate. According to Keryn, Holbrook's visits were arranged by Jagiello, one of the nurses who was secretly loyal to Shari, who would "translate" Sumner's grunts to Holbrook during their encounters. Over time, Keryn alleged that Jagiello controlled Sumner through his access to Holbrook. Sumner's obsession grew so intense that he would sometimes ask for her multiple times a day, forgetting that he had already done so.

Manuela was wary of Holbrook. According to Sumner's lawyers, she had Sumner's doctor tell him that he was only allowed to have sex once a week. When he insisted on seeing Holbrook anyway, Sumner's lawyers claim Manuela made up excuses why she could not come—she was sick, her mother was sick, she had to cancel at the last minute. Holbrook says these were never true. "I told him, 'If somebody tells you that I can't see you, they are lying,'" she said.

Most important, Manuela wanted to keep Sydney away. When, in early October, Sydney's lawyer asked Bishop to hand-deliver a letter for her to Sumner in which she profusely apologized for her infidelity and professed her love, Manuela intercepted the letter and replaced it with one she wrote herself. According to Sumner's lawyers, the letter read:

Sumner
  I did not lie to you everyone else is lying I never had an affair with that man
  It's not true people are just trying to break us up.
  You have to believe me I never lied to you I don't know who he is.

Don't understand why you don't believe me and you believe everybody else.

Sydney

Sumner's lawyers claim that Manuela had the nurses read Sumner that letter instead of the real one. Manuela, in a separate lawsuit, appears to claim that the draft of that letter was planted on her computer by Shari's allies.

Meanwhile, Jagiello was eavesdropping on happenings in the house and sending word back to Tyler. According to Manuela's complaint in one lawsuit, Jagiello even recorded meetings between Sumner and Manuela and Bishop and Dr. James Spar, the geriatric psychiatrist whom Bishop used to give Sumner mental capacity exams, sent the information to Shari and her lawyers. The complaint also alleges that Jagiello got an email address and password from Sumner's driver, Isileli "Isi" Tuanaki, and used it to log on to Manuela's email and the video recordings of the network of cameras that the women—they claimed at Sumner's request—had set up around the house.

On September 18, Jagiello and Tyler texted about their plans to oust Manuela from the house.

"Good morning," Jagiello texted Tyler. "Thanks for talking last night. Seal team commence operation freedom today! FYI! I will keep you posted . . ."

"Ha it kinda does take seal precision! Thanks for the update," Tyler replied.

"Let's hope this goes well. SMR asked me same question this am. Once he knows the truth he is going to be livid! . . . Also do you think it is a good idea to take video footage of Manuela/Keryn post reveal while shit hitting the fan for everyone's protection? Also Philippe working closely with Manuela," Jagiello wrote.

"Video can't hurt (unless you're caught!) . . . may also help protect you if M [Manuela] fires anyone against smr wishe[s]."

When Manuela's ouster did finally come, her response would rock the Redstones' global empire to its foundations.

CHAPTER 21

Sex and Steak

B y October 2015, Sumner's silence on Wall Street was deafening. He had not spoken on an earnings call in nearly a year and attended neither Viacom's nor CBS's annual meetings that year. Meanwhile, media stocks had tanked in August after Disney CEO Bob Iger said that ESPN—long considered so essential to pay-TV distributors that it could charge them a stunning $7 per subscriber, many times more than any other channel—had experienced "some subscriber losses." Investors took those words as confirmation of their long-held fears that the cable bundle was coming apart. Viacom, having delivered disappointing earnings, was hit hardest. By early October, its stock had dropped more than 40 percent over the past year.

For longtime investors who had watched Sumner fire CEO after CEO following far more modest drops in Viacom's stock price, Dauman's continued employment seemed clear evidence that Sumner was no longer himself. At one point, Shari had been so distraught over Dauman's performance that she went to him directly and said they both knew he was not the right person to lead the company. (Dauman replied that he didn't intend to be CEO for life, but the company had some key affiliate deals coming up that he felt were important for him to be involved in.) When that didn't work, she went to the committees of the board, begging them to get rid of Dauman. But Viacom's board was stacked with Sumner intimates like George Abrams and William Schwartz, who had been there since Sumner took over the company in 1987. Those who did not fall into this category had little leverage. Unhappy with the direction of the company but concluding there was little he could do about it under the current governance structure, Bob Kraft, Shari's ally, left the board in August.

On October 7, 2015, the *Wall Street Journal* wrote a front-page story about the growing investor unrest over Viacom's performance and questions about Sumner's mental state. The story counted Shari, who had lost a huge share of her and her children's personal fortune from the stock drop, among the unhappy investors, and included the ominous line for Dauman that, while Shari had not been clearly named as her father's successor, she saw a path to control of the trust. Hours before the story was to be published, Sumner emailed the *Journal* voicing full-throated support for Dauman, saying he "continues to have my unequivocal support and trust." And then he took a swipe at Shari with echoes of the 2007 *Forbes* letter, saying that "the transfer of what I created—my controlling interest in Viacom and CBS—to an independent trust that I set up decades ago will ensure that the assets are professionally managed for the benefit of all shareholders. Recent speculation about personal agendas has only confirmed for me the wisdom of my decision."

This was Daumanese for "Back off, Shari." The idea that Sumner could have written, or even dictated, this statement strained credulity, but Viacom's leadership had closed ranks, pointing to the mental capacity tests that he had recently passed when he wrote Sydney out of his will. The *Journal* later reported that Dauman had written the statement heaping praise on himself with the help of Folta, though there had been some editing changes—from whom it wasn't entirely clear—made at the mansion.

The day after the article ran, Dauman went to visit Sumner. The old man sat in his upholstered armchair watching baseball on mute while Dauman took the seat to his left and Manuela took the seat to his right. In a later affidavit, Dauman claimed that Sumner was "engaged and attentive" during this visit. "We had an extensive business discussion regarding articles that had appeared recently in the *New York Times* and the *Wall Street Journal*, and we also discussed personal matters," he said. Manuela described the scene differently. "During the time that Mr. Dauman was in the room, Sumner looked at him only a few times. Most of the time, Sumner was gazing somewhat vacantly toward the television or me. During the entirety of Mr. Dauman's visit, there was no two-way conversation or discussion between Mr. Dauman and Sumner. None whatsoever . . . It was a monologue by Mr. Dauman that Sumner did not appear to comprehend."

Sumner's mental state during this apparently inconsequential meeting would turn out to be very consequential indeed—because of what happened next. Exactly how Manuela Herzer came to be ejected from Sumner Redstone's mansion less than a week after this meeting is lost in a fog of accusations and counteraccusations, but a few things are clear. The first is that Sumner did not handle the breakup with Sydney well. He cried all the time and was more fragile and vulnerable than at any point in his long life. The second is that Manuela was not beloved by the household staff. She was a tough, demanding boss on a good day, and in the tense weeks following Sydney's departure— when the tabloids were beginning to whisper she was next—she unleashed what staff called a "reign of terror" on the people working in the house. The third is that this terror extended into her wanting to keep rivals out of the house, whether they be Sydney or any of the women who Sumner casually paid for sex.

According to Manuela's legal filings, in the days following Dauman's visit, a group of nurses and staff members loyal to Shari—Tuanaki, Jagiello, and another nurse named Igor Franco—went to Sumner to stage an "intervention" against Manuela. Tuanaki presented Sumner with his will, telling him that he had only planned to leave Manuela $15 million instead of the $50 million that he had left her. According to the filings, Sumner responded with a simple, final statement ending their relationship: "Call Leah."

According to Sumner's legal filings, the staff's mutiny against Manuela was about love, not money. In this version, the staff told Sumner that Manuela had been making them lie about the availability of one of his favorite female companions, Terry Holbrook, and had intercepted Sydney's real letter of apology.

Manuela woke up on the morning of October 12 worried about Sumner's health, according to her legal filings. He had seemed particularly out of sorts at the previous evening's movie night with his friends, CBS board member Arnold Kopelson and his wife, Anne, and had even had to have the room cleared at one point so that his windpipe could be suctioned. Manuela told one of the nurses that his doctor should examine him that day, and then went out to run errands. When she got back later that morning, everything had changed.

"Mr. Redstone doesn't want you here," Tuanaki told her as she approached him in the hallway, according to her filings. She walked past him, down the hall, and into the sitting room, where Sumner, a nurse, several aides, and Bishop were awaiting her. Mayhem broke out. Bishop, who had Andelman on the line, held up her cell phone and yelled, "You can't be here!" And then, to Andelman, "Manuela is here but is not supposed to be here. I don't know how she came in."

Manuela went up to Sumner, who was staring vacantly. "Are you okay?" she asked him. In Manuela's telling, Sumner said nothing. In the telling of Gabrielle Vidal, Sumner's lawyer at Loeb & Loeb, he said, "Yes."

Bishop demanded that Manuela leave the house so that she could talk to him alone. "Do you want me to leave? Are you mad at me?" Manuela asked Sumner. Again, in Manuela's telling, Sumner said nothing. Again, in the telling of Sumner's lawyers, he said, "Yes."

Manuela asked a third time, and Sumner grunted and began to bawl. Manuela asked Jagiello what Sumner said. Jagiello replied that Sumner had said he wanted her to leave. "What do I do?" Manuela asked Bishop. Bishop said that Sumner wanted to talk to her alone and that Manuela could come back later and collect her things. As Manuela left the room, she looked over her shoulder at Sumner, who was still sobbing.

When Manuela called Bishop later to ask why she had been kicked out, Bishop would only tell her that she had "lied" to Sumner. When she asked Dauman, he told her that the "lie" had been the credit card that Sumner had allowed Keryn to use and then forgotten about, and the cameras she had installed, she claimed with Sumner's permission. ("I did not lie," Manuela said in court papers. "Sumner had simply forgotten what he said.")

On October 16, Manuela was removed as Sumner's health care agent and erased from his will, paving the way for Shari and her children to reenter Sumner's life. Dauman was made the health care agent. The house was stripped of photos of Manuela and her family and, according to Manuela's filings, household staff was made to sign loyalty oaths promising not to speak to Sumner about Manuela or communicate with her. Keryn was also banished, unable to visit her "Grumpy" until a lawyer-negotiated visit in February.

But Manuela was not about to go quietly. In the spring, she and Sydney had hired Pierce O'Donnell, a charismatic, high-profile, and wildly expensive Hollywood lawyer expert at using the press as a weapon in litigation, to protect them from the legal challenge they expected from Sumner's family after he died. O'Donnell had just become a household name in Los Angeles for his role in another case that involved a rich, older man of questionably sound mind, a much-younger girlfriend, and a high-profile media asset hanging in the balance. He had represented Shelly Sterling, the wife of Los Angeles Clippers owner Donald Sterling, in a case that led to her selling the team to former Microsoft chief Steve Ballmer after her husband's racist rant was released to TMZ by an ex-girlfriend. Sumner had paid O'Donnell's $100,000 retainer, and for months he had worked closely with Bishop to shore up Sumner's gifts to the women.

Now, with those bequests stripped away, O'Donnell suddenly found himself squaring off against Loeb & Loeb as he tried to get Manuela an audience with Sumner and a chance to reclaim her belongings. Finally, on November 23, after a blizzard of negotiation between their legal teams, Manuela was allowed back into the mansion briefly. The scene resembled "trying to enter the White House," recalled another of her lawyers, Ronald Richards. Plainclothes security guards were all over the grounds, each guard wearing a Secret Service–esque radio earpiece. An opaque black curtain had been hung near Sumner's bedroom with a half-dozen security guards around it so that there would be no visual or auditory contact. "It was as if Mr. Redstone was a prisoner in his own home," Richards said, adding that after they left, the house was swept for bugs.

On November 25, 2015, with her designer clothes now safely in her possession, Manuela dropped the bombshell that would alter the future of two major public media companies. She filed a petition in Los Angeles Superior Court to be reinstated as Sumner's health care agent, arguing that Sumner was non compos mentis when he signed the papers removing her and demanding that his mental capacity be tested by an independent doctor. It was a tricky argument for her to make, because she had to show that Sumner had had his marbles as recently as early September, when he left her $70 million in his will and made her sole health care agent, and then suddenly lost them over the next six weeks. The lawsuit was a stalking horse for her lawyers to be able to gather evidence about Sumner's mental capacity, with the aim of challenging his decision to strip her from his will after he died. Its impact, however, went far beyond that because the question that Manuela was asking—*is anybody in there?*—was the same one that Viacom and CBS investors were asking. The media feasted on her complaint, which was brimming with prurient details about Sumner's life as a spaced-out, incontinent, wholly dependent "living ghost" who was nonetheless obsessed with eating steak and having sex daily. Most damningly for the boards and top management of Viacom, CBS, and National Amusements, Manuela claimed he was "unable to follow plot lines of films or television shows or follow conversations of more than a brief duration," unable to write, unable to converse "except for brief grunted responses to directed questions," and no longer aware of what was going on in world events or the financial markets.

If Manuela's account of Sumner's status was correct—and in this matter, her credibility was greatly aided by the fact that she was calling for an independent doctor to come examine him—then a great fraud had been perpetrated upon the shareholders of Viacom and CBS, who had been paying tens of millions of dollars to an "executive chairman" who could not manage to stay awake until the end of a televised baseball game and sobbed through the opening credits of *Deadpool*. Worse still, his name and quotes were being used to justify the continued employment of a CEO who had just overseen the evaporation of half his company's value in the last two years. Dauman had almost no choice but to respond. And so, immediately after Manuela filed her suit, Sumner's lawyers at Loeb & Loeb filed their response trying to block further discovery, attaching an affidavit from Dauman in which he described finding Sumner "engaged and attentive" during his recent visits.

Wall Street howled in protest, sending Viacom's stocks and, to a lesser degree, CBS's, tumbling. Mario Gabelli, whose funds own the second-largest portion of Viacom voting shares outside the Redstone family, asked Dauman for more disclosure about Sumner's mental competency. "All I know is, you cannot have Philippe Dauman, the CEO of a company that has some business issues, in a position where the press is saying maybe there's some lack of credibility," he said. "I'm just asking for some clarity, which is what any public company has to do."

Sumner's lawyers at Loeb & Loeb furiously fought to keep Sumner from having to submit to a mental exam, but they could not protect Dauman. Because of his earlier affidavit, Manuela's lawyers had grounds to subpoena him seeking his deposition. Dauman was forced to hire his own legal team to try to quash the subpoena. Meanwhile, as Dauman was fighting a legal battle to preserve his credibility, an activist Viacom investor named Eric Jackson attacked his business acumen in a scathing ninety-nine-page slideshow arguing that he should be fired. With just $300 million in assets under management, Jackson's SpringOwl Asset Management could hardly throw its weight around in the tightly controlled company. But Jackson's cheeky slideshow—with its multiple *Weekend at Bernie's* references and sarcastic French cartoons reacting to Dauman's outsize pay ("Oo-la-la, c'est trop cher!")—was a viral hit among the investor class. Bob Kraft's office asked for a copy.

The effect of the slideshow was such that, as Viacom's annual disclosure of its executives' compensation loomed a few days later, the company attempted to bury the news of Dauman's latest pay raise by releasing information about his compensation in pieces. On January 20, Viacom took the highly unusual step of announcing that Sumner's pay had declined 85 percent in fiscal 2015 due to his reduced responsibilities and that Dauman's bonus had declined 30 percent, without any further elaboration. But when the full proxy came out two days later, Dauman's total compensation had actually grown 22 percent to $54.2 million in fiscal 2015, while the company's stock price dropped 44 percent.

It was just too egregious. Wall Street wanted his head on a pike. Instead, it would have to settle for the knowledge than Manuela's hand-picked geriatric psychiatrist would soon be evaluating Sumner's mental state, following the order of a California judge in her case. For the boards of Viacom and CBS, that meant the jig was up. Although the results of the exam were to remain sealed, just days after the doctor drove through the gates of Beverly Park to administer the exam, both Viacom and CBS announced that Sumner was stepping down from his position as executive chairman.

CBS went first, offering a master class in Shari relations. The CBS board offered her the position of nonexecutive chairman, in accordance with her rights, but Shari declined the offer and nominated Moonves for the job of executive chairman. In his statement on the move, he thanked her and praised "her business acumen and knowledge of the media space." At Viacom, which was caught unawares by CBS's move, there were no such niceties. Ahead of Viacom's board meeting to vote on its next chairman, Shari put out a statement saying she didn't believe her father's successor should be "entwined in Redstone family matters, but rather a leader with an independent voice." Briefly believing this meant that Dauman was out, the market sent Viacom's stock up 5 percent on the morning of the board meeting. But when the vote for the next executive chairman was held, Dauman got every vote except for Shari's, sending the stock back down. Wells Fargo analyst Marci Ryvicker wrote that Dauman's "elevation to executive chairman likely means there will not be a change in control," adding that "this is the most likely cause of the stock's pullback." CBS shares, meanwhile, were up 1 percent.

Rarely in American business has an executive gotten such a big promotion under such crushing pressure. Three days after becoming executive chairman, Dauman broke from his typically unflappable decorum and lashed out at his critics on an earnings call with analysts, saying, "Our outlook and the facts have been distorted by the naysayers, self-interested critics and publicity seekers." But these words rang hollow amid reports of yet another catastrophically bad quarter, in which revenue and profit declined, revenue missed analysts' estimates, and the company was forced to lower its earnings guidance for the future because it wasn't going to be able to get as much money from subscription fees anymore. The stock dropped 13 percent on the earnings, close to a five-year low. When an analyst asked what qualities the board had seen in him and his performance to merit his new role, Dauman replied that the stock drop was accentuated by "a lot of noise that's surrounding us," adding, "I think it's obvious to everybody what the noise is."

If Dauman was going to survive, he would need to do something big, and fast. In the last year, he had made several smart deals, including the purchase of the British broadcaster Channel 5, which immediately bolstered Viacom's international division's results, and a forward-looking deal with Snapchat to sell advertising against the vanishing-messages app company's owned and operated content. But none of these could offset the effects of the huge ratings declines and distribution woes that the core cable channels were still suffering. For years, many on Wall Street had grumbled that Viacom ought to get rid of Paramount, which was financially hardly worth the headache it took to run. Paramount had been able to provide some surges of profits at key moments in the past, but by early 2016, it had come in last at the box office for each of the last four years, as Brad Grey pursued a cautious strategy of making fewer movies than competitors in hopes of focusing more on profits. As franchises like Transformers and Paranormal Activity began to age, losses widened. By the end of fiscal 2016, Paramount had lost $445 million.

So, two weeks after becoming executive chairman, Dauman announced that Viacom was looking to sell a minority stake in Paramount by the end of June. The plan made some sense. The market was only assigning Paramount a value of about $1 billion, but Dauman believed that the mystique of the 104-year-old Hollywood studio, along with its vast library of more than three thousand titles, could get a partner to value it at closer to $10 billion—particularly if that partner was of the deep-pocketed, starstruck, Chinese variety like Dalian Wanda Group Co., which had just paid $3.5 billion for Legendary Entertainment, the production company behind *Jurassic World* that wouldn't even qualify as a "mini-major" studio, let alone a major. Indeed, by mid-March, Dauman claimed to have received interest in Paramount from three dozen firms, including "some Asian interest." It would later emerge that Wanda, led by China's richest man and with ambitions to form an entertainment powerhouse with assets like AMC Entertainment and Dick Clark Productions, was in talks to buy a 49 percent stake in Paramount. Analysts and investors largely applauded the idea, especially Gabelli, who had publicly called for Paramount to do a similar deal with Alibaba or Amazon a few months earlier.

But anyone who knew Sumner knew that he would never go for it. Paramount was his baby, his reason for being, the kingdom that made him the "King of Hollywood." Soon after Dauman announced his plans to sell the Paramount stake, Sumner began to repeat the phrase "I don't want to sell Paramount" to anyone who would listen— household staff, Brad Grey, old friends and family. By April, his feelings had made their way onto the front page of the *Wall Street Journal*.

In the meantime, those hoping to keep prying eyes away from Sumner's mental state were dealt a blow: Los Angeles Superior Court Judge David Cowan ruled that Manuela's case challenging Sumner's mental capacity could proceed, and he set a trial date for May 6. In explaining his decision, he referred to the sealed thirty-seven-page report that Dr. Stephen Read had produced after examining Sumner in his mansion, calling it "sufficient to raise a reasonable question about whether Redstone lacked capacity," adding that it was "difficult to read in describing how this man is hanging on to life." He added that he found it "perplexing that Redstone still puts Philippe Dauman, and for that matter, Thomas Dooley, the COO of Viacom, ahead of his own daughter as his agent in case of incapacity," an arrangement that "does not give the Court confidence" that Shari and Sumner had patched up their relationship.

In the wake of this major victory for Manuela on many levels (since her complaint had also been full of allegations about how strained relations between Sumner and Shari were), the Redstones made a crucial decision: they hired a new lawyer named Rob Klieger to Sumner's legal team.

Up to that point, Sumner had been represented by Gabrielle Vidal, a litigator at Loeb & Loeb, the same law firm where Bishop worked as Sumner's estate attorney. They were experts in estate planning and probate cases, but as this case was now headed for a very public trial, Shari and her lawyers had some qualms with Loeb being the sole counsel, given that Vidal and Bishop were on Manuela's witness list. Vidal suggested an attorney, Klieger, who had been introduced to her husband, Aaron May, by a mutual friend. May called up Klieger and found that he was available. Klieger, who had recently joined the law firm of Hueston Hennigan, knew the business side of the empire well and had confidence and press-savvy and storytelling flair that rivaled—and ultimately bested—O'Donnell's.

Despite his gray-flecked temples, Klieger was young and dynamic, with a Gen X cadence to his speech and dark eyebrows that made him look a bit like the actor Bobby Cannavale. He had grown up in Pittsburgh in a family of doctors and graduated from Stanford Law School in 1997 with the second-highest grade point average in his class. Thereafter, he headed for Hollywood, where he represented many Redstone-controlled clients, including Paramount, MTV, Nickelodeon, and Showtime. Along the way, he also dabbled in the creative side of the movie business, cofounding a production company called the Paradise Collective and landing executive producer credits on films like the 2016 sci-fi thriller *Shortwave*. In the promotional shots for the company, he posed with a movie camera in his hand. His legal briefs read like screenplays, with tight pacing, colorful scenes, and masterful attention to character development.

His arrival signaled a major change in strategy. The Redstones were not simply going to fight Manuela in court to keep her away from Sumner. They were going to fight the whole machine—Manuela, Dauman, the boards, the trust, all of it—to put Shari in control, oust Dauman, and stop the destruction of the value of Viacom. The cornerstone of this strategy was to remove Dauman as Sumner's health care agent and replace him with Shari. The disagreement over the Paramount stake provided the perfect illustration of how Sumner and Dauman's long friendship had deteriorated.

"Sumner had become very disillusioned with Philippe, principally not because of Viacom's shitty performance, although that should have been enough, but principally because he didn't listen to him on Paramount," said one person close to Sumner. "As long as you are loyal to Sumner, he will give you leeway. Once he was disloyal to Sumner, Sumner no longer wanted to have anything to do with Philippe. So the first thing he wanted was to get Philippe off his health care agency."

The attorneys at Loeb & Loeb thought this was a highly risky maneuver on the eve of trial, but Klieger pushed for doing it anyway—for moving, in essence, from defense to offense. As Judge Cowan's statement on Shari's role showed, the risks for her were far greater not to be Sumner's health care agent than any risk of complicating the trial.

As the case headed to trial, both Shari and Dauman were subpoenaed to be deposed on the topic of Sumner's mental capacity—something both of them wanted desperately to avoid. And so, by early April, Manuela's and Sumner's legal teams had entered into settlement talks, which Shari helped drive. A deal was hammered out that would have given Manuela $30 million plus the Carlyle Hotel apartment tax-free. And most crucially, in the midst of but not tied to this settlement deal, Shari was made Sumner's health care agent in place of Dauman. The settlement talks fell apart, in part because Manuela came back with a series of demands, including that they cover her legal costs if she was sued by any member of their family, including their cousin Gary Snyder. Snyder, who also lived in Beverly Hills, had filed his own elder abuse complaint on Sumner's behalf against Manuela in March, drawn from the details that Manuela herself had included in her initial petition to be reinstated as Sumner's health care agent. The Redstones also refused to agree to Manuela's demand that they fire Jagiello and Tuanaki, who she believed had been disloyal to her. But most of all, she wanted to see Sumner one last time, and for her and her children to be at his funeral. (Even if she was enriched by her relationship to Sumner, she truly cared about him, according to people who know her.) The Redstones were not having it. Even after the talks fell apart, however, Shari kept her role as health care agent.

Shari was now fully in control. She told the court how her father's health "flourished" since she and her children have been able to visit regularly and taken over responsibility for his medical care.

* * *

The trial on May 6, 2016, was a full-blown media circus. The courtroom in Los Angeles Superior Court was so packed with reporters that officials were checking to make sure there was only one from every media outlet inside, forcing the rest to crowd in the hallway around a tiny, grimy window, where they could just make out PowerPoint slides with titles like "Redstone's Delusions." Shari was there, in a gray suit, with her son Brandon dressed more casually. So was Manuela, in black skirt and jacket, dark stockings, and black clunky heels. Shari shook her head "no" through much of O'Donnell's opening statement, which described his client's ouster as a "palace coup" that was "financed by his daughter Shari."

The main attraction, however, was a videotaped deposition of Sumner, aided by his speech therapist, which was played for a closed courtroom. Reporters were later given a transcript of the video. The transcript makes it impossible to tell exactly how well or authentically Sumner could form words, and where his own words end and the interpreter's begin. In the course of the deposition, Sumner tries and fails to spell out words with a pointer and cannot answer the question of what his birth name was. But the transcript has him answering a question about what he thinks Manuela lied to him about with the phrase "about Terry's availability and Sydney's letter"—words clearly supplied by the interpreter. But one phrase comes across clearly, over and over, parrot-like: "Manuela is a fucking bitch." And when asked whom he wants to make his health care decisions, he stutters but goes on to say "Shari."

"I think he said what he wanted to say," Judge Cowan said after watching the video. "How can I sit here and say, after seeing that video, 'No, you've got to have Manuela'?" The following Monday, the judge dismissed the case, saying Sumner clearly expressed that he didn't want Manuela in charge of his health care. But the judge was careful to note that this did not mean he was making a ruling of any kind on Sumner's mental capacity.

Klieger was triumphant, crowing that "Ms. Herzer bet wrong when she assumed that Mr. Redstone's difficulty communicating would result in her reinstatement in his life and fortune." An associate of O'Donnell's followed Shari from the courthouse to Sumner's mansion, where he served her with a new, $70 million lawsuit against her, her sons, and members of Sumner's staff accusing them of working together to destroy Manuela's relationship with Sumner and deprive her of her inheritance. Manuela's motives were now laid out on the table, and Shari was fully in charge. She was so pleased with Klieger's performance that she asked him to represent her in the lawsuit she knew was coming from Manuela. In the hallway outside the courtroom, she cried with relief. "I am grateful to the court for putting an end to this long ordeal," she said in a statement. "I am so happy for my father that he can now live his life in peace, surrounded by his friends and family."

Around lunchtime the day the trial was dismissed, an audio recording of Sumner pleading with a prospective lover to participate in a four-way with "Bob" and "the most beautiful producer" was posted to the gossip site Radar Online. "Bob's never done a threesome with two men," Sumner says on the recording. "He's done it with two women. So he's a little bit nervous but he's gonna come 'cause I want him to. So what will probably happen will probably really excite you. I'll fuck her and she'll suck Bob off and he'll fuck her and she'll suck me off. Before that, I'll make her jerk off in front of Bob because she's very hot when she jerks off. She's better than what you do. She takes a long time and she moans." The timing of the recording was not clear, but the *New York Post* claimed it was within the last two years. What dignity that had not been destroyed by the lawsuit was now completely gone.

CHAPTER 22

Pandemonium

Philippe Dauman's corner office was mostly filled with toys—
SpongeBob SquarePants dolls, Dora the Explorer tchotchkes,
and, most recently, a long lineup of Teenage Mutant Ninja Turtle
figurines representing the intellectual property–driven, merchandise-
powered global future he envisioned for Viacom. But his most prized
possession was a pair of boxing gloves signed by Mike Tyson and
Evander Holyfield minutes before Tyson bit off a chunk of Holyfield's
ear. The fight aired on Showtime, and Dauman was ringside. "The incident was unexpected and scary," Dauman told the *Financial Times*.
"There was pandemonium."

If Tyson's maneuver could ever have an equivalent within the
hushed and bloodless suites of corporate media, it happened in the
early evening of Friday, May 20, 2016, with the flick of a pen. That
evening, barely two weeks after Sumner's testimony against Manuela
revealed that he didn't even know his own birth name, a Los Angeles lawyer claiming to represent Sumner—someone Dauman had
never heard of—emailed him with news that Sumner had booted him
from the National Amusements board and trust. His replacement
was a media analyst–turned–abstract painter named Jill Krutick who
had been Shari's friend of twenty years. On the document, Sumner's
signature was a nearly straight line veering up toward the top right
corner of the page, as if signaling the direction he wished his stock
price would one day go again. George Abrams met a similar fate. In
a single, shocking instant, Dauman and his ally were removed from
the true seat of power in the Redstone kingdom. With that gone, the
rest—including his job as CEO of Viacom—would surely collapse.

Ever since the women were thrown out of the house and Shari began spending about a third of her time at her father's side, Dauman had been worried that she might try something like this. In January, he and Abrams had hired lawyers to explore what recourse they would have if they were thrown off the trust. (The answer was to prove Sumner was incapacitated and being manipulated by his daughter.) In the weeks after the trial, hints of mechanisms that would be used to oust him—such as the fact that Sumner could throw Dauman off the trust but not Shari—began to filter into the press. So when the blow finally came, shocking as it was, Dauman was ready. Minutes after the emails arrived, Viacom spokesman Carl Folta blasted them to *Fortune* as a "shameful effort by Shari Redstone to seize control by unlawfully using her father Sumner Redstone's name and signature," arguing that the recent trial demonstrated to all that "Sumner Redstone now lacks the capacity to have taken these steps." As soon as Massachusetts government buildings opened on Monday morning, Dauman and Abrams filed a lawsuit in Norfolk Probate and Family Court, where the trust was settled, seeking to block their removal from the trust.

Shari steadfastly maintained she had nothing to do with it. In a brilliantly crafted PR statement, she said simply, "I fully support my father's decisions and respect his authority to make them." Indeed, in the weeks after the trial, the Redstones built a network of lawyers and PR professionals around Sumner that put Shari at a remove from any of the statements or legal filings coming out under Sumner's name. Central to this effort was Rob Klieger, Sumner's lawyer, the creative, aggressive litigator who had won the case against Manuela.

Shortly after joining the legal team battling Manuela in March 2016, Klieger had become a trusted adviser to the Redstone clan. He was, as one of them put it, "engaged" in a way no previous lawyer had been. He saw the big picture. Just as, before the trial, it was his idea to push for making Shari Sumner's health care agent, after the trial, it was his idea to get Sumner a new lawyer—a "corporate counsel"— that Sumner would use to go to war against the men who had been his most trusted confidants for decades.

Part of the reason that Sumner needed a new lawyer was that Paramount was clearly going to loom large in the coming fight, and Klieger was conflicted, as he was still working for Paramount on other matters. Klieger knew Paramount was about to spark a major fight because, before the trial, he was at Sumner's mansion going over estate planning when Sumner asked him to please communicate to Viacom that he did not want to pursue the Paramount sale. Klieger relayed the message to Michael Fricklas, Viacom's general counsel, but Sumner insisted he go higher up the chain of command, directly to the board. So Klieger relayed the message to two board members: George Abrams and Fred Salerno, a former vice chairman of Verizon who had been on Viacom's board since Verizon's predecessor, Nynex, helped Viacom take over Paramount. Salerno heard Klieger out but said that he would need to verify what he was saying with Sumner directly, since he didn't know Klieger and wasn't even sure that Klieger really represented Sumner. (Salerno would try many times to visit Sumner both before and after the trial, to no avail.) Abrams called back a few weeks later, telling Klieger that he was no longer sure that what Sumner said he wanted was really what he wanted. "I'm going to be approaching this from the view of what I think Sumner would want," Abrams told Klieger.

After so many legal maneuvers, claims, and counterclaims—not to mention a rotating cast of lawyers plying their wares—it was hard to know who or what to believe at this point. It was no surprise then that neither Viacom's management nor its board did anything when they received these messages. And that lack of action provided all the reason that Sumner would need to get rid of them.

The day after the trial, Klieger flew to Hawaii on a preplanned vacation but spent most of his time there on the phone, trying to rustle up an unconflicted corporate counsel for Sumner. Through a referral, he found his way to Michael Tu, leader of the shareholder litigation practice at Orrick, Herrington & Sutcliffe, one of the very few Los Angeles firms that did not have some business somewhere with CBS or Viacom and was not daunted by the prospect of going up against the chief executive of one of the world's largest media companies. Through another referral from Shari's spokeswoman, Nancy Sterling, he found a spokesman for Sumner, the Boston-based Michael Lawrence. Tu and Lawrence then set about attacking Dauman and Abrams on behalf of Sumner, largely on the grounds that they were proceeding with the sale of a Paramount stake against his wishes. Viacom countered that they didn't speak for Sumner, who had dialed into a board meeting a few days earlier without voicing any objection to the Paramount stake sale.

In truth, both sides had their work cut out for them. In challenging Sumner's mental capacity, Dauman was now in the awkward position of arguing the opposite of what he had just argued in Manuela's litigation, when he had submitted that affidavit calling Sumner "engaged and attentive." Like Manuela, he had to thread the very fine needle of arguing that Sumner had had capacity very recently—in this case, as recently as February, when he had voted to tap him to succeed him as chairman of Viacom—and then suddenly lost it. Dauman's legal challenges were compounded by Viacom's continuing abysmal performance, which made any move toward removing him as CEO, however indirect, appear logical, in the best interest of shareholders, and very much in keeping with Sumner's history of behavior toward previous CEOs.

But the challenges and risks for Shari were even greater. Like Dauman, she, too, suddenly found herself on the opposite side of her previously held argument about her father's mental capacity. After spending two years so convinced that Sydney and Manuela were taking advantage of her enfeebled father that she had pledged to sue them for undue influence, she was now arguing that he had the mental capacity to make massive changes to his long-held estate planning. (Before the year was out, the women's long-held fear that their inheritance and gifts would be challenged proved well founded, and Sumner would sue Manuela and Sydney for elder abuse and undue influence in a suit the women claimed Shari was behind.) This view essentially put her at odds with the Viacom board, which had recoiled in horror at what Sumner's testimony at Manuela's trial had revealed about his mental state and promptly voted to cut his pay out of well-founded fears that they were vulnerable to shareholder lawsuits if they did otherwise. "You have to ask what you should be paying him, if anything," said one person familiar with the board's thinking. "You question whether he has the mental capacity to be a decision maker on the board."

People close to Sumner pointed to his anger over his pay cut as another reason he was ready to ax Dauman and Abrams. When their replacements were formally announced a few days later along with the appointment of Shari's daughter, Kim, to the National Amusements board, Sumner's statement had an Old Testament quality: "This is my trust and my decision," he said. "I have picked those who are loyal to me and removed those who are not." If you listened hard enough, you could almost hear the theme from *The Godfather* playing in the background.

*   *   *

Fred Salerno knew this movie was unlikely to end well for him. Just a week before, the telecommunications veteran had been named to the newly created position of lead independent director—a role he had played on other public company boards—in a last-ditch effort to quell the critics of Viacom's corporate governance. But as soon as the Redstones made their move against Dauman, Salerno cast his lot with the beleaguered CEO, with whom he had served on Viacom's board for nearly three decades. "We believe that Philippe and the entire management team have a strong and smart plan to move forward and prosper, and we support that plan," he wrote in an email to the entire Viacom staff the weekend of Dauman's ouster.

For weeks, Salerno had been playing a cat-and-mouse game with Sumner's lawyers, trying in vain to get an audience with Sumner so that he could judge for himself whether Sumner really knew what was being done in his name. Before the trial, the lawyers nixed any visits to avoid upsetting Sumner. After the trial, Klieger said any visits had to wait until Sumner had his corporation counsel. Once Tu was hired, he then took up the mantle of keeping Salerno at bay, saying any meeting would "need to be considered carefully" given Salerno's comments to the press about Sumner and Shari, and asking Salerno to submit an agenda of the proposed meeting. Salerno sarcastically followed orders, saying the meeting would open with "greetings and pleasantries about our shared experiences over decades together as colleagues," followed by a "Q&A session" and "anything else Sumner would like to share with us" and finally "good-byes."

But he knew that it was just a matter of time before he and much of the rest of the board would be ousted as well. They laid plans to sue to block their ousters in Delaware, where National Amusements was incorporated. "We know that such an attempt, on its face, would be completely inconsistent with Sumner's lifetime commitment to an independent Board and professional management for Viacom after his incapacity or death," Salerno wrote in an open letter on May 30 responding to speculation about his imminent ouster. "More specifically, it would be equally inconsistent with his stated judgment for many years that his daughter, Shari, should not control Viacom or his other companies." It would be easier to just leave, he said, but "to a person" the board felt morally bound to fight because "of the inexplicable assertion that Sumner was acting of his own free will" while simultaneously dodging a face-to-face meeting with Salerno and another director. The board was unhappy with Viacom's performance, he wrote, which was precisely why it wanted to explore a sale of a part of Paramount to provide much-needed cash and strategic help to aid the company get back on its feet.

Viacom's slump proved to be just the leverage Shari would need. Viacom's stock leaped 13 percent in the week after Dauman was kicked off the trust, signaling that investors were eagerly awaiting his departure. In response to Salerno's attacks, Shari ceased at least part of the charade that she had nothing to do with the shake-up. Through her spokeswoman, she once again reiterated that she had "no desire to manage Viacom nor chair its board" but made a forceful case that an overhaul was needed. "The shareholders whom Salerno and the other independent directors purport to represent have already spoken—they want new management at the top and strong Directors with independent oversight on the Board." Reports began to surface that she was already on the hunt for a CEO to replace Dauman, talking to luminaries from the company's glory days like Judy McGrath and Jeffrey Katzenberg. When Sumner's lawyers filed their motion to block Dauman's suit, arguing that Sumner had been found to have "legal mental capacity," they also mentioned that Dauman had done "a bad job running Viacom." As if to hammer home the point, Paramount's big summer movie, *Teenage Mutant Ninja Turtles: Out of the Shadows*, had just bombed at the box office, opening to an estimated $35.3 million after costing $135 million to make. Its weak performance would force Viacom to lower its profit guidance for the third quarter.

At the same time that Sumner's lawyers were arguing that he had capacity, they were also (rather incredibly) arguing that it didn't matter whether he had capacity or not. A few days before the first Massachusetts court hearing on June 7, Klieger revealed that four of the seven trustees had ratified Sumner's decision to kick Dauman and Abrams off the trust, making the move valid regardless of whether Sumner had capacity. This meant that David Andelman, long in lockstep with Dauman and Abrams against Shari when Sumner was well, had sided with Shari now that Sumner was sick. Several people familiar with the matter said that Andelman's signing off on so much of the money that the women received from Sumner left him vulnerable. "David is not a super-wealthy guy," one of them said. He billed the Redstones over the years, but he couldn't withstand a Redstone lawsuit for the rest of his life. He made the pragmatic decision, 'I'm going to go with Shari.' He was always the weak link . . . That was basically checkmate, once she had David." Andelman denies this was his motivation. "Shari never threatened me with litigation over my role in Sumner's giving money to the women, and I did not 'flip to her side' but continued to represent Sumner and act in his best interests," he said.

The National Amusements vote meant that Dauman and Abrams "literally cannot win," as one person close to the matter put it. Even if the Massachusetts judge found that Sumner lacked capacity, they were not getting back on the National Amusements board or the trust. Nevertheless, on Monday, June 6, Dauman's and Abrams's lawyers pushed for an immediate medical examination of Sumner, who was so unwell, they claimed, that he could not "speak, stand, walk, eat, write or read." Sumner's granddaughter Keryn, who had decided to join the ousted trustees in common cause, said the last time she saw her Grumpy in February, he just "sat there lifeless." Represented by O'Donnell—who was still warring on several legal fronts on behalf of Manuela—Keryn claimed Shari and her children had managed to "effectively kidnap, brainwash and take advantage of my grandfather due to his debilitated state of mind and frail health."

As a beneficiary of her grandfather's trust and a mortal enemy of Shari's, Keryn had a lot to lose if Shari and her allies got control of the trust. The day that Manuela's case got tossed out, she had tweeted a doctored photograph of Shari looking vampirically white-faced with blood dripping down her chin. A more incendiary tweet, accusing Shari of buying "hookers for her father," was deleted immediately, but some screenshots were captured by the *Hollywood Reporter* and the whole episode was enough to earn her a cease-and-desist letter from Klieger.

Dauman and Abrams weren't the only ones in a hurry. On the eve of the first court date, the newly constituted National Amusements board announced that it had changed Viacom's corporate bylaws to require a unanimous vote to approve any sale of any part of Paramount, slamming the brakes on Dauman's last desperate effort to save the company's deteriorating finances. Viacom denounced the move as "illegitimate," but it was increasingly clear that Viacom's management wouldn't be in charge of the company much longer. Jeffrey Sonnenfeld, senior associate dean at Yale School of Management, told the *Wall Street Journal* the move "definitely smacks of a cat playing with its prey before the kill."

*   *   *

On the hot and steamy summer morning of Tuesday, June 7, twenty-two lawyers crammed into the fluorescent-lit courtroom of Norfolk Probate and Family Court in the quiet Boston suburb of Canton, Massachusetts, just down the highway from Mickey's original home-town drive-in in Dedham. On one hand, it seemed appropriate that the fate of the vast Redstone media empire would be decided here, in this faceless office park in the Redstone homeland, inside this curious modernist building resembling a cartridge of film made by the Eastman Kodak Company—the very company that Viacom had been compared to for its inability to adapt to technological change. But on the other hand, the court seemed unprepared for a fight of this scale and import. Dauman and Abrams had named every trustee and beneficiary of the Redstone family trust in their suit, right down to Kim and Jason's two small children, forcing every one of them to hire counsel. The courtroom looked, in the words of one observer, "like a bar association meeting." Judge George Phelan marveled at the sums involved. "I grew up in a housing project where I was lucky to have a quarter in my pocket, so I'm still trying to grasp the concept of billions with a 'B,'" he said.

He proved reluctant to make any fast moves—and fast moves were what Dauman and Abrams needed. While their lawyer, Leslie Fagen of Paul, Weiss, claimed Sumner was "holding on to life by a thread," Klieger countered that he was exercising daily and leaving the house to visit his grandson Brandon and his friends in Malibu. When Judge Phelan probed why Sumner, if upset about Paramount, didn't speak up at the board meeting he was dialed into recently, Klieger said, "Telephone calls are not generally where he expresses his views best." Judge Phelan said he would need a few days to decide whether to allow the expedited discovery, and he "might or might not" make a decision before Sumner's lawyers make their motion to dismiss the suit out-right later in the month. The speed that Dauman and Abrams needed did not seem likely to come from Massachusetts.

CHAPTER 23

"Cleaning House"

Meanwhile, as the armies of lawyers were assembling in Massachusetts and Delaware in early June, Shari's son Tyler wondered if he couldn't defuse the situation in a different way. Without his mother's knowledge, the thirty-year-old start-up CEO quietly reached out to Dauman to see if they could reach a settlement through back channels. Tyler had served alongside Dauman on National Amusements' board, and the two exceedingly polite Manhattanite lawyers shared a nerdish delight in the intricacies of business transaction law. Tyler felt sure that Dauman, being both pragmatic and risk-averse, was a reasonable enough person to come to the negotiating table and find a way to a peaceful exit. He was right.

Soon after, Tyler and his lawyer, David Sloan of Holland & Knight, and Dauman and his lawyer, Bob Schumer of Paul, Weiss, sat down in a conference room at Viacom's headquarters and kicked off what would end up being nearly two months of settlement talks. Tyler felt that the key was to give Dauman some kind of capstone for his long career—for the veteran mergers and acquisitions lawyer, ideally a transaction—that would allow him to leave with dignity. In early talks, Tyler even floated the idea of merging Viacom and CBS, which the National Amusements board had been mulling for three years. But it became clear that the transaction that Dauman felt was most necessary to stabilize Viacom was to find a joint venture partner for Paramount. And so the outlines of the deal came together quickly: Dauman would step down after getting a chance to pitch the benefits of the Paramount deal to the board, and the rest of the troublemaking board members would go, more or less immediately.

*   *   *

Meanwhile, unaware of the peace talks, Dauman's enemies escalated their attacks. In an effort to disprove the argument that Sumner was "holding on to life by a thread," Shari loaded Sumner into a minivan and drove him to the Paramount lot. Around eleven a.m. on Friday, June 10, they parked in front of the Sumner Redstone Building, which had once housed Adolph Zukor's office—Sumner had crowed during the naming dedication in 2012 that they hadn't waited for him to die to name it after him because "I will never die"—and, for ten brief minutes, welcomed Brad Grey into the vehicle for a visit. A source told the *Hollywood Reporter* that Sumner took a tour of the lot afterward, marking the first time he was seen in public in a year. He and Shari performed a similar maneuver at CBS's West Coast offices in Studio City the following Tuesday, with CBS CEO Leslie Moonves coming down for a roughly ten-minute chat, according to the *Wall Street Journal*. When Salerno, who had still made no progress in his quest to see Sumner in person, called the visits "staged legal and publicity ploys," Sumner's spokesman released a statement saying, "I no longer trust Philippe [Dauman] or those who support him."

Up to this point, Tom Freston had mostly kept his dismay over the decline of Viacom to himself, busying himself instead with philanthropy, investing, and helping Vice Media take over the world. But during a June 15 interview with CNBC, he went public with his low opinion of Dauman. "I don't think he's been the optimal leader for the company," Freston said, adding, "There's been a series of pretty serious errors." His critique was so scathing, from the folly of the YouTube lawsuit to the corporate culture that had driven all the creative people from the building—including the departure of megastars Jon Stewart, Stephen Colbert, and John Oliver from Comedy Central in a matter of months—that Viacom felt it had to respond. "Viacom is significantly bigger, more global and generates far more profits today than when Philippe Dauman's predecessor left office in 2006," Viacom's spokesman told CNBC.

In a subsequent interview, Freston said he had not gone on television intending to take down Dauman, but when they started asking him questions, he could not help but answer them truthfully. As to whether Shari put him up to it, he told CNBC that, although they are friendly, "she doesn't even know I'm on TV." But after he got off, she sent him an email filled with smiley-face emojis. In the court of public opinion, Dauman was losing.

Against this backdrop of extraordinary public sniping, the next day's sudden overhaul of Viacom's board, which would have been shocking on any other day, seemed almost normal. As the various players in the drama had been expecting for weeks, National Amusements announced that it was booting Dauman, Abrams, Salerno, and two other independent directors from the Viacom board. In their place, it put forth a formidable crop of new directors with more media industry experience, including Ken Lerer, the longtime MTV PR consigliere who had gone on to cofound the *Huffington Post* and chair the board of BuzzFeed; Judith McHale, the former CEO of Discovery Communications; Ronald Nelson, the former COO of DreamWorks SKG who had since become chairman of Avis Budget Group; Nicole Seligman, a former president of Sony Entertainment; and Tom May, the chairman of Boston's Eversource Energy. Salerno immediately sued in Delaware to block the overhaul, calling it a "brazen and demonstrably invalid attempt" by Shari to get control of Viacom against her father's wishes. Shari denied orchestrating the move but said, through her spokeswoman, that she supported the shake-up that "has nothing to do with power or personalities and everything to do with maximizing value for all Viacom shareholders." Dauman was not officially out as CEO yet, as that decision was technically up to the board, but there was no question where that train was heading. That same day, according to a later report in the *Wall Street Journal,* Shari called Tom Dooley to ask him to be interim CEO when Dauman left. Dooley agreed, and padded the few steps over to Dauman's office to let him know. Dauman was resigned to his fate, saying, "If that's her plan, that's her plan."

But that didn't stop him from trying to seal one last deal before he had to hand in his badge. As both the secret settlement talks and the litigation dragged on in multiple states through July, Dauman continued to press for a partner for Paramount, entering into advanced talks to sell a 49 percent stake in the studio to China's Dalian Wanda Group, a deal he felt would add as much as $10 to Viacom's stock price. But when news of the talks leaked to Reuters, National Amusements was quick to reject the idea—apparently regardless of the price—arguing that such a deal would limit Viacom's ability to take on other partners and "chill the interest of parties that may be interested in a larger transaction involving all of Viacom." Analysts expected that the first of these "larger transactions" would likely be a merger with CBS, which many analysts had been pushing for years. Earlier in July, Moonves—who was known to have expressed interest in running a movie studio and been annoyed when Paramount went to Freston in the 2006 split—had been spotted at the annual Allen & Co. media industry conference in Sun Valley, Idaho, driving Shari to dinner in his rented Buick.

*   *   *

By July 27, Dauman had negotiated his gentleman's surrender with Tyler and the rest of the Redstones and was ready to share the news with the rest of the Viacom board. It went over like a lead balloon. Salerno and his fellow independent directors were livid that Dauman had been negotiating behind their backs and even less pleased that the deal had a soft landing for himself but an abrupt departure for his fellow directors. "I think they were very upset with what Philippe had been doing," said one person familiar with the negotiations. "They did not reject it out of hand, but they slow-played it to see what was going to happen in Massachusetts and Delaware."

What happened in Massachusetts and Delaware were big wins for Dauman and the other beleaguered directors, which changed the power dynamic behind the settlement talks. In both cases, the Viacom directors' charges that Sumner was being manipulated were taken seriously enough that trials were set in October. Judge Andre

Bouchard in Delaware was particularly dismissive of the argument that Sumner's mental capacity was irrelevant because they had the votes without him. "There could be total exploitation of somebody who had no desire to do this, and it would be totally unreviewable," he said. Talks went dormant.

They were revived by Viacom's apocalyptically bad third-quarter earnings report, which, when it was delivered, on August 4, managed to set in motion what dozens of lawyers in multiple states were unable to do. Profit had plunged 29 percent in the quarter. Weak ratings at the cable networks sent advertising revenue down 4 percent. And most troublingly, affiliate sales—those supposedly ever-rising fees from cable and satellite companies that were the engine of Viacom's growth for decades—were down 10 percent. Paramount, executives warned, was going to operate at a loss for the year—a loss that ultimately turned out to be nearly half a billion dollars. After the earnings call, National Amusements, acting more like a particularly aggressive activist investor instead of the controlling shareholder that it was, put out a statement saying that Viacom's management had "failed to articulate a credible long-term plan to reverse the company's decline."

For several players caught up in the drama, this earnings call was the last straw. On its heels, Lerer asked Shari for permission to be the go-between for her and his friend Aryeh Bourkoff, the founder of the boutique media-focused investment bank LionTree, who had been informally advising Salerno for months. Having watched Sumner's battles with his daughter over decades, Salerno started out deeply skeptical that Shari could really act on behalf of her father in reorganizing his empire. But as Viacom's performance worsened, he began, with Bourkoff's help, to see that his responsibility to Viacom's independent shareholders and Shari's desire to replace Dauman were not such different objectives. Moreover, Dauman's secret settlement talks had left Salerno with a bad taste. So on August 7, Salerno accepted Bourkoff's invitation to Lerer's house in Quogue, New York, where the three men hashed out the groundwork for a new settlement. Wanting to be a gracious guest, Bourkoff picked up pastries at Tate's Bake Shop

in Southampton on his way to the meeting. No one touched them—
they were too scared of carbs—but the meeting later became known
as the "muffin summit" after tales of the pastries made their way into
the *Wall Street Journal*. Within two weeks, all parties had signed off
on the settlement.

It varied little from the original, except that it let most of the ousted
board members stay until the company's annual meeting the following February and did not specify which ones would be leaving in the
announcement. Dauman would step down as CEO on September 13,
and the new board members would start on that date, with Tom May
becoming the new chairman of the board. Dooley would become interim chief executive through September 30, when Viacom's fiscal
year ended. After all the Sturm und Drang about Dauman's desire to
make a final presentation to the board about the wisdom of selling a
stake in Paramount, in the end, he quietly handed out a memo, sold a
bunch of his Viacom stock, and vanished into life as a civilian, cush-
ioned by the silky folds of his $72 million golden parachute.

The weekend of the peace accord, Paramount and MGM's $100 mil-
lion remake of the 1959 classic *Ben-Hur* opened in theaters and
flopped in epic fashion, bringing in a breathtakingly paltry $11.4 mil-
lion in domestic box office. Produced by Mark Burnett and Roma
Downey, who had struck gold with *The Bible*, the film was pitched to
the religious audiences who had flocked to *The Passion of the Christ*
but failed to elicit a similar response. Paramount vice chairman Rob
Moore explained the failure as part of a broader industry trend, telling
the *New York Times*, "Movies like 'Ghostbusters,' 'Independence Day'
and 'Ben-Hur' certainly looked like they were going to be big going
into the summer, but audiences, especially in the world of remakes,
have been very tough." Hollywood had run out of ideas, nowhere more
acutely than at Paramount.

*   *   *

On Wednesday, September 14, the new board met for the first time in
New York, and the new directors discovered that the financial situation

was even worse than they had thought. Viacom's credit was nudging into junk territory, and Paramount's eye-popping losses were accelerating. Over a week of grim budget and strategy meetings, executives formulated a plan to stanch the bleeding: halve the dividend, tap debt markets to give the company some immediate breathing room, and, in an extraordinary preemptive step, write down $115 million for an unnamed film that had not yet been released but was apparently so unequivocally appalling that executives felt no need to guess about how it would perform in theaters. The film was later revealed to be *Monster Trucks*, a live-action CGI (computer-generated imagery) feature about a monster that gives a teenager's truck special powers, inspired by a top Paramount executive's observation that his three-year-old liked playing with trucks. The new board officially nixed the Paramount stake sale and accepted Dooley's resignation—and $60 million payout—wiping away the major vestiges of the old regime. "It was pretty clear what needed to be done," said one person familiar with the board's thinking. "The board decided to do it all now, and have a restart of sorts moving forward."

But who would lead the new regime? The only obvious candidate was Leslie Moonves, CEO of CBS, programmer with the golden touch, consummate Wall Street crowd-pleaser, and expert navigator of corporate politics. For years, analysts and investors had spoken longingly about the potential to have Moonves's creative chops guiding Viacom's beleaguered brands, not to mention the CBS broadcast network's all-powerful rights to the NFL and other sports when it came time to negotiate distribution agreements with cable and satellite companies for the sportsless likes of MTV, Nickelodeon, and Comedy Central.

In television, NFL rights are the equivalent of nuclear weapons—expensive, yes, but also delivering the priceless peace of mind that nobody is going to push you around. CBS had done a masterful job using them and other sports rights, along with its stable of hit shows like *The Big Bang Theory*, to extract favorable deals with cable companies that carried its television stations' signals. Meanwhile, it had also used them to squeeze ever-rising fees from the local CBS affiliates that it didn't own, creating an investor-friendly business model that was gradually shifting CBS away from reliance on the volatile advertising market toward steady subscription revenue. At the same time, under Moonves, CBS had broken from the rest of the broadcast network owners and created its own $5.99-per-month, direct-to-consumer streaming service called CBS All Access. When it was launched, initially devoid of NFL games because CBS did not yet have the digital rights, most industry executives considered it a prop weapon with which to threaten cable and satellite companies in distribution negotiations. But CBS began feeding the service with original content, holding back some of its best-loved franchises, like the latest iteration of *Star Trek*, for the platform, and eventually getting the rights to show NFL games on it. After two years, it had more than one million subscribers, with projections for four million by 2020. These were hardly Netflix numbers, but they were a promising indication that quality content and brands, properly tended, just might be able to survive on their own if and when the crumbling pay-TV castle falls into the sea. This was just the glimmer of hope that Viacom's investors needed to see.

Moonves, meanwhile, had always coveted having a studio of his own to run, the ultimate seat of power in the entertainment industry. Over the years, he and Shari had worked out a respectful, if sometimes wary, alliance, brought together by their common rival, Dauman. When rumors began to swirl in early 2015 that Sumner's health was slipping, which always got the media bankers licking their chops in anticipation of the potential sale or reunification of Viacom and CBS, reports surfaced that Moonves was talking to private equity firms about ways to buy out National Amusements' controlling stake in CBS Corp. But as Viacom's performance deteriorated and Shari rose to prominence, he set about wooing her in preparation for a potentially very different post-Sumner future—one without Dauman.

Meanwhile, there were many other purely industrial elements of the original split of Viacom and CBS in 2006 that didn't make sense. Movie studios and premium cable channels need each other. When Paramount and Showtime were owned by the same company, they represented an elegant vertical integration. Separating them in the split meant that Viacom had to go start another premium channel, Epix, from scratch after its deal with Showtime lapsed. While Paramount's prestigious movie studio had gone with Viacom in the split, its television production arm had gone to CBS, leaving a hole at Paramount that Brad Grey had only recently—and really too late—focused on filling by building Paramount TV again from scratch. CBS, meanwhile, had launched CBS Films to underwhelming results.

And so, on September 29, 2016, barely two weeks after Dauman had vacated his office, National Amusements sent a letter to the boards of Viacom and CBS asking them to explore a merger, saying such a combination "might offer substantial synergies." It preferred an all-stock transaction and warned panting bankers that it wasn't going to entertain any deal that didn't leave it with control of both, or the combined, companies. It was signed by both Sumner Redstone, CEO, and Shari Redstone, President, of National Amusements.

In principle, it made sense. "We never thought they should ever be separated," Michael Nathanson, an analyst at MoffettNathanson, told the *Wall Street Journal*, adding that the 2006 split "destroyed tons of family value over a decade." But such a public announcement handed Moonves a lot of leverage, and he had already been cool to the prospect of being saddled with Viacom's problems. He would only want to do a deal in which CBS shares were valued at a premium to Viacom shares, and in which he could be assured the same level of autonomy to which he had become accustomed. While there were some rumors that Shari might place voting shares on the table to get the deal done, the reality was that, like her father, she was not about to dilute the Redstone family's control over the companies.

Nonetheless, the boards of both companies set up special committees, which hired an army of bankers and lawyers to weigh the merits of a combination. In private meetings, Viacom outlined a rosy future for CBS in which Viacom's company stock, then trading in the mid-$30 range, would soon be trading at $60 a share, thanks to 5 percent annual growth in advertising revenue and other turnarounds. "CBS essentially said, Great, then go do it, and come back to us when you have," said one person close to the talks. With little enthusiasm from Moonves, the investment bankers never got far. "It takes two to tango," said one person close to the talks. "Shari went through a summer of fighting to replace a CEO of one of those companies. It's very hard to turn around and battle another CEO. I'm not sure she had it in her to go all the way."

But when it came to protecting her father against the women she felt had preyed on him, Shari did have it in her—and then some. While the special committees and their advisers weighed the future of the media empire, Rob Klieger prepared a blockbuster lawsuit to go after Manuela and Sydney in exactly the way they had always feared. On October 25, 2016, Sumner sued the women in Los Angeles Superior Court for elder abuse, seeking to reclaim the full $150 million he had given them "with interest." Klieger insisted that, despite Shari's past threats to sue the women, "Shari implored her father not to file his elder abuse suit. Had Sydney and Manuela kept Sumner from his family until his death, Shari would have gladly gone to war with them. Now that she had her father back, she wanted nothing more than for Sydney and Manuela to be gone from their lives forever. She would rather have them keep the money than continue to be part of the mix."

Sydney's and Manuela's lawyers, meanwhile, allege that Shari is behind the entire thing. They note that the suit was filed at a time when Sumner could not even talk, let alone hire counsel for complex litigation.

It was a highly risky maneuver for someone who had just pulled off an astonishingly successful corporate coup. By arguing that Sumner had been so susceptible to undue influence that the women were able to drain his bank accounts without his true approval, Klieger was stepping dangerously close to undermining the argument for Sumner's current mental capacity upon which many of the decisions from the last year—and indeed Shari's rise to power—rested. (Though in this context, Klieger's argument that it didn't matter whether Sumner had capacity or not since Shari had the votes takes on greater meaning.)

It also raised the question of why Shari, as a member of Viacom and CBS's boards, did not voice her concerns about her father's mental state sooner, if she was getting reports as far back as 2014 about him being routinely reduced to tears by women half his age.

The suit against the women dismayed some members of Shari's inner circle, who felt that Shari should quit while she was ahead. But as the months of litigation turned to years, a funny thing happened: nothing. Sumner's legal team was able to fight back the women's attempts to have him deposed. Manuela was ejected from the Carlyle Hotel apartment. As of spring 2018, the litigation is still pending, but so far, the risks that Klieger took for the Redstones have all paid off. In July 2017, he was voted onto the CBS board.

*　　*　　*

With Dooley gone, somebody needed to keep the trains running at Viacom while the special committees weighed the merger. The job required a rare combination of competence and humility, since it was entirely possible that Moonves would soon come along and make this person redundant. Bob Bakish fit the bill perfectly. As the CEO of Viacom's international division, he had run the one corner of the company that had a positive story to tell, while being mercifully shielded from the past year's drama.

Tall, ruddy, and broad-chested, with a bit of chest hair often peeking up from his open-collared shirt, Bakish exuded an affable everyman quality. He was a technocrat, not a creative visionary, but his time overseas in countries with markedly different television distribution systems had given him creative ideas about how Viacom's channels could be packaged and distributed. Most important, he was not a bullshitter. He became acting CEO on Halloween.

Six weeks later, with Moonves still unenthusiastic about the merger idea and Viacom's latest quarterly earnings showing a 25 percent drop in profit, National Amusements called off the merger talks and named Bakish permanent CEO of Viacom. Wall Street whispered that Moonves had dug in, but Shari gushed that it was the strength of Bakish's turnaround plan that made her change her mind. Bakish promised to restore Viacom's creative culture, fix its frayed relationships with distributors, and rein in Paramount's finances while pushing the studio to mine Viacom's channel brands like MTV and Nickelodeon for more of its movie ideas.

Most important, if unsaid, was that he was Shari's guy. He welcomed her input, and she, in turn, rhapsodized over his brilliance. After years of caginess and spotlight-dodging, she seemed to visibly relax and began to do more public speaking, taking questions in live settings on everything from the need for scale among big media companies to the opportunities that blockchain technology presents to tech investors. Every now and then, she would toss off her father's old adage that "content is king." But mostly she would praise Bakish, bragging that he was restoring the culture that defined Viacom in her father's heyday. This is literally true: under Bakish, MTV has rebooted *TRL, Unplugged,* and even the Jersey Shore franchise, hoping to reclaim its lost magic.

By the end of 2016, with her hand-picked CEO installed, the media and entertainment industries had settled into the realization that Shari was finally her own mogul. The *Hollywood Reporter* named her its "Women in Entertainment Executive of the Year" for her "success at cleaning house in the family's business—both public and private." Even as, with lawsuits pending, everyone continued to tiptoe around exactly how she did it, the industry was deeply impressed by this gladiator in its midst. She bent her head gratefully for the laurels. "This was a really difficult year for me personally, my family, professionally—and looking back on what we were able to achieve is incredible," she told the magazine. Media columnist Michael Wolff dubbed her an "accidental mogul" but noted that she was also "the first woman as media mogul," bringing with her all the supposedly womanly—if decidedly un-Redstonian—qualities of patience, humility, open-mindedness, and empathy. She continued to insist that she didn't want to run the companies, only to ensure they had good CEOs and strong boards.

"When they need me, I'm there, and when they don't need me, I'm on to my nonprofit work and the work that I do at Advancit."

As a mogul, her most important responsibility was to ensure that the nightmare of the last year did not play itself out again in thirty years. And so, in the midst of all the fighting, she quietly brought her son Brandon aboard National Amusements as a director. Now all three of her children served on the National Amusements board, poised to take up the mantle of another generation of oversight over the family media empire. While each has a distinct personality—Kim is a do-gooder, Brandon a showman, Tyler a fixer—there are no signs of the kind of dissension between them that marked Shari's relationship with her brother, Brent. They run a charitable foundation together and, as court documents showing their efforts to gather information about Manuela and Sydney revealed, work together as a team. Shari and Ira's marriage might not have worked out in the end, but it was not the daily screamfest that Sumner and Phyllis's was when Shari and Brent were growing up. While Sumner loved his children, he also made clear to them in ways large and small that they always came second to his first love, his business. By contrast, the people whom Shari prioritized when she insisted on being home for dinner every evening are now her fellow board members and trustees.

With Bakish installed in Dauman's old office on the fifty-second floor of Viacom's headquarters, Shari set about refurbishing her father's old office down the hall, with its dizzying wraparound view of One World Trade Center looming above the lower half of Manhattan like an obelisk. Her taste is spare, if not Spartan, a subdued symphony of cream and beige. Among the few decorations is a painting by her friend Jill Krutick, a blurred abstraction in mauve and gray that mirrors the hazy skyline in the distance; a framed jersey of the New England Patriots quarterback Tom Brady; framed photos of her cherubic, dark-haired grandchildren; and a small snapshot of her next to her father, both dressed in Patriots jerseys. She's giving a thumbs-up. He looks like a corpse.

Epilogue:
The First Female Media Mogul

With their purple hair, torn jeans, and expectant chatter, the teenagers spilling out of Viacom's headquarters into Times Square on the afternoon of November 30, 2017, might have been mistaken for their counterparts a generation ago, had they not all been staring down at their phones. They were, after all, lined up for a very late-'90s ritual: a live taping of MTV's *Total Request Live*, or *TRL*, the music video countdown show that had once held young audiences in thrall with stars like Britney Spears, Eminem, and Beyoncé. After nearly a decade off the air that coincided with the rise of smartphones and social media, Viacom's new management had decided to bring the show back, featuring a handful of fresh-faced hosts with large Instagram followings. The most piercing screams were reserved for the handsome Dolan Twins, a pair of seventeen-year-old YouTubers with five million social media followers. Their specialty that afternoon was shaving each other's beards and eating pizza topped with bugs. (Were Mickey Redstone on the scene, no doubt he would have recognized them as vaudevillians.) The reboot of *TRL* was just one of the first of many efforts of the new Viacom, now helmed by Bob Bakish, to reassert itself as an arbiter of popular culture, a ratings winner, and a media behemoth to be reckoned with.

Bakish had spent the previous decade running the company's international channels overseas, where the MTV brand is still a beacon of youth culture and pay-TV is still growing. That vista had given him a unique appreciation of the staying power of many of Viacom's older hits even as he recognized that, with the advent of smartphones and social media, simply replaying Viacom's greatest hits wouldn't be enough to revive the company. In Bakish's first twelve months, MTV had revamped *Unplugged, My Super Sweet 16*, and, nearest and dearest to Bakish's New Jersey–native heart, the Jersey Shore franchise. The original show only ran in the United States from 2009 to 2012, but globally it has had dozens of spin-offs that remain on the air to this day, including *Geordie Shore* and, Warsaw's landlocked geography notwithstanding, *Warsaw Shore*. "The U.S. team five years ago walked away from it, and that was really dumb," Bakish had told the Business Insider Ignition conference in November 2017. At Paramount, Jim Gianopulos, the studio chief Bakish installed in March 2017 after firing Brad Grey (who died of cancer two months later), was banking on sequels to *Top Gun* (1986) and *The Terminator* (1984) to pull the studio out of its slump.

Such are the plans of a man with very little room to maneuver. When Bakish first stepped into the corner office, he found a company so levered that its debt was teetering on junk territory, Paramount had just finished losing half a billion dollars in a single year, and the ratings at iconic channels like MTV hadn't grown in five years. With such weak ratings, the company was no longer in a position to play the bully with its distributors, who loathed the way Viacom had forced them for years to take dozens of channels they mostly didn't want just so they could have *SpongeBob* and *The Daily Show*. Some analysts assumed it was only a matter of time before a major distributor dropped Viacom altogether. Nearly as bad, Viacom wasn't having a lot of luck getting its programming on the new generation of cheaper, smaller pay-TV bundles delivered online by services such as Hulu or YouTube.

Bakish's solution was to get real: the future had no space for Viacom's two dozen channels, and so in February he announced that Viacom would narrow its focus to six core networks—Nickelodeon, Nick Jr., MTV, Comedy Central, BET, and Spike, which was renamed the Paramount Network. In addition to getting resources to improve programming and global distribution, each of these would also have Paramount make movies out of their best intellectual property. Other channels weren't necessarily killed outright, but many of the weakest would likely shrivel up and die. He overhauled the leadership of the six key channels, personally recruited money-minting producer Tyler Perry to make shows for BET and movies for Paramount, and started a new digital studio for short-form mobile content. He paid down debt and quietly said good-bye to about four hundred employees (in a company of more than nine thousand) while making plans for a more substantial restructuring. He tried to reset the company's frayed relationships with distributors by taking a more conciliatory approach, offering them help with advertising and content creation—as well as a softer line on raising fees, represented by a new distribution team. As a result, Viacom did not get dropped from any major distributors during Bakish's first year, and, in fact, wooed back Suddenlink, the small operator whose early decision to drop all of Viacom's channels had been the initial signal that Viacom was in very big trouble.

Through it all, Bakish benefited from Shari Redstone's full support. He emailed with her regularly, listened to her advice, and frequently took it. Shari, for her part, found that all the connections she had made in the digital world through Advancit were finally starting to pay off. Not long after tapping Bakish as CEO, she mentioned to him that he should go meet Brian Robbins, the cofounder of AwesomenessTV, a producer and distributor of YouTube content aimed at teenagers to which the Dolan Twins are signed. Bakish flew to Los Angeles to meet Robbins and was impressed. A few months later, Robbins was hired to lead the newly created Paramount Players, a division set up to mine Viacom's cable channels for characters and storylines to turn into movies.

And yet, despite all this newfound synergy and good feeling, the stock continued to drop. By November 2017, it had bottomed out at $23—a far cry from the $60 a share that Bakish and his colleagues had suggested was possible when they had gone a year earlier to pitch Viacom's prospects to CBS. The nice-guy approach to distribution kept the channels on enough people's televisions to prop up the advertising business, but it meant that Viacom was now beginning to accept a reduction in fees charged to distributors—essentially shifting the engine that had driven the industry for decades into idle. And unlike in Dauman's time, Bakish's Viacom could not patch up holes in distribution revenue with fat checks from Netflix and Hulu. Bakish had made a strategic decision to pull back from these platforms, out of concern that they were bad for the pay-TV ecosystem. The focus on the six core networks yielded some early ratings gains, with MTV seeing its first summer ratings growth in six years, but by the end of Bakish's first year, these had mostly been erased by the accelerating erosion of the entire industry's ratings and distribution. Nearly all the major players in television suffered double-digit ratings declines in the last quarter of 2017, while the number of people who cut the cord that year grew 30 percent to 22 million. It was not just Viacom that was looking increasingly beyond repair—it was cable television itself. According to an analysis of Nielsen ratings by Pivotal research analyst Brian Wieser, the episode of *TRL* with the bug-eating Dolans drew just ninety-two thousand total viewers, roughly an eighth as many as the show got at its peak. MTV saw a surge of activity on social media as a result of the new *TRL*, but it didn't make money from any of it.

Viacom's bigger competitors responded to these pressures by merging. In the span of a year, CNN owner Time Warner agreed to sell itself to AT&T; Discovery Communications agreed to buy Food Network owner Scripps Networks Interactive; and, in a move precisely no one in the industry saw coming, Twenty-First Century Fox agreed to sell the bulk of its assets to the Walt Disney Company. The idea that Rupert Murdoch would agree to dismantle the sprawling empire he had spent his life building struck many as extraordinary. And yet his explanation was matter-of-fact: there is simply no way that he would ever have the scale to compete with Netflix and Amazon, as they shovel ever more billions into making TV shows and movies. "New technologies, competitors and shifting consumer preferences have redrawn the whole media map," he said.

Murdoch's move shocked Shari back into action. She had never stopped believing that merging Viacom and CBS made sense, but now the media's game of musical chairs was entering a potentially dangerous finale. "The Fox-Disney thing changed the landscape for everybody," said one person close to her. Ultimately, she suspected National Amusements' media assets might complete the puzzle for some still-larger company—a cash-rich telecom like Verizon, say, or paired with a studio like Lionsgate—but none of those deals could be done until Viacom and CBS were recombined. "Scale matters now, and it's going to continue to matter in the future," she told an audience at New York's Paley Center for Media in October 2017. By January, she had urged Moonves to kick-start a new round of merger talks.

Moonves was no more interested in the idea than he had been a year earlier, but the world around him had changed. Wall Street still regarded him as the most talented programmer in the business, but the industry's problems were now looking bigger than anything his distinct talents could fix. Although Viacom was by far the sicker patient, both CBS and Viacom did worse in 2017 than analysts had expected. Moonves was valuable, yes, but was he indispensable? Privately, Shari and other members of the CBS board began to grumble that CBS's management hadn't done the kind of succession or long-range planning that was best practice in the industry, despite the fact that CBS chief operating officer Joe Ianniello was widely understood to be Moonves's heir apparent. By mid-January, some of this discontent was reported by the *Wall Street Journal*, which noted that Shari was pressing for "new blood" on the CBS board and already taking names for some potential replacements. Among the people she thought might make good successors to Moonves in a merged company was Bakish. In response to the *Journal* story, which horrified the management of CBS, one Viacom executive whispered to *Variety*, "Here we go again."

Within days, Reuters reported that Moonves and Bakish had met for a preliminary conversation about merging. Shari's point had been made. Moonves might have a great deal of leverage—Wells Fargo estimated that CBS's stock price would fall 10 percent if he left the company—but he still served at her pleasure. By February, the CBS and Viacom boards announced they were once again exploring a merger.

*   *   *

Shari turns out to be her father's daughter: doggedly determined, shrewd, and not particularly patient. In her first full year in power, she has shown the world its first true female media mogul, a de facto owner of major assets who is neither a passive family steward nor in some way "talent"—as Oprah Winfrey and, to a lesser degree, Arianna Huffington have been—but rather a strategist, an aggressive operator, and a deal maker. With $5 billion in family assets and companies worth $36 billion under her control—including the storied CBS News division of Edward R. Murrow and Walter Cronkite—Shari is the most significant woman in the history of media ownership since Katharine Graham became the first female CEO and chairman of the Washington Post Company in the 1970s.

Shari's story has many parallels to Graham's: both of their fathers amassed great media assets, which they then handed, not to their own flesh and blood, but to their daughters' Harvard-trained husbands. (Graham's father explained that he made arrangements in the late 1940s for his son-in-law to own more stock in the company than his daughter because "no man should be in the position of working for his wife.") For a time, both Shari and Graham were content to play the roles of wife and mother, a role Graham once called being the "tail to his kite." Shari often says she was happy baking cookies, telling the *Worcester Telegram & Gazette* in 1995 that she thought the family theater chain "was a business I'd never go into." It took calamity— Graham's husband's 1962 suicide and Shari's 1992 divorce—to create the opportunity for both women to join, and ultimately lead, their family's business.

Graham wrote that she was "pleased" that her father thought of her husband instead of her as a successor, while Shari began to chafe at the plaudits being heaped upon her father and husband after Sumner's daring takeovers of Viacom and then Paramount. People who know the family point to the moment that Shari informed her father of the divorce, only to hear him bemoan the loss of his son-in-law from the company, as the root of Shari's difficult relationship with her father, a man for whom business was the most vivid thing in life. Some describe Shari's involvement in the business as motivated entirely by family dynamics: it was the only way that she could actually become a person in her father's eyes. The irony was that Shari's professional ascent could only come about by battling her own father, who obstinately refused to be succeeded. "He didn't want her in the company, he didn't want her to succeed him, but when she was there, he caved," said one person close to the family. Any power that he did give her, she had to wrest from him, as he had wrested it from others.

And yet, once Shari made her way into the boardroom of her family's business, she was forced to reckon with some of the same dynamics Katharine Graham experienced a generation before. Both were belittled, talked over, and snickered at behind closed doors—in Shari's case, often by her own father. Even well into the twenty-first century, a female media owner remains a kind of unicorn. Women own less than 7 percent of the television stations in the United States, despite decades of federal regulation attempting to increase diversity among station owners. Other parts of the media are so devoid of female ownership for it not to even be a topic of discussion. From this fundamental imbalance flows the litany of sad, stale facts of women's seemingly permanently junior role in the business of telling the world's stories: they are only on camera on TV news about a third of the time, only write about a third of the newspaper stories, only make up 6 percent of film directors.

And then, about a year into Shari's reign, the dam broke. The *New York Times* and the *New Yorker* uncovered decades of Harvey Weinstein's sexual abuse and harassment of women, opening a torrent of allegations against other men in the entertainment industry and beyond. No one knows what Hollywood will look like after this flood, but there will certainly be more women in charge. After seeing the brutality and misogyny of the media industry exposed, is it any wonder that a woman had to ferociously fight her way to power within it?

During her first year as a proper media mogul, Shari continued her family's legal fight against her father's former companions, not flinching even as embarrassing personal emails were dredged up in discovery and alarming accusations were hurled at her alleging she was part of a conspiracy to break California law. (Her lawyers deny the allegations and maintain that Shari has nothing to do with Sumner's lawsuit against the women.) Her own legal training and upbringing in a family of legal infighters had prepared her well: so far, the lawsuits against her have made little progress. She even scored a victory in October when a judge ousted Manuela Herzer from her penthouse apartment in the Carlyle.

However messy the details, in the court of public opinion, few blamed Shari for reclaiming her birthright. Her years spent running the theater chain, serving on Viacom and CBS's boards, and investing in start-ups had given her a unique understanding and a broad set of relationships in an industry that was now in a state of total upheaval. If she didn't have the answers, nobody else did either. In business, she shared her father's interest in the next thing—the cable that would overtake the movies, the video games that would overwhelm the cable, the digital media that would overtake them all—but she faced a far more complicated landscape than he ever did.

If Sumner had had his full faculties, would he have recognized the great wave that was overwhelming his companies—Viacom in particular—and done something differently? Would he, too, have come to a Murdochian realization that the deck was now stacked against traditional media companies competing directly against unregulated, automated, and ballooning tech giants and decided to cash in his chips? It's hard to imagine that he wouldn't have surveyed the landscape in which Google and Facebook accounted for 84 percent of global digital advertising spending in 2017—a situation that the business press dispassionately refers to as "the duopoly"—and tried to cook up some kind of antitrust suit, his trusty weapon of choice. But would he have had the flexibility of mind to upend his own estate planning documents, which go to elaborate lengths to bar his heirs from selling

his companies, in order to preserve the wealth he built for future
generations?

He may still have the chance. These days, Sumner rests comfortably in his hilltop mansion, tended to by nurses loyal to his family, in
touch with his family via FaceTime and occasional visits, but otherwise cut off from the world in every measurable way. Unable to eat or
talk, he communicates via buttons on a tablet loaded with recordings
of his voice from stronger days—"yes," "no," and, his favorite, "fuck
you." The man who always wanted total control, who believed in his
own abilities above those of anyone else, who vowed to never sell Viacom, who swore he would never die—as of this writing, this man,
Sumner Redstone, still draws breath, thanks, perhaps, to a lifetime
of healthy eating and, even more likely, his own iron will. It is he, not
Shari, who owns the majority of the controlling shares in the companies, and so long as he is not declared incapacitated, it will be he who
must technically decide the increasingly urgent question of whether
to merge or sell Viacom and CBS. Because while content may still be
king, kings, it turns out, can be bought just like anybody else.

Acknowledgments

This book exists, first and foremost, because of the insights of my *Wall Street Journal* editor, Amol Sharma, who presciently saw in the late summer of 2015 that the question that had long peppered investors' conversations about Viacom—"How's Sumner doing?"—was about to become a very big story. I am grateful for the time and space he gave me to dig into the story at the *Journal*, and for the support he has given this project at every step.

Nearly as forward-looking was my HarperCollins editor, Hollis Heimbouch, who reached out about the possibility of a book before the real power struggle for the Redstone media empire had even begun, and who helped me envision a more ambitious book than I had thought possible. Working with her was a delight.

Still the book would not have happened without my agent, Alice Martell, for whose faith, encouragement, and savvy I will always be grateful.

Beyond any individual, I owe the institution of the *Wall Street Journal* a great debt. When telling a business tale that stretches for more than a century, there is no greater resource than the archives of a 129-year-old business newspaper. While much of the reporting in the later chapters originated in my own reporting for the paper, much of the earlier chapters is built on the work of my predecessors and colleagues on the beat, including Laura Landro, Merissa Marr, and Martin Peers. In the present day, I am fortunate to be able to collaborate on this story with talented colleagues like Joe Flint, Joann Lublin, Ben Fritz, Erich Schwartzel, and Sarah Rabil, and on the broader media beat with Shalini Ramachandran, Jeffrey Trachtenberg, Lukas Alpert, Suzanne Vranica, Alex Bruell, Ben Mullin, and Laura O'Reilly. Thank you to Jim Oberman and Lisa Schwartz for their research help. I am particularly grateful to Joe Flint and Amol Sharma for covering for me while I was on maternity leave.

Thank you to Raju Narisetti for nudging me toward the *Journal* and to Martin Peers for hiring me, mentoring me, and giving me a great beat. I am grateful to Gerry Baker for giving me leave to work on this book, and to Jason Anders and Jamie Heller for supporting my commitment to both this book and the bigger story.

Thanks to the many members of the Redstone, Rothstein, and Ostrovsky families who spoke to me, and to their advisers who were generous with their time. In particular I want to thank Keryn Redstone and Gary Snyder for their patience and generosity.

Many historians and history enthusiasts helped me in my research, most notably Duane Lucia at the West End Museum, and Stephanie Schorow, David Kruh, and Amy Bentley at the Valley Stream Historical Society. Thank you to Kay Nguyen for patient and energetic research help. Thanks to Brian Wieser for ratings research.

I'm grateful to Luke Kummer, David Enrich, Lisa Dallos, Mike Spector, and Michael Wolff for their wise advice, to Lindsay and Steve Bronstein for their encouragement, and to all my friends—especially Nita Praditpan, Julie Alexander, Derik Riesche, Leah and Tal Gozhansky, Kirsten Osur, Michelle and Nigel Noyes, Lauren Lancaster, and Michael DelGrosso—for putting up with me and cheering me on over the last two years. I'm grateful to my brother, Foster Hagey, and his wife, Stephanie, for having our backs.

Thank you to Margie and Bill Harris, who provided child care at several critical junctures and have been so warmly encouraging throughout this project. Thank you to my grandmother Diane Igleheart, who let me camp out in her house and write for a week—with lunch provided. Thank you to Daiane Rezende, our au pair, whose wisdom and creativity have made all of our lives better, and to Griffin Bancroft-Baines for crunch time babysitting help and friendship.

I want to thank my parents, Jingle and Chandler Hagey, who showed me how to derive great pleasure from books and gave me the foundation for a satisfying intellectual life. I am grateful for the priority they placed on my education and the enthusiastic support they have given this project.

And most of all, I want to thank my husband, Wesley Harris, whose sacrifices made this book possible, and whose peerless advice has improved it. To our daughters, Belle and June, thank you for your patience and for filling our lives with so much joy.

Author's Note

This book is based primarily on more than 170 interviews with family, friends, lovers, colleagues, advisers, employees, and competitors of Sumner Redstone and his family's media empire, conducted between 2015 and 2018. While the bulk of these interviews were conducted for this book, a few—notably with Shari Redstone and Philippe Dauman—were conducted originally for the *Wall Street Journal*.

Quotations that are not otherwise credited are from these interviews. Some of them were on the record. Many more were on background, due to the sensitive nature of the topic. For the sake of clarity, facts that were corroborated by multiple sources do not have attribution. Where facts came from a single source, I note that.

A great deal of this saga is also drawn from court papers from five decades of legal infighting among members of the Redstone clan, as well as a series of high-profile lawsuits involving Sumner Redstone's former companions, top lieutenants, and his daughter. These, as well as the many other newspapers, magazines, books, and other documents I used as source material are detailed in the book's notes.

However, I owe particular debts of gratitude to the excellent reporting of the *Boston Globe*, *Wall Street Journal*, *New York Times*, *Variety*, and *BoxOffice*; the Courtroom View Network; and the formidable journalism of Judith Newman, Gretchen Voss, Bryan Burrough, William D. Cohan, Ken Auletta, Julia Angwin, David Kirkpatrick, Peter Elkind, and Marty Jones. Most of all, this book owes a great debt to Sumner Redstone's 2001 autobiography, *A Passion to Win*, written with Peter Knobler, which captures the fighting spirit of the mogul at his peak.

Notes

PROLOGUE: "I Don't Want to Sell Paramount"

4   Sumner's protestations would not: Keach Hagey, "The Relationship That Helped Sumner Redstone Build Viacom Now Adds to Its Problems," *Wall Street Journal*, April 11, 2016.

CHAPTER 1: Rain at Sunrise

10   For weeks leading: "Outdoor Auto Movie House, First in State, Being Erected on Highway at Valley Stream," *New York Times*, July 3, 1938.
10   So when they turned: "Parking-Film Theater Started in Valley Stream," *Brooklyn Daily Eagle*, July 3, 1938.
10   "World's Biggest Movie Screen for Outdoor Theater": *Popular Science*, 1938.
11   Drive-ins mainly served: "Drive-In Theater; State's First Auto Movie Theater Opens Wednesday on Sunrise Highway," *Brooklyn Daily Eagle*, August 7, 1938.
11   The chairman of the board: "Outdoor Theatre Protest in Dedham," *Boston Globe*, October 1, 1937.
12   The ad in the local papers: Sunrise Drive-In Theatre advertisement.
12   By 1938, drive-ins were not quite as novel: Kerry Segrave, *Drive-In Theaters: A History from Their Inception in 1933* (Jefferson, NC: McFarland, 1992), 1–11.
13   The Sunrise was the first: William E. Geist, "Drive-In Movies: An Innovation Hits 50 and Passes Its Prime," *New York Times*, June 7, 1983.
13   Foreseeing this boom: Sunrise Auto Theatre, Inc., business entity summary, Secretary of the Commonwealth of Massachusetts.
13   Despite what a *New York Times* reporter: *New York Times*, August 14, 1938.
13   The bad weather: "Drive-In Theatre Open Until Mid-November," *Wave*, September 4, 1938.
14   Under the leadership: "Profile: A Night at the Movies; the Rise and Fall and Possible Rise Again in the Popularity of Drive-in Theaters," *CBS News: Sunday Morning*, June 30, 2002.
15   Although he was the straggler: "Harry Rohtstein of Mattapan; Services Today," *Boston Globe*, August 27, 1967.
15   Boston's immigrant population: Reed Ueda, *West End House, 1906–1981* (Boston: West End House, 1981), 4.
15   From 1880 to 1920: Daniel J. McGrath, "Politicians, Planners and the Dilemmas of Urban Redevelopment: Boston's West End and the Consequences of

Rebuilding an Old City" (undergraduate thesis, Harvard University, March 23, 2000).

16   early, private form of affordable housing: Robert I. Rotberg, *A Leadership for Peace: How Edwin Ginn Tried to Change the World* (Palo Alto, CA: Stanford University Press, 2007).

16   By age seventeen: Joseph F. Dinneen, Spilling the Beans, *Boston Globe*, March 12, 1943.

18   It went by a variety: "'Nigger Pool' Agents Are Now Being Fined $250," *Boston Globe*, November 11, 1930; "Nigger Pool Arrest Made on Lynn Wives' Plaints," *Boston Globe*, July 12, 1935.

18   By July 29, 1932: "Lottery Ring Raid Nets 26," *Boston Globe*, July 30, 1932.

19   "Belle worshipped her father": Judith Newman, "Fort Sumner," *Vanity Fair*, November 1999.

20   Bootlegging in Boston: Emily Sweeney, *Boston Organized Crime* (Charleston, SC: Arcadia Publishing, 2012), 23–24.

20   The son of Russian Jews: Albert Fried, *The Rise and Fall of the Jewish Gangster in America* (New York: Columbia University Press, 1980), 104.

20   He became a member: Stephanie Schorow, *Drinking Boston* (Wellesley, MA: Union Park Press, 2012), 103–8.

21   So, too, was Linsey: Nicholas Gage, "Ex-Head of Schenley Industries Is Linked to Crime 'Consortium,'" *New York Times*, February 19, 1971.

21   At age nineteen: "Explanations Due from Max; Must Uncover Mystery of Stolen Bag," *Boston Post*, May 22, 1921.

22   He bought a used truck: Interview with Judith Newman.

22   he got a bank loan: "Real Estate Transactions," *Boston Globe*, September 30, 1925.

22   "I remember when": Belle Redstone to Edward Redstone, 1971.

22   By this point, in 1930: 1930 census records.

22   "My father peddled linoleum": Sumner Redstone with Peter Knobler, *A Passion to Win* (New York: Simon & Schuster, 2001), 41.

23   By the end of the decade: Schorow, *Drinking Boston*, 115–19.

CHAPTER 2: The Conga Belt

24   The club had an impeccable: Schorow, *Drinking Boston*, 103–20, 136.

25   After another change of ownership: "Restaurant License on Site of Mayfair," *Boston Globe*, January 10, 1934.

25   In the wake of repeal: "Restaurant License on Site of Mayfair; Declared 'Probationary' by Boston Board," *Boston Globe*, January 29, 1934.

25   "New Owner-Manager of Mayfair": *Boston Globe*, January 29, 1940.

25   In the United States, where the increasingly anti-Semitic: Susan Welch, "American Opinion toward Jews during the Nazi Era: Results from Quota Sample Polling during the 1930s and 1940s," *Social Science Quarterly* 95, no. 3 (September 2014): 615–35.

26   In an ironic twist: Nick Tosches, "A Jazz Age Autopsy," *Vanity Fair*, May 2005.

26 His cousin Irving Rothstein: "Gaming Raids Result in 12 Arrests," *Boston Globe*, September 19, 1947.

26 Another cousin, Edward Rothstein: Frank Mahoney, "U.S. Links Rothstein to Bootlegging Gang," *Boston Globe*, April 8, 1960.

27 A few months after Mickey: Redstone, *A Passion to Win*, 46.

27 The Sunrise had been a success: Interview with Bob Sage.

27 By the late 1930s: "Club Mayfair Gets Special 3-Day Permit," *Boston Globe*, February 26, 1943.

27 Mickey told the *Boston Globe*'s: Joseph F. Dinneen, Spilling the Beans, *Boston Globe*, September 9, 1942.

28 It would come out in court: "Club Mayfair Gets Special 3-Day Permit."

28 Mickey had a good feel: Joseph F. Dinneen, Spilling the Beans, *Boston Globe*, September 9, 1942.

28 The Latin Quarter was the brainchild: Barbara Walters, *Audition: A Memoir* (New York: Vintage Books, 2009), 26–29.

29 In July 1942, Walters sold: Boston property records.

30 Winer would go on to cofound: "Louis Winer, 79, Was Boston Lawyer," *Boston Globe*, March 12, 1993; Julia Collins, "The Double Life of George Abrams '57," *Harvard Law Today*, April 25, 2000.

30 On September 10, 1942: Joseph F. Dinneen, Spilling the Beans, *Boston Globe*, September 9, 1942.

30 Within a little more than a month: "Boston Niteries and Hotel Spots Expand Due to Best Biz in Years," *Billboard*, October 24, 1942.

30 Sagansky's other businesses were also: Testimony of Virgil Peterson, operating director of the Chicago Crime Commission, to the Kefauver Committee, U.S. Senate Special Committee to Investigate Organized Crime in Interstate Commerce, July 7, 1950.

30 Along with Costello, Erickson: Nicholas Pileggi, "Crime at Mid-Century," *New York* magazine, December 30, 1974–January 6, 1975.

31 Sagansky had similar relationships: Kefauver Committee testimony.

31 A Hollywood cowboy movie star: Stephanie Schorow, *The Cocoanut Grove Fire* (Beverly, MA: Commonwealth Editions, 2005), 10–26.

32 Within less than a half an hour: Samuel Cutler, "400 Dead in Hub Night Club Fire," *Boston Globe*, November 29, 1942.

32 City officials launched: John Esposito, *Fire in the Grove: The Cocoanut Grove Tragedy and Its Aftermath* (Cambridge, MA: Da Capo Press, 2006), 129.

33 "The whole thing constitutes": Leslie Ainley, "Grove a 'Death Trap'—Bushnell," *Boston Globe*, March 17, 1943.

33 The Latin Quarter had to yank: Schorow, *Drinking Boston*, 145.

CHAPTER 3: "The Whole Situation"

34 January 12, 1943, started out: Leslie Ainley, "24 Held in Racket Drive; Curley Confirms $8500 Loan from Dr. Sagansky," *Boston Globe*, January 14, 1943.

34 But there had been a fire: "Scores Arrested in Multi-Million Dollar Lottery," Associated Press, January 14, 1943.

35 Indeed, a hint about those priorities: "24 Held in Racket Drive."

36 Curley had been mayor: Jack Beatty, *The Rascal King: The Life and Times of James Michael Curley, 1874–1958* (Reading, MA: Addison-Wesley, 1992), 273.

36 The financial ties between: Esposito, *Fire in the Grove*, 15.

36 Within forty-eight hours of the raid: Leslie Ainley, "Probe of Department's Anti-Gaming Work for Last 2 Years Indicated," *Boston Globe*, January 15, 1943.

36 A week after Sagansky's: Leslie Ainley, "Sagansky Rearrested; Pool Code Solved in Boston Area," *Boston Globe*, January 17, 1943.

37 One of his first acts: Massachusetts State Senate Special Commission to Investigate Organized Crime and Organized Gambling, Second Report, July 1955, 11.

37 The American government: "Dec 1, 1942: Mandatory Gas Rationing, Lots of Whining," *Wired*, November 30, 2009.

37 When Bushnell's investigators caught: Ainley, "State Police Strike at Boston Rackets."

38 "Obviously, these things converge": Leslie Ainley, "Timiltys, Fallon and Long before Grand Jury Today," *Boston Globe*, February 5, 1943.

38 As Bushnell built the two cases: Esposito, *Fire in the Grove*, 208.

38 And as he unveiled: Ainley, "State Police Strike at Boston Rackets."

39 Second, in a stunning: "7 Police Heads Indicted; Commissioner on Leave; Others Are Suspended," *Boston Globe*, March 28, 1943.

39 But on the morning: Ainley, "Timiltys, Fallon and Long before Grand Jury Today."

39 The proceedings laid out: Leslie Ainley, "Grand Jury Calls Comr. Timilty and Capt. Sheehan," *Boston Globe*, February 7, 1943.

39 After he and associates: "Indicted as Leaders of Huge Liquor Ring: Four Men Accused in Brooklyn Said to Have Operated Fleet from Canada and Europe," *New York Times*, January 5, 1933.

39 Once known as the "King": "Louis Fox Rites Today in Brookline," *Boston Globe*, October 27, 1963.

39 Only one small line: "Fox's Testimony," *Boston Globe*, March 22, 1957.

40 During the grand jury: "Timiltys Move to Restrict Their Books to Jury Use," *Boston Globe*, February 9, 1943.

40 During the trial, two Malden: Leslie Ainley, "Sagansky Offered Bribes for Beano, Malden Officials Say," *Boston Globe*, February 9, 1943.

40 He added that Club Mayfair: Leslie Ainley, "Sagansky and Carrigan Deny Beano Bribe Offers," *Boston Globe*, February 12, 1943.

41 Within a week: "Club Mayfair Gets Special 3-Day Permit."

41 After the lawyer: "Club Mayfair Keeps All of Its Licenses," *Boston Globe*, March 9, 1943.

41 Barely a week after Sagansky: "2 Men Wounded in Night Club Mystery Shooting," *Boston Globe*, March 26, 1943.

41 The police, mindful: "Timilty Recommends All Latin Quarter Licenses Be Ended," *Boston Globe*, March 27, 1943.

42 When Sumner entered Harvard: *Harvard Freshman Red Book*, 1940.

42 During the summers: Redstone, *A Passion to Win*, 48.

42 Sumner was one of about: George Packard, *Edwin O. Reischauer and the American Discovery of Japan* (New York: Columbia University Press, 2010).

42 Sumner left Harvard: Redstone, *A Passion to Win*, 50.

43 After the war ended in September: Ibid., 55.

43 His Harvard yearbook: *Harvard College Yearbook 1943–1944.*

43 Instead of stars, he offered: Joseph F. Dinneen, Inside Boston, *Boston Globe*, August 11, 1943.

44 With Sagansky in prison: Joseph F. Dinneen, Spilling the Beans, *Boston Globe*, March 10, 1943.

44 Timilty managed: Esposito, *Fire in the Grove*, 189.

44 He became what: Ronald Kessler, *The Sins of the Father: Joseph P. Kennedy and the Dynasty He Founded* (New York: Warner Books, 1996), 45.

44 Bushnell never made it: "Robert T. Bushnell Dies Suddenly in N.Y. Hotel," *Boston Globe*, October 24, 1949.

44 He continued to have: "Legendary Boston Bookmaker Dead at 99," Associated Press, January 31, 1997.

44 Even after power: Tom Long, "Harry Sagansky, 99, Masterminded Bookmaking Empire in the '30s and '40s," *Boston Globe*, January 20, 1997.

44 On his ninetieth birthday: Richard J. Connolly, "At 90, Alleged Bookmaker Begins His Jail Term," *Boston Globe*, January 8, 1988.

44 By the end of his life: "Dr. Harry Sagansky, 99, of Brookline, Dentist," *Boston Herald*, January 29, 1997.

45 And he still had enough: Paul Sullivan, "Crafty Bookie's Kids Come Out $9.5M Ahead," *Boston Herald*, March 27, 1997.

45 In the 1950s, as the mob: "The Dunes," Online Nevada Encyclopedia, http://www.onlinenevada.org/articles/dunes-hotel.

45 Despite help from friends: "Ruling Delays Foreclosure against Dunes," *Reno Gazette-Journal*, July 25, 1987.

45 Years later, as the FBI was investigating: JFK Assassination System Identification Form, FBI, Record Number 124-10342-1000.

46 The nightclub business suffered: John Riley, "Latin Quarter Offers a New Kind of Entertainment for Night Clubs," *Boston Globe*, November 16, 1949.

46 By 1948, they had bought: "Revere Drive-In Theatre Opens, with 'Swordsman,'" *Boston Globe*, August 25, 1948.

46 The same year, they opened: "Redstone Pushes Hub Plans; Points Up Over-Expansion," *Billboard*, April 15, 1950.

46 But in the final weeks: "Councilors Blast Curley for OK on Drive-In Theatres," *Boston Globe*, September 13, 1949.

46 In any other year: McGrath, "Politicians, Planners and the Dilemmas of Urban Redevelopment."

47 Curley was not one: William J. Lewis, "Woman Serves Injunction in Drive-In Row," *Boston Globe*, December 31, 1949.

47 On January 1, 1950: "Mulligan to File Bills to Regulate Drive-In Theatres," *Boston Globe*, January 1, 1950.

47 But when Hynes was sworn in: "Hynes Can't Halt Curley Drive-Ins, Baxter Decides," *Boston Globe*, January 21, 1950.

47   Still, Hynes had promised: McGrath, "Politicians, Planners and the Dilemmas of Urban Redevelopment."

CHAPTER 4: The Next Generation

49   It should have been: "Redstone Pushes Hub Plans; Points Up Over-Expansion."

49   Leading up to 1950: Bettye H. Pruitt, *The Making of Harcourt General: A History of Growth through Diversification, 1922–1992* (Boston: Harvard Business School Press, 1994), 18.

50   The decline would continue: Alex Ben Block, *George Lucas's Blockbusting: A Decade-by-Decade Survey of Timeline Movies, Including Untold Secrets of Their Financial and Cultural Success* (New York: itBooks, 2010).

50   although as a percentage of population: Michelle Pautz, "The Decline in Average Weekly Cinema Attendance: 1930–2000," *Issues in Political Economy* 11 (2002): 54–65.

50   The cause was a perfect storm: Tino Balio, *The American Film Industry* (Madison: University of Wisconsin Press, 1976), 401.

50   Television then exacerbated the trend: Ibid.

50   Also, in May 1948: Ibid., 253.

51   In the decade after *Paramount*: Pruitt, *The Making of Harcourt General*, 49.

51   Profits at the ten biggest companies dropped: Balio, *The American Film Industry*, 402.

51   Many of these trends: Pruitt, *The Making of Harcourt General*, 18.

52   "Our problem": "Redstone Pushes Hub Plans; Points Up Over-Expansion."

52   "Our apartment": Redstone, *A Passion to Win*, 41–45.

53   These reminiscences: US City Directories, Boston, 1932, entry for Morris Rohtstein; US City Directories, Boston, 1933, entry for Rebecca Rohtstein.

53   given that his father: "Real Estate Transactions."

54   "everything from fixing septic fields": Edward S. Redstone and Madeline Redstone v. Mark Schuster, George Duncan and Samuel Rosen, Middlesex Probate Court, Massachusetts, Deposition of Edward Redstone, November 16, 2004.

54   The next year: "Miss Leila B. Warren of New York Engaged to Edward Redstone of Cohasset," *Boston Globe*, December 2, 1951.

54   The only child: David H. Warren obituary, *New York Times*, November 3, 1966.

54   Eddie got his MBA: *Variety*, July 16, 1952.

54   At Eddie and Leila's wedding: "Miss Leila B. Warren Is Bride of Edward S. Redstone in New York," *Boston Globe*, November 16, 1952.

54   the brothers had always been close: Redstone v. Schuster, Deposition of Edward Redstone.

54   Though he worked: Pruitt, *The Making of Harcourt General*, 3.

54   As Doc Sagansky's: Newman, "Fort Sumner."

55   In his autobiography: Redstone, *A Passion to Win*, 43.

55   Eddie remembered her: Redstone v. Schuster, Deposition of Edward Redstone.

55   Sumner credits his mother's: Sumner Redstone speech at Boston University, March 31, 2010, https://www.youtube.com/watch?v=11zypIc5QMY.

55   Founded in 1635: Boston Latin School website, http://www.bls.org/apps/pages/index.jsp?uREC_ID=206116&type=d.

57   His first year: Redstone, *A Passion to Win*, 45–46.

57   Over many decades: Robert Lenzner, "True Grit," *Boston Globe*, March 17, 1981.

57   "highest grade point average": Redstone, *A Passion to Win*, 46.

57   Debating Council: *Harvard College Yearbook 1944–1944*.

58   Immediately after taking the bar: Redstone, *A Passion to Win*, 57.

58   Phyllis's parents: 1920 census document for Hilda Cherry.

58   Eli Raphael: Eli Raphael naturalization document.

58   Her only pet peeve: Gretchen Voss, "The $80 Billion Love Affair," *Boston* magazine, January 12, 2000.

58   Two years Sumner's junior: Redstone, *A Passion to Win*, 57.

58   she returned to Boston: Marriage Announcement 7, *Boston Globe*, January 26, 1947.

58   Belle Redstone approved: Voss, "The $80 Billion Love Affair."

59   by January 1947: Marriage Announcement 7, *Boston Globe*.

59   July 4, 1947: Harvard Class of 1944, 10th Anniversary Report and 25th Anniversary Report.

59    $43 a week: Marla Matzer and Robert Lenzner, "Winning Is the Only Thing," *Forbes*, October 17, 1994.

59   "I was not interested": Redstone, *A Passion to Win*, 57–58.

59   On September 7, 1948: "Atty Redstone Named to Washington Post," *Boston Globe*, August 15, 1948.

59   In the wake of the Supreme Court's decision: United States v. Paramount Pictures, Inc., 334 U.S. 131.

59   Though Sumner was assigned: Redstone, *A Passion to Win*, 60; "2 Ex-Justice Aides Put under Inquiry," *New York Times*, August 7, 1952.

59   Later in 1951: Matzer and Lenzner, "Winning Is the Only Thing."

60   The media industry: "2 Ex-Justice Aides Put under Inquiry"; Redstone, *A Passion to Win*, 62.

60   After that merger: Ruth Marcus, "Death of a Law Firm: D.C. Partnership a Victim of Changing Times," *Washington Post*, April 7, 1986.

60   The crowning achievement: Redstone, *A Passion to Win*, 64–66.

60   He went on to say: Ibid., 65–66.

61   That's an odd way: Matzer and Lenzner, "Winning Is the Only Thing."

62   One front-page profile: Jane Fitz Simon, "Sumner Redstone," *Boston Globe*, October 5, 1986.

62   In 1998, he told *Forbes*: Frank Rose, "There's No Business Like Show Business," *Forbes*, June 22, 1998.

62   In his autobiography: Redstone, *A Passion to Win*, 69.

62   In court testimony in 2009: Thomas N. O'Connor et al. v. Sumner M. Redstone et al., Suffolk Superior Court, Massachusetts, Testimony of Sumner Redstone, July 27, 2009.

62   the Dedham and Revere: "Redstone's Boston Drive-In Bows Okay," *Billboard*, September 1, 1948.

62   the Whitestone Bridge Drive-In: "Whitestone Drive-In Will Open on Friday," *Brooklyn Daily Eagle*, August 10, 1949.

62   the Neponset Drive-In: "Redstone Pushes Hub Plans; Points Up Over-Expansion."

62   Lee Highway Drive-In: Redstone, *A Passion to Win*, 68; and Cinema Trea-sures, http://cinematreasures.org/theaters/12250.

62   By October 1955: "Lake Shore Drive-In Sold to Boston Man for $110,000," *Democrat and Chronicle* (Rochester, NY), October 22, 1955.

62   Drive-in owners: Segrave, *Drive-In Theaters*, 73.

62   Sumner said his father: Redstone, *A Passion to Win*, 67.

63   In 1954, the average drive-in: Segrave, *Drive-In Theaters*, 77.

63   "For instance, I flew into Louisville": Redstone, *A Passion to Win*, 70.

63   The Kenwood Drive-In opened: "Wall Able to Resist 100-Mile-an-Hour Wind," *Courier-Journal* (Louisville, KY), June 12, 1949.

63   Northeast's successor company: Charlie White, "Theater Is for Sale but Po-tential Buyer Says Information Scarce," *Courier-Journal* (Louisville, KY), Decem-ber 30, 2009.

63   The same was true in Cincinnati: Cinema Treasures, http://cinematreasures.org/theaters/9787.

63   For all of Sumner's talk: Guy Livingstone, "Boston," *Variety*, March 14, 1956.

63   or his brother to answer questions: "Dates Set to Open Drive-Ins," *Democrat and Chronicle* (Rochester, NY), June 6, 1956.

64   But as the broader film: Pruitt, *The Making of Harcourt General*, 49.

64   His official role: "San Francisco Drive-In Agenda TOA's 'Conventionette' Expects Attendance of 250 Ozone Operators," *Variety*, March 3, 1958.

64   but when the press reported: "Frisco Forum's Faith in Trust Fund; Rue Un-wanted Results of Divorce," *Variety*, April 2, 1958.

64   He pinned the woes: "Film Industry Own Worst Enemy, Exhibitors Allege," *Los Angeles Times*, March 28, 1958.

64   By the time the Theatre: "Prime TOA's 11th Year: Convention Set for Miami Beach," *Variety*, June 25, 1958.

65   And by July 1958: *Variety*, July 16, 1958.

65   At the convention: "Dept. of Justice's Open-Ears to Ideas but No Return to 'Favored Theatres,'" *Variety*, October 29, 1958.

65   In theory: Andy W. Smith Jr., "Greater Exhib-Demand for A's; Drive-Ins' Plus Values," *Variety*, January 4, 1950; Pruitt, *The Making of Harcourt General*, 21.

66   That same year, drive-ins won: Segrave, *Drive-In Theaters*, 57.

66   In March 1959: Gene Arneel, "'Exploding' an Import at the Waldorf," *Vari-ety*, March 25, 1959.

CHAPTER 5: National Amusements

67   On August 28, 1959: Estate of Edward S. Redstone, Deceased, Madeline M. Redstone, Executrix v. Commissioner of Internal Revenue, U.S. Tax Court, 2015.

68   The company used its: Redstone, *A Passion to Win*, 71.

68   Meanwhile, across town: Pruitt, *The Making of Harcourt General*, 47.

68   Phil Smith, three years: Ibid., 2.

68   Like Mickey, he opened: Ibid., 9.

68   Like Sumner, Phil's son: Ibid., 22.

68   Like Eddie, Richard: Ibid., 23.

68   By the late 1950s: Ibid., 37.

68   This let the Smiths: Ibid.
69   But by the time: Ibid., 51.
69   "I never felt I had to": Ibid., 40.
69   "While others were building": Redstone, *A Passion to Win*, 71.
69   By 2000: Joseph Pereira and Nikhil Deogun, "Parent of General Cinema Chain Files for Chapter 11; Top Executives Resign," *Wall Street Journal*, October 12, 2000.
69   They opened their first: "$250,000 Renovation for Redstone Indoor," *Box-Office*, November 5, 1962.
69   Riseman, who had designed: "William Riseman, Architect of Numerous Movie Theaters," *New York Times*, June 21, 1982.
70   On a clear, breezy: Marjory Adams, "'Great Race' to Open New Cleveland Circle Cinema," *Boston Globe*, November 21, 1965.
70   In September 1960: "Theater Owners Told of Fight on Pay-T," *Los Angeles Times*, September 16, 1960; convention schedule from *Variety*, September 12, 1960.
70   Still, exhibitors were: "TOA's Sumner Redstone Raps Toll as Detriment to Pix, Regular TV," *Variety*, May 24, 1961.
71   In 1964: "TOA Elects Redstone Prexy; Inches Nearer Allied Merger," *Variety*, September 29, 1964.
71   getting his picture taken: "Three Files Establish Andrews as TAO's Darling of the Year," *Variety*, October 20, 1965.
71   Eddie was cutting ribbons: "Reopen Milford Drive-In," *Bridgeport (CT) Post*, April 25, 1962.
71   "I cannot be held responsible": "Proposed Drive-In Upsets Township," *Variety*, March 6, 1968.
71   Eddie also took on: "Edward Redstone at Helm of N.E. Exhibs," *Variety*, April 20, 1966.
71   By the end of the decade: "The Real Estate Front," *Boston Globe*, June 29, 1969.
71   Nevertheless, Mickey maintained: Sumner Redstone v. Commissioner of Internal Revenue, Testimony of Sumner Redstone.
71   He had begun: "Manchester," *Bennington (VT) Banner*, September 9, 1964.
72   He began creating a plan: Redstone v. Commissioner of Internal Revenue, 2015–237, United States Tax Court, 5 (2015).
72   The grandchildren would receive: O'Connor v. Redstone, Amended Complaint.
72   Sumner's son, Brent: Brent D. Redstone v. National Amusements, Inc., Baltimore Circuit Court, Maryland, 2006, Complaint.
73   Without Eddie's knowledge: Edward S. Redstone and Madeline Redstone v. Mark Schuster, George Duncan and Samuel Rosen, Middlesex Probate Court, 2004, Deposition of Edward S. Redstone, 7.
73   "When I was four": Redstone v. Schuster, 24.

CHAPTER 6: "From One Catastrophe to Another"

75   Michael Redstone had not wanted to go: Interview with Eliot Finn.
75   In fact, it had been the recommendation: Redstone v. Schuster, Deposition of Michael Redstone, 25.

75 Within two hours: Ibid., 29.
76 Founded in 1817: Alex Beam, "The Mad Poets Society," *Atlantic*, July/August 2001.
76 In one poem: Robert Lowell, "Waking in the Blue," in *Selected Poems* (New York: Farrar, Straus and Giroux, 1976).
76 Thorazine: Redstone v. Schuster, Deposition of Michael Redstone, 30.
76 "I was often locked in a room": Ibid., 58.
76 Mickey and Belle were horrified: Estate of Edward S. Redstone v. Commissioner of Internal Revenue, 264.
77 "My grandparents didn't like my parents": Redstone v. Schuster, Affidavit of Michael Redstone, 57–58.
77 Jerry Swedroe: "Jerry Swedroe Is Promoted," *Journal News* (White Plains, NY), April 26, 1967.
77 He demanded his 100 shares: Sumner Redstone v. Commissioner of Internal Revenue, U.S. Tax Court, 2015, 7.
77 there was none: Sumner Redstone v. Commissioner of Internal Revenue, Testimony of Sumner Redstone, 2009.
77 "evil, scheming cunt": Redstone v. Schuster, Affidavit of Michael Redstone, 66.
78 Well aware that: Sumner Redstone v. Commissioner of Internal Revenue, Memorandum of Findings of Fact and Opinion, 9.
78 Eddie, his heart ever: Letter from Edward Redstone to Mickey Redstone, July 19, 1971.
78 In his autobiography: Redstone, *A Passion to Win*, 69.
79 In his testimony: O'Connor v. Redstone, Testimony of Sumner Redstone.
79 Indeed, it was Sumner: Memorandum by Jim DeGiacomo regarding Edward Redstone, June 16, 1972.
79 The two sides explored: Sumner Redstone v. Commissioner of Internal Revenue, Memorandum of Findings of Fact and Opinion, 10.
79 Belle, excitable already: Letter from Belle Redstone to Edward Redstone, 1972.
80 Eddie, against his: Letter from Edward Redstone to Belle Redstone, February 18, 1972.
80 While the increasingly adversarial: Sumner Redstone v. Commissioner of Internal Revenue, 11–13.
80 Years later, Eddie was: Redstone v. Schuster, Deposition of Edward Redstone, 28.
81 Once again he made: O'Connor v. Redstone, Complaint, 10.
81 By 1972, Sumner was firmly: Ibid., 11.
82 The small liberal arts college: Lynn Sherr, "Brandeis: A Breeding Ground for Rebels?" *Chicago Tribune*, December 6, 1970.
82 Around the same time: "Final Report on the Activities of the Children of God to Hon. Louis J. Lefkowitz, Attorney General of the State of New York," submitted by the Charity Frauds Bureau, September 30, 1974.
82 a band of self-described "Jesus freaks": Roy Rivenburg, "25 Years Ago, the Children of God's Gospel of Free Love Outraged Critics," *Los Angeles Times*, March 21, 1993.

83 By 1970, having: Gordon Shepherd and Gary Shepherd, *Talking with the Children of God: Prophecy and Transformation in a Radical Religious Group* (Urbana: University of Illinois Press, 2010), 7.

83 By 1971, it boasted: James T. Wooten, "Ill Winds Buffet Communal Sect," *New York Times*, November 29, 1971.

83 By 1972: Family International website, https://www.thefamilyinternational .org/en/about/our-history/.

83 In 1973: "The Christmas Monster," letter from David Berg to his followers, September 8, 1973.

83 "She took . . . off": Redstone v. Schuster, Deposition of Edward Redstone, 27.

83 According to a 1974 report: "Final Report on the Activities of The Children of God," 8, 21, 22.

84 Around the time Ruth Ann joined: Shepherd and Shepherd, *Talking with the Children of God*, 9.

84 Berg called it: Ed Priebe, "Prostitution and Political Seduction," exfamily .org, March 2002, http://www.exfamily.org/art/exmem/ffing_ed.shtml.

84 Over the years: Redstone v. Schuster, Deposition of Edward Redstone, 51.

84 but she escaped: Steve Bailey, "A Family Argument," *Boston Globe*, February 25, 2005.

85 In the spring of 1980: Lonnie Isabel, "Woman Links Attackers to Her Stand on Cult Bills," *Boston Globe*, April 11, 1980.

85 He spent a little more than a year: Redstone v. Schuster, Deposition of Michael Redstone, 59.

85 "I had broken into an office": Ibid., 31–32.

86 Eddie, a New England: Barbara Kantrowitz, "'Woodstock' Beats Censorship Bid," *Boston Globe*, July 25, 1970.

87 "Primarily, he was pushing me": Redstone v. Schuster, Deposition of Michael Redstone, 70.

CHAPTER 7: "Artful Dealings"

---

88 "Contrary to popular assumption": Harvard Class of 1944, 25th Anniversary Report, 1969.

88 clutching a cigar: "Para Sesh a Rousing Success," *Independent Film Journal*, October 11, 1976.

88 lunching in Hollywood: "Redstone Present as Fox Up; He's Close to Yablans," *Variety*, March 12, 1975.

88 dancing the hora: "Inside Stuff—Pictures," *Variety*, November 1, 1972.

88 playing tennis: Robert Lenzner, "Hollywood's Hermit Seeks to Go It Alone Professionally, Too," *Boston Globe*, April 12, 1981.

88 "He screams and argues": Robert Lenzner and Marla Matzer, "Late Bloomer," *Forbes*, October 17, 1994.

88 Sumner had always been close: Redstone, *A Passion to Win*, 69.

89 When corporate raider Herbert Siegel: Abel Green, "Par Exec Comm. Ousts Duo," *Variety*, August 25, 1965.

90 With Sumner having completely: "Multiplex Cinemas," Trademark Electronic Search System, 1984.

90 Starting with 52 drive-ins: George McKinnon, "Redstone Movie Chain Expands," *Boston Globe*, July 10, 1973.

90 Sumner had more than doubled: Cecille Markell, "Redstone Opens Tenplex Cinemas in Revere," *Jewish Advocate*, August 5, 1982.

90 The Redstone Theaters: Jim Robbins, "Two Redstone 10-Plexes Expected to Heat N.Y. Environ Competition," *Variety*, October 26, 1983.

90 Most important, the Redstone: Doris Whitbeck, "Suburban Movie Theaters Scramble for Films, Some Lose," *Hartford Courant*, September 25, 1977; "Patrons Switch to Suburban Cinemas, New Issue for New Haven Exhibitors," *BoxOffice*, March 17, 1975.

91 In East Hartford: "Nice Movies Didn't Pay Way," *Hartford Courant*, March 10, 1974.

91 In New Haven: "Patrons Switch to Suburban Cinemas New Issue for New Haven Exhibitors," *BoxOffice*, March 17, 1975.

91 After five theaters: Whitbeck, "Suburban Movie Theaters Scramble for Films."

91 In 1975, three small-time: "File Anti-trust Suit against Major Movie Firms," *Ames (IA) Daily Tribune*, March 13, 1975.

92 Dubinsky and his fellow plaintiffs: Steve Weinberg, "Some of Cast Walk Off Court Stage in Movie Theater Dispute," *Des Moines Register*, December 31, 1977.

92 The response from Sumner: "Redstone Smacks Exhibs, Attorneys with $10M Suit," *Independent Film Journal*, December 23, 1977.

92 "I have not discovered": "Goodrich Apologizes to Redstone, Yablans," *BoxOffice*, February 26, 1979.

92 The DOJ put a few mild restrictions: "Blind Bidding Agreement Signed," *Variety*, August 21, 1968.

93 The argument fell mostly on deaf ears: Redstone, *A Passion to Win*, 86.

93 In April 1978: "New York Seen Key State: Exhibs, Distribs, Clash on Bids in Albany," *Variety*, April 25, 1978.

93 In June 1979: Aljean Harmetz, "15th State Outlaws Blind Bidding on Film," *New York Times*, June 19, 1979.

94 Under Sumner's direction: Laura Landro, "National Amusements Inc.'s Redstone Is Known for His Tenacity and Timing," *Wall Street Journal*, April 12, 1986.

94 buying at $8 a share: Matzer and Lenzner, "Late Bloomer."

94 Sumner fared similarly well: Redstone, *A Passion to Win*, 102–3.

94 No one is sure exactly: Voss, "The $80 Billion Love Affair," 58.

94 The protagonist of the novel: Delsa Winer, *Almost Strangers* (New York: Simon & Schuster, 2000).

95 After graduating: "Miss Eisenberg Engaged," *New York Times*, August 7, 1949.

96 Her protagonists: Delsa Winer, "Spaces in the New Year," *Tikkun*, November/December 1996. Also Winer, *Almost Strangers*.

CHAPTER 8: Forged in Fire

98 The Variety Club of New England: "Boston Welcome to Film Row Execs," *Variety*, March 28, 1979; "Roger Hill's WB Post," *Variety*, March 3, 1976.

98 As the day wore on: Redstone, *A Passion to Win*, 15; interview with Virginia Mulcahy.

99 "The fire shot up my legs": Redstone, *A Passion to Win*, 16.

99 Both were taken: William R. Cash, "List of Those Hospitalized after Fires," *Boston Globe*, March 30, 1979.

100 He was taken: Ibid.

100 Hill held on: "Fire Victim Sues Copley Plaza for $12m," *Boston Globe*, August 24, 1979.

100 Sumner's doctors: Redstone, *A Passion to Win*, 16.

100 By early June: "Father Gives Graphic Details of Sumner Redstone's Ordeal," *Variety*, June 6, 1979.

100 The fire roaring: "Julio Valentin Rodrigues, 19, of West Springfield," *Boston Globe*, October 1, 1980.

101 the presence of which: Sumner Redstone interview for the Archive of American Television, https://www.youtube.com/watch?v=ZunBI9O3ZsU.

101 Nearly two thousand people: Pamela Merritt and Victor Lewis, "Hundreds Flee 2 Hub Hotel Fires," *Boston Globe*, March 29, 1979.

101 Boston's fire commissioner: Sean Murphy, "An Uncertain Time for Julio Rodrigues," *Boston Globe*, July 22, 1979.

101 Sumner and Phyllis jointly sued: Avery Mason, "Redstones File $12 Million Suit for Fire Injuries," *BoxOffice*, September 3, 1979.

101 Her presence in the hotel: Voss, "The $80 Billion Love Affair."

101 Yet her debut novel: Winer, *Almost Strangers*, 94.

102 For years afterward: Redstone, *A Passion to Win*, 18.

102 almost as soon as: Ralph Kaminsky, "Redstone Denouncing Blind Bidding, Calls for Fight," *BoxOffice*, November 5, 1979.

102 two thousand exhibitors: "Two Bostonians: Both Fairly Long-Winded, Will Open NATO Convention," *Variety*, October 31, 1979; "Sumner Redstone Honored at Theatre Owners Convention," *Jewish Advocate*, November 15, 1979.

102 "If I had any talent and ability": Lenzner, "True Grit."

103 "I don't see movie": Ibid.

103 Over the course of 1981: Robert E. Dallos, "Theater Owner Acquires More Columbia Stock," *Los Angeles Times*, November 19, 1981.

103 When Coca-Cola: Landro, "National Amusements Inc.'s Redstone Is Known for His Tenacity and Timing"; "Columbia Board Approves High-Priced Takeover Bid from Soft-Drink Company," *Variety*, January 20, 1982.

103 That year, Sumner: "America's Jewish Billionaires. How Rich! How Charitable?" *Moment*, December 31, 1996.

103 As early as 1981: Sumner Redstone, "Redstone Theatres," *Film Journal International*, November 9, 1981.

104 In a *Boston Globe* profile: Bruce A. Mohl, "Coming Soon: Movie War," *Boston Globe*, January 12, 1982.

104 Nevertheless, he continued: Markell, "Redstone Opens Tenplex Cinemas in Revere."

104 The next year: Robbins, "Two Redstone 10-Plexes Expected to Heat N.Y. Environs Competition."

104 By then, the eleven-theater multiplex: Nan Robertson, "Multiplexes Add 2,300 Movie Screens in 5 Years," *New York Times*, November 7, 1983.

104 He told *Newsweek*: Toby Thompson, "The Twilight of the Drive-In," *American Film*, July 1, 1983.

106 When a pogrom: "Nathan Korff, 91, Milton Rabbi Known for His Generous Spirit," *Boston Globe*, February 3, 2010.

106 All three of his sons: Eric Page, "Baruch Korff, 81, Rabbi and Defender of Nixon," *New York Times*, July 27, 1995.

106 By the time Ira met: "Announce Betrothal," *Jewish Advocate*, March 27, 1980.

107 Like Sumner, Korff: "To Speak at 54th Annual Union Guest Day in Needham," *Jewish Advocate*, April 17, 1980.

107 "President Reagan's Foreign Policy": "Rabbi Korff on Foreign Policy," *Jewish Advocate*, December 4, 1980.

107 As Sumner put it to a profiler: Marian Christy, "The Redstone Scenario," *Boston Globe*, May 22, 1985.

108 Sumner of course had no: "National Amusements Raises Its Viacom Stake," *Los Angeles Times*, June 2, 1986.

109 On March 8, 1984: O'Connor v. Redstone, Complaint.

109 Michael got $7.5 million: Robert Lenzner and Devon Pendleton, "Family Feud," *Forbes*, October 27, 2007.

109 As a hint: O'Connor v. Redstone, Complaint, 15.

110 Years later, Brent would: Redstone v. National Amusements, Complaint.

110 "I think she's a simple": Voss, "The $80 Billion Love Affair."

110 The newly merged company: Landro, "National Amusements Inc.'s Redstone Is Known for His Tenacity and Timing."

111 Sumner, keenly aware: "National Amusements Discloses 5.1 Percent Stake in Unit of MGM/UA," *Wall Street Journal*, July 11, 1984.

111 The company raised: Redstone, *A Passion to Win*, 105–6.

CHAPTER 9: Defeating the Viacomese

---

112 the most profitable and fastest-growing: Laura Landro, "Viacom Is Increasingly Seen as Takeover Play Despite Firm's Lack of Acknowledged Suitors," *Wall Street Journal*, October 11, 1985.

112 Meanwhile, the broader company: William Knoedelseder Jr., "MTV Considers $469 Million Bid," *Los Angeles Times*, August 9, 1985.

113 They had formed Warner-Amex: "Cable TV Joint Venture Will Launch Company to Distribute Programs," *Wall Street Journal*, November 9, 1979.

113 But by the mid-'80s: Craig Marks and Rob Tannenbaum, *I Want My MTV: The Uncensored Story of the Music Video Revolution* (New York: Dutton, 2011), 227–331.

113 For weeks, it seemed: Laura Landro and David B. Hilder, "Warner Communications Is Expected to Sell Cable-TV Interests to Viacom," *Wall Street Journal*, August 26, 1985.

113 Instead, MTV Networks: Michael A. Hiltzik, "Viacom to Buy MTV and Showtime in Deal Worth $667.5 Million," *Los Angeles Times*, August 27, 1985.

113 a bunch of financial guys: Interview with Tom Freston.

113 the "Viacomese": Interview with Geraldine Laybourne.

113 Viacom International Inc.: Laura Landro, "Viacom Is on the Prowl for Purchases," *Wall Street Journal*, August 16, 1985.

113 Starting with a base: Dan Dorfman, "Oilman Davis Rumored to Be after Viacom," *Minneapolis Star Tribune*, April 17, 1986; Redstone, *A Passion to Win*, 108.

114 It was led by: Paul Richter, "Viacom Quietly Becomes Major Force in TV," *Los Angeles Times*, September 22, 1985.

114 As he told: Landro, "Viacom Is on the Prowl for Purchases."

114 But his aggressive bidding: Richter, "Viacom Quietly Becomes Major Force in TV."

114 In 2016, the average cable bill: Leichtman Research Group, http://www.leichtmanresearch.com/press/090315release.html.

115 The tone was set: Marks and Tannenbaum, *I Want My MTV*, 16.

115 The idea was deceptively: Ibid., 41.

117 more founding executives: Ibid., 233–36.

117 Little did they know: Jane Fitz Simon, "Sumner Redstone," *Boston Globe*, October 5, 1986.

117 But an interview: Christy, "The Redstone Scenario."

117 So when Sumner, Mickey: "Viacom Stake Raised to 8.73 Percent by a Group Led by Theater Firm," *Wall Street Journal*, September 15, 1986.

117 Sumner's growing stake: Geraldine Fabrikant, "Viacom Chief Leads Group's Buyout Bid," *New York Times*, September 17, 1986.

117 Sumner woke up on the morning: Ibid.; Redstone, *A Passion to Win*, 109.

118 and hit the roof: Redstone, *A Passion to Win*, 109.

118 The bid was only about: Ibid.

118 He had skipped: Thomas S. Mulligan, "Viacom CEO May Lack Cool, but He Has Clout," *Los Angeles Times*, October 7, 2007.

119 Within twenty-four hours: Redstone, *A Passion to Win*, 110.

119 He immediately bought more stock: Geraldine Fabrikant, "At Least Two Investors Report Stakes in Viacom," *New York Times*, September 18, 1986; Redstone, *A Passion to Win*, 110.

119 "It's a whole new world": Geraldine Fabrikant and Dee Wedemeyer, "Viacom Investor Puzzles Wall Street," *New York Times*, October 13, 1986.

120 On February 2, 1987: Laura Landro, "Viacom Gets Counteroffer to Buyout Bid," *Wall Street Journal*, February 3, 1987.

120 Viacom's management's: Wendy Fox, "Sumner Redstone Goes for Viacom," *Boston Globe*, February 3, 1987.

120 Nevertheless, Viacom's board: "Viacom Rejects Bid by Redstone Unit," *New York Times*, February 11, 1987.

120 Sumner wanted to go higher: Redstone, *A Passion to Win*, 125.

120 By now, Bob Pittman was well-ensconced: "Pittman's Plans for MCA-Backed Outfit Include Acquisitions," *Variety*, January 21, 1987.

121 The elegant Upper East Side: Alexandra Wolfe, "The Never-Ending Glamour of the Carlyle Hotel," *Wall Street Journal*, September 12, 2013.

122 He raised his bid: Peter Barnes, "Two Rival Suitors for Viacom Sweeten Bids Again," *Wall Street Journal*, March 3, 1987.

122 "The management must have": Redstone, *A Passion to Win*, 134–36.

122 On March 4, 1987: Peter Barnes, "National Amusements Wins Bidding War for Viacom with Its Offer of $3.4 billion," *Wall Street Journal*, March 4, 1987.

123 "This could add another 10": Laura Landro, "Theater Magnate Redstone May Find Running Viacom Is Toughest Act Yet," *Wall Street Journal*, March 6, 1987.

123 But Sumner said all: Geraldine Fabrikant, "His Toughest Challenge Yet," *New York Times*, March 15, 1987.

123 The same month that Sumner seized: "Mystery Multiplex Plan Fueled Redstone UK Launch Rumours," *Screen International*, March 28, 1987.

123 The *Journal* noted: Landro, "Theater Magnate Redstone May Find Running Viacom Is Toughest Act Yet."

124 The *Boston Globe* heralded: "Michael Redstone, Owned Theaters, Latin Quarter Nightclub; At 85," *Boston Globe*, April 6, 1987; Michael Redstone obituary, *New York Times*, April 6, 1987.

124 The consulate informed: Ruth Ann Redstone obituary, *New York Times*, April 30, 1987.

125 "The discovery sent shock waves": Ed Priebe, "Prostitution and Political Seduction," exfamily.org, March 2002, http://www.exfamily.org/art/exmem/ff ing_ed.shtml.

125 Although Ruth Ann was in: Redstone v. Schuster, Deposition of Edward Redstone, 48–49; Lenzner and Pendleton, "Family Feud."

125 "When she was in her late 70s": Newman, "Fort Sumner."

125 "One of the great regrets of my life": Redstone, *A Passion to Win*, 142.

125 On December 1: Redstone v. Schuster, Deposition of Edward Redstone; "Leila W. Redstone," *Lowell (MA) Sun*, December 3, 1987.

125 On June 17, 1986: Voss, "The $80 Billion Love Affair."

126 They picked out a: Declaration of Trust of the Twin Pond Trust, August 24, 1988; Mortgage for 4 Twin Pond Lane, August 30, 1988.

126 "I despair": Delsa Winer diary from 1988–89, courtesy of Winn Wittman.

CHAPTER 10: Scaling Paramount

129 "I have a great feeling for the company": Landro, "Theater Magnate Redstone May Find Running Viacom Is Toughest Act Yet."

129 "I didn't really know the full difference": "Redstone Tells Showeast Exhibs He Still Holds Pix/Theaters Dear," *Variety*, September 23, 1987.

129 During a three-day retreat: Interview with Ken Gorman.

129 A child of the New Jersey: Kathryn Harris, "Entertainment Mega-Merger: Biondi: 'Glue' for Media Colossus?" *Los Angeles Times*, February 16, 1994.

130 Sumner had Dauman: Redstone, *A Passion to Win*, 147; Ken Auletta, "Redstone's Secret Weapon," *New Yorker*, January 16, 1995.

130 Sumner called Biondi's wife, Carol: Redstone, *A Passion to Win*, 147.

131 On top of that, reruns: Auletta, "Redstone's Secret Weapon."

132 A little over a year after: Robert Lenzner, "Redstone's Entertainment Empire: It All Adds Up to a Family Worth between $1.5 and $2 Billion, Possibly the Wealthiest in Boston," *Boston Globe*, August 7, 1988.

132 The company was still operating at a loss: Lisa Gubernick, "Sumner Redstone Scores Again," *Forbes*, October 31, 1988.

132 For the first time, Sumner joined fellow newbies Donald Trump: "The Rich Get a Little Richer," Associated Press, October 11, 1988.

132 The *Boston Globe* figured the Redstones: Lenzner, "Redstone's Entertainment Empire."

132 By 1989, *Forbes* pegged him: Jack Thomas, "He Lives by His Own Rules," *Boston Globe*, November 6, 1989.

133 Over deafening screams: "MTV Inaugural Ball Bill Clinton," YouTube, https://www.youtube.com/watch?v=ort9oy-wbAo&t=206s.

133 Even amid the glow: "Redstone Tells Showeast Exhibs He Still Holds Pix/Theaters Dear."

134 "The only thing we lack is a studio": "Redstone Cautious about Buying Studio," *Boston Globe*, October 7, 1989.

134 Hollywood was built by exhibitors: Neal Gabler, *An Empire of Their Own* (New York: Doubleday, 1988).

134 But just as he was making his move: Andrew L. Yarrow, "The Studios' Move on Theaters," *New York Times*, December 25, 1987.

134 In 1989, Time Inc., the publisher: Robert Lenzner, "Super Merger Proposed," *Boston Globe*, March 12, 1989.

134 "There will emerge on a worldwide basis": John Cassidy, "Whatever Happened to Time Inc.?" *New Yorker*, March 7, 2013.

135 Very soon afterward: Kathryn Harris, "Viacom Seeks a Role in the Land of Media Giants," *Los Angeles Times*, November 19, 1989.

135 From the moment he seized Viacom: Redstone, *A Passion to Win*, 175.

135 Paramount was not just the last: Ken Auletta, "The Last Studio in Play," *New Yorker*, October 4, 1993.

135 Paramount had been the first truly dominant: Douglas Gomery, *The Hollywood Studio System: A History* (London: British Film Institute, 2005), 1–25.

136 Davis then set about unmaking: Michael Cieply, "Martin Davis on the Prowl," *Los Angeles Times*, November 12, 1989.

136 "He was acting like": Bryan Burrough, "The Siege of Paramount," *Vanity Fair*, February 1994.

137 Davis knew: Ibid.

137 The studio had suffered: Auletta, "The Last Studio in Play."

137 This time it wasn't Herb Allen: Randall Smith, "How Greenhill Bagged First Megadeal in New Role at Smith Barney Shearson," *Wall Street Journal*, September 13, 1993.

137 In April 1993, Sumner and Dauman: Redstone, *A Passion to Win*, 180.

138 Paramount was slightly larger: Laura Landro and Johnnie L. Roberts, "Paramount, Viacom Discuss a Stock Swap," *Wall Street Journal*, September 10, 1993.

138 From that evening onward: Redstone, *A Passion to Win*, 183.

138 "You know, Sumner": Ibid., 190.

138 At seven forty-five a.m. on Sunday: Geraldine Fabrikant, "Sumner Redstone Lands the Big One," *New York Times*, September 13, 1993.

139 The next day, wearing: Jonathan Weber, "Viacom, Paramount See Smooth Merger," *Los Angeles Times*, September 14, 1993.

139 Although many of the questions: Geraldine Fabrikant, "Martin Davis Finds His Deal," *New York Times*, September 13, 1993.

139 Sumner declared: Beth Belton, "Paramount, Viacom Celebrate Marriage," *USA Today*, September 14, 1993.

CHAPTER 11: Killer Diller

---

141 The day after his bombastic: Randall Smith and Johnnie L. Roberts, "Viacom's Proposal to Buy Paramount Got a Helping Hand," *Wall Street Journal*, September 14, 1993.
141 Viacom argued that: Redstone, *A Passion to Win*, 195.
141 Diller had grown up the son: Aaron Zitner, "The Intangible Assets of Barry Diller," *Boston Globe*, September 26, 1993.
142 When he left Fox: Kim Masters and Paul Farhi, "Fox Chairman Barry Diller Resigns," *Washington Post*, February 25, 1992.
142 Diller invested $25 million: John Lippman, "Shopping Network's Potential Attracted Diller," *Los Angeles Times*, December 11, 1992.
142 Four days after announcing: Johnnie L. Roberts and Randall Smith, "QVC and Diller Consider a Bid for Paramount," *Wall Street Journal*, September 16, 1993.
142 Sumner had been worried: Redstone, *A Passion to Win*, 193.
143 As for Diller: Geraldine Fabrikant, "Shuffling Hollywood's Deal Deck," *New York Times*, November 6, 1993.
143 When the formal bid came: Redstone, *A Passion to Win*, 194.
143 The bid was overwhelming: Kathryn Harris and John Lippman, "Diller Seeks to Outbid Viacom for Paramount," *Los Angeles Times*, September 21, 1993.
143 As Mario Gabelli: Laura Landro and Johnnie L. Roberts, "QVC's $9.5 Billion Bid for Paramount Brings Industry Titans to Fray," *Wall Street Journal*, September 21, 1993.
144 When the *Journal*: Laura Landro and Johnnie L. Roberts, "Viacom Vows to Buy Paramount but Asserts It Won't Raise Bid," *Wall Street Journal*, September 23, 1993.
144 Three days after QVC: Johnnie L. Roberts and Laura Landro, "Viacom Files Suit to Halt QVC's Bid for Paramount," *Wall Street Journal*, September 24, 1993.
144 Altogether, his market power: "John Malone's TV-Dinner," *Economist*, July 10, 1993.
145 In the meantime, Sumner: Kathryn Harris, "Defending the Deal," *Los Angeles Times*, September 27, 1993.
145 They wooed: Rayne Boyce, "Blockbuster Entertainment Enters into Strategic Relationship with Viacom," *Business Wire*, September 29, 1993; Geraldine Fabrikant, "Nynex Aid for Viacom in Its Bid, $1.2 Billion Added to Paramount Fight," *New York Times*, October 5, 1993.
145 Just as whispers: Ken Auletta, "John Malone: Flying Solo," *New Yorker*, February 7, 1994.
145 Sumner, who had testified: Michael L. Rozansky, "Malone Assailed by Viacom Chief at Senate Hearing," *Philadelphia Inquirer*, October 28, 1993.
145 Meanwhile, Diller's side: Randall Smith and Johnnie L. Roberts, "Court Blocks Acquisition of Paramount by Viacom," *Wall Street Journal*, November 26, 1993.

145 Paramount's board: Burrough, "The Siege of Paramount."

145 The haggling between: John Lippman, "QVC Raises Per-Share Bid to $90 Merger," *Los Angeles Times*, November 13, 1993.

145 Analysts started to complain: Laura Landro, "Redstone, Diller Show That Egos Are Paramount," *Wall Street Journal*, December 20, 1993.

146 Wall Street hated the: Geraldine Fabrikant, "Viacom Announces Merger and Raises Bid for Paramount," *New York Times*, January 8, 1994.

146 Huizenga was the kind: James Cox, "Work Is Play for Huizenga," *USA Today*, January 10, 1994.

146 Although he saw the writing on the technological wall: Anita Sharpe, "Graceful Exit; Blockbuster Merger Viewed as Bailout for Chairman," *Wall Street Journal*, January 11, 1994.

146 As the February 1: Kathryn Harris, "Viacom Raises Paramount Bid by $80 Million in Cash, Stock Mergers," *Los Angeles Times*, January 19, 1994.

147 Diller raised his bid: Skip Wollenberg, "Viacom, QVC Alter Bids at Deadline," *Austin American-Statesman*, February 2, 1994.

147 A few months earlier: Johnnie L. Roberts, "Redstone's Wife Filed for Divorce but Dropped Suit," *Wall Street Journal*, December 22, 1993.

147 As the final shares: James Bates, "Paramount Deal: A Show Closes, a Look at the Script," *Los Angeles Times*, February 16, 1994.

CHAPTER 12: Immortality

149 single slab of dried corned beef: Elizabeth Lesley, Gail Degeorge, and Ronald Grover, "Sumner's Last Stand," *Businessweek*, March 2, 1997.

149 "I'm one of those people": Steve Fainaru, "Multimedia Man: Born before TV, 71-year-old Sumner Redstone Leads a Communications Empire into a New Era," *Boston Globe*, January 22, 1995.

149 Days after the deal was done: Stephen Galloway, *Leading Lady: Sherry Lansing and the Making of a Hollywood Groundbreaker* (New York: Crown Archetype, 2017), 205.

150 The Paramount fight: Lesley, Degeorge, and Grover, "Sumner's Last Stand."

150 In order to service this debt: Ibid.

151 When the *New Yorker*: Auletta, "Redstone's Secret Weapon."

151 "I would have thought": David Lieberman, "Redstone Kids Not in Line for Viacom," *USA Today*, January 10, 1995.

152 Brent was the first Redstone: "Viacom Inc.," *Wall Street Journal*, November 25, 1991.

152 Early in his career, he won: "18-Year Term in Child Rape," *Boston Globe*, March 28, 1982.

152 Toward the end, he prosecuted: John H. Kennedy, "Cocaine Psychosis Cited in Boy's Beating Death," *Boston Globe*, July 12, 1989.

152 The man was charged: Doris Sue Wong, "Killer of Boy Given 18–20 Year Term," *Boston Globe*, July 18, 1989.

152 Brent inherited his father's height: Background interviews.

153 Sumner had come: Lloyd Grove, "Sumner's Discontent: The Tale of a Latter-Day King Lear," *Portfolio*, February 2009.

154 In May 1994: "Former Redstone Son-in-Law Quits Theater Chain," *Los Angeles Times*, May 20, 1994.

154 Once a clean-shaven business: Mark Jurkowitz, "Transformed by Tradition," *Boston Globe*, April 1, 1999.

155 Shari, who had once: "New Bus Service from Dover Area to Local Day Schools," *Jewish Advocate*, May 24, 1990.

157 As she recounted to *Forbes*: Matzer and Lenzner, "Winning Is the Only Thing."

CHAPTER 13: "Remember, I'm in Control!"

159 Viacom was the toast: John Batelle, "Viacom Doesn't Suck," *Wired*, April 1, 1995.

159 The stock was down 27 percent: Laura Landro and Mark Robichaux, "Biondi Is Forced Out at Viacom," *Wall Street Journal*, January 18, 1996.

159 Viacom executives told the *New York Times*: Mark Landler and Geraldine Fabrikant, "His Place Among the Moguls," *New York Times*, January 19, 1996.

160 Several other Viacom: Mark Landler, "Viacom Chief Ousted, Paramount's Performance a Factor," *New York Times*, January 18, 1996.

160 In his autobiography: Redstone, *A Passion to Win*, 268.

160 In the wake of Biondi's: Ken Auletta, "That's Entertainment," *New Yorker*, February 12, 1996.

160 Many Viacom executives: Tom Freston and background interviews.

160 According to a subsequent: Auletta, "That's Entertainment."

160 As one person who was part of the discussions: Background interview.

161 Sumner responded to queries: Mark Landler and Geraldine Fabrikant, "The Media Business: His Place Among the Moguls," *New York Times*, January 19, 1996.

161 He got off to a strong start: Geraldine Fabrikant, "TV Agreement Gives Viacom Greater Access to Germany," *New York Times*, April 9, 1996.

161 Viacom had to take a staggering: Eben Shapiro, "Viacom Plans Big $100 Million Charge for Closing 50 Blockbuster Music Stores," *Wall Street Journal*, January 8, 1997.

161 "I was shocked": Geraldine Fabrikant, "A Question of Skills: Viacom's Deal Maker Falters in Running What He Buys," *New York Times*, April 23, 1997.

162 Most troublingly: Eben Shapiro, "How Viacom's Deal for Blockbuster Chain Went Sour So Fast," *Wall Street Journal*, February 21, 1997.

162 But the worst blow for: Lesley, Degeorge, and Grover, "Sumner's Last Stand."

162 "I could hardly sleep at night": Redstone, *A Passion to Win*, 39.

162 He ousted Bill Fields: Ibid., 40.

162 They nixed Fields's: Eben Shapiro, "Blockbuster Rescue Bid Stars Viacom Top Guns," *Wall Street Journal*, May 7, 1997.

162 "We are out of the retail business": Eben Shapiro, "Viacom Posts Loss of $195 Million as It Attempts to Fix Blockbuster," *Wall Street Journal*, August 6, 1997.

163 Within a year, the stock was back up: Claudia Eller and Mark Saylor, "At 74, Mogul Redstone Still Finds Running Viacom Entertaining," *Los Angeles Times*, April 29, 1998.

164 The son of Eastern European: Mark Gunther, "King of All Radio," *Fortune*, April 14, 1997.

164 Along the way, Karmazin: Michael Hiltzik, "Company Town: Creating a Media Giant; the Leaders; Shared Vision, Contrasting Styles," *Los Angeles Times*, September 8, 1999.

164 By 1997, Westinghouse: Ken Auletta, "The Invisible Manager," *New Yorker*, July 27, 1998.

164 He went from running: Claudia Eller, "Infinity Chief Seen as Shrewd Manager," *Los Angeles Times*, June 21, 1996; Kyle Pope and Timothy Aeppel, "CBS Shake-Up Now Has to Play a Tough Crowd," *Wall Street Journal*, May 27, 1997.

165 When CBS announced: Geraldine Fabrikant, "At CBS News of a New Chairman and a Strong Earnings Report Quickly Lifts Share Prices," *New York Times*, October 30, 1998.

166 "We felt it was important": Kyle Pope and Martin Peers, "Merging Moguls: Redstone, Karmazin Both Like to Be Boss; Now, They Must Share," *Wall Street Journal*, September 8, 1999.

166 But as he was launching: Hiltzik, "Company Town: Creating a Media Giant."

167 And then, a few years: Kim Masters, "Sumner Redstone Gal Pal Says She Got Nothing," *Hollywood Reporter*, July 28, 2010.

167 When Evans suffered: Michael Cieply, "A Hollywood Player Inspires a Broadway Play," *New York Times*, February 10, 2010.

168 When Sumner vacationed: Mitchell Fink, "Chief's Sizzling Sumner Vacation," *New York Daily News*, September 8, 1998.

168 She hired a private detective: Jeane MacIntosh, "Viacom Mogul Could Be Sumner $quashed—Wife Calls Him Cheater, Wants Half His Fortune," *New York Post*, September 19, 1999.

168 Just outside the frame: Masters, "Sumner Redstone Gal Pal Says She Got Nothing."

168 Phyllis had the evidence: Redstone, *A Passion to Win*, 310.

168 Instantly, analysts began to fret: "Viacom Inc. Makes Announcement," *Business Wire*, September 19, 1999.

169 The statement was a bluff: Redstone v. National Amusements, Complaint, 7; Pope and Aeppel, "CBS Shake-Up Now Has to Play a Tough Crowd."

CHAPTER 14: The Hotshot

171 Shari, who contributed: "CineBridge to Launch Hip, New Movie Venture in Los Angeles," *Business Wire*, February 14, 2001.

171 The posh theater wasn't quite: Ibid.

172 The previous year: Claudio H. Deutsch, "Now Playing: Invasion of the Multiplex," *New York Times*, June 25, 1995.

172 They didn't just build more: Kevin Lally and Ed Kelleher, "Megaplex Mania," *Film Journal International*, August 1, 1996.

173 True to her word: "The Latest Coming Attraction: Movie House in East New York," *New York Times*, April 12, 1997.

173 Shari continued to build: Ed Kelleher, "National Amusements Is Home to Shari Redstone," *Film Journal International*, December 1, 1995.

173 "I got involved": "Shari E. Redstone: Taking National into the 21st Century," *Film Journal International*, November 1, 1996.

173 began the company's first push into South America: "Chile Showcase," *Film Journal International*, September 1, 1998.

173 By 1997, she had 360 screens: "Media Moguls Putting on Heirs," *Variety*, April 14–20, 1997.

173 From the time she joined: Dyan Machan, "Redstone Rising," *Forbes*, May 13, 2002.

174 By 1998, Shari was: "Location, Location, Location," *Film Journal International*, April 1, 1998.

174 All of the big guys: "Movie Theaters of the Absurd," *Forbes*, March 2, 2001.

175 From the moment the Viacom-CBS deal was announced: Pope and Peers, "Merging Moguls: Redstone, Karmazin Both Like to Be Boss; Now, They Must Share."

175 Karmazin's idea: Ibid.

175 A little over a year into: Geraldine Fabrikant and Seth Schiesel, "At Viacom, Rumors Persist of Tension at the Top," *New York Times*, January 21, 2002.

176 From the moment she got: Shlomo Schwartzberg, "National Amusements: The Next Generation," *BoxOffice*, April 1, 1995.

176 She even posed: "Showmandizer Promotion of the Month," *BoxOffice*, June 1, 1996.

176 Yet she was also: Machan, "Redstone Rising."

176 A month after the piece: Claudia Eller, "To Russia with Theaters (and Digital Sound)," *Los Angeles Times*, June 25, 2002.

177 One month later, Sumner: "Redstone Divorce Granted," PR Newswire, July 26, 2002.

177 Ever since: Brent D. Redstone v. National Amusements, Inc., Complaint.

177 As part of the settlement: Sumner M. Redstone National Amusements Trust Declaration of Trust, June 28, 2002.

177 During Sumner's lifetime: Term Sheet for proposed buyout of Shari Redstone's stake in National Amusements, 2014.

178 It got so bad that Viacom's: Sallie Hofmeister, "Viacom's Board Tells Top Executives to Work It Out," *Los Angeles Times*, January 31, 2002.

179 Like many people who: Bryan Burrough, "Sleeping with the Fishes," *Vanity Fair*, December 2006.

179 bringing her to his company-owned: "Another Woman for Sumner?" *New York Post*, July 27, 2000.

180 After a nearly two-year: Geraldine Fabrikant, "More Than a Sumner Romance, But Not a 50–50 Marriage," *New York Times*, August 25, 2002.

180 Of course there was a prenup: Ibid.

180 Sumner moved into: Burrough, "Sleeping with the Fishes."

181 In February 2004: Lloyd Vries, "Blockbuster Split," Associated Press, February 10, 2004.

181 But by 2004: "Midway Games: Viacom's Redstone Adds to His Stake," Bloomberg News/*Chicago Tribune*, March 4, 2004.

182 Sumner, however, knew: John Crudele, "Redstone's Portfolio Picks: Holds

Major Stakes in WMS Industries & Midway Games," *New York Post*, July 19, 2000; Laura Rich, "A Succession Plan. Well, Almost," *New York Times*, June 20, 2004.

182 So in March 2004: "Midway Plans Board Revamp; Redstone Acquires Majority Stake," *Chicago Tribune*, May 12, 2004.

182 Even Shari, whom he soon elevated: Jim Kirk, "Redstones' Midway Strategy Thus Far Known Only to Them," *Chicago Tribune*, June 27, 2004.

182 "It was always my": Geraldine Fabrikant, "A Younger Redstone Takes a Role at Viacom," *New York Times*, May 10, 2004.

183 Viacom missed its earnings: Joe Flint, "Final Cut: Karmazin Leaves Viacom Post, Ending a Story Marriage," *Wall Street Journal*, June 2, 2004.

183 By June 2004, the price had: David Lieberman and Michael McCarthy, "Ex-CBS Chief Chooses to Be No. 2 No More," *USA Today*, June 2, 2004.

183 He would later explain: Ibid.

184 As long as Sumner: Flint, "Final Cut."

184 As chairman and CEO: Martin Peers, Joe Flint, and John Lippman, "Stability of Power Trio Is Critical to Viacom's Future," *Wall Street Journal*, February 4, 2002.

184 Through it all, he maintained: Bill Carter, "And Now, Enter the Two Who Would Be One," *New York Times*, June 2, 2004.

185 A former actor: Christopher S. Stewart, "King of TV for Now, CBS Girds for Digital Battle," *Wall Street Journal*, November 30, 2012.

186 Sumner said he would break: Galloway, *Leading Lady*, 321.

CHAPTER 15: "Sumner in a Skirt"

187 Adam Redstone's life was just beginning to turn around: Redstone v. Schuster, Deposition of Edward Redstone.

187 Eddie and Madeline were: Redstone v. Schuster, Deposition of Madeline Redstone.

188 When they began to suspect: Redstone v. Schuster, Depositions of Edward and Madeline Redstone.

188 "We were inseparable": Schuster v. Redstone, Deposition of Edward Redstone.

188 When Ruth Ann died: Redstone v. Schuster, Complaint.

188 On Thursday, May 27: Redstone v. Schuster, Deposition of Madeline Redstone; interview with Madeline Redstone.

189 By Sunday, the day of the funeral: "Redstone, Gabriel Adam," *New York Times*, May 30, 2004.

189 A month later, they filed: O'Connor v. Redstone, Amended Complaint.

190 Two days later: Flint, "Final Cut."

190 The performance worked: Lieberman and McCarthy, "Ex-CBS Chief Chooses to Be No. 2 No More."

190 The problem was that: Geraldine Fabrikant, "Viacom Considers a Plan to Split into 2 Companies," *New York Times*, March 17, 2005.

190 He was joined by an army: Ibid.

190 One analyst dubbed: John Higgins, "ViaSlow vs. ViaGrow," *Broadcasting & Cable*, May 9, 2005.

190 That meant that Simon & Schuster: Ibid.

191 The same day the Viacom board voted: Sallie Hofmeister, "Viacom OK's Plan to Split, but 1 Man Will Still Run the Show," *Los Angeles Times*, June 15, 2005.

191 Rumors swirled: Ibid.

191 But by 2005: Carol Hymowitz and Joe Flint, "Shari Redstone Waits in Wings to Head Viacom," *Wall Street Journal*, March 21, 2005.

192 "Sooner or later": Hofmeister, "Viacom OK's Plan to Split, but 1 Man Will Still Run the Show."

192 It was at this moment: Hymowitz and Flint, "Shari Redstone Waits in Wings to Head Viacom."

192 In early 1999, a year before: Jim Cooper, "The Ghost in the Machine," *Media-Week*, April 17, 2000.

192 With an eye toward: Joseph Gallivan, "MTVi Faces the Music," *New York Post*, September 28, 2000.

193 At the same moment: Julia Angwin, *Stealing MySpace: The Battle to Control the Most Popular Website in America* (New York: Random House, 2009), 119.

193 When Freston and Moonves held: Ibid.

193 Freston, who had declared: Interview with Jason Hirschhorn.

193 In early December: Angwin, *Stealing MySpace*, 119.

193 Like pre-Redstone: Ibid., 99.

195 Over a frantic two weeks in early July: Ibid., 163–67.

196 This time, Freston went to Sumner: Ibid., 170.

196 By Thanksgiving of 2005: David Kirkpatrick, *The Facebook Effect: The Inside Story of the Company That Is Connecting the World* (New York: Simon & Schuster, 2010), 159–60.

198 Around midnight on December 8: Merissa Marr, Kate Kelly, and Kathryn Kranhold, "Hollywood Rewrite: Viacom Outbids GE to Buy DreamWorks," *Wall Street Journal*, December 12, 2005.

199 He had borrowed $425 million: Michael Hiltzik and Claudia Eller, "'Kombat' Split Redstones," *Chicago Tribune*, August 5, 2007.

199 In a document filed: National Amusements, Inc. Security and Exchange Commission 13D filing, December 28, 2005.

199 Sumner abruptly stopped buying: Mike Hughlett, "Midway Shares on Steady Downfall," *Chicago Tribune*, February 11, 2006.

199 Out of the blue, Brent, armed: Brent D. Redstone v. National Amusements, Inc., Circuit Court of Maryland for Baltimore City, February 6, 2006, Complaint.

200 Brent did not succeed: Robert Lenzner, "Redstone Blasts Daughter," *Forbes*, July 20, 2007.

CHAPTER 16: "This Is Crazy!"

201 "It's nothing to do with his": Merissa Marr, "Sumner Redstone Gives Tom Cruise His Walking Papers," *Wall Street Journal*, August 23, 2006.

202 His first quarterly earnings: Matthew Karnitschnig and Brooks Barnes, "Viacom Split Offers No Panacea," *Wall Street Journal*, July 24, 2006.

202 By July, just six: Richard Greenfield, "How Viacom Lost Its Mojo," Pali Research, July 10, 2006.

203 As Hollywood's best-sourced: Nikki Finke, "Who's Crazier: Viacom or Tom Cruise?" *Deadline Hollywood*, August 22, 2006.

203 Sumner would later claim: Burrough, "Sleeping with the Fishes."

203 An hour after: Matthew Karnitschnig, "Ouster of Viacom Chief Reflects Redstone's Impatience for Results," *Wall Street Journal*, September 6, 2006.

203 Freston was busy: Burrough, "Sleeping with the Fishes."

204 When he got there: Sumner Redstone interview with Charlie Rose. *Charlie Rose*, PBS, October 2006.

204 Just six weeks earlier: Karnitschnig and Barnes, "Viacom Split Offers No Panacea."

204 "I have worked": "Viacom Names Philippe Dauman President and CEO," *Business Wire*, September 5, 2006.

204 this final indignity: "Viacom's Ex-Chief Getting $85 Million," Bloomberg News, October 19, 2006.

204 Sumner desperately missed: Cooper, "The Ghost in the Machine."

204 to reclaim them: Sumner Redstone interview with Charlie Rose.

204 But the rise: Jonathan Levy and Anne Levin, "The Evolving Structure and Changing Boundaries of the U.S. Television Market in the Digital Era," Federal Communications Commission, https://transition.fcc.gov/ownership/materials /newly-released/evolving060106.pdf.

205 But Sumner's digital beef: Sumner Redstone interview with Charlie Rose.

205 In the wake of his firing: Patricia Sellers, "The Most Wanted Man on the Planet," *Fortune*, February 6, 2009.

205 At a previously scheduled: "Freston Flock Rips Redstone," *New York Post*, October 26, 2006.

205 Viacom's stock dropped: Geraldine Fabrikant and Bill Carter, "Another Split at Viacom," *New York Times*, September 6, 2006.

206 Merrill Lynch analyst: Karnitschnig and Barnes, "Viacom Split Offers No Panacea."

206 Bruce Greenwald, a finance professor: Fabrikant and Carter, "Another Split at Viacom."

206 As he emerged: "Viacom Mob Gives Tom Freston a Touching Send-Off," *Gawker*, September 7, 2006.

206 Grey, as Freston's hire: Merissa Marr, "Will Brad Grey Fade to Black at Paramount?" *Wall Street Journal*, September 6, 2006.

207 Dauman and Dooley pledged: Johnnie I. Roberts, "Viacom Shuffle: Redstone's Search for Youth," *Newsweek*, September 18, 2006.

207 By the summer: "YouTube Serves Up 100 Million Videos a Day Online," Reuters, July 16, 2006.

207 Despite the audience overlap: Andrew Ross Sorkin and Jeremy W. Peters, "Google to Acquire YouTube for $1.65 Billion," *New York Times*, October 9, 2006.

208 In the meantime, Viacom licensed: Kevin J. Delaney and Matthew Karnitschnig, "Media Titans Pressure YouTube over Copyrights," *Wall Street Journal*, October 14, 2006.

208 Caught up in his marriage: Lloyd Grove, "Sumner's Discontent," *Portfolio*, January 7, 2009.

209 This time it was his nephew, Michael: O'Connor v. Redstone, Complaint.

209 He wanted $4 billion: Julia Angwin, "Sumner Redstone's Nephew Sues over Management of Family Trusts," *Wall Street Journal*, November 21, 2006.

209 Painting Michael as crazy: Michael Redstone's death certificate, Office of the Boulder County Coroner.

209 He earned his GED: Redstone v. Schuster, Deposition of Michael Redstone.

210 "My duties range": Ibid.

210 He and Shelley had wanted: Ibid.

210 In the same lawsuit, Eddie: Redstone v. Schuster, Deposition of Edward Redstone.

210 During Eddie and Madeline's: Redstone v. Schuster, Deposition of Michael Redstone.

210 According to Michael's complaint: O'Connor v. Redstone, Complaint.

210 As a result, he argued: Michael A. Hiltzik and Claudia Eller, "A Dynasty in Dysfunction," *Los Angeles Times*, July 23, 2007.

211 Seizing on these words: Peter J. Reilly, "Sumner Redstone Liable for Tax on Long Ago Gift," *Forbes*, December 12, 2015.

CHAPTER 17: "Good Governance"

212 After Sumner, Freston, and Moonves: Matthew Karnitschnig, "Viacom Lawsuit on Executive Pay Can Go Forward," *Wall Street Journal*, June 30, 2006.

213 Shortly after Freston's: "Viacom Cuts Chairman's Pay in Half to $10.5m," *Calgary Herald*, September 26, 2006.

213 When CBS followed suit: Mike Barris, "CBS Links Redstone Pay to Shareholder Returns," *Wall Street Journal*, March 14, 2007.

213 In an interview with recently: "Conversations with Michael Eisner," interview with Sumner Redstone, CNBC, October 19, 2006.

214 In February, National Amusements bought another: Hiltzik and Eller, "'Kombat' Split Redstones."

214 "Unfortunately I have come": Letter from Sumner Redstone to the Trustees of the Sumner M. Redstone National Amusements Trust, February 8, 2007, included in Sydney Holland's cross-complaint in Los Angeles Superior Court, Sydney Holland v. Shari Redstone, Jeremy Jagiello, Joseph Octaviano, and Giovanni Paz, December 15, 2016.

215 Meanwhile, the tensions: Steve Baily, "Redstone, Continued," *Boston Globe*, April 27, 2007.

215 On July 20, 2007: Robert Lenzner, "Redstone Blasts Daughter," *Forbes*, July 20, 2007.

215 In a dig: Claudia Eller, "Redstone's Letter Takes Public Slap at Daughter," *Los Angeles Times*, July 21, 2007.

216 Dauman was once again: Tim Arango, "New Crack in the House of Redstone," *Fortune*, July 19, 2007.

216 By the end of the year: Wailin Wong, "Redstones' Family Feud Cools Off," *Chicago Tribune*, December 22, 2007.

216 Unbeknownst to Viacom: Merissa Marr, "Redstone Rejects Viacom, CBS Sale," *Wall Street Journal*, October 23, 2008.

217 Sumner tried to get out in front: Merissa Marr, "Redstone Company in Talks over Debt after Sale of Shares," *Wall Street Journal*, October 20, 2008.

217 Sumner tried to calm them: Marr, "Redstone Rejects Viacom, CBS Sale."

217 Not surprisingly, Sumner came: Tim Arango, "Redstone Weighs Sale of Theaters," *New York Times*, November 25, 2008.

217 At the start of December: Merissa Marr, "Redstone Sells Control of Midway to Ease Debt," *Wall Street Journal*, December 1, 2008.

218 But the sale doomed: Wailin Wong, "Midway Games Faces Default," *Los Angeles Times*, December 6, 2008.

218 Two months after the sale: Lauren Pollock, "Midway Games Files for Chapter 11," *Wall Street Journal*, February 13, 2009.

218 Although Shari was leading the negotiations: Merissa Marr, "Redstones Move Closer to a Deal with Creditors," *Wall Street Journal*, December 19, 2008.

218 The situation grew so tense: Ibid.

218 By February, the Redstones struck a deal: Meg James and Claudia Eller, "Redstone Deal Lifts Threat to Empire," *Los Angeles Times*, February 28, 2009.

218 In October 2009: Claudia Eller, "Sumner Redstone's National Amusements Closes Deal to Sell 29 Theaters to Rave Cinemas," *Los Angeles Times*, December 22, 2009.

219 Amid these crises: Merissa Marr, "Redstones File to Obtain a Divorce," *Wall Street Journal*, October 22, 2008.

219 She felt isolated: Nikki Finke, "Redstone Family Woes: Now His Marriage," *Deadline Hollywood*, August 3, 2007.

CHAPTER 18: Strange World

---

220 One summer evening in 2011: "Crazy Night Out with the Electric Barbarellas," *RumorFix*, July 27, 2011, https://www.youtube.com/watch?v=YZXyS1KCM-Q.

220 A little over a year earlier: Peter Lauria, "Sumner Redstone and His All-Girl Band, the Electric Barbarellas," *Daily Beast*, June 2, 2010.

221 A few weeks after: Peter Lauria, "Sumner Redstone Offers Reward to Get the Electric Barbarellas Leak," *Daily Beast*, July 20, 2010.

221 The voice mail only made matters worse: Richard Johnson, "Sumner Basks in Bribe Uproar," *New York Post*, July 22, 2010.

221 Another of Sumner's: Sumner M. Redstone v. Manuela Herzer, Sydney Holland, and DOES 1–10; Sydney Holland's Answer to Plaintiff Sumner M. Redstone's Complaint, Los Angeles Superior Court, December 12, 2016, p. 20.

222 Since beating prostate cancer: Sumner Redstone interview with Larry King at the Milken Institute Global Conference in 2009.

222 "I have the vital statistics of a 20-year-old man": Ibid.

222 He began work: Merissa Marr, "Redstone Daughter in Succession Mix," *Wall Street Journal*, October 26, 2012.

222 "Viacom is me": Redstone, *A Passion to Win*, 23.

223 It gave Dauman cover: Amy Chozick, "The Man Who Would Be Redstone," *New York Times*, September 21, 2012; Michael Cieply, "Paramount Pictures Finds Long-Sought Balance," *New York Times*, December 13, 2009.

223 While Viacom's stock had: Loch Adamson, "Philippe Dauman Transforms Viacom," *Institutional Investor*, September 2009.

223 MTV had its first: Dave Itzkoff, "Gym, Tan, Later: MTV Ending 'Jersey Shore,'" *New York Times*, August 30, 2012.

223 Along with other grittier: Matthew Flamm, "MTV Gets Groove Back," *Crain's New York Business*, January 24, 2011.

223 Things were even turning around: Cieply, "Paramount Pictures Finds Long-Sought Balance."

223 Meanwhile, Viacom's top brass promised: Sandra Ward, "When Sumner Met Betty," *Barron's*, March 29, 2010.

223 By the end of 2010: Nat Worden, "Viacom CEO's Pay More Than Doubled," *Wall Street Journal*, January 24, 2011; Chozick, "The Man Who Would Be Redstone."

223 In 2009, MTV Networks signed: "Netflix and MTV Networks Announce Deal to Stream 'South Park' and Trove of Nickelodeon Shows on Netflix," PR Newswire, April 6, 2009.

224 In 2010, Viacom strengthened: Sue Zeidler and Jennifer Saba, "Netflix, Epix Strike Programming Deal," Reuters, August 10, 2010.

224 "When satellite came": Sam Schechner, "Boss Talk: Viacom CEO Tries to Keep the Party Going," *Wall Street Journal*, November 1, 2010.

224 Paramount already had: Claudia Eller, "Paramount Extends Deal with Marvel," *Los Angeles Times*, September 30, 2008.

224 Analysts initially believed: Matthew Ingram, "Six Years Later, Disney's Acquisition of Marvel Looks Smarter Than Ever," *Fortune*, October 8, 2015.

224 Sometimes Viacom missed out on hits: Hagey, "The Relationship That Helped Sumner Redstone Build Viacom Now Adds to Its Problems."

225 One of Dauman's first: Ibid.

225 Today, with investment from: Lukas I. Alpert and Shalini Ramachandran, "Vice Media Secures $450 Million Investment from Private-Equity Firm TPG," *Wall Street Journal*, June 19, 2017.

225 Vice has since: Emily Steel, "At Vice, Cutting-Edge Media and Allegations of Old-School Sexual Harassment," *New York Times*, December 23, 2017; Lukas I. Alpert and Amol Sharma, "BuzzFeed Set to Miss Revenue Target, Signaling Turbulence in Media," *Wall Street Journal*, November 16, 2017.

226 He had her direct reports: Claire Atkinson, "Dauman Digs In," *New York Post*, May 6, 2011.

226 The contract negotiations: Chris Smith, *The Daily Show: An Oral History* (New York: Grand Central Publishing, 2016), 318–19.

227 "Girls around here just": Eric Bailey, "Silence Protects Youths Who Shattered a Girl's Life," *Los Angeles Times*, January 17, 1988.

227 After graduating from: William D. Cohan, "Who Controls Sumner Redstone?" *Vanity Fair*, June 2015.

227 By 2004, she appeared under: *Los Angeles* magazine, February 2004, classifieds.

227 She and her partner: Peter Elkind with Marty Jones, "The Disturbing Decline of Sumner Redstone," *Fortune*, May 5, 2016.

228 In court papers, Sydney described: Holland v. Redstone, Complaint.

228 Sumner was, by his own lawyer's description: Redstone v. Herzer, Complaint.

228 By early 2011, he asked: Ibid.
229 She handled: Redstone v. Herzer, Sydney Holland's response.
229 By March 31, 2011: Redstone v. Herzer, Complaint.
229 Around this time, according to: Claire Atkinson, "The Explosive, Plotting Emails of Sumner Redstone's Girlfriend," *New York Post*, May 19, 2015.
230 "My grandfather was a visionary": "De Lux Launch: National Amusements Showcases Its Legacy," *Film Journal International*, September 17, 2009.
230 This same year, Shari began thinking about legacy: Interviews with Shari Redstone and Jason Ostheimer.
230 They were married in the garden: Carol Beggy, "Names," *Boston Globe*, September 4, 2007.
230 Kim, a classic beauty: Keach Hagey, "Redstone Family's Next Generation Takes on Bigger Roles, Influence in National Amusements," *Wall Street Journal*, November 15, 2016.
230 Jason worked in private equity: Interview with Jason Ostheimer and Advancit biography.
230 In June 2011: Nat Worden, "Redstone Sells Russian Movie-Theater Chain," *Wall Street Journal*, June 6, 2011.
231 Two months later: Meg James, "Shari Redstone Launches Her Own Investment Firm," *Los Angeles Times*, August 27, 2011.
231 After a year: Merissa Marr, "Shari Redstone Adds Partner to Firm," *Wall Street Journal*, July 9, 2013; SEC filing.
231 A third fund would aim to raise: SEC filing.
231 In August 2011, Netflix: Sam Schechner, "Viacom Net Falls 65 Percent Due to Charge, Lower Ad Revenue," *Wall Street Journal*, February 2, 2012.
231 Almost immediately, Nickelodeon's ratings: Claire Atkinson, "Nicked by Nielsen 'SpongeBob' Net's Ratings Squeeze," *New York Post*, December 1, 2011.
231 Analysts who had fretted: John Jannarone, "Viacom's SpongeBob Crisis," *Wall Street Journal*, May 2, 2012.
232 Dauman rejected this narrative: Schechner, "Viacom Net Falls 65 Percent Due to Charge, Lower Ad Revenue."
232 But when ratings sank: Jannarone, "Viacom's SpongeBob Crisis."
232 Anticipating this criticism, Dauman: George Szalai, "Viacom CEO: Netflix Content Is Not Hurting Nickelodeon Ratings," *Hollywood Reporter*, February 2, 2012.
232 The company said: Schechner, "Viacom Net Falls 65 Percent Due to Charge, Lower Ad Revenue."
234 Viacom stock kept: Chozick, "The Man Who Would Be Redstone."
235 A month after the *Journal*: Holland v. Redstone.
236 In 2009, he bought her: In Re Advance Health Care Directive of Sumner M. Redstone, Los Angeles Superior Court, Petition for Determinations Re Advance Health Care Directive of Sumner M. Redstone, November 25, 2015.

CHAPTER 19: "Our Family"

237 But, according to Manuela's: Advance Health Care Directive.
238 By the time the red-haired: Redstone v. Herzer.

238 In April 2013: Holland v. Redstone.

238 While Sydney was in San Diego: Sydney Holland v. Heather Naylor, Los Angeles Superior Court, August 30, 2013, Complaint.

238 Naylor sat Sumner: Elkind and Jones, "The Disturbing Decline of Sumner Redstone."

238 Naylor denied having the laptop: Heather Naylor v. Sydney Holland, Los Angeles Superior Court, February 6, 2014, Cross-complaint.

238 She also alleged: Matthew Belloni and Eriq Gardner, "Sumner Redstone Embroiled in Girlfriend's Legal War," *Hollywood Reporter*, July 4–18, 2014.

239 In the wake of this dustup: Redstone v. Herzer.

239 Sumner's lawyers alleged that Sydney and Manuela asked: Redstone v. Herzer, Complaint.

240 Sumner's lawyers alleged that Sydney and Manuela blocked: Ibid.

241 Each got $45 million: Redstone v. Herzer and Herzer v. Redstone.

241 But Andelman had: Redstone v. Herzer, Deposition of David Andelman.

242 On May 26, 2014: Holland v. Redstone.

242 With this maneuvering in the background: Elkind and Jones, "The Disturbing Decline of Sumner Redstone."

242 Keryn wouldn't find out: In Re Advance Health Care Directive, Declaration of Keryn Redstone, April 14, 2016.

242 Shari's spokeswoman: Keach Hagey, "Family Fight Heats Up in Redstone Lawsuit," *Wall Street Journal*, April 20, 2016.

242 Over the summer of 2014: Holland v. Redstone.

243 Shari refused to sign: Redstone v. Herzer.

243 Nevertheless, at its annual: Viacom Inc. 2014 proxy statement.

243 CBS held its annual: Merissa Marr, "Media Mogul Sumner Redstone Cashes In," *Wall Street Journal*, May 23, 2014.

243 CBS did not hike: CBS Corp. 2014 proxy statement.

CHAPTER 20: "Sharp as a Tack"

245 In September 2014: Redstone v. Herzer, Complaint

246 I want my $45 million back: Redstone v. Herzer, Declaration of Giovanni Paz.

246 Paz turned out: Ibid.

246 In the wake of his firing: Holland v. Redstone, Complaint.

246 A few days later: Redstone v. Herzer, Complaint.

247 And perhaps worst: Manuela Herzer v. Shari Redstone, Tyler Korff, Brandon Korff, Isileli 'Isi' Tuanaki, Jeremy Jagiello, Joseph Octaviano, Giovanni Paqz, Igor Franco, Faleolo Toia, DOES 1-50, Los Angeles Superior Court, May 9, 2016, Complaint.

247 "I just called": Holland v. Redstone.

247 The next day: Redstone v. Herzer.

248 As the missives ostensibly from: Holland v. Redstone.

249 Viacom had performed better: Keach Hagey and Chelsea Delaney, "Viacom Aims to Bolster Ad Business," *Wall Street Journal*, November 13, 2014.

250 Two months later, Dauman's: Keach Hagey and Tess Stynes, "Viacom Extends CEO's Contract by Two Years," *Wall Street Journal*, January 15, 2015.

250 A week later, the company: Keach Hagey, "Viacom CEO Gets Increase of 19 Percent in Pay," *Wall Street Journal*, January 26, 2015.

251 These incidents fit into: Redstone v. Herzer, Declarations of Jeremy Jagiello, Joseph Octaviano, and Giovanni Paz.

252 In Manuela's legal filings: Herzer v. Redstone, Complaint.

252 In one email: Holland v. Redstone, Complaint.

252 Adult Protective Services: Redstone v. Herzer, Declaration of Jeremy Jagiello.

253 Given Sumner's extreme: Holland v. Redstone, Complaint.

253 Octaviano got a peek: Redstone v. Herzer.

253 On April 9: Keach Hagey, "Year-Old Email Raises Questions about Sumner Redstone's Condition," *Wall Street Journal*, April 12, 2016.

254 At least two of these people: Keach Hagey, "Doctors Have Key Role in Fate of Sumner Redstone's Company Stakes, Like Viacom," *Wall Street Journal*, February 6, 2016.

254 In the end, calmer heads prevailed: Cohan, "Who Controls Sumner Redstone?"

255 Among the people shocked: William D. Cohan, "Why Sumner Redstone Really Kicked Sydney Holland Out," *Vanity Fair*, September 21, 2015.

257 But in late August: Redstone v. Herzer.

258 On September 3, Sumner called in Bishop: Herzer v. Redstone.

258 He also removed Sydney: In Re Advance Health Care Directive, Declaration of Manuela Herzer in Support of Petition for Determination Re Advance Health Care Directive of Sumner M. Redstone.

258 Sumner agreed to loan her: In Re Advance Health Care Directive, Declaration of Keryn Redstone.

258 To make sure the changes stuck: Keach Hagey and Amol Sharma, "Battle Brews Atop Media Giant Viacom," *Wall Street Journal*, October 7, 2015.

258 Soon after she arrived: In Re Advance Health Care Directive, Declaration Re Urgency and Notice on Ex Parte Application, Los Angeles Superior Court, November 25, 2015, Exhibit: "Removal and Replacement of Trustee Keryn Redstone 2015 Irrevocable Trust."

259 Manuela claimed to Holbrook: Manuela Herzer v. Shari Redstone, Tyler Korff, Brandon Korff, Isileli "Isi" Tuanaki, Jeremy Jagiello, Joseph Octaviano, Giovanni Paz, Igor Franco, Faleolo Toia, and DOES 1–50, Los Angeles Superior Court, May 9, 2016, Complaint.

260 According to Sumner's lawyer: Redstone v. Herzer.

260 Meanwhile, Jagiello was eavesdropping: Manuela Herzer v. Shari Redstone, Tyler Korff, DOES 1–10, United States District Court, Central District of California, October 16, 2017, Complaint.

CHAPTER 21: Sex and Steak

261 Meanwhile, media stocks: Frank Bi, "ESPN Leads All Cable Networks in Affiliate Fees," *Forbes*, January 8, 2015.

262 On October 7, 2015: Hagey and Sharma, "Battle Brews Atop Media Giant Viacom."

262 The *Journal* later reported: Hagey, "The Relationship That Helped Sumner Redstone Build Viacom Now Adds to Its Problems."

262 The day after the article: In Re Advance Health Care Directive of Sumner M. Redstone, Los Angeles Superior Court, Opposition of Sumner Redstone to Ex Parte Application Seeking Evidentiary Hearing, November 25, 2015.

263 According to Sumner's legal filings: Redstone v. Herzer.

263 According to Manuela's: Herzer v. Redstone.

264 Manuela woke up: Ibid.

265 On October 16, Manuela was removed: Ibid.

265 Finally, on November 23, after a blizzard: In Re Advance Health Care Directive of Sumner M. Redstone, Los Angeles Superior Court, December 14, 2015, Declaration of Ronald Richards in Support of Petitioner's Ex Parte Application for Discovery in Support of Response to Respondent's Request to Dismiss Petition.

267 And so, immediately after Manuela: In Re Advance Health Care Directive of Sumner M. Redstone, Los Angeles Superior Court, November 25, 2015, Opposition of Sumner Redstone to Ex Parte Application Seeking Evidentiary Hearing.

267 Mario Gabelli, whose funds own: Keach Hagey, "Mario Gabelli Wants More Disclosures on Sumner Redstone's Health," *Wall Street Journal*, December 2, 2015.

267 Because of his earlier affidavit: Keach Hagey, "Viacom CEO Dauman Tries to Keep Distance from Redstone Lawsuit," *Wall Street Journal*, January 19, 2016.

268 On January 20, Viacom: Keach Hagey, "Viacom Says Sumner Redstone's Compensation Fell 85% in Fiscal 2015," *Wall Street Journal*, January 20, 2016.

268 But when the full proxy: Keach Hagey, "Viacom CEO's Total Compensation Rose 22 Percent in Fiscal 2015," *Wall Street Journal*, January 22, 2016.

268 Instead, it would have to settle: Keach Hagey, "Viacom Chairman Must Face Acuity Test," *Wall Street Journal*, January 23, 2016.

268 CBS went first, offering: Joe Flint, "Redstone Resigns as CBS Executive Chairman," *Wall Street Journal*, February 3, 2016.

268 Briefly believing this meant: Keach Hagey, "Redstone Confidant Dauman Wins Power Struggle at Viacom," *Wall Street Journal*, February 4, 2016.

271 In the wake of this major victory: Eriq Garner, "Sumner Redstone Hires New Lawyer in Battle over His Health Care," *Hollywood Reporter*, March 16, 2016.

272 And so, by early April, Manuela's: Keach Hagey, "Sumner Redstone's Team in Settlement Talks in Competency Case," *Wall Street Journal*, April 5, 2016.

272 A deal was hammered out: Hagey, "Year-Old Email Raises Questions about Sumner Redstone's Condition."

273 The main attraction: In Re Advance Health Care Directive of Sumner M. Redstone, Los Angeles Superior Court, May 5, 2016, Videotaped Deposition of Sumner M. Redstone, 31 Beverly Terrace, Beverly Hills, CA.

274 The following Monday: Joe Flint and Keach Hagey, "Sumner Redstone's Competency Suit Dismissed," *Wall Street Journal*, May 9, 2016.

274 In the hallway: Peter Elkind and Marty Jones, "Philippe Dauman's Protector Has Turned against Him and Now, It Seems the CEO's Days Are Numbered," *Fortune*, June 3, 2016.

274 Around lunchtime the day: Dylan Howard and Melissa Cronin, "Dirty Old

Man! Billionaire Sumner Redstone Caught on Tape Arranging Raunchy Orgies," Radar Online, May 9, 2016.

CHAPTER 22: Pandemonium

276 But his most prized: Emma Jacobs, "20 Questions: Philippe Dauman, Viacom," *Financial Times*, July 1, 2010.

276 On the document: In the matter of the Sumner M. Redstone National Amusements Trust, Los Angeles Superior Court, Petition for Order Confirming Validity of Removal and Appointment of Trustees, May 23, 2016, Exhibit A, Removal and Appointment of Trustee "Sumner M. Redstone National Amusements Trust."

277 In January, he and Abrams: Emily Steel, "Redstone's Lawyers Argue That His Mental Health Is Irrelevant in Dispute," *New York Times*, June 3, 2016.

277 In the weeks after the trial: Jessica Toonkel, "Sumner Redstone Has Power to Remove Viacom CEO from His Trust," Reuters, May 17, 2016.

277 Minutes after the emails: Peter Elkind, "Exclusive: Sumner Redstone Ousts Viacom CEO from Trust That Will Control Viacom and CBS," *Fortune*, May 20, 2016.

277 Shari steadfastly maintained: Keach Hagey, "Viacom CEO Calls Attempt to Remove Him from Redstone Trust 'Illegal,'" *Wall Street Journal*, May 21, 2016.

280 When their replacements: Amol Sharma, "Redstone Taps New Stewards for His Viacom, CBS Holdings," *Wall Street Journal*, May 24, 2016.

280 "We believe that Philippe": Claire Atkinson, "'Philippe'ing Out," *New York Post*, May 24, 2016.

281 They laid plans to sue: Joe Flint, "Viacom CEO Gets June Hearing in Lawsuit over Redstone Trust," *Wall Street Journal*, May 27, 2016.

281 "We know that such": David Lieberman, "Viacom Directors Vow to Fight Ouster Effort and Sell Paramount Stake," *Deadline*, May 30, 2016.

281 In response to Salerno's attacks: Joe Flint, "Shari Redstone Says Viacom Shareholders Want New Management," *Wall Street Journal*, June 1, 2016.

282 Reports began to surface: Claire Atkinson, "Shari Is on a Safari," *New York Post*, June 5, 2016.

282 When Sumner's lawyers filed: Meg James, "Examination: Redstone Competent," *Los Angeles Times*, June 4, 2016.

282 As if to hammer home the point: Ben Fritz, "'Ninja Turtles' Sequel Is Latest Disappointment at Box Office," *Wall Street Journal*, June 5, 2016.

282 At the same time that Sumner's lawyers: Steel, "Redstone's Lawyers Argue That His Mental Health Is Irrelevant in Dispute."

283 Nevertheless, on Monday: Tom Kludt, "Viacom CEO Calls for 'Immediate Medical Examination' of Sumner Redstone," CNN Wire Service, June 6, 2016.

283 Sumner's granddaughter Keryn: Emily Steel, "Sumner Redstone's Granddaughter Sides with Viacom Directors," *New York Times*, June 1, 2016.

283 A more incendiary tweet: Robert N. Klieger letter to Keryn Redstone, May 10, 2016, Demand to Cease and Desist.

283 On the eve of the first: Michael J. de la Merced and Emily Steel, "National

Amusements Alters Viacom Bylaws to Stymie Sale of Paramount," *New York Times*, June 6, 2016.

283 Jeffrey Sonnenfeld, senior associate dean: Joe Flint, Ben Fritz, and Joann Lublin, "Paramount Sale Hits Wall," *Wall Street Journal*, June 7, 2016.

284 On the hot and steamy summer morning: Nathalie Tadena, "Judge to Decide in Days on Expedited Process in Redstone Suit," *Wall Street Journal*, June 8, 2016.

284 While their lawyer, Leslie Fagen: Emily Steel, "Sumner Redstone Legal Battle Moves to a Massachusetts Court," *New York Times*, June 8, 2016; Tadena, "Judge to Decide in Days on Expedited Process in Redstone Suit."

284 When Judge Phelan: Tadena, "Judge to Decide in Days on Expedited Process in Redstone Suit."

CHAPTER 23: "Cleaning House"

285 Meanwhile, as the armies: Keach Hagey, "Redstone Family's Next Generation Takes on Bigger Roles, Influence in National Amusements," *Wall Street Journal*, November 14, 2016.

286 Around eleven a.m. on Friday, June 10: Kim Masters, "Sumner Redstone Visits Paramount Lot amid Viacom Drama," *Hollywood Reporter*, June 14, 2016.

286 He and Shari performed a similar: Joe Flint, "Sumner Redstone Makes Rare Appearances at CBS, Paramount," *Wall Street Journal*, June 15, 2016; Joe Flint, "Sumner Redstone Says He No Longer Trusts Viacom Board or CEO," *Wall Street Journal*, June 16, 2016.

286 But during a June 15 interview: Brian Price, "Former Viacom CEO Tom Freston Speaks Out on Company's 'Serious Errors,'" CNBC, June 15, 2016.

287 Against this backdrop: Joe Flint, Amol Sharma, and Joann S. Lublin, "Sumner Redstone's National Amusements Moves to Oust Five Viacom Directors," *Wall Street Journal*, June 16, 2016.

287 That same day, according to a later report: Joe Flint, "Viacom Détente Yields Promotion for New Interim CEO," *Wall Street Journal*, August 21, 2016.

288 But when news of the talks: Liana B. Baker and Jessica Toonkel, "China's Wanda Shows Interest in Viacom's Paramount," Reuters, July 13, 2016; Rick Carew, Amol Sharma, and Ben Fritz, "Viacom in Talks to Sell Paramount Pictures Stake to Chinese Group," *Wall Street Journal*, July 13, 2016; Emily Steel, "Viacom's Owner Says Sale of Paramount Would Harm Shareholder Value," *New York Times*, July 16, 2016.

288 Earlier in July: Joe Flint, "Can CBS and Viacom Merge? It Depends on the Redstone-Moonves Dance," *Wall Street Journal*, September 29, 2016.

288 What happened in Massachusetts: Peg Brickley and Joe Flint, "Viacom Board Suit Against Sumner Redstone's Holding Company to Proceed," *Wall Street Journal*, July 29, 2016.

289 They were revived by: Emily Steel, "Viacom's Profit Slumps 29 Percent, Providing a Lens into a Business in Turmoil," *New York Times*, August 4, 2016.

289 After the earnings call, National: Joe Flint and Amol Sharma, "Viacom's Results Further Stoke Feud," *Wall Street Journal*, August 5, 2016.

290 It varied little: Flint, "Viacom Détente Yields Promotion for New Interim CEO."

290 After all the Sturm und Drang: Claire Atkinson, "Bon Voyage, Philippe," *New York Post*, September 14, 2016.

290 The weekend of the peace accord: Brooks Barnes, "'Ben-Hur' Is Latest Flop for Paramount," *New York Times*, August 21, 2016.

291 Over a week of grim: Keach Hagey and Joshua Jamerson, "Viacom's Interim CEO Tom Dooley to Depart," *Wall Street Journal*, September 21, 2016.

292 Over the years, he and Shari had: Flint, "Can CBS and Viacom Merge? It Depends on the Redstone-Moonves Dance."

292 When rumors began to swirl: "CBS's Moonves Plans to Buy a Company ahead of Potential Viacom Deal," *New York Post*, February 5, 2015.

293 And so, on September 29, 2016: "National Amusements, Inc., Proposes Combination of CBS and Viacom," National Amusements press release, September 29, 2016.

293 Nonetheless, the boards of both companies: Keach Hagey, Joann S. Lublin, and Joe Flint, "Viacom and CBS Boards Name Special Committees to Review Merger," *Wall Street Journal*, September 30, 2016.

294 On October 25, 2016, Sumner sued: Redstone v. Herzer.

295 He became acting CEO on Halloween: Keach Hagey, "Viacom Taps Bob Bakish as Acting CEO," *Wall Street Journal*, October 31, 2016.

296 The *Hollywood Reporter* named her: Kim Masters, "Shari Redstone Named THR's Women in Entertainment Executive of the Year," *Hollywood Reporter*, December 6, 2016.

296 Media columnist Michael Wolff dubbed her: Michael Wolff, "Shari Redstone Has a Plan for Viacom (Really)," *Hollywood Reporter*, January 20, 2017.

EPILOGUE: The First Female Media Mogul

299 Nearly as bad: Shalini Ramachandran, "Sony to Drop Viacom Channels from Streaming TV Service," *Wall Street Journal*, November 8, 2016.

299 Bakish's solution: Keach Hagey, "Viacom to Narrow Focus to Six Key Cable-TV Channels," *Wall Street Journal*, February 8, 2017.

301 Nearly all: Todd Spangler, "Cord-Cutting Explodes," *Variety*, September 13, 2017.

302 "Scale matters": Jessica Toonkel, "Viacom, CBS Owner Shari Redstone Says Media Companies Need Scale," Reuters, October 3, 2017.

302 By January: Keach Hagey and Joe Flint, "Shari Redstone Wants New CBS Directors, Renews Push for Merger with Viacom," *Wall Street Journal*, January 17, 2018.

302 Although Viacom was: Marci Ryvicker, "CBS-VIAB? No Thank You," Wells Fargo Equity Research, January 28, 2018.

302 Privately, Shari and: Hagey and Flint, "Shari Redstone Wants New CBS Directors."

302 In response to the *Journal*: Cynthia Littleton, "Revival of CBS-Viacom Merger Talk Sows Tension within Redstone Empire, Again," *Variety*, January 17, 2018.

302 Within days: Jessica Toonkel, "Exclusive: Viacom, CBS CEOs Discuss Potential Merger—sources," Reuters, January 25, 2018.

303 Graham's father: Marilyn Berger, "Katharine Graham of Washington Post Dies at 84," *New York Times*, July 18, 2001.

303 Shari often says: Richard Ducket, "Theatrical Blood: For Shari Redstone, Movies Are a Family Affair," *Worcester Telegram & Gazette*, August 10, 1995.

304 Women own less: "Report on Ownership of Commercial Broadcast Stations," Federal Communications Commission, June 27, 2014.

304 From this fundamental: "The Status of Women in the U.S. Media 2017," Women's Media Center, March 21, 2017.

305 She even scored: Julia Marsh, "Sumner Redstone's Ex Won't Be Getting His NYC Penthouse," *New York Post*, October 25, 2015.

305 It's hard to imagine: Matthew Garrahan, "Google and Facebook Dominance Forecast to Rise," *Financial Times*, December 3, 2017.

Bibliography

Angwin, Julia. *Stealing MySpace: The Battle to Control the Most Popular Website in America*. New York: Random House, 2009.

Bart, Peter. *Fade Out: The Calamitous Final Days of MGM*. New York: Doubleday, 1990.

Baruch, Ralph, with Lee Roderick. *Television Tightrope: How I Escaped Hitler, Survived CBS, and Fathered Viacom*. Los Angeles: Probitas Press, 2007.

Beatty, Jack. *The Rascal King: The Life and Times of James Michael Curley, 1874–1958*. Reading, MA: Addison-Wesley, 1992.

Esposito, John. *Fire in the Grove: The Cocoanut Grove Tragedy and Its Aftermath*. Cambridge, MA: Da Capo Press, 2006.

Fried, Albert. *The Rise and Fall of the Jewish Gangster in America*. New York: Columbia University Press, 1980.

Gabler, Neal. *An Empire of Their Own*. New York: Doubleday, 1988.

Galloway, Stephen. *Leading Lady: Sherry Lansing and the Making of a Hollywood Groundbreaker*. New York: Crown Archetype, 2017.

Hersh, Seymour M. *The Dark Side of Camelot*. New York: Little, Brown, 1997.

Kessler, Ronald. *The Sins of the Father: Joseph P. Kennedy and the Dynasty He Founded*. New York: Warner Books, 1996.

Marks, Craig, and Rob Tannenbaum. *I Want My MTV: The Uncensored Story of the Music Video Revolution*. New York: Dutton, 2011.

Pruitt, Bettye H. *The Making of Harcourt General: A History of Growth through Diversification, 1922–1992*. Boston: Harvard Business School Press, 1994.

Redstone, Sumner, with Peter Knobler. *A Passion to Win*. New York: Simon & Schuster, 2001.

Sanders, Don, and Susan Sanders. *The American Drive-In Movie Theatre*. New York: Crestline, 2013.

Schorow, Stephanie. *Drinking Boston*. Wellesley, MA: Union Park Press, 2012.

Segrave, Kerry. *Drive-In Theaters: A History from Their Inception in 1933*. Jefferson, NC: McFarland, 1992.

Shepherd, Gordon, and Gary Shepherd. *Talking with the Children of God: Prophecy and Transformation in a Radical Religious Group*. Urbana: University of Illinois Press, 2010.

Sweeney, Emily. *Boston Organized Crime*. Charleston, SC: Arcadia Publishing, 2012.

Ueda, Reed. *West End House, 1906–1981*. Boston: West End House, 1981.

Walters, Barbara. *Audition: A Memoir*. New York: Vintage Books, 2009.

Winer, Delsa. *Almost Strangers*. New York: Simon & Schuster, 2000.

Index

About the Author

Keach Hagey is a reporter at the *Wall Street Journal*, covering television and large media companies. Her team's reporting on the power struggle at Viacom won a "Best in Business" award from the Society of American Business Editors and Writers. Previously, she covered media for *Politico*, the *National*, CBSNews.com, and the *Village Voice*. She lives in Irvington, New York.